Y0-AAA-682

GROWTH AND STABILITY OF THE POSTWAR ECONOMY

Growth and Stability of The Postwar Economy

by Bert G. Hickman

The Brookings Institution · Washington, D. C.

Published December 1960

Library of Congress Catalog Card Number 60-53654

Printed in the United States of America
George Banta Company, Inc.
Menasha, Wisconsin

THE BROOKINGS INSTITUTION is an independent organization engaged in research and education in the social sciences. Its principal purposes are to aid in the development of sound public policies and to provide advanced training for students in the social sciences.

The Institution was founded December 8, 1927, as a consolidation of three antecedent organizations: the Institute for Government Research, 1916; the Institute of Economics, 1922; and the Robert Brookings Graduate School of Economics and Government, 1924.

The general administration of the Institution is the responsibility of a self-perpetuating Board of Trustees. In addition to this general responsibility the By-Laws provide that, "It is the function of the Trustees to make possible the conduct of scientific research and publication, under the most favorable conditions, and to safeguard the independence of the research staff in the pursuit of their studies and in the publication of the results of such studies. It is not a part of their function to determine, control, or influence the conduct of particular investigations or the conclusions reached." The immediate direction of the policies, program, and staff of the Institution is vested in the President, who is assisted by an advisory council, chosen from the professional staff of the Institution.

In publishing a study, the Institution presents it as a competent treatment of a subject worthy of public consideration. The interpretations and conclusions in such publications are those of the author or authors and do not necessarily reflect the views of other members of the Brookings staff or of the administrative officers of the Institution.

Foreword

THIS STUDY of "Growth and Stability of the Postwar Economy" was begun in 1956 as an empirical examination of major factors affecting the growth and stability of the American economy since World War II. The author compares recent experience with that of the 1920's and examines the importance of structural changes in the economy and their influence on economic fluctuations. Although he concludes that a prolonged and severe contraction like that of the early 1930's is unlikely, he finds no reason to suppose that serious contractions of lesser magnitude may not recur.

During the progress of this research the author published several relatively self-contained portions of the analysis. He has drawn freely on these published materials in the present volume, although none of the papers was incorporated in its entirety or without revision. Similar use was made of portions of an earlier study done for the National Bureau of Economic Research. These prior publications, and the chapters in which they figure, are as follows: *The Korean War and United States Economic Activity, 1950–1952,* Occasional Paper 49 of the National Bureau of Economic Research, 1955 (Chapter 5); "Federal Spending and the Stability of the Postwar Economy," *Federal Expenditure Policy for Economic Growth and Stability,* Papers Submitted by Panelists Appearing before the Subcommittee on Fiscal Policy, Joint Economic Committee, 85 Cong. 1 sess., November 5, 1957 (Chapter 9); "The Contraction of 1953–1954," *The Review of Economics and Statistics,* February 1958, copyright 1958 by the President and Fellows of Harvard College (Chapter 6); "An Interpretation of Price Movements Since the End of World War II," *The Relationship of Prices to Economic Stability and Growth,* Compendium of Papers Submitted by Panelists Appearing before the Joint Economic Committee, 85 Cong. 2 sess., March 31, 1958 (Chapters 4 and 14); "Postwar Cyclical Experience and Economic Stability," *American Economic Review,* May 1958 (Chapter 2).

An Advisory Committee, consisting of Robert A. Gordon, Geoffrey H. Moore, and Walter S. Salant, contributed helpful criticisms and suggestions. John G. Gurley and Hyman P. Minsky also made helpful comments on Chapter 13. The author had the able research assistance of William R. Belmont and later Charlene Semer. Mrs. Semer also prepared the index. The manuscript was edited by Virginia Parker. To all of them the author and the Institution are deeply indebted.

The study was financed with funds provided by the Ford Foundation for general support of the Institution. The findings and conclusions are those of the author and should not be interpreted as necessarily reflecting the views of the Brookings trustees, officers, or other staff members, or of the foundation providing financial support.

ROBERT D. CALKINS
President

December 1960

Table of Contents

PART III KEY FACTORS IN THE POSTWAR CYCLES

Tables

Charts

PART I / The Problem and the Background

1 / *Introduction*

THIS STUDY ANALYZES the cyclical experience of the United States economy between 1946 and 1958, in an attempt to appraise the importance of the major forces which shaped that experience and to account for its principal features. The analysis has been guided by three main questions. Were the business cycles of the postwar period primarily the result of the normal functioning of a free enterprise economy, responding to much the same forces in much the same manner as in other years? How important were the abnormal disturbances caused by war and the cold war? To what extent were postwar developments affected by structural changes in the economy —changes which might be expected to endure and to alter permanently the character of American business cycles? These are difficult questions, for which complete and conclusive answers are not offered. Perhaps the major contribution of this volume is that it asks them, since in grappling with them, it provides additional perspective for evaluating the meaning of the present and its promise for the future.

Although the principal characteristics of postwar economic performance are measured and compared with earlier experience in the next chapter, the results are summarized briefly at this point. By historical standards, a good, but not unusual, rate of growth of real income per capita has been achieved during the postwar years. Between 1946 and 1958 the economy passed through three complete business cycles and began a fourth, but a major depression was avoided. Again, this record while good was not unique, for there have been past spans of comparable length in which no major contraction occurred. As a corollary of satisfactory growth and stability of production, a low average level of unemployment was also a feature of the postwar period. Finally, though the period was marked with two war-induced inflationary episodes and a gentler uptrend of prices after 1955, the economy escaped the major price deflation which had been a sequel of past wars.

Why did the postwar business cycles display these characteristics and not others? What forces prevented a severe contraction, so that the growth of physical activity was interrupted only by minor setbacks? What factors were responsible for the inflationary pressures of 1946-48, 1950-51, and 1955-57, and for the resistance to deflation exhibited by the economy in other years? It is because of an interest in such questions as these that this study was undertaken. That is why the focus is on postwar experience, and why Part II of the book contains a chronological analysis of the course of economic activity from 1946 through 1958.

But a study of recent experience is not enough. It is not until the postwar era is compared with other periods in American history that maximum advantage will have been taken of the opportunity to assess the importance of war influences, changes in economic structure, government policies, and other factors in postwar developments. And it is not until this assessment is made that an informed judgment is possible of the implications of those developments for the future stability and growth of the economy. Liberal use is accordingly made of historical comparisons in Part III, which analyzes key factors in prewar and postwar business fluctuations.

The aim, then, is a broad interpretation of recent experience in the light of the previous history of growth and fluctuation in the economy. One could easily get lost in a welter of fascinating detail and descriptive material in such an endeavor. Historical analogies, moreover, are potentially as misleading as they are informative. It is essential, therefore, that the inquiry be shaped by an analytic framework showing what to look for and, if possible, what mistakes to guard against.

Analytic Framework of the Study

The framework rests on the usual conception that business cycles result from autonomous disturbances acting upon an economic system which responds to them in such manner as to give rise to cumulative, and possibly self-reversing, expansions and contractions of aggregate economic activity. Disturbances may occur sporadically—wars, for example—or fairly continuously—as in the case of inventions. Disturbances could be the sole cause of business cycles, but only if they themselves followed a cyclical pattern and if no response mechanism tended to spread their effects throughout the economy. Economic systems are conceivable, in contrast, for which the response to a single disturbance would be a series of self-generating cyclical fluctuations. In the real world, however, business fluctuations result from a combination of the two types of cause. Disturbances arise frequently, but they act upon an economic structure that tends systematically to convert them into cumulative movements which sometimes reverse themselves and at other times are brought to an end by new disturbances. One important consequence is that the individual cycles of experience exhibit varying characteristics because of differences in originating impulses, structural responses, or both. Sufficiently pronounced and enduring structural changes, moreover, may effect a lasting alteration of cyclical characteristics.

An attractive feature of this emphasis on the coordinate importance of impulse and response in the cyclical process is that the analysis of fluctuations merges readily with that of secular change. This is because the same forces that contribute to long-term economic growth—population increase, resource discovery and development, and technological change are perhaps basic[1]—also influence short-term cyclical movements and in turn are influenced by them. When cycles are explained largely in terms of the structural characteristics of the economy—that is, when attention is concentrated on the response mechanism—the role of growth factors as partly autonomous sources of expansionary or contractionary impulses tends to be minimized. The population does not increase at a constant rate, however, nor does its age composition or geographic distribution remain fixed. Similarly, the pace of technological change may be uneven and its impact varies among industries. It seems wisest to adopt an analytical scheme that keeps to the forefront the potentional effects of such factors on the duration, amplitude, and other characteristics of business cycles. This

[1] These factors are basic, given an institutional and social structure favorable to economic development. The structural requirements are also "basic."

is especially important because of the considerable body of evidence that the deep and prolonged depressions of the past were partly caused by a deficient stock of investment opportunities stemming from autonomous factors.

War is the most powerful of all disturbances, and there is no doubt that World War II and the Korean War were among the major forces molding cyclical experience during the recent past. Several times the economy was called upon to adjust to abrupt and substantial changes in the composition of demand and production as a result of war or its aftermath. These adjustments were accomplished with what, in retrospect, appears to have been remarkable ease; yet they accounted for much of the instability that did occur. Thus, the period was marked by two violent inflationary episodes in 1946-48 and 1950-51. The first was a response to the release of war-induced inflationary pressures; the second to the forces set in motion by the outbreak of hostilities in Korea. Similarly, the contractions of 1945-46 and 1953-54 came during periods of retrenchment of military expenditures, while that of 1948-49 was also a kind of postwar adjustment—in this case, adjustment to the cessation of war-induced inflationary pressures.

The economic effects of war, however, are not limited to the shocks imposed by the expansion or contraction of military expenditures. Major wars also modify trends in growth factors like population increase and technological development and they may foster changes in economic structure. In practice it may not be possible to separate war from other causes of secular growth or structural change. Although desirable this separation is not essential as long as the influence of growth factors and structural changes is recognized directly in the analysis of postwar developments.

With regard to structural change, two broad types need to be distinguished for present purposes. The first consists of those continual shifts in the composition of output and employment which are the hallmark of a growing economy. This type of structural change is significant as a determinant of aggregate investment demand. This significance arises from the fact that the volume of investment undertaken by rapidly expanding industries probably will more than compensate for the diminished investment of lagging industries. Aggregate investment is likely to be larger when the composition of output is changing rapidly than when it is not. When economy-wide business fluctuations are being studied, it is convenient to treat this sort of detailed change in structure or composition of output and its causes in the class of autonomous factors, and that will be my procedure.

The other type of structural change is more pervasive, cutting across particular activities or industries and embracing wide sectors of the economy. Such changes usually take the form of the development or modification of economic institutions or habitual economic practices, although they may also occur for other reasons. No matter what their causes, they are important if they alter the responses of businessmen, workers, consumers, and other economic agents—including government policy makers—to changes in income or other relevant variables, or if they affect the degree to which the economy is exposed to disturbances. A given structural change may have effects in both these directions.

Throughout the study I have relied heavily on an informal use of income-expenditure theory, both for its direct explanatory value in some connections and for its value as an organizing and focusing device in others.[2] Among other things, this means that the structural changes with which I will deal are primarily those which can be interpreted as altering the parameters of the aggregate consumption function or of the aggregative relationships between national income and the inducements for businessmen to invest or for the government to spend or otherwise take contracyclical action.

The Concept of Economic Stability

Diagnosis, more than prescription, is the concern of this study. If prescription were the immediate goal, it would be necessary to establish a norm of optimum performance, to compare actual experience with the norm, and to decide upon actions to correct deviations from the ideal. My purpose is at once less ambitious and more neutral in

[2] There is no attempt, however, to make quantitative use of formal aggregative cycle models or to fit nonincome variables into a complete model.

respect to issues of public policy. The very concept of economic stability is charged with different meanings to different people, and many disagreements over policy can be traced to that fact. It will suffice here to distinguish the more important of these differences of meaning, without attempting once for all to resolve the conflicts.

First, what aspects of economic activity are to be measured for stability or to serve as objectives for stabilization? The stability I have in mind in these pages is that of the aggregate and not of its parts. The stability of a given industry, occupation, or region will be of interest only insofar as it affects that of the entire economy. Basic social questions of equitable income distribution and efficient resource allocation are thereby ignored. This would be intolerable if the purpose were to weigh social alternatives, but as it is, I merely note that over-all stabilization objectives may sometimes conflict with other economic (or noneconomic) goals, and that such conflicts must be reconciled—either consciously or unknowingly—by policy makers.

Aggregate economic activity itself has more than one dimension, however. At least three aspects are relevant: production, employment, and prices. Production is important because it is the basic determinant of the level of living of the population; employment, because unemployment means an irrecoverable loss of production and because it shifts the income distribution against the unemployed; prices, because inflation may induce depression and because price movements alter the distribution of real income and wealth. Since the three variables tend to fluctuate together cyclically, it may be considered redundant to list each separately. That would be true except for the vital fact that their cyclical amplitudes and their trends may differ considerably, with attendant implications for economic welfare.

Once it is decided that several aspects of aggregate activity are involved in the notion of over-all economic stability, new questions arise. An absolutely stable level of production, for example, would be inconsistent with full employment for more than a few weeks or months. Population growth enlarges the labor force, and advances in productivity add to potential output per man-hour. For these reasons, production must increase over time if full employment is to be maintained with a constant labor force and a given workweek, and it must rise even more rapidly if the labor force grows. Evidently, then, in its physical aspects economic "stability" does not mean "constancy." There is asymmetry between downward and upward stability. Losses of population, territory or resources aside, a decline of production or employment is evidence of instability, but this is not necessarily the case with an increase.

If the norm of physical stability is restated as steady advance at a rate determined by the secular growth of population and productivity, instability can be defined in terms of deviations of actual from potential production. On this definition, most deviations would be below the trend line of potential production, since the actual could rise above the potential only for brief periods of overfull utilization of manpower and equipment. Apart from such exceptional periods, a given movement of production would be destabilizing if it increased the deviation below the growth line, and stabilizing if it diminished it. Any decrease of production would be evidence of instability, of course, but so would an increase which was too small to match the growth of potential output during the same period. Somewhat paradoxically, an increase at a faster rate than the potential rate must be described as stabilizing on this criterion, for it would return the economy more quickly to its full potential.

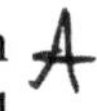

The basic idea of a growth norm may be applied loosely or rigorously in actual practice. Loose application consists of remembering the fact of economic growth, and its implications about the asymmetry of stability and the difference between increases of employment which reduce unemployment and those which do not. Rigorous use of the concept in empirical work implies ability to determine the trend of potential output in order to compare it with the path of actual production.

Statistical determination of the growth potential from past experience is a decidedly risky undertaking. Even if the growth rate of potential output could be estimated reliably for a given historical epoch, it could only be applied properly to a different period if the basic determinants of population and productivity were unchanged. Similarly, even if the average annual growth rate were reliably determined for a given epoch, it could be applied to a particular year in that span only under the decidedly unrealistic assumption that growth of the labor force and of productivity occurred steadily at the average rate. Of

course, if a way could be found to estimate potential output independently of historical trends, and to allow for such unevenness in its development as is intrinsic in the growth process, these difficulties would disappear. Stability could then be measured relative to a path of potential output which was determined by prevailing conditions, but was itself flexible over time.

It would be easy to overstress the possible pitfalls in this approach as a tool of historical research. Errors in estimation of former growth potentials are unlikely to alter significantly the *relative* rankings of past business fluctuations. The issues become critical, however, when this approach is applied to current developments as a tool for the formulation or evaluation of stabilization policy. At this point, also, the issue of predictive accuracy merges with that of control over the growth rate as a policy end in itself.

In contrast with physical activity, when people speak of stable prices, they usually mean a constant price level. If the ideal for physical activity be steady secular growth at a constant rate determined by population and technology, that for prices, it is thought, is a horizontal trend. It is too much to expect either in the real world, but the goal is clear: minimal fluctuation of output along a rising trend and of prices around a horizontal one.

This formulation is not beyond question. In the first place, if a choice could be made without affecting the behavior of production, there is no prima facie case for steady prices as against prices which rise or fall gradually over the long run. Runaway inflation or deflation is to be avoided, but for the rest, it is not obvious that the redistribution of real wealth and income which would occur because of a rising or falling price trend would be undesirable. That depends on the character of the redistribution, and on its desirability according to individual value judgments or the collective judgment of the society as expressed in custom or law.

Furthermore, it is by no means certain that rising production and constant prices are consistent long-run objectives. In past years, business contractions have tended to be more severe during periods of secularly falling prices than in epochs of rising prices. The loose positive correlation between long upswings of prices and long periods of "stable" real growth does not in itself show that rising prices are necessary to prolonged prosperity, of course. Both factors are interacting, and they may be largely the passive joint result of other, more basic, determinants. Even if rising prices are not a necessary condition for prolonged prosperity under a free enterprise system, however, it may be impossible to prevent a "natural" price uptrend and still preserve full employment. This is because prices usually rise during business expansions and hold steady during mild contractions. Fiscal and monetary actions powerful enough to curb any increase of average prices during an upswing would probably prompt a downturn of physical activity, and deflationary action during the ensuing contraction would depress production as much or more than prices.

In view of the foregoing complexities, what meaning can be given to a statement that the economy is now more stable than before? Most of us would agree that absence of severe cyclical contraction is the major criterion of stability. Thus, an economy in which there were frequent but small deviations from a satisfactory growth trend would be more stable than one in which contractions occurred less often, but were substantial when they did come. Some ambiguity would arise if small oscillations were combined with a chronic condition of unemployment, but such behavior could scarcely be considered satisfactory even if thought to be stable. Growth, in other words, is a basic criterion of satisfactory economic performance, whether embodied directly in the concept of stability or handled separately. It is also necessary to recognize that an economy in which severe contractions did not occur, might have an inflationary bias and, therefore, be less stable than another with regard to prices, especially if the criterion of price stability stressed the secular trend of prices more than their cyclical movements.

Enough has been said about the concept of over-all economic stability, but it remains to emphasize that complications also arise when one asks whether a certain factor in the economy, or a change in the factor, augments or diminishes stability. The automatic fiscal stabilizers, for example, damp induced movements of consumption demand and, hence, of prices and output. They tend thereby to reduce cyclical amplitudes—on upswings as well as contractions. This is obviously beneficial as long as other factors make for strong recoveries, but what if they do not? Then the damping effect of the stabilizers might

prevent the economy from reaching full employment without discretionary intervention by the fiscal or monetary authorities. Similarly, an increase in the relative importance of an autonomous factor may or may not be stabilizing, depending upon its own stability, its tendency to move with or against other determinants of aggregate demand and supply, and whether there is a gain or loss of stability from the factors which have diminished in relative importance. These considerations argue for the comprehensive coverage and analysis of structural changes and autonomous forces in the postwar economy attempted in Part III.

Significance of the Findings for the Future

As a rule, I have suppressed the temptation to peer into the future in the pages that follow, concentrating instead on a comparative analysis of the cyclical forces at work in the recent and the more distant past. Two main difficulties stand in the way of extending the results of this analysis to the future, apart from the possibility that some important influence has inadvertently been left out of account. The first difficulty is that the relative importance of some factors cannot be determined objectively, even for the past. The second is that future values of some key variables are either unknowable because affected by unsystematic causes or else unpredictable without more intensive investigations than are undertaken in the present volume. It may nevertheless be useful to set down briefly the broad judgments to which I have been led by the analysis, if only to assist the reader in his own interpretation of what I mean to say or imply at one or another point in the following chapters.[3]

First, it is extremely unlikely that the United States will again experience a prolonged and severe contraction like that of the early 1930's. But it would not be surprising in the future to experience brief but severe contractions on the order, say, of those of 1907-08,

[3] The principal support for these judgments will be found in Chapters 2, 9, and 11-14.

1920-21, or 1937-38. Certainly there is no assurance that the contractions of 1948-49, 1953-54, and 1957-58 were as severe as any that might occur in the future. They were considerably milder than the earlier severe ones, partly because of the damping effects of such recent structural changes as the growth in importance of automatic fiscal stabilizers. The degree of improvement in this respect is frequently exaggerated, however, and it is well to remember that the economy proved to be quite resistant to deflationary pressures during numerous minor recessions before 1929. Moreover, the recent contractions were kept mild partly by nonstructural factors that need not always be present—factors such as demand backlogs, plentiful liquidity, and a large stock of investment opportunities in important growth industries. Thus the possibility of a deeper contraction than any yet experienced in the postwar years cannot be lightly dismissed.

Nevertheless, our defenses against prolonged depressions are stronger than ever before. The long cycle of residential building is not as great a threat as formerly to general economic stability, owing to the diminished relative importance of residential construction in private investment and national output and to structural changes both inside and outside the housing market. The financial structure of the economy has more built-in resistance to deflationary forces than in prewar years. Most significant of all, the federal government is now large enough to afford powerful leverage to its fiscal actions, and modern knowledge of the consequences of such actions should prevent recurrence of the cyclically perverse policies sometimes followed in the past. Powerful antideflationary instruments are available in federal tax reductions, expenditure increases, or both, should private investment prove inadequate to prevent severe contraction because of temporary exhaustion of investment opportunities or because it fails for some other reason to respond to expansionary monetary influences. Indeed, were it not for the problems of imperfect foresight and possible conflict between antirecession and anti-inflation policies, fiscal actions could probably be instituted promptly enough to make even sharp, though brief, contractions a remote possibility.

Just as the chances of avoiding severe contraction without direct government intervention in the expenditure stream depend primarily on the existence of an adequate stock of private investment opportunities, so also do chances of achieving a full-employment growth rate of national output during business expansions. Investment opportunities are created not only by growth of national output but also by factors which are autonomous with regard to the level or rate of change of national output, and I have given considerable stress to income-autonomous investment determinants both in the analysis of postwar experience and with regard to the possible causes of past depressions. I have not, however, had space or time to provide the empirical basis for a scientific judgment on whether private investment opportunities will remain adequate to sustain a satisfactory level of employment and growth rate of output during, say, the decade of the 1960's. I, therefore, must remain content with urging the vital importance of this question for research on business cycles, for correct appraisal of unfolding events during the years ahead, and for wise decisions on public policy.

Finally, the price level is more likely than not to rise gradually over future years. It may not be possible to prevent price increases during business expansions without unduly curbing output and employment, and prices will decline little or not at all during business contractions unless the latter assume severe proportions because of a failure of antirecession policy. In the absence of international political or military disturbances, however, there is little reason to expect rapid inflation.

2 / *Postwar Cycles in Historical Perspective*

NO SERIOUS DEPRESSION has occurred since World War II. This impressive postwar record is partly responsible for the widespread tendency to emphasize aspects of recent experience that are believed to be new or abnormal and are thought to have contributed importantly to economic stability. The structural changes of the past quarter century, it is often asserted, have so altered the response mechanism of the economy that wide swings are a thing of the past. At the other pole is the argument that postwar prosperity has been due to war or cold war influences, which are not only autonomous but abnormal in their persistence for nearly two decades. If correct, either of these explanations has obvious implications for future stability. So also does a third possibility: Although the postwar economy differs from its predecessors in details of structure and the mixture of autonomous factors at work, there has been no essential change in the nature or causes of business fluctuations.

A direct attack on these problems of structural change and autonomous forces must await Part III. The major purpose in the present chapter is to gain perspective on the postwar performance of the economy through historical comparisons. An obvious first question for a study like this is whether the recent business fluctuations have differed so much in outward aspects from those of earlier years that abnormal factors or decisive structural changes must clearly be the cause of contemporary behavior.

CHART 1. *Manufacturing Production, Real Gross National Product, and Wholesale Prices, Annually, 1866-1958*

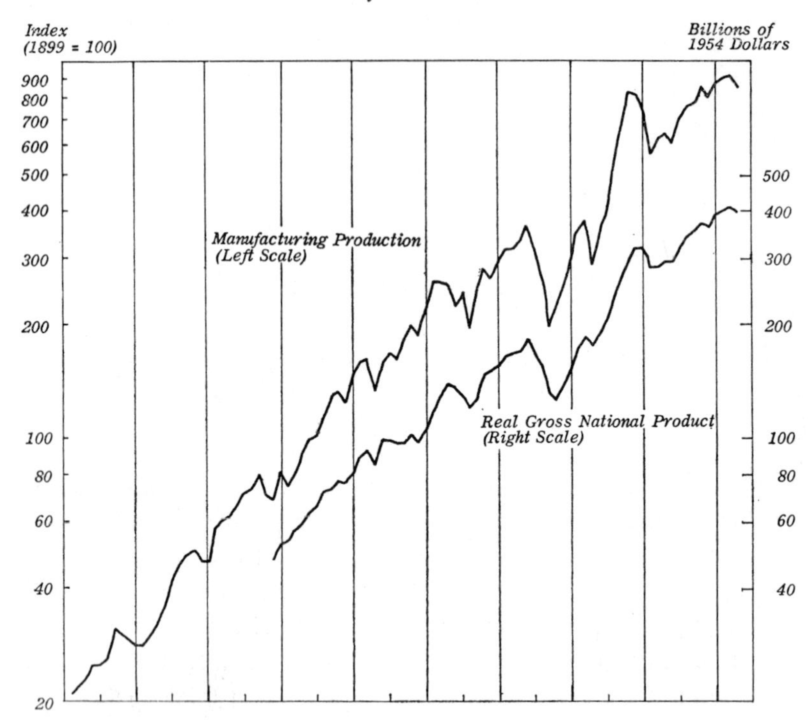

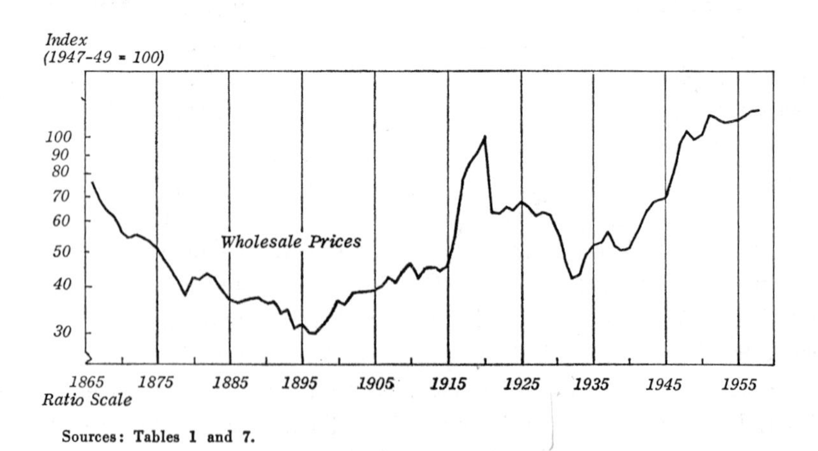

Sources: Tables 1 and 7.

Growth and Stability of Production

A long-run view of the development of production in the United States will help in finding an answer to this question. Two dominant impressions emerge from a study of the measures of manufacturing production, extending back to the Civil War, and real gross national product pictured in Chart 1. On the one hand, the long-term gains are striking; on the other, growth has been far from steady, for marked fluctuations appear in both series.

A closer look reveals two sorts of fluctuation. Growth has sometimes proceeded for long stretches with only minor and short-lived interruptions. Such interruptions—which in these annual data occasionally take the form of mere retardations instead of actual declines—are the traces left by minor business recessions. At times, however, severe contractions have occurred, and in some instances several years have elapsed before the preceding peak was exceeded and growth to new levels resumed. One of the noteworthy features of the post-World War II era is that it has escaped a major depression, though experiencing minor contractions in 1949, 1954, and 1958.

Because growth has been so uneven, it makes a substantial difference which periods are selected for comparison with the postwar years. Various criteria are possible, but one has particular appeal. Since the absence of a major contraction is a distinctive feature of the postwar era, the most comparable intervals with regard to stability and continuity of growth lie between the severe contractions of the past. Among these may be ranked the contractions of 1873-78, 1882-85, 1892-94, 1907-08, 1920-21, 1929-32, and 1937-38.[1] The contraction of 1944-46, while large in terms of production, was mild insofar as the development of unemployment or excess capacity is concerned.

It is evident that the postwar period is not in a class by itself in its

[1] The dates are from the annual business cycle chronology of the National Bureau of Economic Research as reproduced in Table 7 below. They do not necessarily agree with the peaks and troughs of the corresponding contractions in the production series included in Chart 1, although the disagreements are few.

freedom from depression, though not far from it. Beginning with the segment of 1866-73, the intervals between major contractions before World War II measured respectively 8, 4, 7, 13, 12, 8, and 5 years, while the postwar experience has spanned 14 years (1946-59) thus far.[2] If the comparatively mild (in terms of production), though long-lived, contraction of 1882-85 is excluded from the class of major contractions, moreover, the two short periods which are second and third on the foregoing list would be replaced by a single interval of 14 years. As against this observation it may be argued, however, that the 12-year span ending in 1920 is not comparable to the other periods because it bridges World War I. Furthermore, the duration of the contemporary period becomes 21 years if it is extended to include World War II. The vital question, however, is whether by virtue of structural change or abnormal forces the economy has been inherently more stable in the postwar years. The influence of World War II and its aftereffects cannot be neglected, but the fact remains that the relevant period for study and comparison begins in 1946 instead of 1939.

It is somewhat surprising to discover that the average annual rate of increase of production has been smaller in the postwar years than in most of the other comparison periods (Table 1).[3] Most of the earlier periods, however, began with recoveries from deep troughs in which surplus capacity had developed on a large scale, permitting rapid advances until the slack was eliminated. Allowance should be made for this fact, since the present period did not begin from a position of under-utilization.

A correction for the capacity factor may be made by selecting intervals of approximately equal labor force utilization, on the reasonable assumption that utilization rates of the labor force and of total

[2] The first and last segments date respectively from the end of the Civil War and World War II, even though no major contraction occurred at either time. Hence the initial year is included in the duration of each segment. The durations of the other intervals are computed from the first year after the trough of a major contraction to the peak year which precedes the next major contraction.

[3] The year 1958 was excluded from the comparison, not because 1957-58 was a severe contraction, but because the other periods all ended in cyclical peaks, and I did not want to bias the postwar growth rate by including a terminal year of contraction.

TABLE 1. *Average Annual Percentage Rates of Increase of Production, Periods Between Severe Contractions, 1866-1957*[a]

Period	Manufacturing Production[b] (1899=100)	Gross National Product[c] (1954 Dollars)	
		Total	Per Capita[d]
1866–73	5.7	—	—
1878–92	5.8	—	—
1878–82	11.3	—	—
1885–92	6.5	—	—
1894–1907	6.9	5.0	3.0
1908–20	5.0	3.8	2.2
1908–13	7.1	2.2	0.4
1914–20	2.6	5.2	4.1
1921–29	6.3	4.7	3.2
1932–37	14.3	8.3	7.6
1938–44	20.0	11.1	9.9
1946–57	4.4	3.8	2.1

[a] Percentage growth rate computed from an exponential curve fitted to the annual data by the use of Glover's mean value table (J. W. Glover, *Tables of Applied Mathematics* [1923], pp. 468 ff.). The first period in the table did not initiate from a severe contraction, nor did the last period terminate in one. The subperiods during 1908–20 are included to isolate the influence of World War I and are not broken by a severe contraction. The combined period 1878–92 is included because the contraction of 1882–85 was relatively mild and the reader may wish to treat the entire period as comparable to 1946–57.

[b] Index of manufacturing production for years 1860–99 is from Edwin Frickey, *Production in the United States, 1860–1914* (1947), Table 6; for 1900–1937, from Solomon Fabricant, *The Output of Manufacturing Industries, 1899–1937* (1940), Table 1; and for 1938–57 from *Economic Report of the President* (January1959), Table D-29, converted to 1899=100.

[c] Gross national product for years 1897–1928 is from Raymond W. Goldsmith, *A Study of Saving in the United States*, Vol. III (1956), Table N-2. The series was adjusted to the level of the Department of Commerce estimate for 1929 and converted to 1954 dollars. Extrapolated to 1894 by unpublished estimates of Simon Kuznets. The 1929–57 GNP is from Department of Commerce estimates as given in *U. S. Income and Output*, a supplement to *Survey of Current Business* (November 1958), and *Survey of Current Business* (July 1960).

[d] Figures for the per capita adjustment for 1897–1928 are from Bureau of the Census, *Historical Statistics of the United States, 1789–1945* (1949), p. 26; and for 1929–57, from *Economic Report of the President, op. cit.*, Table D-14.

productive capacity are closely correlated. Estimates of the percentage of the labor force which was unemployed during the various comparison periods since 1900 are shown in Table 2. These figures are of interest in their own right because of their direct bearing on economic welfare. By this important welfare criterion, the economy has fared well in the postwar years, and indeed better than in any comparison period covered by the unemployment data with the exception of 1900-1907. The average unemployment ratio for the 1920's, however, is raised by the high rates of 1921 and 1922. If those years of initial expansion are disregarded, the resulting ratio for 1923-29 (3.8 per cent) is about equal to 1946-57.

Here, then, are two periods—1900-1907 and 1923-29—during which over-all resource utilization was comparable to present times, according to one criterion. Unfortunately, the same test cannot be applied to the nineteenth century for lack of data on unemployment. I therefore fall back on an alternative criterion for the nineteenth

TABLE 2. *Ratio of Unemployment to Civilian Labor Force, Selected Periods, 1900-1957*[a]

Period	Percentage Unemployed	Period	Percentage Unemployed
1900–1907......	2.9	1932–37........	20.2
1908–20........	5.4	1938–44........	9.8
1921–29........	5.1	1946–57........	3.9

[a] Data for 1900–1928 are from Stanley Lebergott, "Annual Estimates of Unemployment in the United States, 1900–1954," *The Measurement and Behavior of Unemployment*, a Conference of the Universities—National Bureau Committee for Economic Research (1957), p. 215; for 1929–57, *Economic Report of the President* (January 1959), Table D-17. Unemployment estimates based on old definitions.

century and eliminate those early years of each expansion, if any, in which the economy remained below the preceding peak of production. This adjustment for initial under-utilization may be incomplete in cases where capacity continued to increase despite the depression, but exclusion of additional years would be arbitrary in the absence of reliable measures of capacity.[4]

A combination of both criteria yields six comparison periods of assumed high-level capacity utilization. When growth rates are computed for these periods the spread between the earlier rates and that of 1946-57 is considerably diminished (Table 3). As for the 1920's, exclusion of the early years from the computation reduces the growth

[4] Capacity is unlikely to decline from previous peak levels even during severe contractions, because net investment seldom becomes negative and because physical destruction of capital is a drawn-out process even if capital is losing value.

rate of gross national product from 4.7 per cent in 1921-29 to 3.5 per cent in 1923-29. Therefore, contemporary growth at 3.8 per cent, while still slower than around the turn of the century, has been faster than in the middle and late 1920's. The excess, however, is too small to be considered a difference in kind.

Attention now shifts from speed to stability of growth. The growth rates considered so far were computed from exponential (constant-percentage) curves fitted to the annual observations during each period. Fluctuations about the line of constant-percentage increase are evidence of unstable growth—accelerations or retardations in the rate of increase from year to year, or in some years, actual declines. Therefore, an index of instability of growth may be computed by averaging the annual percentage deviations of the actual data from the growth line.[5] The larger the index, the more unstable was growth.

TABLE 3. *Average Annual Percentage Rates of Increase of Production, Periods of Assumed High-Level Capacity Utilization, 1866-1957*[a]

Period	Manufacturing Production (1899=100)	Gross National Product (1954 Dollars)	
		Total	Per Capita
1866–73	5.7	—	—
1878–82	11.3	—	—
1886–92	5.6	—	—
1895–1907[b]	6.5[c]	4.9	2.9
1923–29	4.8	3.5	2.0
1946–57	4.4	3.8	2.1

[a] See text for method of selecting periods. For sources of data and methods of computation, see Table 1.

[b] The growth rates for manufacturing production, GNP, and GNP *per capita* during 1900–1907 are respectively 6.3, 4.6, and 2.6 per cent.

[c] Calculated for 1898–1907 because the 1892 peak of manufacturing production was barely exceeded until 1898. The growth rate for 1895–1907 is 6.8 per cent.

Unfortunately, the estimates of real GNP before the 1920's are subject to technical deficiencies which make them unsuitable for the study of year-to-year variations. As compared with 1921-29, how-

[5] This measure is discussed in Frederick C. Mills, *Economic Tendencies in The United States* (1932), pp. 46-49.

TABLE 4. *Indexes of Instability of Growth of Production, Selected Periods, 1921-57*[a]
(In per cent)

Period	Manufacturing Production (1899=100)	Gross National Product (1954 Dollars)	
		Total	Per Capita
1921–29	4.9	2.9	2.8
1923–29	2.8	1.3	1.4
1946–57	3.4	2.2	2.1

[a] The indexes of instability of growth are the mean percentage deviations of the annual observations from the exponential curves fitted to the data, as explained in Table 1.

ever, production growth has proceeded more steadily since 1946 (Table 4). But growth was more stable in 1923-29 than in 1946-57, since 1921 and 1922 were years of under-utilization and, hence, of rapid production gains. Thus real GNP increased slightly more rapidly but slightly less steadily in 1946-57 than in 1923-29, whereas the reverse is true in comparison with 1921-29.

The record of annual deviations from steady growth can be pushed back further for manufacturing alone. Table 5 contains the instability indexes for periods of assumed high-level utilization. The differences among the several periods are relatively slight except in 1878-82 and 1886-92. With those exceptions, growth during 1946-57 was about as stable as in earlier comparable periods.

TABLE 5. *Indexes of Instability of Growth of Manufacturing Production, Periods of Assumed High-Level Capacity Utilization, 1866-1957*[a]

Period	Index (Per cent)	Period	Index (Per cent)
1866–73	2.7	1898–07	3.5
1878–82	1.9	1923–29	2.8
1886–92	1.1	1946–57	3.4

[a] For sources and methods, see Tables 3 and 4.

Duration and Amplitude of Cycles

The two sorts of fluctuation revealed in Chart 1 have been noted. Growth was fairly steady between the major contractions, but even then it often proceeded by fits and starts and was frequently interrupted by "mild" downswings. These "minor" deviations from steady growth were measured with the indexes of instability of growth, of course. It is time to take a closer look at them.

Table 6 lists the durations of American business cycles since 1854, as dated by the National Bureau of Economic Research. The Bureau does not distinguish between major and minor cycles in its dating procedures, although recognizing that wide disparities exist among individual cycles with regard to length and severity. Thus the post-World War II period contains three complete business cycles, with the first beginning in October 1945 and the last ending in April 1958. How do these cycles compare with their predecessors?

All three expansions since 1945 have been considerably longer than the average of previous upswings, though they were not the longest on record. The Korean expansion of 1949-53 was exceeded in length by three earlier expansions and nearly equaled by a fourth. Three of these earlier long expansions occurred during the civil and world wars, of course, but the expansion of 1949-53 was probably also prolonged by the war in Korea. Comparison of the expansions of 1945-48 and 1954-57 with previous peacetime experience, shows that they exceeded the average duration of earlier peacetime expansions by 50 per cent. There were several earlier peacetime expansions of comparable length, however, in 1870-73, 1879-82, 1904-1907 and 1933-37.

Similarly, the contractions of the past decade were briefer than the average—either of all previous contractions or of minor contractions alone—but there were several earlier downswings of approximately the same duration.

With regard to amplitude, the crude comparisons yielded by the average rise and fall of three indexes of business activity during business cycles are given in Table 6. Apart from the substantial concep-

TABLE 6. *Duration of Business Cycle Expansions and Contractions and Average Amplitude of Three Indexes of Business Activity During Expansions and Contractions, 1854-1958*[a]

EXPANSIONS

Business Cycle		Duration (Months)	*Amplitude (Per Cent)*
Trough	Peak		
December 1854	June 1857	30	*12.3*
December 1858	October 1860	22	*16.8*
June 1861	April 1865	46	*18.1*
December 1867	June 1869	18	*6.9*
December 1870	OCTOBER 1873	34	*18.4*
MARCH 1879	MARCH 1882	36	*27.6*
MAY 1885	March 1887	22	*22.7*
April 1888	July 1890	27	*16.6*
May 1891	JANUARY 1893	20	*16.3*
JUNE 1894	December 1895	18	*25.3*
June 1897	June 1899	24	*26.6*
December 1900	September 1902	21	*14.2*
August 1904	MAY 1907	33	*20.2*
JUNE 1908	January 1910	19	*25.6*
January 1912	January 1913	12	*13.6*
December 1914	August 1918	44	*29.8*
March 1919	JANUARY 1920	10	*17.9*
JULY 1921	May 1923	22	*38.0*
July 1924	October 1926	27	*17.8*
November 1927	AUGUST 1929	21	*16.7*
MARCH 1933	MAY 1937	50	*63.7*
JUNE 1938	February 1945	80	*72.7*
October 1945	November 1948	37	*14.7*
October 1949	July 1953	45	*23.9*
August 1954	July 1957	35	*13.9*
Averages			
All expansions before 1945		29	*24.4*
All peacetime expansions before 1945[b]		24	*22.0*

[a] Dates are from National Bureau of Economic Research. Peaks and troughs of major business cycles are indicated in capital letters. The amplitudes are averages of three trend-adjusted indexes of business activity: AT&T, Persons-Barrons, and Ayres. Before 1879, the entries are for the Ayres index alone. The amplitudes for each index are based upon the specific cycles in the index. The method by which specific cycle amplitudes are computed is explained in Arthur F. Burns and

TABLE 6 (continued)

CONTRACTIONS

Business Cycle		Duration (Months)	*Amplitude (Per Cent)*
Peak	Trough		
June 1857	December 1858	18	*21.0*
October 1860	June 1861	8	*14.1*
April 1865	December 1867	32	*11.4*
June 1869	December 1870	18	*7.9*
OCTOBER 1873	MARCH 1879	65	*26.9*
MARCH 1882	MAY 1885	38	*27.9*
March 1887	April 1888	13	*11.2*
July 1890	May 1891	10	*17.0*
JANUARY 1893	JUNE 1894	17	*30.7*
December 1895	June 1897	18	*24.3*
June 1899	December 1900	18	*14.4*
September 1902	August 1904	23	*14.4*
MAY 1907	JUNE 1908	13	*29.5*
January 1910	January 1912	24	*12.0*
January 1913	December 1914	23	*23.2*
August 1918	March 1919	7	*22.0*
JANUARY 1920	JULY 1921	18	*34.7*
May 1923	July 1924	14	*21.8*
October 1926	November 1927	13	*9.3*
AUGUST 1929	MARCH 1933	43	*75.1*
MAY 1937	JUNE 1938	13	*45.4*
February 1945	October 1945	8	*41.0*
November 1948	October 1949	11	*17.5*
July 1953	August 1954	13	*14.3*
July 1957	April 1958	9	*22.7*
Averages			
All contractions before 1948		21	*24.3*
All minor contractions before 1948[c]		16	*17.7*

Wesley C. Mitchell, *Measuring Business Cycles* (1946), Chap. 2.

[b] Excludes June 1861–April 1865, December 1914–August 1918, and June 1938–February 1945.

[c] Excludes October 1873–March 1879, March 1882–May 1885, January 1893–June 1894, May 1907–June 1908, January 1920–July 1921, August 1929–March 1933, and May 1937–June 1938.

tual problems involved in the very notion of aggregate economic activity, these indexes are based on slender samples for the years before World War I. Thus, differences in coverage may have affected the amplitude of the indexes as between earlier and later business cycles. In general, increasing coverage tends to reduce amplitudes, but this may well be offset by other changes. Notice also that the indexes are adjusted for secular trend, with the result that the amplitude of contractions is increased relative to that of expansions.[6] For this reason comparisons over time will be confined within contractions as a class and expansions as a class.

For what they are worth, then, the amplitude measures indicate that the first and third of the upswings since the end of World War II were among a number of mild expansions on record, while the second was about average. The downswings of 1948-49 and 1953-54 had amplitudes below the average of all prior contractions but well within the upper range of previous minor recessions, including that of 1923-24.[7] The contraction of 1957-58 was among the more severe of minor contractions.

Thus far, I have compared like phases of business cycles—expansions against expansions, contractions against contractions—and have found the postwar fluctuations to be similar in amplitude and duration to a number of their forerunners. The differences between them and earlier fluctuations are no greater than the differences among earlier fluctuations. But what about full cycles and runs of full cycles?

As for full cycles, each of the three recent expansions was not only

[6] Indeed, because of the trend adjustment the average amplitudes are equal for expansions and contractions. Unadjusted measures would show, of course, that contractions are typically much milder than expansions, in view of the pronounced secular uptrend of production.

[7] It is worth noting that the amplitude measures of Table 6 yield the same ranking of contractions between 1920 and 1954 as that resulting from a consensus of seven broad measures of aggregate activity, provided that the abnormal reconversion contraction of 1945 is eliminated from either ranking. Geoffrey H. Moore in "Measuring Recessions," *Journal of the American Statistical Association* (June 1958), pp. 259-316 (reprinted by National Bureau of Economic Research as Occasional Paper 61), Table 261, gives the amplitudes of the seven series and the ranking of the several contractions. It should not be inferred that the same agreement would necessarily be found if the seven broad measures were available for years before 1919, of course.

longer than the average, but also was followed by only a minor contraction. The earlier long expansions during peacetime, in contrast, all terminated in major contractions—the contractions of 1873-78, 1882-85, 1907-1908, and 1937-38. Here, then, is at least one unusual feature of recent cycles: long expansions which did not end in severe contractions. If one ignores durations and looks only at amplitudes, on the other hand, there are a number of earlier expansions which were apparently quite as vigorous as the recent ones and which also ended in mild contractions.

Finally, consider runs of business cycles. Have there been earlier periods like the present one, in which three consecutive business expansions terminated in mild contractions? Inspection of Table 6 reveals that a similar sequence occurred during 1854-69, when there were four consecutive expansions without an intervening severe contraction. This period bridges the Civil War, of course. Similarly, the series of three cycles with minor downswings during 1908-19 spans World War I. There was, however, a peacetime sequence of three such cycles in 1894-1904.[8] Nor should the substantial influence of the Korean War during the middle expansion of the present sequence be overlooked.

Behavior of Prices

To judge from the historical record, the absence of postwar deflation is an outstanding characteristic of the contemporary era (Chart 1). It means that there has been neither an attempt to reestablish the prewar price level by deflationary monetary policies nor a severe business contraction to drag prices down along with production and employment. Nonetheless, contemporary price behavior cannot be accepted as prima facie proof of a basic change in the nature of business cycles since prewar years. There are numerous precedents for the sort of cyclical price fluctuations recently observed. There is nothing unusual about price increases during business expansions,

[8] The economic effects of the Spanish-American War were too small to be significant in this connection.

TABLE 7. *Amplitude of Wholesale Prices During Business Cycles, 1834-1958*[a]

Expansions				Contractions			
Business Cycle[a]		Amplitude (Per Cent)[b]		Business Cycle[a]		Amplitude (Per Cent)[b]	
Trough	Peak	Total	*Per Year*	Peak	Trough	Total	*Per Year*
1834	1836	27.5	*13.8*	1836	1838	− 5.0	*− 2.5*
1838	1839	5.2	*5.2*	1839	1843	−26.0	*− 6.5*
1843	1845	1.2	*0.6*	1845	1846	3.4	*3.4*
1846	1847	0.2	*0.2*	1847	1848	− 4.7	*− 4.7*
1848	1853	7.5	*1.5*	1853	1855	3.7	*1.8*
1855	1856	0	*0*	1856	1858	−10.0	*− 5.0*
1858	1860	− 1.7	*− 0.8*	1860	1861	0.5	*0.5*
1861	1864	89.4	*29.8*	1864	1867	− 9.5	*− 3.2*
1867	1869	−10.8	*− 5.4*	1869	1870	− 7.4	*− 7.4*
1870	1873	− 3.4	*− 1.1*	1873	1878	−26.3	*− 5.3*
1878	1882	7.2	*1.8*	1882	1885	−14.4	*− 4.8*
1885	1887	− 0.3	*− 0.2*	1887	1888	1.6	*1.6*
1888	1890	− 2.1	*− 1.0*	1890	1891	− 0.5	*− 0.5*
1891	1892	− 6.6	*− 6.6*	1892	1894	− 8.3	*− 4.2*
1894	1895	1.9	*1.9*	1895	1896	− 4.7	*− 4.7*
1896	1899	12.3	*4.1*	1899	1900	7.7	*7.7*
1900	1903	6.0	*2.0*	1903	1904	0.3	*0.3*
1904	1907	9.3	*3.1*	1907	1908	− 3.5	*− 3.5*
1908	1910	12.0	*6.0*	1910	1911	− 7.9	*− 7.9*
1911	1913	7.6	*3.8*	1913	1914	− 2.4	*− 2.4*
1914	1918	92.6	*23.2*	1918	1919	5.6	*5.6*
1919	1920	11.3	*11.3*	1920	1921	−36.8	*−36.8*
1921	1923	3.2	*1.6*	1923	1924	− 2.4	*− 2.4*
1924	1926	1.9	*1.0*	1926	1927	− 4.6	*− 4.6*
1927	1929	− 0.2	*− 0.1*	1929	1932	−32.0	*−10.7*
1932	1937	33.3	*6.7*	1937	1938	− 8.9	*− 8.9*
1938	1944	32.3	*5.4*	1944	1946	16.4	*8.2*
1946	1948	32.7	*16.4*	1948	1949	− 5.0	*− 5.0*
1949	1953	11.0	*2.8*	1953	1954	0.2	*0.2*
1954	1957	7.3	*2.4*	1957	1958	1.6	*1.6*

[a] The business cycle dates are from the chronology of the National Bureau of Economic Research. The annual peak and trough dates may not agree with the monthly dates shown in Table 6 because "the annual reference dates purport to state the years in which general business reached a high or low point when comparisons are made by full years; these need not be the same as the years in which business activity on a monthly basis made cyclical turns." (Arther F. Burns and Wesley C. Mitchell, *Measuring Business Cycles* [1947], p. 81.)

[b] The percentage changes during expansions are computed from trough to peak and those during contractions from peak to trough. Index of wholesale prices (1947–49=100) is from a mimeographed release of the Bureau of Labor Statistics.

and although prices have fallen more often than not during business contractions, they nevertheless rose during seven of the 26 contractions which occurred between 1836 and 1938 (Table 7).

All this is not to say that the characteristics of business cycles are unrelated to price trends. On the contrary, it is firmly established that business contractions tend to be long or short according as the trend of prices is rising or falling.[9] For example, between 1854 and 1938 the average duration of United States business contractions during periods of falling prices was 25 months, as compared with only 17 months for periods of rising prices.[10] Moreover, the contraction phase was longer relative to the expansion phase for those business cycles occurring during the periods of price decline.

As already noted, the business expansions since World War II were not only longer than the average but were different from previous long expansions in that they ended in minor contractions. It must now be emphasized that it is not unusual for expansions to be long relative to contractions during periods of rising prices. It still remains true, however, that the recent expansions were not only above average in length but were also above average in the relationship of their length to that of the recent contractions. Thus, between 1854 and 1938 the average length of expansions and contractions during the periods of price uptrend was respectively 26 and 17 months, whereas the corresponding figures for 1946-58 are 39 and 11 months. Whether this difference in degree is indicative of a difference in kind is a moot question that ultimately can be settled only by experience.

The avoidance of postwar deflation is to be viewed with satisfaction, since a drastically lower price level could have been attained only at considerable sacrifice of real income and employment, barring currency reforms of the European variety. The continued uptrend of prices during the 1950's is less gratifying considered by itself. As we shall see in Chapter 14, however, the inflationary bias of the postwar American economy is largely a by-product of its expansionary bias, and should be judged with that fact in mind.

[9] Arthur F. Burns and Wesley C. Mitchell, *Measuring Business Cycles* (1946), pp. 431-40; Wesley C. Mitchell, *Business Cycles, The Problem and Its Setting* (1927), pp. 410-11.

[10] Burns and Mitchell, *op. cit.*, p. 437, Table 167.

"The Breakup of the Business Cycle": A New Phenomenon?

Contemporary observers have not overlooked an interesting feature of recent business fluctuations: that is the tendency for offsetting movements to occur among various sectors of the economy. Sustained declines of business fixed investment occurred during the contractions of 1948-49 and 1953-54, but residential construction and personal consumption led on both recoveries. The outbreak of Korean hostilities stimulated private as well as public demand, and the subsequent reaction to the early speculative buying diminished the pressure on resources just as an accelerated mobilization program got well underway. After lagging behind home building and consumption on the 1954 upturn, business fixed investment rose steeply as residential construction declined, and when business investment began to taper off in 1956, federal spending commenced to rise. Again, declines of business fixed investment, net exports, and purchases of consumer durable goods were principal factors in the contraction of 1957-58, but these adverse factors were quickly counteracted by increases in consumer nondurables and services, government expenditures, and a bit later, residential construction.

It is tempting to speculate that these tendencies are a reflection of new structural developments which have inhibited the transmission of inflationary or deflationary impulses from one sector to another. As an example, Sumner Slichter's influential views were set forth in an article in late 1954:

> Perhaps the most encouraging fact about the recent boom in stock prices is that it provides an additional bit of evidence that the old-fashioned business cycle is being broken up into a number of more or less independent cycles which do not move up and down together. Certainly it has not been usual for stock prices to rise—or for expenditures on housing to rise and outlays on industrial plant and equipment to remain steady—while production and employment were dropping. And yet these things have happened during the recession [of 1953-54].
>
> What has been going on during the last few years has been a

gradual loosening up of the entire economy so that the different parts of industry (construction, consumption, the purchase of plant and equipment) move more or less independently of each other.[11]

Slichter goes on to discuss some of the structural factors, including the built-in government stabilizers and long-range investment planning by business firms, which have loosened the economy.

These structural influences and others will be analyzed in Part III. For the present, I will confine myself to an indirect approach to the problem, by again asking whether the observed phenomenon is a new one which necessarily requires or supports a new explanation.

The answer is that it is not, which will surprise few students of business cycles and none who has stressed the importance of disaggregation. There are similar instances of counterbalancing movements during earlier cycles. Residential construction reached a peak of the long building cycle in 1925; it therefore rose during part or all of the business contractions of 1920-21 and 1923-24, but fell during the expansion of 1927-29. Simon Kuznets' estimates of annual consumption expenditures in 1929 prices show increases during the contractions of 1923-24 and 1926-27, although sales of semidurables fell during the former contraction and those of durables during the latter.[12] Annual expenditures for plant and equipment declined less than 5 per cent over-all during the same contractions, and sizable increases occurred in several important industrial sectors.[13]

These illustrations are drawn, of course, from the minor fluctuations of the twenties. But that is just the point. Let us accept the hypothesis that the contractions of the forties and fifties were mild because of independent offsetting movements within the economy. Since offsetting movements were also a feature of the mild contractions of the middle twenties, contemporary experience can hardly be cited as proof that recent structural changes have eliminated old-fashioned business cycles. Evidently the economy was sufficiently loose to permit "a number of more or less independent cycles which do not move up

[11] Slichter, "Wall Street As a Barometer: An Analysis," *New York Times Magazine* (October 3, 1954), p. 40.

[12] Simon Kuznets, *National Product Since 1869* (1946), Table 15.

[13] George Terborgh, "Estimated Expenditures For New Durable Goods, 1919-1938," *Federal Reserve Bulletin* (September 1939), p. 732, Table 2.

and down together" at least as early as the twenties. The key question is whether there has been sufficient improvement in this respect so that it is safe to assume that major contractions can no longer occur. That question cannot be settled, if at all, by casual observation of the superficial aspects of business fluctuations.

Summary

Several aspects of postwar economic performance were set against the perspective of history in the preceding pages. By historical standards, the record since 1946 has been good with regard to rate and stability of growth, maintenance of a high ratio of employment to labor force, and absence of severe contraction, although it is not unique in any of these respects taken alone. Nor was the period unusual in its combination of brief business contractions and a rising price trend. Finally, none of the recent expansions or contractions was outside the range of durations and amplitudes established by previous business fluctuations. These findings must be qualified in two important respects, however. First, the recent expansions have been longer and the contractions shorter than in earlier epochs of rising prices. Second, although there were earlier intervals of comparable length during which severe contraction was avoided, growth was not as stable nor employment as satisfactory throughout those periods as recently, since production was recovering from deep troughs at the beginning of each of the earlier periods.

What is the proper interpretation to place on the fact that in a number of important ways the post-World War II business cycles fall within the range of their predecessors? The contrary finding would establish a presumption in favor of the hypothesis that business cycles have changed significantly since prewar years because of abnormal autonomous factors, changes in the response mechanism, or both. And yet that hypothesis is not disproved by the outward similarities between recent and earlier business fluctuations. It is entirely possible for varying combinations of autonomous factors or for different economic structures to yield the same general outcome. The multiplicity of theories of the business cycle is evidence of that, as is the stubborn persistence of the phenomenon in the real world. At the same time, one cannot be as confident that a fundamental change has occurred as he would be if contemporary experience were entirely outside of the previous range; and the mere fact that business cycles have persisted during a long history of institutional development and economic growth cautions especially against uncritical inferences that lasting structural changes are responsible for recent stability and will continue to induce stability in the future.

3 / *The Breakthrough to Postwar Prosperity*

WAR AND ITS AFTEREFFECTS must rank high on any list of factors affecting economic activity in the postwar era. Major wars always unleash powerful economic forces, but the transformation wrought by World War II was particularly impressive because of the magnitude and duration of the conflict and because it followed a decade of depression. The super-depression of the 1930's had left its mark on virtually every aspect of economic life. Long-established growth trends had been interrupted and economic activity was little higher at the end of the decade than at its beginning. During the war, however, production, employment, and incomes rose so swiftly and carried so high that war's end found the economy at a level undreamed of in 1939. As a result of the wartime surge, the economy was established on a new high plateau of prosperity from which growth could be resumed.

The magnitude of the breakthrough from prewar to postwar levels may be judged from Chart 2. Annual population increase, gross national product, nonagricultural employment, consumer prices—each of these curves traces out the depressed contours of the 1930's, the steep rise of the war years, and the continued growth of the postwar era. This does not mean that the recovery from the depression is to be attributed exclusively to World War II, for the curves all turned upward after 1932 or 1933. Nor does it mean that a decade and more of postwar prosperity can be explained as a sort of conditioned response to war—the contrast with earlier postwar experience should be enough to disabuse anyone who held it of that notion.

What it does mean is that as a result of wartime developments, conditions were created which were favorable to growth and which helped to sustain growth during much of the postwar decade. These effects

CHART 2. *Population Increase, Real Gross National Product, Nonagricultural Employment, and Consumer Prices, Annually, 1919-58*

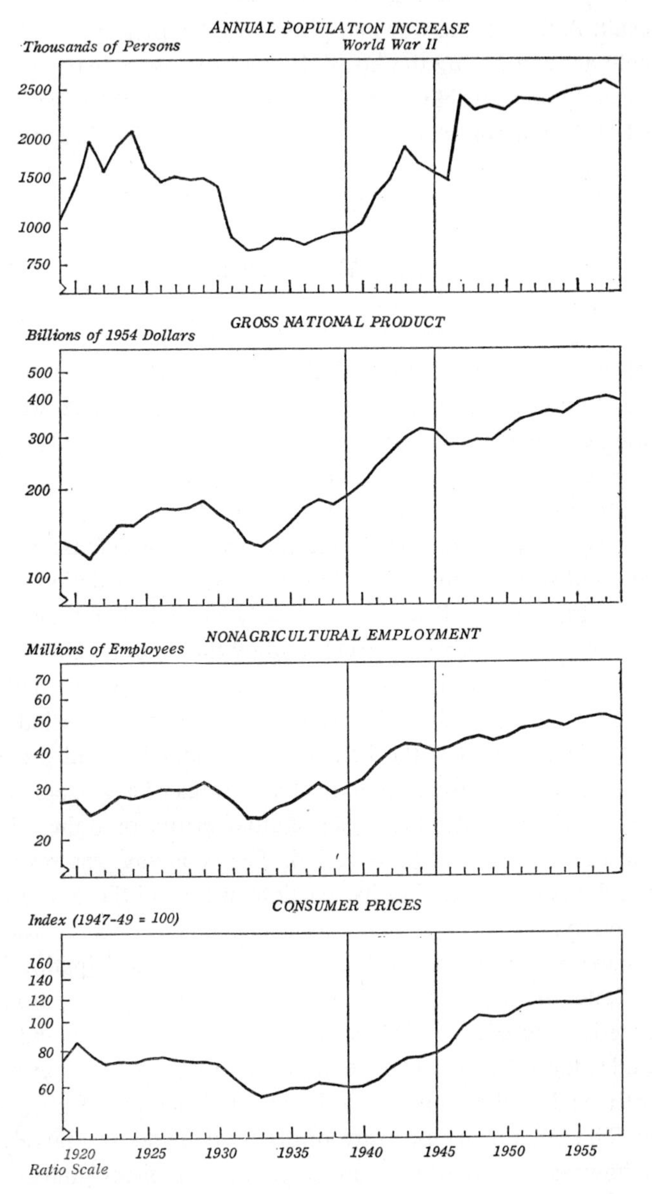

Sources: Bureau of the Census, Bureau of Labor Statistics, and National Bureau of Economic Research.

of the war can and will be analyzed below; but it does not follow that because a particular cause contributed to a result, it was necessary to that result. Although the war had pronounced expansionary effects on economic activity during the hostilities and for some years thereafter, it is certainly conceivable that vigorous growth would have resumed in the 1940's and continued in the 1950's even in its absence.

The War Years

It was not until the defense mobilization got underway in mid-1940 that the economy was decisively affected by the war. A weak and vacillating expansion had been in progress since June 1938 but, even so, 15 per cent of the civilian labor force was unemployed in the second quarter of 1940, just before the mobilization began. The pace of the expansion accelerated under the impact of the defense program, however, and with so much slack in the economy, production and employment rose swiftly. Prices were steady at first, but they too advanced rapidly after February 1941, and by the time the United States entered the war in December average consumer prices had risen 9.6 per cent. What needs to be emphasized about this period of defense mobilization is that the behavior of production and prices can be explained with the usual theoretical apparatus of aggregate demand and supply without introducing substantial errors or doing violence to the institutional facts of the period. The economy was reacting to a powerful external force, but its reactions were still those of a peacetime economy.

The same cannot be said of the phase of active participation by the United States in the war. During this period aggregate output was determined by supply. A chronic condition of excess demand developed under the spur of war expenditures, so that production pressed constantly against the limit set by the available supply of physical resources. The inflationary pressure of excess demand was largely contained, however, by the elaborate apparatus of direct controls over prices, wages, credit, production, and distribution. This set of wartime controls constituted a drastic though temporary change in structure which greatly modified the response mechanism of the economy. One result was that prices rose considerably less during the four war years than in the preceding 18 months of defense mobilization. Another consequence was the creation of a strong inflationary potential that was discharged upon the postwar removal of the controls.

The change in the character of the expansion when the economy went on a full wartime footing is reflected in the movements of consumption, investment, and government expenditures. All three components increased during 1939-41, but private investment fell to a trickle in 1942-45, and consumption advanced much less than in proportion to gross national product. Meanwhile, the government component swelled enormously and at the height of the war effort in 1943-44 amounted to nearly one-half of total output, as compared with 15 per cent in 1939 and 1946.

The financial counterpart of the wartime diversion of resources to government use is illustrated in Chart 3, which shows the balance of income and expenditures within each of the three main sectors of the economy. The sum of expenditures for the three sectors is the gross national product in current dollars, and the sum of receipts is the gross national income, consisting of gross retained business earnings, disposable personal income, and taxes. Since aggregate income must equal aggregate expenditure, an excess of spending over income in one or more sectors (dissaving) must be balanced by an equal excess of income over expenditure (saving) in some other sector or sectors.

The huge margin by which government expenditure came to exceed tax receipts during 1942-45 stands out clearly in the chart. Equally apparent is the fact that owing to wartime controls over expenditures, retained business earnings substantially outstripped investment outlays, thus reversing the behavior typical of cyclical expansions during peacetime. Finally, it is evident that the volume of consumer saving swelled considerably above normal proportions during the war years.

In essence, the World War II policy was to finance a large portion of war expenditures by deficits and to compel or persuade consumers and business firms to hold idle the liquid assets thereby generated; that is, to accumulate financial claims rather than goods. The deficits were financed by issuing new Treasury securities, and the funds raised

CHART 3. *The Nation's Income, Expenditure, and Saving, Annually, 1939-50*[a]

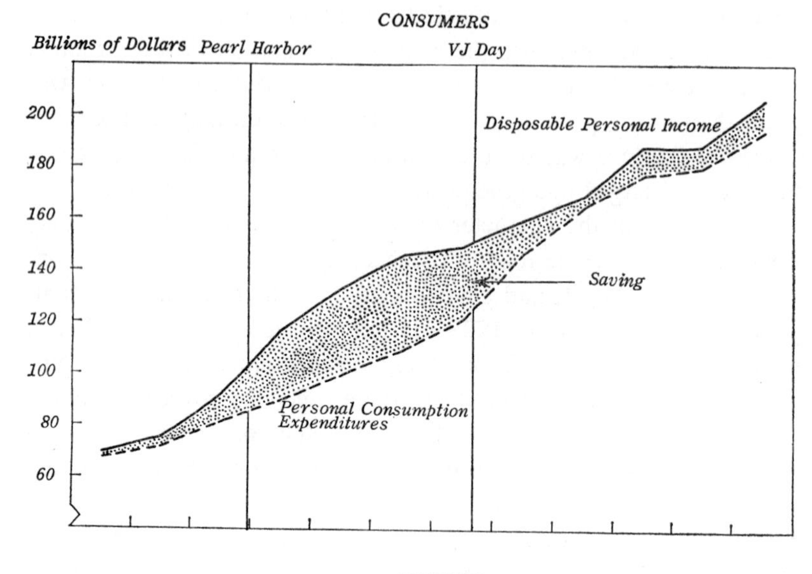

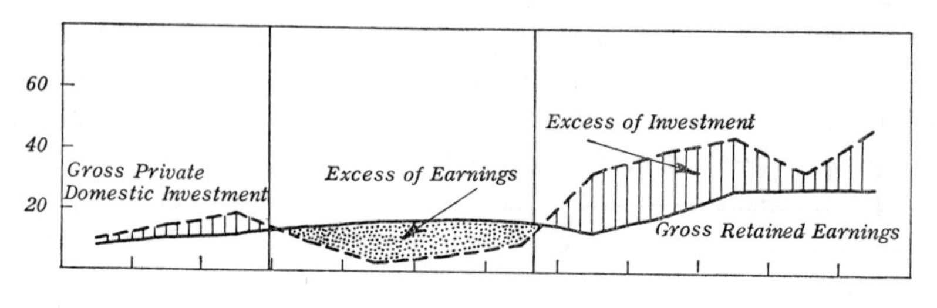

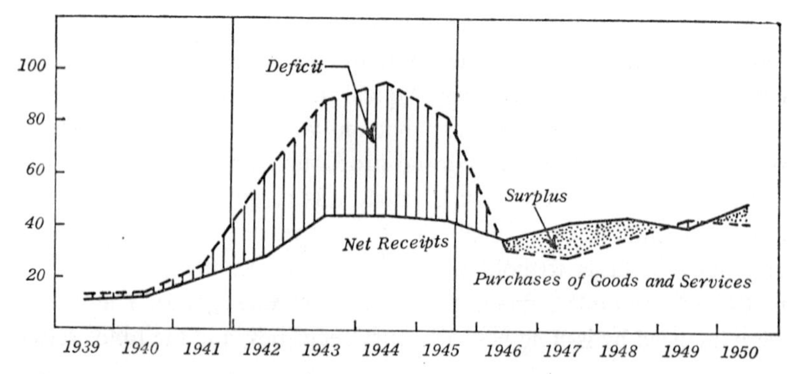

[a] Gross retained earnings are undistributed corporate profits, inventory valuation adjustment, and capital consumption allowances. Government receipts are net of transfer payments.

Source: Office of Business Economics, Department of Commerce.

in this fashion were then paid out as income to the private economy when the government made its purchases. Part of the additional income thus created was absorbed by taxes, but the remainder was available for spending or saving. Since expenditures for goods were restricted by shortages and controls, consumers and businesses perforce saved substantially, and held their savings in liquid form. The principal forms taken by these financial accumulations were currency, bank deposits, and government securities.

Two features of these financial processes require emphasis because of their bearing on postwar developments. First, the dramatic wartime rise of total debt was due entirely to the financial activities of the federal government. The federal debt rose nearly $200 billion between 1941 and 1945, while the private debt was practically unchanged and that of state and local governments declined about $2.5 billion.[1] Second, the added federal debt arose in the succession of wartime deficits, but this does not mean that the savings of consumers and businesses took the form predominantly of government securities. This would have been the case if the new securities had been sold only to the sectors which did the actual saving. As it was, however, large amounts of government bonds were sold to financial intermediaries, and especially to banks, which purchased half of the issues. When the deposits created by banks to purchase new bonds were spent by the government, they swelled the private money supply. Businesses and consumers thereby came to hold a substantial part of their wartime savings as money or time deposits instead of bonds, whereas banks ended the war with huge portfolios of government securities.

What position had the economy attained by the end of the war? As compared with the prewar situation, three major changes had occurred: the economy was operating at full capacity with respect to human and capital resources; important backlogs of demand had accumulated during several years of enforced saving and deferred expenditures on durable goods; and the financial condition of consumers and businesses had improved markedly. A few key measures will substantiate these points (Table 8).

[1] E. J. Bonnel and J. A. Gorman, "Changes in Public and Private Debt," *Survey of Current Business* (September 1953), Table 1.

TABLE 8. *Indicators of Economic Activity, Resource Utilization, and Financial Condition in 1929, 1939, and 1945*[a]
(All measures are relatives with base 1939 = 100)

Series	1929	1945
Population and Production		
1. Population	93	107
2. Gross national product at 1953 prices	96	166
3. GNP per capita at 1953 prices	103	155
Labor Force and Employment		
4. Total labor force	89	117
5. Armed forces	70	3,089
6. Civilian labor force	89	98
7. Civilian employment	104	115
8. Unemployment	16	11
9. Unemployment as per cent of civilian labor force	19	11
Prices		
10. Index of consumer prices	123	129
11. Index of wholesale prices	124	137
Capital Stock		
12. Stock of privately owned plant and equipment at 1953 prices	97	104
13. Privately produced GNP at 1953 prices	98	151
14. Ratio of stock of privately owned plant and equipment to privately produced GNP	99	69
Stock of Consumer Durable Goods		
15. Stock at 1929 prices	99	106
16. Stock at 1929 prices per capita	106	99
Money Supply		
17. Demand deposits adjusted and currency	72	283
18. Time deposits adjusted	106	179
19. Total deposits adjusted and currency	87	238
Debt		
20. Net public and private debt	104	222
21. Federal debt	39	593
22. State and local debt	81	84
23. Private debt	130	113
Financial Condition of Consumers		
24. Disposable personal income in current prices	118	213
25. Personal saving	145	1,000
26. Saving as a per cent of disposable personal income	123	469
27. Liquid asset holdings of individuals	91	295
28. Mortgage and consumer debt of individuals	104	99
29. Ratio of liquid assets to disposable personal income	77	138
30. Ratio of mortgage and consumer debt to disposable personal income	88	46
Working Capital of Corporations		
31. Current assets	n.a.	179
32. Current liabilities	n.a.	153
33. Net working capital	n.a.	211
34. Ratio of cash and government security holdings to current liabilities	n.a.	216

n.a. Not available.

[a] The sources and notes for lines 1 through 34 are as follows:

1. *Economic Report of the President* (January 1959), Table D-14.

2. *U. S. Income and Output*, a supplement to *Survey of Current Business* (November 1958). Current dollar estimates from Table I-1 *divided by* implicit price indexes from Table VII-4, converted to 1953 as base year.

3. Line 2 *divided by* line 1.

4–9. *Economic Report of the President, op. cit.*, Table D-17.

10–11. Releases of the Bureau of Labor Statistics.

12–14. Releases of the Machinery and Allied Products Institute. Stock estimates derived by cumulating estimated survivals from past installations of plant and equipment measured at constant prices. Privately produced GNP is GNP less compensation of employees of government and government enterprises.

15. Raymond W. Goldsmith, *A Study of Saving in the United States*, Vol. III (1956), Table W-3.

16. Line 15 *divided by* line 1.

17–19. *Federal Reserve Bulletin* (February 1959), p. 164.

20–23. *Survey of Current Business* (September 1953), Table 1.

24–25. *U. S. Income and Output, op. cit.*, Table II-1.

26. Ratio of line 25 to line 24.

27–28. Releases of Securities and Exchange Commission. Liquid assets comprise currency and bank deposits, saving and loan shares, and government securities.

29. Line 27 *divided by* line 24.

30. Calculated from data in releases of SEC.

31–34. From release (November 1, 1954) of SEC. Current assets include cash, government securities, accounts receivable, inventories, and other current assets. Current liabilities include accounts payable, government advances and prepayments, federal income tax liabilities, and other current liabilities. Net working capital is the difference between current assets and current liabilities.

We note first the sizable increases in employment and production during the war. These increases were facilitated by population growth, but the total labor force increased more rapidly than the population and a notable gain resulted from the elimination of prewar unemployment. Clearly, the nation's human resources were utilized intensively in the war effort.

So also were its capital resources. Privately produced output increased by half between 1939 and 1945, whereas the capital stock rose only slightly, owing to the small amount of net private capital formation during the war years. Thus, the war fostered and sustained an extraordinary expansion of income and output without adding commensurately to the capital stock. Unlike a peacetime expansion driven by private investment, in which the possibility always exists that the capacity created by the very investment required to increase aggregate demand may eventually outpace demand, the wartime expansion created a shortage of capacity to be made good after the war. True, it was only a potential shortage with respect to postwar output, since a sufficiently large reduction of output from wartime levels would have eliminated the need for additional capacity. But as matters stood in 1945, the capacity factor was favorable to business investment rather than the reverse.

The same situation prevailed in the housing field. Accurate estimates of the physical stock of dwelling units at the end of the war are unavailable, but we do know that by April 1, 1947, there were 4,925,000 more nonfarm households (occupied dwelling units) than on the same date seven years earlier, and that only 2,643,300 private nonfarm dwelling units were started in the intervening period.[2] The deficit was made up by such devices as conversions of existing structures and occupation of seasonal dwelling units and units formerly classified as farm dwellings, and perhaps by some reduction in vacancies—but these are all manifestations of short supply in the housing market.

[2] Housing and Home Finance Agency, *Housing in the Economy, 1955* (1957), Tables A-1 and A-64. Of the 2,643,300 estimated private housing starts in 1940-46, 1,149,100 occurred in 1940-41; 831,700 in 1942-45; and 662,500 in 1946.

A physical basis was also laid during the war for a strong postwar upsurge of consumer demand. During 1942-45, expenditures for consumer durable goods averaged $9 billion per year in 1947 dollars, as compared with $13.5 billion in 1939-41 when incomes were substantially lower. The stock of consumer durables increased between 1939 and 1941 and declined thereafter because of the wartime restrictions on production. On balance, there was a small net increase between 1939 and 1945, but this was just enough to match population growth, and in the meantime personal income had risen sharply. There can be no doubt that consumers emerged from the war with a physical stock of durable goods which they regarded as inadequate at given levels of personal income and wealth.

The general nature of the process by which the national debt and the money supply came to be swollen during the war has already been sketched. A significant aspect of this development was a marked improvement in the financial condition of consumers. Even though disposable personal income doubled between 1939 and 1945, the ratio of liquid assets to income increased 38 per cent. Over the same interval, the ratio of mortgage and consumer debt to disposable income was halved. A similar increase in liquidity was to be found in the business sector. The net working capital of corporations, for example, more than doubled during the war, as did the ratio of corporate holdings of cash and government securities to current liabilities.

Thus, whether one examines real or financial factors, it is apparent that the war fostered conditions which favored a postwar upsurge of private demand for goods and services. With the end of hostilities in Europe, however, a new problem was posed. Would not the imminent cutback in military expenditures reduce income and in turn depress private demand, perhaps plunging the economy into a cumulative contraction? This was certainly a possibility, but to judge from their actions it was never considered likely by either consumers or businessmen. After years of wartime restrictions, consumers were in a frame of mind to spend freely and they had the financial ability to do so. Moreover, businessmen expected them to do so. A survey of investment plans of manufacturers conducted early in 1945 pointed to large and expanded capital outlays in the first year to follow V-E Day, in war and nonwar industries alike.[3] The nonwar industries had experienced substantial increases in sales between 1939 and 1944 and anticipated small reductions—or even increases—in postwar sales, yet their capital expenditures had been severely restricted during the war.[4] Government-owned facilities had been constructed in large volume in the war industries, and the companies expected sales to decline rather substantially from the wartime levels, but they too planned large postwar investments.[5] Among these, the consumer durable goods industries required the capital expenditures to reconvert facilities to the production of peacetime products for which profitable markets were apparently expected. Reconversion demand was less important in the other war industries, but those businesses, too, planned substantial outlays, presumably for replacement and modernization of existing facilities and for expansion of capacity in lines which had been comparatively neglected during the war but which would be important in peacetime.

The Reconversion Period

The optimistic expectations of businessmen about the near-term future were justified in the actual event partly because they were founded upon correct estimates of real elements of strength in the economy, and partly because the actions based upon the expectations conserved those elements of strength. The first postwar expansion of aggregate economic activity was not to begin without an intervening period of contraction while war production was cut back, but the contraction

[3] D. S. Wilson, "Planned Capital Outlays by Manufacturers," *Survey of Current Business* (June 1945), pp. 5-9.

[4] The nonwar industry groupings included food and kindred products; textile, apparel, and leather products; paper and products and printing and publishing; lumber and furniture products; and stone, clay, and glass products.

[5] The war industries were comprised of chemicals and allied products; products of petroleum, coal, and rubber; iron and steel and their products; transportation equipment, including automobiles; machinery; nonferrous metals and their products; and miscellaneous manufacturing industries.

was a peculiar sort which did not spread to other sectors of the economy. The decline was confined entirely to production for government use and private expenditures actually rose strongly.

The smoothness of the transition from wartime to peacetime economy seems the more remarkable when one considers the magnitude of the changes in demand, production, and employment which transpired within a few brief months. The peak in federal expenditures was reached in the first quarter of 1945, when they totaled $91 billion at a seasonally adjusted annual rate and accounted for 41 per cent of GNP. Federal spending then dropped slightly in the second quarter and plummeted thereafter, sinking to a level of $26 billion by the first quarter of 1946. How did the economy withstand this abrupt and powerful deflationary shock?

It did not fully withstand it, of course. Somewhat less than two-thirds of the $65 billion decline in federal expenditure was offset by increases elsewhere in the economy, so that gross national product still fell $24.5 billion, or approximately 10 per cent. Even this was a sizable reduction, but its effect on unemployment was softened by a concomitant shrinkage of the labor force and workweek. Although 6.5 million men were discharged from the armed forces in late 1945 and early 1946, the total labor force declined by the same amount from its wartime peak. Some of the returning servicemen stayed out of the job market for a time, and the influx of others to the civilian labor force was counterbalanced by a withdrawal of "wartime" workers as munitions production diminished. The result was that the civilian labor force changed scarcely at all, and the growth of unemployment was confined to that caused by reduced employment. This meant that unemployment increased only 1.5 million between the first quarters of 1945 and 1946, and in the latter period amounted to but 4 per cent of the civilian labor force.

Expenditures, production, and employment did decline under the impact of economic and military demobilization, then, but the adjustment was mild when compared with the shock. This was partly because employment and production had been abnormally high during the war, so that a portion of war production could be foregone without the need to replace it in order to maintain full voluntary employment. It was as if the normal United States economy had been enlarged during the war by the addition of a supplementary economy with its own labor force and that after the war the supplementary economy was discarded as unwanted.

Another factor contributed to the mildness of the decline. The contraction of demand did not become cumulative, since the loss of income from the production and sale of goods or services to the government did not reduce the demand for private capital formation or consumer goods. On the contrary, even as federal expenditures were declining at an annual rate of $65 billion, the following increases occurred in other components of gross national expenditure: gross private domestic investment, $13 billion; net foreign investment, $6 billion; personal consumption, $20 billion; and state and local expenditures, $1 billion; or $40 billion in all. These increases were an outgrowth of the expansionary forces built up during the war, and an early symptom of the postwar reversion toward patterns of economic behavior typical of peacetime.

An examination of the main avenues by which a contraction in one sector of the economy may be transmitted to other sectors, permits better assessment of the conditions which prevented this from occurring when government spending was reduced in 1945-46. First, the decline in expenditures for, say, goods and services on government account will result in corresponding fall of gross income in the industries producing those end-products or their components. This fall in gross income may reduce disposable personal income, thereby inducing a decline in consumption expenditures and depressing activity in the consumer goods industries. Second, investment demand may be adversely affected by the primary decline in government expenditure or the induced secondary declines in consumption. The adverse response of investment might have a physical basis in the development of excess capacity as production falls off; or the deterioration of sales and profits might depress expectations about the future profitability of present investments; or firms might curtail investment programs in order to preserve their liquidity as profits decline; or lenders might become more cautious about financing risky loans; etc.

To begin with the first possibility, why was there no induced decline in consumer demand as a result of the loss of income from war production during the transition period? This did not occur for two prin-

TABLE 9. *Relationship Between Change of Gross National Income and Change of Disposable Personal Income, Seasonally Adjusted Annual Rates, First Quarter of 1945 to First Quarter of 1946*[a] (In billions of dollars)

Item		Change
Reduction in gross national product or income		24.5
Less: Reduction in gross business saving		3.7
Capital consumption allowances	1.8	
Undistributed corporate profits	1.9	
Less: Reduction in corporate profits tax liability		6.9
Less: Net reduction in other items[b]		1.2
Equals: Reduction in personal income receipts from production[c]		12.7
Less: Reduction in personal tax and nontax payments		3.5
Less: Increase in transfer payments		9.7
Government transfer payments	8.6	
Business transfer payments	0.0	
Net interest paid by government	1.1	
Equals: Increase in disposable personal income		0.5

[a] Calculated from data in Tables 43, 47, 49, and 52 in *National Income, 1954 Ed.*, a supplement to *Survey of Current Business.*

[b] Includes indirect business taxes, corporate inventory valuation adjustment, business transfer payments, contributions for social insurance, excess of wage accruals over disbursements, subsidies *minus* current surplus of government enterprises, and the statistical discrepancy.

[c] Consists of wage and salary disbursements, other labor income, dividends, personal interest income excluding net interest paid by government, proprietors' and rental income. Excludes personal contributions for social insurance.

cipal reasons: (1) Autonomous increases of private demand served directly to offset two-thirds of the reduction in federal spending, so that GNP fell only $24.5 billion instead of $65 billion. (2) Disposable personal income rose slightly despite the $24.5 billion decline of gross national income. Table 9 shows why.

Almost one-half of the decline in gross income was absorbed by reductions in business saving, corporate profits taxes, and other items, so that personal income receipts from production fell only $13 billion. Corporate profits before tax decreased $8 billion as a result of diminished business activity, but the reduction was split between corporate profits taxes and undistributed profits, and dividends actually increased somewhat. About two-thirds of the drop in taxes on corporate profits was induced by lower earnings and the remainder resulted from repeal of the excess profits tax and from reductions in the rates at which corporate incomes were taxed. It is normal for induced declines in corporate profits taxes and undistributed corporate profits to act as automatic personal income stabilizers during contractions—the former because tax rates are fixed for discrete intervals and the latter because corporate managements tend to maintain dividend payments even in the face of diminished net earnings. Automatic stabilizers are only somewhat less automatic if they depend upon habitual behavior rather than upon legislated properties of government fiscal systems. It will be noted that capital consumption allowances also declined during the transition period, owing to the expiration of wartime allowances for accelerated amortization. This was unusual, of course, since depreciation charges seldom decrease during minor downswings.

Although part of the impact of reduced defense expenditures was borne by corporate profits and other items, personal income receipts from production nevertheless fell about $13 billion. Increased transfer payments swelled income receipts by nearly $10 billion, however, largely because of mustering-out payments and other financial assistance given to discharged servicemen. Personal tax payments decreased $3.5 billion, moreover, with approximately $1 billion of the decline induced by smaller earnings and about $2.5 billion due to legislated tax reductions. These offsets to diminished receipts from production were sufficient to yield a small increase in disposable personal income.

Since disposable income did not fall in the contraction, the principal route by which consumer demand might have been depressed was closed. It was to be expected that expenditures would be maintained under these circumstances. In actual fact, however, personal consumption expenditures were not simply maintained, but rose $20 billion. This was an autonomous rise, caused by demand backlogs and excess liquidity instead of an increase of current income. It was important both as a direct offset to the reduction in military spending, accounting for half of the autonomous increase of private demand mentioned above, and because it confirmed the favorable business expectations about postwar markets and strengthened investment incentives, thereby preventing any induced decline of investment demand.

With demands for consumer goods, housing, business plant and equipment, net exports, and inventories all rising strongly, the deflationary force of falling defense outlays was quickly spent. The initial postwar expansion was well underway by the early months of 1946, although some technical problems of reconversion remained to be solved and the wartime apparatus of economic controls was not fully dismantled. The expansion began, moreover, from a level of activity far exceeding prewar performance and with a war-fostered heritage of unsatisfied demands and excess liquidity. For a time, at least, inflation rather than depression was to be the paramount concern of the postwar economy.

PART II / Chronological Analysis of the Postwar Cycles

4 / *The Cycle of 1946-49*

THE FIRST POSTWAR EXPANSION began in November 1945, a little over two months after the surrender of Japan, and did not reach a peak until three full years had passed. It differed from most expansions chiefly because of its pronounced inflationary character, which was due to elements having their genesis in the preceding years of war production and war finance—elements usually absent from peacetime business cycles. Thus, real gross national product increased merely 3.8 per cent from 1946 to 1948, whereas the implicit index of prices of goods and services comprising the national output rose 18.6 per cent. The ensuing contraction was short-lived—lasting only 11 months from November 1948 to October 1949—and mild, as national output and implicit prices each declined 2 per cent from peak to trough. This chapter will deal briefly with the progress of the inflation, the causes of the downturn, and the factors responsible for early recovery.

Postwar Inflation: 1946-48

As 1946 opened, the economy was still operating under the wartime "disequilibrium system," although the mild reconversion had largely run its course. So long as prices were controlled, the economy could not seek a market equilibrium. The removal of controls during the second half of 1946 freed the economy for reaction to the accumulated demand pressures which had been contained previously by administrative devices. The result was a powerful inflationary shock (Chart 4).

CHART 4. *Indexes of Prices, Industrial Production, and Nonagricultural Employment, Monthly, and of Real Gross National Product, Quarterly, 1946-50*[a]

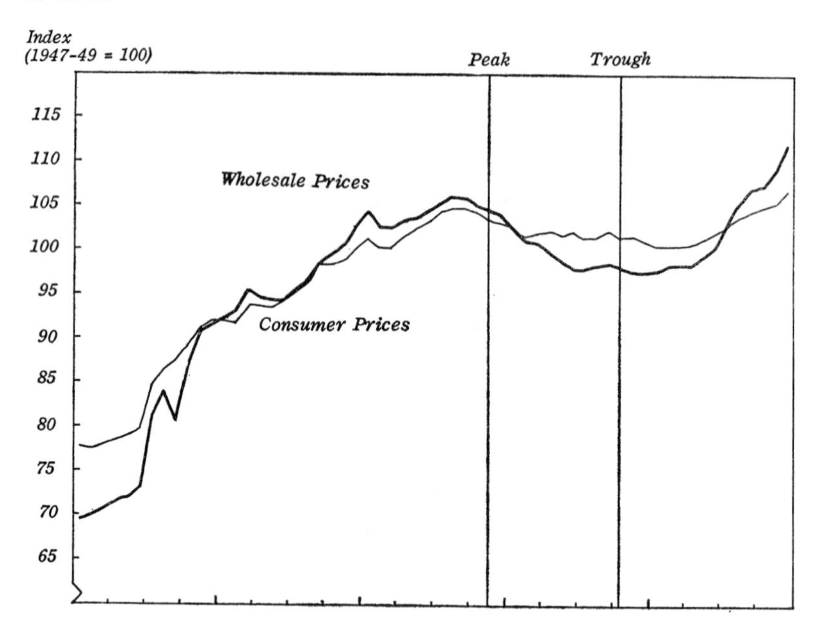

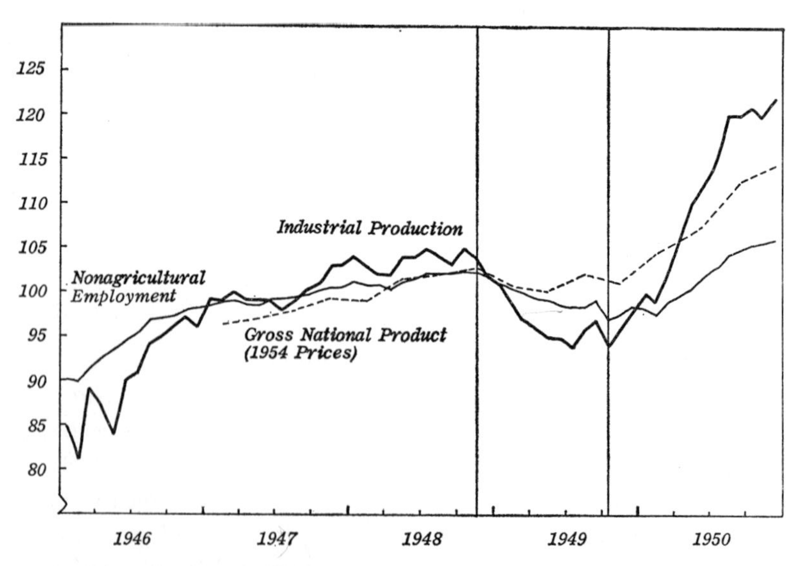

[a] All series except prices are adjusted for seasonal variation. Vertical lines appearing in this and subsequent charts indicate business cycle peaks and troughs as dated by the National Bureau of Economic Research. The exact dates are shown in Table 6.

Sources: Bureau of Labor Statistics; Board of Governors of the Federal Reserve System; Office of Business Economics, Department of Commerce.

Partly because of the wartime heritage of financial liquidity and deferred demands which characterized alike the household, business, and foreign sectors, aggregate demand was extraordinarily high at the time of decontrol. It was augmented also by the "first round" of wage increases of early 1946. Higher wage incomes increased the post-decontrol money demand for consumer goods, and since it is unlikely that other income receivers diminished their consumption or investment demands correspondingly, if at all, this meant that prices rose more than they would have at the old wage rates.

Thus, although the first round of wage increases was by no means the sole cause of the price inflation of mid-1946–early-1947, it contributed to it. To argue that it was the sole cause would be to assert that autonomous wage increases disturbed an initial equilibrium in which there was no excess demand, which is absurd. Similarly, to cite the lag of prices behind wages as evidence of a cost-price spiral is to ignore the fact that the lag was really determined by the timing of price decontrol relative to wage decontrol.[1]

The pace of the inflation slowed noticeably in the second quarter of 1947. The index of wholesale prices actually declined somewhat and the average of consumer prices was stable. A corresponding deceleration occurred in physical activity, as Chart 4 also reveals. The period of tranquility was short-lived, however, and with the coming of summer, production recovered moderately and prices again shot upward. If the respite is regarded as a temporary equilibrium, two questions come naturally to mind: What conditions produced the equilibrium? Why was it unstable?

With regard to the cause of the lull, the first possibility is that financial stringency resulting from the price increases after decontrol may have retarded the expansion of demand in one or more parts of the economy during the spring of 1947. The essence of the sort of excess-demand inflation now under discussion is that it results from competition among the various claimants on the national product for a larger share of a highly inelastic aggregate supply of goods and services. Gradual increases of supply aside, the inflation will continue

[1] Wage decontrol began in August 1945, whereas price decontrol did not begin until the summer of 1946. Wage-price interactions during the inflation of 1946-48 are analyzed in Chapter 14.

CHART 5. *The Nation's Income, Expenditure, and Saving, Seasonally Adjusted Quarterly Totals at Annual Rates, 1946-50*

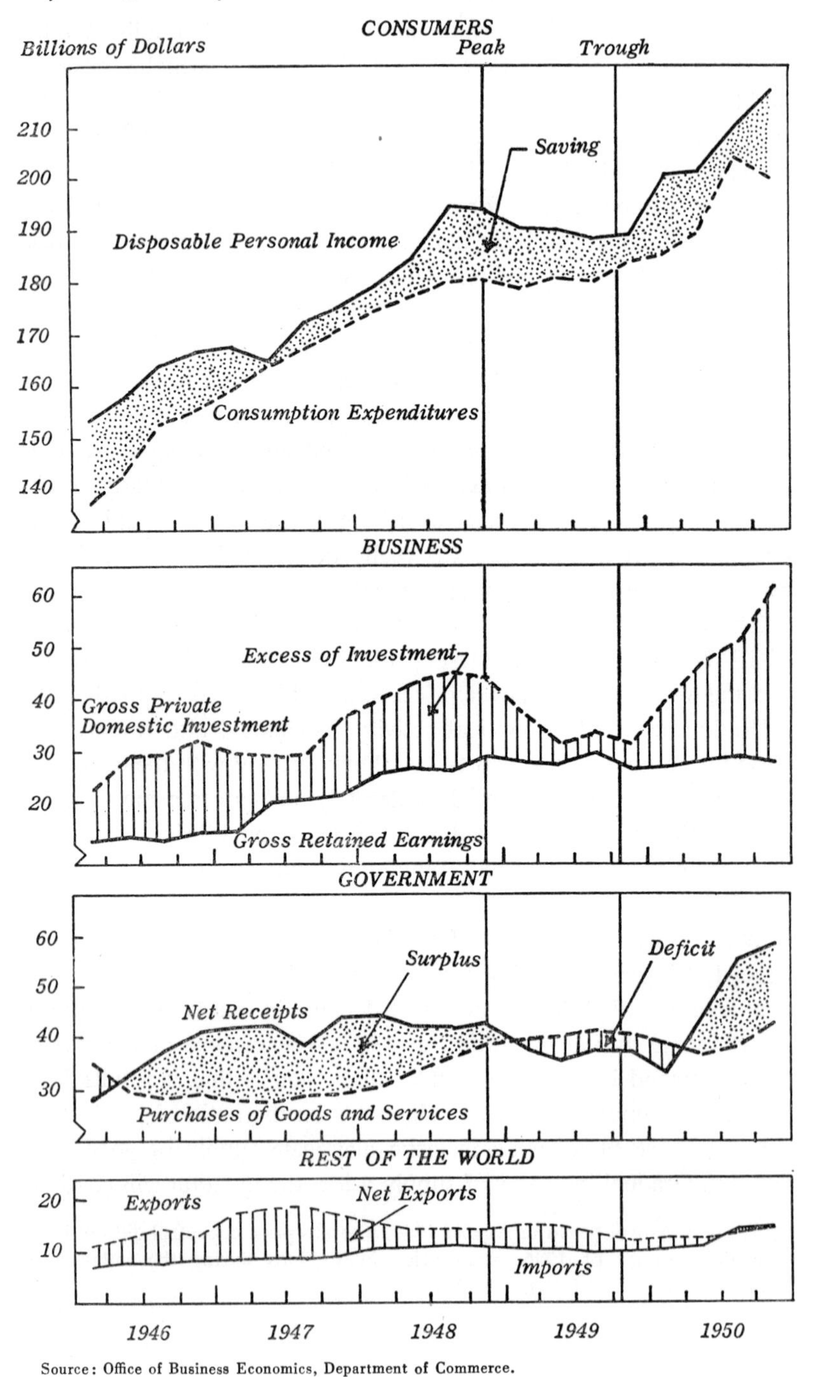

Source: Office of Business Economics, Department of Commerce.

as long as some spending units are displeased with their level of real expenditures—their share of total output—and are able to increase money expenditure in an attempt to bid goods and services away from rival spending units. Conversely, the inflation will be halted if all spending units become satisfied—perhaps better, reconciled—with their current real expenditure in the sense that they cannot, or will not, find the means to finance a large money outlay.

Any spending unit, be it in the household, business, government, or foreign sector, has two sources from which to finance current purchases of goods and services, barring sales of real assets already in its possession. It can spend out of current income receipts; or it can alter its net financial wealth, either by borrowing or by drawing upon its financial assets. Thus, financial stringency could take the form either of an income limitation or of a constraint on the desire or ability to diminish net holdings of financial assets.

Let us examine the incomes and expenditures of the major sectors in turn for evidence of financial constraints on spending, beginning with consumers. Chart 5 shows how expenditures for personal consumption rose continuously from 1945 to mid-1947 and beyond. Furthermore, throughout 1946 and early 1947, expenditure climbed more rapidly than income—a symptom of the excess demand for consumer goods which was released by decontrol and of the determination of consumers to maintain their real purchases after decontrol. Even the diminished increase of disposable income in the first quarter of 1947 and its actual dip in the second quarter—itself largely a reflection of the lull in production and prices—failed to deter the rapid expansion of expenditure. The fall in the rate of personal saving during the first postwar wave of inflation was accompanied by some deterioration in the financial position of consumers as a group, of course.[2] The moderate reduction of consumer liquidity during 1946 may have inhibited the growth of spending in the first half of 1947, just as the retardation of disposable income may have done, but the fact remains that neither force was powerful enough to prevent substantial increases of consumer expenditure in those months. Signs of flagging demand, must be sought elsewhere.

[2] The ratio of individuals' liquid assets to disposable personal income declined 4.5 per cent during 1946.

CHART 6. *Gross Private Domestic Investment and its Components, Seasonally Adjusted Quarterly Totals at Annual Rates, 1946-50*

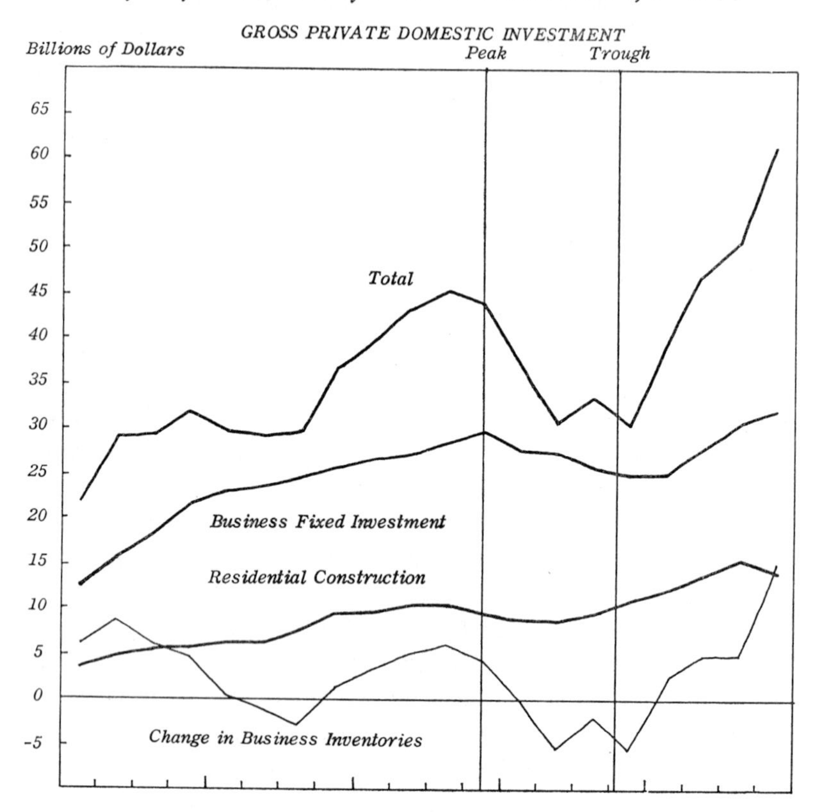

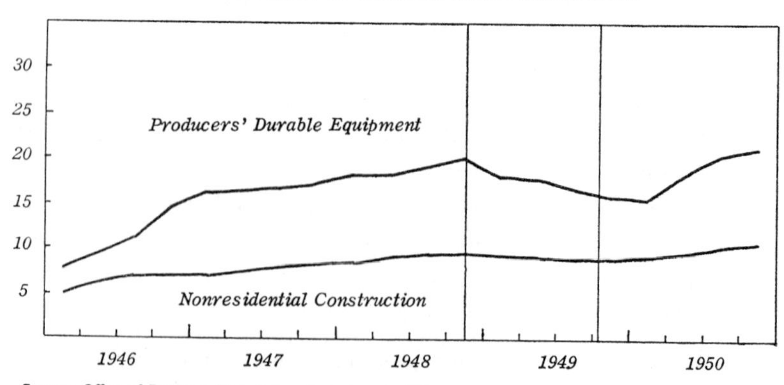

Source: Office of Business Economics, Department of Commerce.

Nor do we fare much better when we turn to the government and foreign sectors shown in Chart 5. Government purchases of goods and services did diminish during the first half of 1947, but relatively little in comparison with the increases in other categories of final expenditure. The reduction came entirely in the federal sector and reflected primarily the further progress of war demobilization rather than any financial constraint. Net tax receipts (receipts less transfer payments) were substantially in excess of government purchases during the last half of 1946 and in 1947. Incidentally, the government surplus served as a partial restraint on the progress of the inflation, but it was not, of course, enough. The sharp rise of receipts during 1946 was largely induced by the expansion of money incomes, and hence was itself a reflection of the inflation which automatic increases of tax receipts could mitigate but not prevent.

No assistance against inflation was forthcoming from foreign sources. On the contrary, net foreign investment rose substantially during 1947 under the spur of postwar needs for relief and rehabilitation in war-ravaged countries.

That leaves domestic investment and its finance. It is apparent from Chart 5 that gross private domestic investment fell in the early months of 1947 and remained relatively depressed until late in the year. Since gross retained earnings continued to rise, private deficit financing for purposes of investment was reduced. This last development was effect rather than cause, however, for there was no shortage of external funds to restrict investment during this period.

A breakdown of gross private domestic investment reveals that its decline after the fourth quarter of 1946 was due entirely to the inventory component (Chart 6). Business fixed investment and residential construction continued to rise along with consumption and net foreign investment. Hence, the lull during the spring of 1947 primarily reflected diminished demands for inventory and not a deficiency of final demands. The lull was not, in other words, the induced result of diminished liquidity arising from the inflationary process itself, at least insofar as the demand for final goods is concerned. Nor is it likely that the decline of inventory investment was caused by financial constraints.

The reason for believing that financial constraints had little to do

CHART 7. *Inventory-Sales Ratios, Monthly, Seasonally Adjusted, 1945-50*

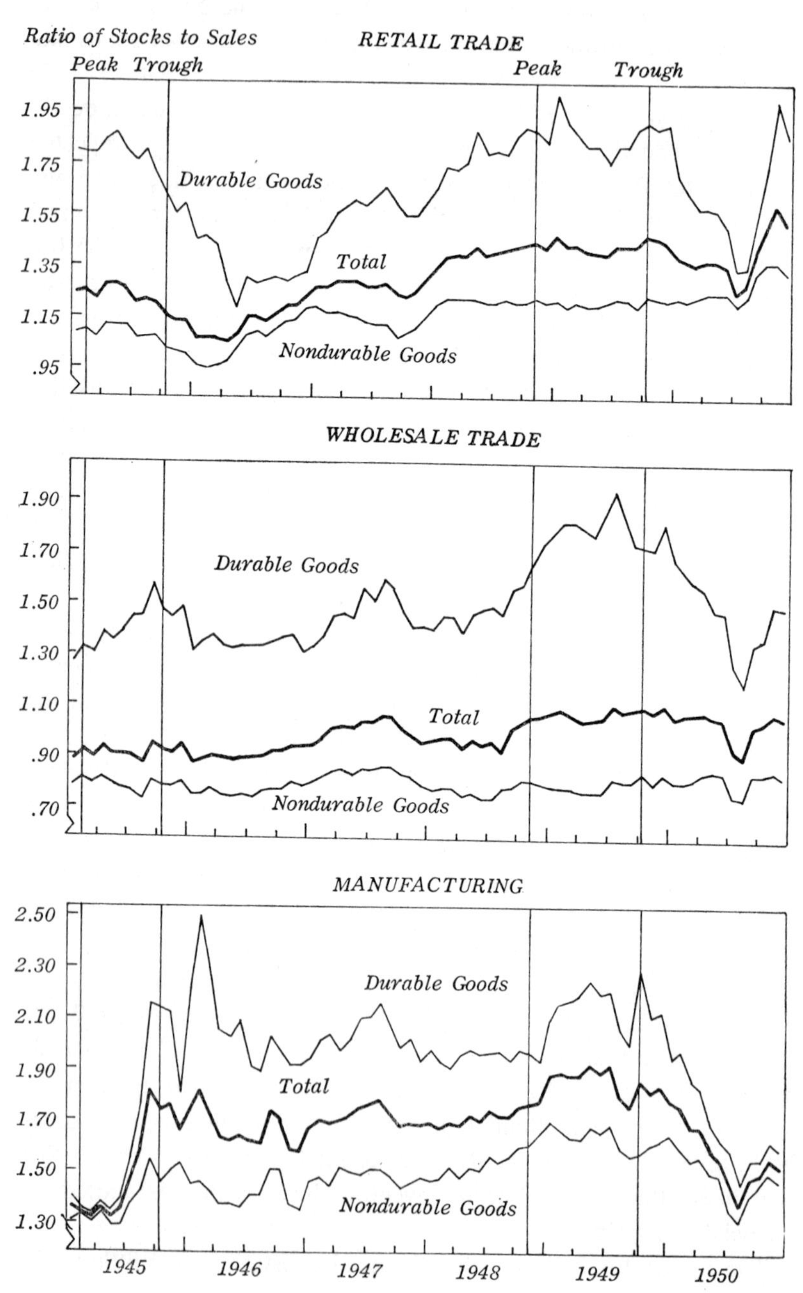

Source: Derived from data of Office of Business Economics, Department of Commerce.

with the behavior of either fixed or inventory investment during 1946-47 is, of course, that the entire economy was quite liquid and bank credit was readily available at generous terms. Since the monetary authorities accepted the goal of stable interest rates, they were unable to act to prevent an expansion of bank credit and the money supply. Any increase in the demand for loanable funds which could not be satisfied from current saving or by dishoarding had to be met by the banking system if interest rates were to be kept from rising.

As it happened, the contribution of additional money supplies to increased spending was comparatively small during the period under review. Thus gross national expenditure increased 11 per cent and the private portion of it 15 per cent between the second quarters of 1946 and 1947. The money supply, consisting of currency outside banks and adjusted demand deposits, rose less than 3 per cent over the same interval. A rise in the income velocity of circulation of money therefore accounted for three-fourths of the increased spending on national output and four-fifths of the rise of private spending. This implies a sharp reduction in the proportion of the money supply held idle. The dishoarding occurred, moreover, at low and stable rates of interest. Here is ample testimony of the involuntary nature of much of the liquid asset accumulation of the war years, which resulted by wars' end in holdings which were considerably larger than desired, given current prices for goods and going interest rates and incomes.

What, then, does account for the reduced inventory demand and consequent lull during the spring of 1947? In the first place, the rate of inventory accumulation had been exceptionally high relative to total production during 1946, owing to the need to replenish war-depleted stocks of civilian goods. Some decline of inventory investment was virtually inevitable once stocks were rebuilt sufficiently to provide appropriate selections and acceptable delivery schedules.[3] To judge from the levels maintained in later years, the appropriate "technical" ratio of stocks to sales was approximated in retail stores selling nondurable goods by early 1947 (Chart 7). This was not true of durable goods retail stores, however, since important durable goods were

[3] An offsetting increase of inventory demand could have occurred if final sales had accelerated during the early months of 1947, but instead they rose more slowly than in 1946. See Charts 7, 8, and 9.

CHART 8. *Indexes of Personal Income, Sales, Inventories, and New Orders, Monthly, Seasonally Adjusted,*[a] *1946-50*

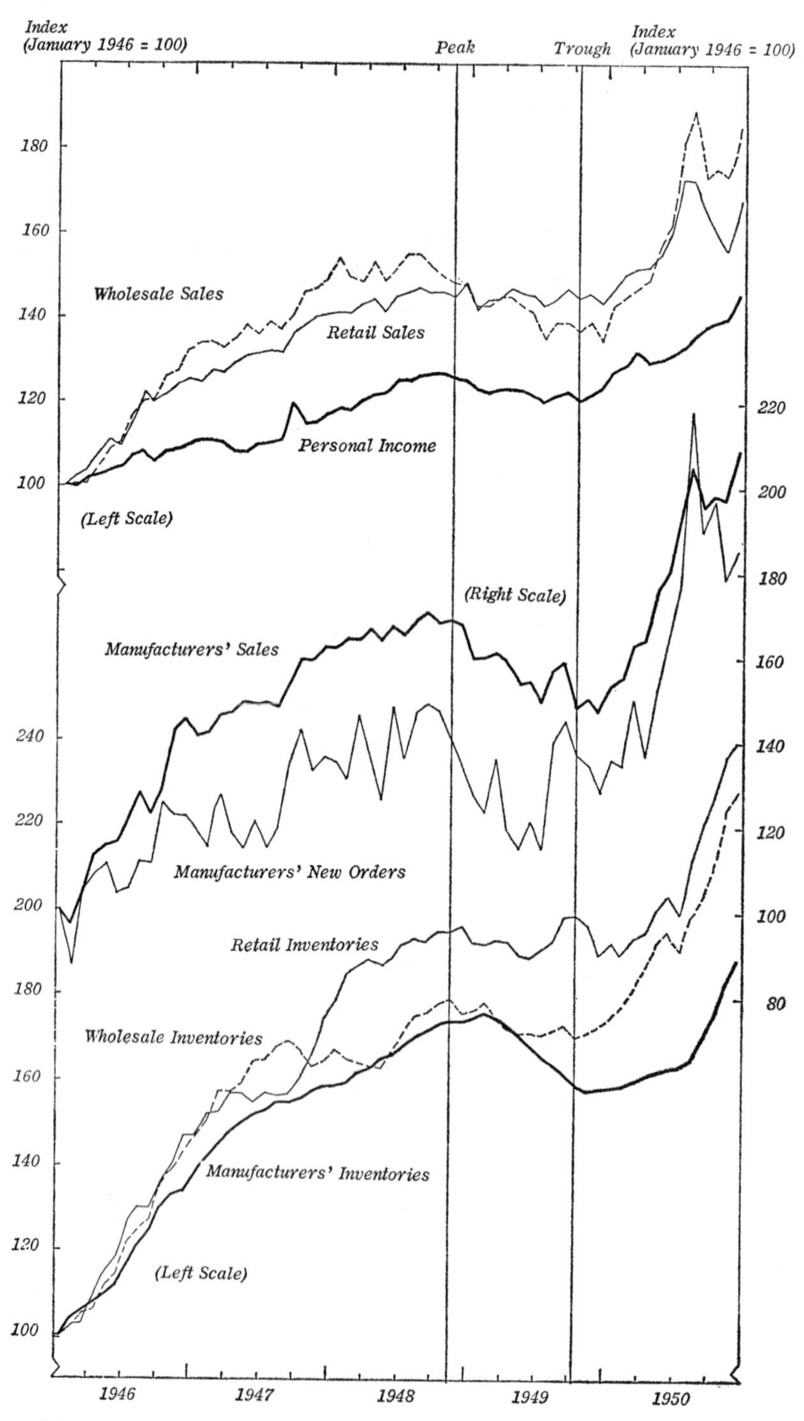

[a] Index of manufacturers' new orders not seasonally adjusted.

Source: Office of Business Economics, Department of Commerce.

still in short supply owing to the reconversion problems and capacity limitations which had restrained their production during the previous year. Thus the decrease in derived demand which was implicit in a shift from rising to stable inventory-sales ratios was confined largely to nondurables during the first half of 1947.

The expectations of businessmen also were probably involved in the diminution of inventory demand during this period. In his *Economic Report* of January 8, 1947,[4] the President felt obliged to take notice that "threatening the continuation and expansion of business investment is the fear that a drop of general consumer demand may be in the offing." The fear rested upon the knowledge that inflation had diminished the real value of disposable personal income during 1946 and that consumers had maintained real expenditure only by increasing money outlay sharply relative to money income. This process could not go on indefinitely and might be near its limit, especially since real demands for specific commodities could be expected to increase more slowly or even to decrease once backlog demands were satisfied. Again, however, it is probable that nondurables were affected more than durables by such expectations.

It is unnecessary to assume that businessmen anticipated an imminent deflation in order to give some independent weight to the factor of expectations as a depressant of inventory demand. Probably expectations of imminent price declines were fairly widespread during the early spring of 1947, especially in those markets where prices are known to respond quickly to shifts of demand or supply. Be that as it may, a shift merely from expectations of rising prices to expectations of stable prices would be enough to eliminate any margin of speculative inventory demand which may have been present in former months.

The dip in wholesale prices during the lull was confined principally to foods and other nondurable goods,[5] both because inventory demand eased more for those goods than for durables and because as a class the prices of nondurables are more sensitive than those of durables to changes in market demand or supply. In contrast, average wholesale prices of finished durable goods rose more during the sec-

[4] Page 16.
[5] See Chart 42.

CHART 9. *Government Purchases and Personal Consumption Expenditure, Seasonally Adjusted Quarterly Totals at Annual Rates, 1946-50*

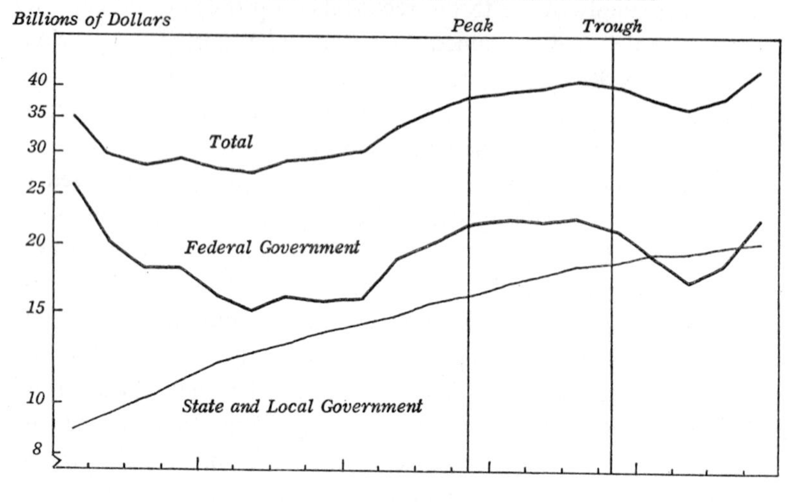

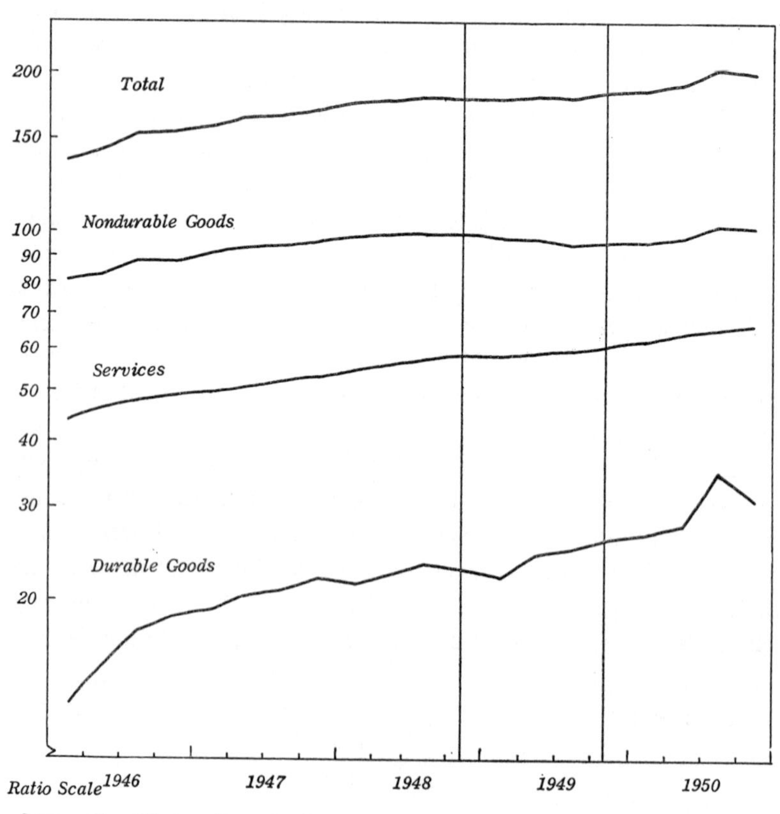

Source: Office of Business Economics, Department of Commerce.

ond quarter of 1947 than in the first, although prices of intermediate durable materials advanced more slowly than before. The latter retardation may reflect some easing in the intensity of demand, since unfilled orders of durable goods manufacturers leveled off in the first quarter and dropped in the second. Perhaps the most interesting development in this sector, however, was the stability of steel prices during the first six months of the year.

What makes it particularly interesting is that steel prices were not raised at the time of the April 1947 increase in wages of steelworkers, and did not rise until three months had passed. On no other occasion during the 13 years covered by this study did steel prices lag a general increase of steel wages. Because of their key position in the industrial price structure, the stability of steel prices probably contributed substantially to the shift away from expectations of rising prices which appears to have characterized the period. It seems likely that steel and other administered prices were, in turn, strongly influenced by the public attention which was focused on the desirability of voluntary restraint in setting prices in the State of the Union Message and Economic Report of January 1947, and again in speeches made by the President in April. Be that as it may, price stability was short-lived in these cases and most others, for it could not persist in the face of the resurgence of demand which soon developed. The next task is to identify the factors back of that resurgence.

Reduced inventory demand consequent upon successful postwar restocking in some lines and upon uncertainty about the short-term course of sales and prices was primarily responsible for the precarious balance of aggregate supply and demand in the spring of 1947. The balance was upset and inflationary pressures revived during the summer partly because expectations were recast. The recasting of expectations, however, did not occur for independent psychological reasons. Quite the contrary, it was due to a sequence of concrete economic events which first removed the drag exerted by uncertainty about short-term developments and a bit later contributed directly to an acceleration of final expenditure.

First, there was the fact that the pessimism about final demand had proved to be unjustified. Consumer expenditures, business investment in plant and equipment, residential construction, purchases of state and local governments, and net exports all increased during the first half of 1947. Fears that new homes would be priced out of a market by rising building costs were lessened when new housing starts rose more than seasonally during the spring. It had been anticipated that the drain on gold and dollar assets of foreign countries and the exhaustion of United States government loans to them would soon force a substantial reduction in net exports, but the prospects in this area were improved by the announcement of Secretary of State Marshall early in June that the United States would support a joint program for European recovery.

The acceleration of prices did not await actual increases of final demand. Specific factors boosted prices in two prominent sectors during the early summer. Food prices rose during July and August 1947 owing to a combination of short domestic and foreign crops and normal seasonal influences. A widely publicized wage increase in coal mining was accompanied by a simultaneous advance in coal prices in July and was followed by a steel price increase in August. These specific increases fostered expectations of a new wave of generalized price advances, the more so because it now appeared that earlier wage gains would be reflected in prices, as indeed they were. Thus, it is probable that speculative purchases were partly responsible for the steep rise of manufacturers' new orders and sales which commenced in September (Chart 8).

Retail sales also spurted strongly in September, providing still another stimulus to orders and prices. Legislation passed late in July permitted redemption of Armed Forces leave bonds on or after September 2. Quick advantage was taken of the opportunity to supplement current incomes, as transfer payments leaped more than $10 billion at an annual rate in September and produced corresponding bulges in personal income and retail sales which persisted for several months. The spurt of final demand was augmented by substantial inventory accumulation at the retail level, and although the latter was partly offset by inventory reductions of wholesalers, factory sales and production nonetheless moved strongly upward. As production mounted, so also did earned incomes, further feeding the expansion of retail sales.

The expansion was given new vigor by the events just reviewed. The underlying sources of strength which stemmed from backlogs of consumer and investment demand, and which had been present all along, now asserted themselves for a time without the debilitating offset of inventory disinvestment. When these forces began to weaken, moreover, fresh stimuli came forward to prolong the movement.

The year 1948 had scarcely begun before the economy experienced a jolt which raised anew the possibility of imminent deflation. Farm and food prices broke sharply downward in February. The reductions were apparently the result of favorable crop prospects at home and abroad—prospects which were disproportionately influential because of expectations that the extraordinary height to which agricultural prices had risen by the end of 1947 could not be sustained under normal conditions. This episode could have touched off a wave of deflationary inventory disinvestment had it created expectations of a generalized price decline, but it did not do so, and industrial prices remained largely unaffected. Expectations remained unshaken, partly because the potential decline of agricultural prices was limited by support programs, and partly because important shortages of durable goods and materials persisted and the response of prices in those sectors to augmented supplies or diminished demands could be expected to take place slowly in any event.

Although final demand was sufficiently high to support prices and outputs of most goods in the face of the February drop of farm and food prices, the first quarter nevertheless marks the emergence of important deflationary factors. These factors were of more than transitory importance because they reflected a change in the basic conditions which had fostered the inflation. I refer to the weakening of real investment demand in the business and housing sectors and to the acceleration of the decline of net exports which had set in earlier.

Business fixed investment increased every quarter in 1948 (Chart 6), but the moderate over-all advance conceals early declines in important industries. Expenditures on new plant and equipment by manufacturing business declined nearly $800 million between the first and fourth quarters of 1948, and the nonrail transportation, trade, service, finance, and construction industries together accounted for an additional decrease of almost $500 million during the same period.[6]

[6] *Survey of Current Business* (June 1956), p. 7. The figures are adjusted for seasonal variation and expressed as annual rates.

The early decline of manufacturing investment probably reflected diminished needs for deferred replacements and for capacity expansion to meet postwar levels of demand; modernization and expansion programs had progressed more rapidly in manufacturing than in railroading or electrical utilities, to name two important sectors in which investment continued upward during 1948. Some reduction of investment demand was to be expected once firms had attained satisfactory postwar relationships between capacity and output, even if output continued to increase as rapidly as before, since the investment required to raise a capacity-output ratio at any given rate of increase of output is greater than that required merely to sustain the ratio. Actually, manufacturing production increased rather slowly during 1947, and this fact may have influenced the formation of investment plans at the turn of the year. In some industries the retardation during 1947 was due to inadequate plant capacity or shortages of materials, but in many product lines it must be traced to a diminution of consumer demand as backlog needs were satisfied for durable or semidurable goods.

The foregoing reflections serve as a reminder that the inflation was driven throughout by demand elements which were to an important degree independent of the level or rate of change of real national income. Satisfaction of backlog investment or consumption demands would in itself tend to reduce inflationary pressures at any given level of real income and independently of financial considerations.

This is not to say that the early investment reductions in manufacturing and other sectors were completely unrelated to financial developments, but the latter influences were secondary at most. Although corporate liquidity had decreased as the inflation progressed, investment funds from current operations improved as the ratio of gross retained earnings to corporate investment increased from 48 per cent in 1946 to 69 per cent in 1947 and 81 per cent in the following year. External funds, moreover, were easily obtainable. Long-term interest rates had been allowed to rise by the Board of Governors of the Federal Reserve System in the closing months of 1947. The increase was moderate, however, and the monetary authorities took the necessary steps then and later to supply reserves to the banking system whenever the stability of interest rates was threatened. The money supply declined slightly after the first quarter of 1948, but bank loans rose substantially and income velocity and total spending continued to increase.

Financial constraints were more important in the areas of home building and foreign trade. The rise of gilt-edge interest rates had the effect of making GI mortgage loans at fixed rates less attractive to lenders, many of whom tightened up on loan applications.[7] From April 30 to August 10, 1948, there was no statutory authority for action by the Federal Housing Administration on the most liberal type of mortgage for lower priced houses or on mortgage insurance for multifamily rental housing units. Housing starts fell sharply beginning in July, and it appears that tightened purchase terms and reduced availability of lower quality mortgage credit should receive a good deal of weight in an explanation of the decline. Uncertainty about the content of future housing legislation may also have inhibited the activities of speculative builders during the hiatus of April 30 to August 10.

Net exports form the third important category of final demand which weakened well before the downturn of aggregate activity (Chart 5). Exports plummeted between the third quarters of 1947 and 1948 because foreign gold and dollar holdings had been depleted by the extraordinary purchases of 1946-47 and because loan-financed aid by the United States government was exhausted.[8] Fortunately, most of the decline in the export surplus came before mid-1948 while other elements of demand were still favorable to the maintenance of physical activity, so that its major effect was to relieve inflationary pressures rather than to initiate a contraction.

After this lengthy recital of early developments that sapped the strength of the underlying forces which had fostered the inflation in previous years, the reader may be surprised to learn that the indexes of wholesale and consumer prices spurted yet again after March 1948, and by September had risen respectively another 3.5 per cent and 4.6 per cent. This last fillip was given to the inflation by a combination of forces, including a supply-induced increase of meat prices, the actual and anticipated effects of government fiscal actions, and wage increases which were partly related to the foregoing factors and partly

[7] Housing and Home Finance Agency, *First Annual Report, 1947,* p. I-21.

[8] These reductions were incompletely offset by increases during 1948 of foreign assistance in the form of gifts under interim aid and the Marshall Plan.

induced by the earlier rise of consumer prices between mid-1947 and early 1948.

The February decline of food prices was followed by a renewed rise beginning in March at wholesale and in April at retail. The food component of the consumer price index increased 7 per cent between March and August. The latter advance was due principally to meats, which continued in short supply and which increased 18 per cent at retail over the same period. Meanwhile, prices of cereal products remained steady at retail and drifted downward at wholesale, owing to abundant crops.

Prices were also influenced by government fiscal actions. These included final approval of a new foreign aid program under the Marshall Plan, enactment of a stepped-up defense program, and a reduction of personal income taxes effective April 2. The bulk of the substantial increase of federal expenditures between the first and third quarters of 1948 (Chart 9) resulted from grants under foreign aid programs and from agricultural price support operations. Domestic defense expenditures rose only in the final quarter of the year. The economic stimulus provided by the defense program did not await the increase of expenditures, however, but was partly felt during the spring when its discussion and enactment affected business expectations and when substantial orders for aircraft were placed. There were also expectations that the tax reduction would have an early effect on retail sales because withholding from wages and salaries would be decreased at an annual rate of $3 billion beginning in May.

It was in the context of these expectations that prices of foods turned upward again in April and that springtime wage negotiations were conducted in the large durable goods industries. Heavy industry had resisted wage increases following the agricultural price break of February, since it appeared that the cost of living would stabilize or decline and that demand pressures were easing.[9] When food prices recovered and the defense program and tax reduction were announced, the determination of labor to win wage increases was augmented and that of management to resist them diminished. The result was a series of wage-price increases in major heavy industries during the spring and summer. For durable manufacturing as a whole, average hourly

[9] *Midyear Economic Report of the President* (July 1948), p. 33.

earnings and average prices of finished goods both advanced 6 per cent between May and September. Most of the 1948 wage increases were roughly equal to the rise in the cost of living during the life of the prior labor contract.[10] Perhaps a substantial increase of money wages would have occurred in any event, but it would probably have been smaller had food prices continued to drop after February and had not management resistance been weakened by favorable demand expectations engendered by government fiscal decisions. (Wage-price interactions are discussed in greater detail in Chapter 14.)

During the second half of 1948, the forces of deflation gained final ascendancy. The downturn developed gradually from an accumulation of depressing factors, each mild in itself, but in sum sufficient finally to cause a decline of aggregate activity. The decline of residential construction after midyear has already been mentioned. Another depressant was added when retail sales leveled off during the third quarter (Chart 8). The retardation affected particularly sales of nondurables, and since stock-sales ratios were being closely controlled by retailers (Chart 7), new orders were immediately trimmed to prevent further accumulation of stocks, wholesale trade in nondurables declined after July and factory sales after September, and manufacturing production of such goods eased during the third quarter and again in the fourth.

The retardation of retail sales was the more disappointing because it followed the April tax cut. Price and wage increases augmented personal incomes during the second and third quarters, and the tax reduction boosted disposable personal income even more, but these developments had the effect mainly of raising saving instead of consumption expenditure (Chart 5). Personal saving increased from an annual rate of $4.8 billion in the first quarter to $11.4 billion in the second and $14.4 billion in the third. The corresponding saving percentages were 2.7, 6.0, and 7.4. Thus, the retardation of consumer spending occurred because spending did not keep pace with income and not because income failed to increase as rapidly as before; on the contrary, disposable income increased faster during the spring and summer than during the preceding half year.

[10] *Ibid.*, p. 34; "Annual Economic Review, A Report to the President by the Council of Economic Advisers," *Economic Report of the President* (January 1949), p. 8.

The decline of consumption expenditures relative to income was primarily a consequence of the diminution of pent-up consumer demands. To the extent that it was an expression of a general easing of demand, it was probably influenced by the progressive decline of liquidity during the preceding years of inflation. Individuals' holdings of liquid assets had increased more slowly than disposable income, inflation had reduced their real value 15 per cent between the end of 1945 and 1947, and there may have occurred a shift of assets to firmer hands. Certainly the intense desire to increase expenditures in any and all directions which had characterized the first year or more of the inflation was no longer manifest, and this argues for the presence of some general constraint such as diminished liquidity.

Diminished liquidity was not the only factor responsible for the failure of aggregate consumption expenditure to rise proportionately with income, however. A supply restraint was also involved. Backlog demands for most goods had been eliminated by 1948, but automobiles were still in short supply. The rate of real expenditure on new automobiles depended upon production and showed no signs of flagging during the spring and summer of 1948 or indeed for many quarters thereafter. Consumer credit controls had been dropped in November 1947 and were not reimposed until September 1948. It is quite probable that had more cars been produced in mid-1948, more would have been purchased—and at higher prices if desired by sellers. Other expenditures would not have decreased correspondingly, moreover, because any current retrenchment of consumption outlays which might be made by families purchasing new automobiles would be smaller than the total outlay for the automobile, the bulk of which would be financed by asset liquidation or new credit. Thus, aggregate consumption expenditure would have been larger at given levels of income and liquidity had more automobiles been produced in 1948.

The emerging inventory problems of retailers were not confined to nondurables. Expenditures for furniture and household equipment also leveled off in the third quarter, and they actually dropped in the fourth, following the reimposition of curbs on installment credit. Inventories of durable goods were not quite so closely controlled by distributors, however, and factory production of major durable household goods was maintained a few months longer than was true of nondurables, before joining the general decline after October.

Thus by the final quarter of 1948 aggregate activity was being depressed by a reduction in residential construction, by stable or falling retail sales, and by diminished inventory demand. Government spending and business fixed investment were still increasing, but insufficiently to prevent a downturn of aggregate physical activity in November or December. Prices fell along with physical activity as inflationary pressures ebbed. The peaks of wholesale and consumer prices led the October peak of industrial production by one month. Agricultural prices had started downhill for certain in July because increased production at home and abroad augmented domestic supplies at the same time that retail sales of food and other nondurables stabilized. Retail food prices dropped in concert with farm prices. Wholesale prices of products other than farm commodities and foods did not fall until December, however, and the consumer price index of all items less food also held firm until year end. Reductions of industrial finished goods prices at wholesale and retail awaited the further easing of demand which came after the turn of the year.

Contraction and Recovery: 1948-49

The truly remarkable feature of the 1948-49 contraction of business activity was that it was so mild. What factors were responsible for the "unique and fortunate experience of liquidating a major inflation without falling into a severe recession,"[11] and why was the price decline so moderate in comparison with the increase which came before (Chart 4)? These are interrelated questions, for the moderate price decline was both consequence and cause of the mildness of the contraction in physical activity.

The contraction was mild enough to be called an inventory recession, and it has often been described by that term. Insofar as the term is taken to mean that final demand declined little and that most of the moderate fall in gross national product was accounted for by inven-

[11] "The Economic Situation at Midyear 1949, A Report to the President by the Council of Economic Advisers," p. 3, *Midyear Economic Report of the President* (July 1949).

tory change, it is quite accurate. This leaves unsettled the question, however, of whether inventory investment exerted more than a passive influence over the course of events. The amount of decline of inventory demand depends in the first instance, after all, on the behavior of final expenditure—that is, on the behavior of gross national expenditure exclusive of inventory investment. If final expenditure drops only moderately, current production will soon fall below sales, attempts to adjust stocks to the smaller volume of sales will meet with early success, and new orders and production will quickly revert to equality or more with sales. Minor contractions are kept minor by those factors—not always the same in every contraction—which foster stability of final demand. What were these factors in 1949?

The behavior of the major components of final expenditure is summarized in Charts 6 and 9. These facts stand out: State and local government expenditures rose strongly throughout the contraction, just as they have done every year of the postwar era under the impetus of population growth and migration and because of the stubborn persistence of backlogs of needs for community services. Federal expenditures increased slightly during the first six or seven months of the contraction, and the subsequent decline of defense spending was small and did not begin until other sectors were assuming active importance in the recovery. Thus autonomous demands on the part of governmental units moderated the decline and favored a prompt upturn.

The early revival of residential construction and personal consumption expenditure is also noteworthy. In both cases, backlogs of real demand remained large—automobiles were at the forefront in the improvement in retail sales—and easier credit facilitated renewed expansion. Mortgage and consumer credit became more readily available because of the cyclical fall of demand for funds for business investment. In addition, there were selective changes in terms on mortgages and consumer instalment contracts.

The initial steps to ease terms on housing mortgages were not part of a conscious antirecession policy, and the early upturn of housing starts in 1949 was a happy accident from the contracyclical point of view. The liberalized provisions under the permanent program of FHA insurance for lower priced sales housing and the restored program for rental housing were contained in the Housing Act of 1948 (August

10), which was passed at a time when inflation was thought to be the near-term threat for the economy. The concern was with the housing problem in itself and not with the level of aggregate activity. The effects were nonetheless favorable to early recovery after the contraction was underway, when the industry was stimulated by the new mortgage insurance programs, easier supply conditions in the capital markets, an induced decline in building costs, and a shift in composition toward inexpensive sales housing and the construction of rental units. Since real disposable personal income was virtually unchanged from 1948 levels, all these factors facilitated the tapping of the additional demand which existed for less expensive housing at the given level of aggregate income.

Regulation of down payments and maturities on instalment credit had been authorized by Congress as an anti-inflationary measure and reimposed by the Federal Reserve in September 1948. The regulations were relaxed in March 1949 and ended in June. Automobile sales would doubtless have risen strongly in any event—they increased during the period of controls—but easier terms probably drew some marginal buyers into the market for automobiles and for other consumer durables as well.

The special factors favoring consumption demand during 1949 were powerfully reinforced by income stability. When measured in constant (1954) dollars, disposable income dropped only $2 billion in the first quarter of 1949 and real consumption changed scarcely at all. Real disposable income then increased $1 billion between the first and third quarters of the year, although still declining in current dollars, whereas real consumption rose $5 billion. Thus consumption demand became an autonomous force for expansion, running far ahead of income.

Automatic stabilizers cushioned the contraction of income and helped foster the expansion of consumption. National income before inventory valuation adjustment declined $15.5 billion between the third quarters of 1948 and 1949, but induced reductions of undistributed corporate profits and corporate profit taxes absorbed about $6.5 billion of the decline, while $1.5 billion was offset by smaller personal taxes, and $2 billion by increased transfer payments which supplemented the flow of production income. Incidentally, the de-

TABLE 10. *Indicators of Capacity Utilization in Selected Years*[a]

Indicator	Year		
	1929	1937	1948
		(1929=100)	
1. Ratios of national output to fixed capital			
a) Goldsmith	100	107	120
b) Machinery and Allied Products Institute	100	96	129
2. Ratios of output to fixed capital, manufacturing			
a) Creamer	100	125	141
b) Department of Commerce	100	115	152
		(*Per Cent*)	
3. Ratios of output to capacity, selected industries			
a) Steel ingots	*88*	*72*	*93*
b) Pig iron	*82*	*73*	*88*
c) Beehive coke	*31*	*43*	*82*
d) By-product coke	*89*	*79*	*93*
e) Electrolytic copper	*94*	*72*	*77*
f) Portland cement	*68*	*46*	*82*
g) Electric power	*36*	*38*	*59*
h) Wheat flour	*57*	*53*	*77*
i) Paper	*81*	*82*	*94*
j) Petroleum refining	*78*	*82*	*92*

[a] The sources and notes for lines 1 through 3j are as follows:

1a. Capital stock from Raymond W. Goldsmith, *A Study of Saving in the United States*, Vol. III (1956), Table W-3. Sum of stocks of nonresidential and nongovernmental structures and producer durables in 1929 prices. Output is measured by privately produced gross national product in 1929 prices.

1b. Government-owned plant and equipment and residential structures are excluded from capital, and the output measure is the privately produced gross national product. The data are corrected for price changes.

2a. Reciprocals of estimates of the ratio of fixed capital to output as given in Daniel Creamer, *Capital and Output Trends in Manufacturing Industries, 1880–1948*, National Bureau of Economic Research, Occasional Paper 41 (1954), p. 49. Fixed capital comprises structures and equipment net of depreciation. Output is measured by gross operating receipts. Both items are corrected for price changes.

2b. Real net value of manufacturing structures and equipment from Donald G. Wooden and Robert C. Wasson, "Manufacturing Investment Since 1929," *Survey of Current Business* (November 1956), Table 4. Federal Reserve index of manufacturing production.

3a–j. The Brookings Institution, U. S. Bureau of Mines, American Iron and Steel Institute, American Bureau of Metal Statistics, Edison Electric Institute, American Paper and Pulp Association, Bureau of the Census. For detailed citations and characteristics of the data, see Bert G. Hickman, "Capacity, Capacity Utilization, and the Acceleration Principle," *Problems of Capital Formation*, Studies in Income and Wealth, Vol. XIX (1957), Appendix A.

cline in net tax receipts and the increased purchases of goods and services by all levels of government were reflected in a shift of $9.5 billion from a surplus to a deficit in the government sector (Chart 5).

Business fixed investment fell about 15.5 per cent in physical volume between the fourth quarter of 1948 and the first quarter of 1950. Thus it was by all odds the major depressant of final expenditure at work in the contraction. The point which deserves greatest stress, however, is not that it declined, but that it did not decline much more. This is a good part of the explanation of how the inflation was liquidated without a severe contraction. The inflationary waves of 1946-48 had not engendered overly optimistic long-term investment expectations and had not caused an unwarranted expansion of productive facilities. The available data on capital stock in relation to production and on capacity utilization by industry indicate that capital facilities were used more intensively before the contraction began than they had been in 1929 or 1937 (Table 10). Fixed investment might have declined more had other elements of final demand decreased sharply during the contraction, of course, but the independent strength of government and consumer spending prevented the development of any widespread condition of seriously excessive capacity.

The situation was much the same with regard to inventory investment. Inventories were not excessive before the downturn began—partly, of course, because they had been watched so very carefully during 1948, with mildly deflationary results during the latter months of that year in the nondurable goods industries. Even by the end of 1948, inventories were below the prewar relationship to sales in manufacturing and distributing alike. The restocking of 1946-48 had been needed to re-establish normal working relationships between stocks and sales, and speculative inventory purchasing in anticipation of advancing prices had not gotten out of hand. This meant that inventory disinvestment during 1949 was confined largely to that required to bring stocks down to the reduced level of sales and production and was uncomplicated by any need to liquidate speculative holdings. Even the feedback effect of inventory disinvestment on production income and, hence, upon final demand was limited by the automatic changes in profits, taxes, and transfers mentioned earlier.

Inventory disinvestment could still have become a powerful independent force in the contraction had adverse price expectations and a psychology of liquidation-at-any-cost developed as it progressed. The initial absence of speculative holdings in itself inhibited such a development, however, and other factors were at work as well, including some significant changes in the institutional structure. I refer to the agricultural price support programs, the government commitment to promote full employment contained in the Employment Act of 1946, and the augmented importance and strength of labor unions in the mass production industries dating from the mid-1930's. Taken altogether, these factors limited actual and potential price declines, thus undercutting such nascent fears as may have existed about the stability of prices.

In summary, production and prices declined comparatively little during 1949 because speculative excesses had not been a feature of the inflation; because institutional factors and public policies minimized actual and expected declines of incomes, sales, and prices and prevented cumulative deterioration of short-term expectations; and because, in those favorable circumstances, the forces for expansion inherent in the postwar population upsurge and remaining backlogs of public and private demand could quickly assert their influence. The deflationary force of inventory disinvestment was largely spent by midyear, and a recovery led by government spending, home building, and automobiles actually began at that time.

The upswing of industrial production was interrupted during the autumn by coal and steel strikes, but expansion was quickly resumed and developed rapidly during the first half of 1950. The recovery of final demand induced a sharp increase of inventory investment during the first quarter, and national income rose correspondingly. As income rose, so also did consumer demand and, after a brief lag, business expenditure for plant and equipment. With the induced revival of business fixed investment in the spring, a cumulative expansion was assured.

Employment recovered along with production during the latter months of 1949 (Chart 10). At first, however, employment increased more slowly than the labor force, so that the peak rate of unemployment was not reached until January 1950. Unemployment fell rapidly thereafter, but 5 per cent of those in the labor force were still seeking

CHART 10. *The Labor Force, Employment, and the Unemployment Ratio, Monthly, Seasonally Adjusted, 1947-50*

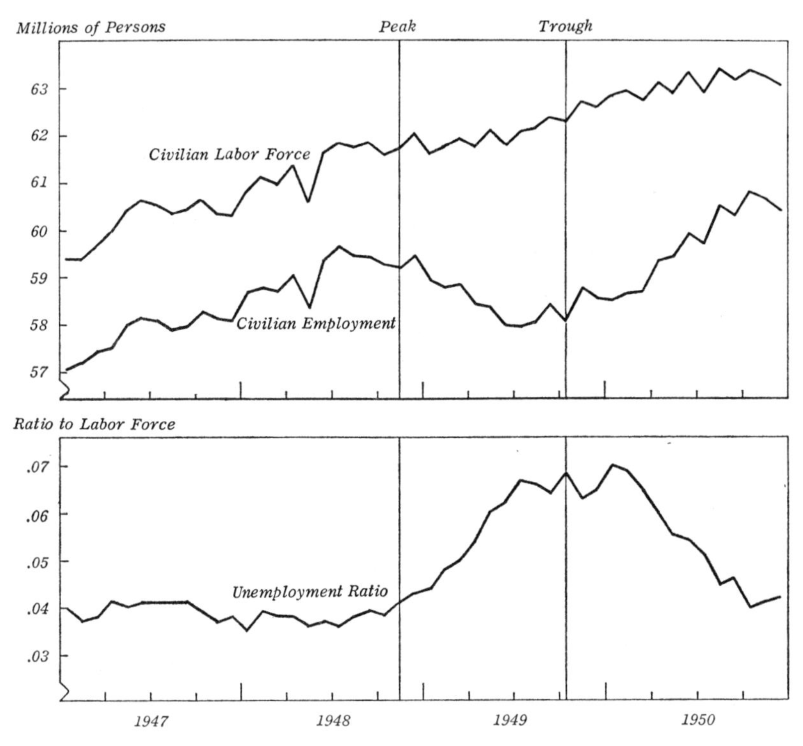

Source: Derived from data of Bureau of the Census.

jobs when the Korean War began in June 1950. By that time, real gross national product was already 5 per cent higher than at the 1948 cyclical peak and continuing expansion was assured, but employment had not yet caught up with the growth of the labor force since 1948.

At its inception, the new expansion was a muted echo of the one which had gone before. The underlying autonomous public and private investment opportunities were the same as those operating in 1946-48, although now present in attenuated degree. There no longer existed a general, pressing excess demand for consumer goods and there had occurred a corresponding diminution of excess liquidity as the stock of individuals' holdings of liquid assets shrank in real value and in relationship to income, though not in absolute amount. Substantial backlogs of demand were still making themselves felt in the important markets for automobiles and residential housing, however, and the same was true of services supplied by state and local governments and privately owned public utilities. And, with the dissipation of acute inflationary pressures and the upturn which followed, the adverse short-term expectations which had been depressing business fixed investment were reversed and investment programs were revised upward. There can be little doubt that the exploitable investment opportunities in the private and public sectors were sufficiently rich to support a normal business expansion before the Korean War created a new situation, although it appears unlikely that the expansion would have lasted as long as it did, were it not for Korea.

5 / *Korean Inflation: 1950-52*

NORMAL PROCESSES of cyclical recovery from the 1949 trough had carried the economy most of the distance toward full employment by mid-1950, at which time the economic forces set in motion by the Korean conflict intervened to alter radically the character of the expansion. Prices were forced up violently in two consecutive waves of forward buying which swept over the country during the first nine months of hostilities, and, although wholesale prices subsequently receded, the average of consumer prices did not (Chart 11). Warfare in Korea and mobilization at home did more than lend an inflationary cast to the expansion, however. The defense mobilization stimulated the economy for several years and prolonged the expansion considerably beyond the usual peacetime duration even of lengthy expansions (Chapter 2). From 1951 through mid-1953, moreover, the civilian unemployment ratio was in the neighborhood of 3 per cent (Chart 17)—an abnormally low ratio by peacetime standards. Finally, the cutback of military spending after Korea was a principal cause—though, as discussed in the next chapter, not the only important cause—of the contraction of 1953-54.

First Nine Months: Expansion and Inflation

A war mobilization may foster economic expansion in several ways. Unless offset by fiscal or monetary measures, public expenditures for defense will augment aggregate demand at any given level of national income. Expansion need not await the actual growth of government

CHART 11. *Indexes of Prices, Industrial Production, and Nonagricultural Employment, Monthly, and of Real Gross National Product, Quarterly, Seasonally Adjusted,*[a] *1950-54*

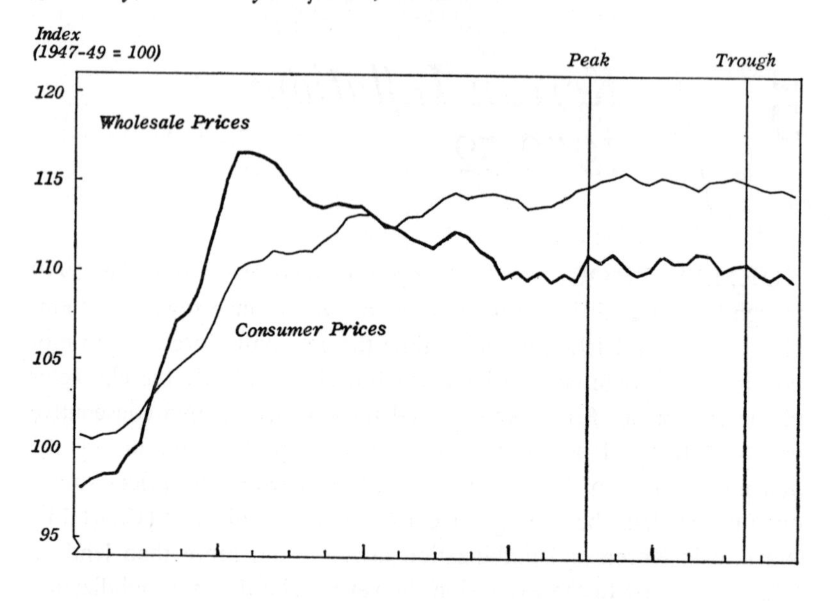

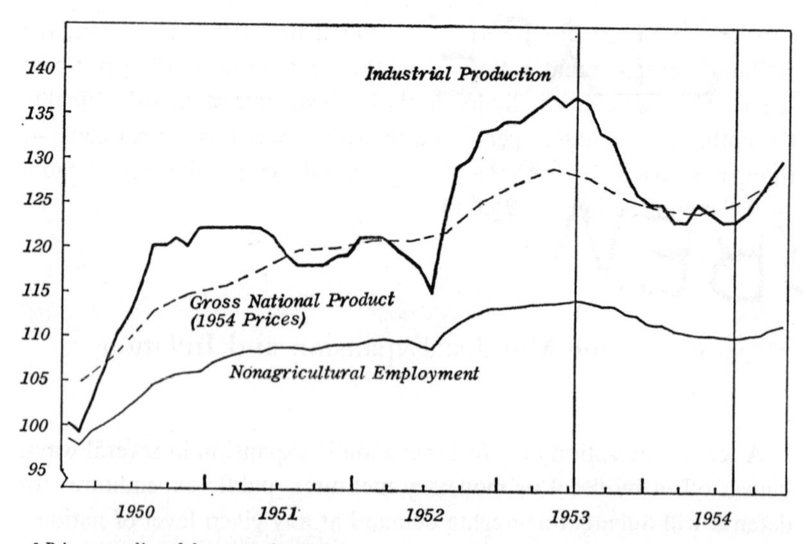

[a] Prices not adjusted for seasonal variation.

Sources: Bureau of Labor Statistics; Board of Governors of the Federal Reserve System; Office of Business Economics, Department of Commerce.

outlays, however. In the first place, the placement of orders will precede actual expenditures. For a time, the increased production consequent on the orders will be reflected in private inventory investment rather than in government expenditure. Second, private fixed investment may be encouraged in industries related to defense not only because of orders for defense goods but also by such devices as accelerated tax amortization, direct loans, and loan guarantees. Such private investment, while resulting directly from the defense program, is not included in federal purchases of goods and services. Finally, the outbreak of hostilities or the announcement of mobilization may quicken demand by affecting the expectations of investors or consumers. This last was an especially important influence in the initial inflationary months of the Korean expansion. Military spending was not the sole or even the principal cause of the early buying waves, although the placement of defense orders doubtless stimulated business activity in late 1950. Rather, it was the forward buying of consumers and businessmen in anticipation of potential shortages which created acute inflationary pressures.

South Korea was invaded in June 1950. Consumer expenditures accelerated immediately. In the third quarter, the surge in durable goods was especially pronounced, but there was also a noticeable spurt in nondurables (Chart 12). Businessmen were not prepared for the flood of sales, and inventory investment, which had been increasing in the first half of the year, decreased slightly in the third quarter (Chart 13).

These swift-moving events may be followed more closely with the aid of the monthly data recorded in Chart 14. Retail sales increased 8 per cent in July, or five times as much as the rise of personal income. Although retailers simultaneously increased their own purchases—wholesale trade rose 16 per cent in July—their stocks were nonetheless reduced by the spurt of sales. Wholesalers also reacted swiftly. Manufacturers' new orders jumped 15 per cent and their sales 7 per cent. In short, buying was extremely active on all market levels in the first few weeks of the war.

The July level of retail sales was maintained through August. Meanwhile, the sales of wholesalers and manufacturers continued to increase, and retail and wholesale stocks were therefore enlarged.

Retail sales broke sharply downward in September and continued to

CHART 12. *Government Purchases and Personal Consumption Expenditures, Seasonally Adjusted Quarterly Totals at Annual Rates, 1950-54*

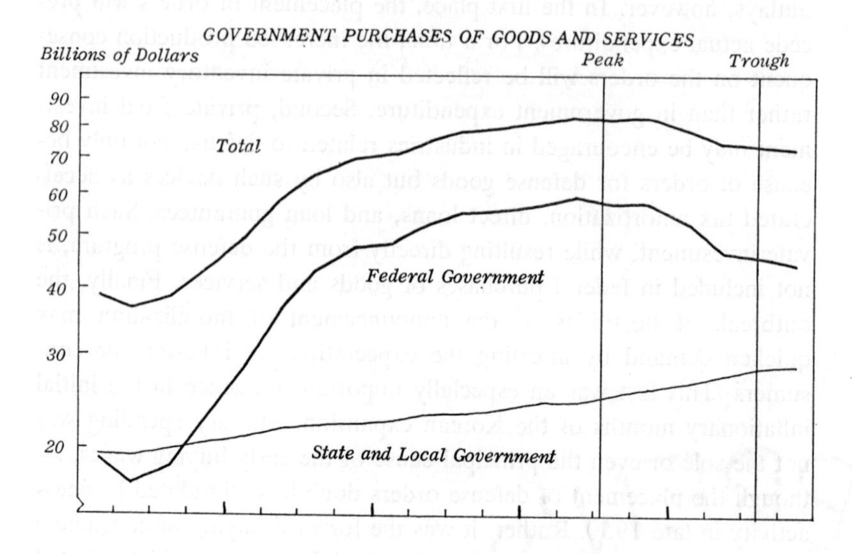

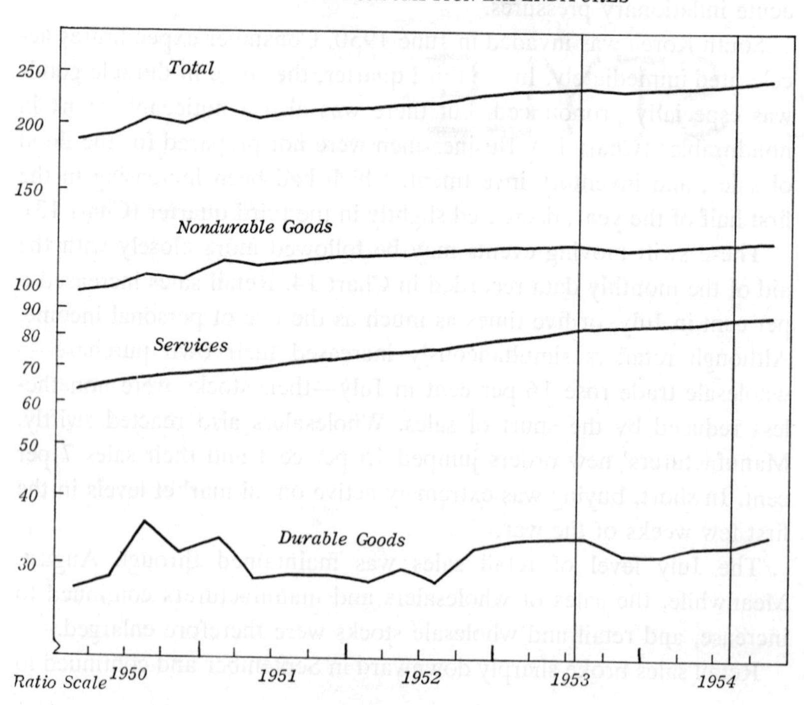

Source: Office of Business Economics, Department of Commerce.

fall through November. The fourth quarter decline in consumer spending affected durables and nondurables alike. Wholesale trade followed retail sales downward, but in neither case did merchandise receipts decline proportionately, so that stocks continued to rise. Manufacturers' stocks also increased, primarily because of increases in purchased materials and goods in process. Thus, manufacturers and distributors alike were making large additions to inventories in the fourth quarter despite, or because of, the lull in consumer spending. The absolute increase in nonfarm inventories was greater than the decrease in consumer expenditures. The ratio of inventory to sales increased substantially on all market levels, with a particularly large rise at retail (Chart 15). There is no indication here of a physical shortage of consumer goods at the year's end.

Nonetheless, another consumer buying wave began in December, following reversals in the Korean campaign. Once again expenditures for durables increased, although not to the level of the third quarter of 1950. Expenditures for nondurables were larger than in the first wave, however. The big spurt in retail sales came in January 1951, but distributors were prepared and the goods were available. Sales by manufacturers and wholesalers increased along with those at retail, and stocks rose all along the line from manufacturer to retailer. Sales at retail and wholesale fell off once more in February and March, but manufacturers' sales were maintained, and distributors' stocks mounted rapidly.

The speculative nature of these successive reversals of consumer demand is readily apparent in the wide swings of expenditure relative to income, timed as they were with the onset of hostilities, the favorable military developments which followed the landing at Inchon on September 15, and the subsequent setback when the Chinese Communists entered the war and the retreat from the Yalu began in late November (Charts 14 and 16). In technical terms, the consumption function shifted upward in the third quarter of 1950, downward in the fourth, and upward again in the first quarter of 1951, as expectations changed. Changes in individual expectations may often be offsetting but, during this period, memories of wartime shortages were still fresh, there was talk of rationing (which was authorized in the De-

CHART 13. *Gross Private Domestic Investment and Its Components, Seasonally Adjusted Quarterly Totals at Annual Rates, 1950-54*

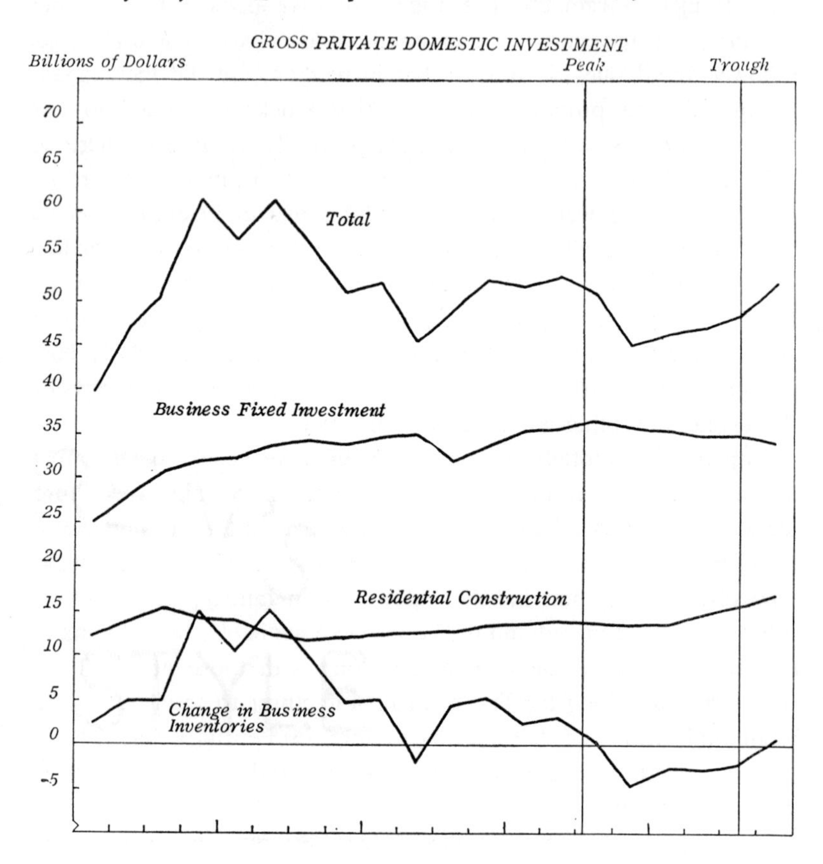

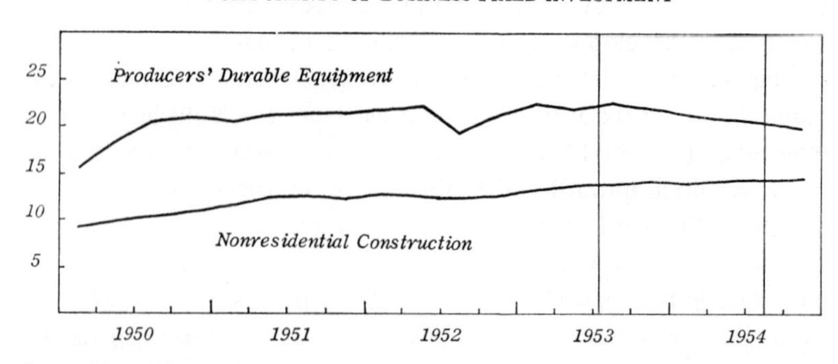

Source: Office of Business Economics, Department of Commerce.

fense Production Act of 1950, approved September 8), and there were dramatic reversals in the military situation, so that shifts in individual expectations were general and in the same direction.

Two associated expectations doubtless influenced households and businesses: the fear that shortages would develop as a consequence of formal or informal rationing and the belief that prices would increase. From time to time, such anticipations may form in the market for a particular product as a result of special conditions which affect that market alone. When many groups hold such expectations at the same time, affecting many markets, the short-period potential for inflation is great. That was the situation during the buying waves. The volume of demand generated by the forward buying was itself sufficient to create temporary shortages at existing prices, and as a result prices advanced rapidly. As it turned out, serious physical shortages of consumer goods did not develop in 1951. However, this might have happened if consumers and businessmen had not accumulated stocks in 1950 and early 1951, since the central government substantially increased its claim on the nation's resources in 1951.

The mobilization itself made comparatively little direct contribution to inflationary pressures at the times when the pressures were most active. Federal purchases of goods and services were stable during the first buying wave. It is true that government expenditures rose in the fourth quarter, and together with inventory investment, accounted for the entire increase of gross national product between the third and fourth quarters. It should be noted, however, that wholesale prices rose only 2 per cent from September to November, but jumped 5 per cent between then and January 1951, after the second buying spree got underway. The rapid advance during December and January may have resulted in part from an effort by sellers to raise prices before a price freeze could be announced, but this merely means that businessmen shared the expectations upon which consumers acted. Whatever direct stimulus to price advances was provided by the defense program during 1950 stemmed largely from the effects of military orders on the purchase plans and production schedules of defense contractors.

CHART 14. *Indexes of Personal Income, Sales, Inventories, and New Orders, Monthly, Seasonally Adjusted, 1950-54*

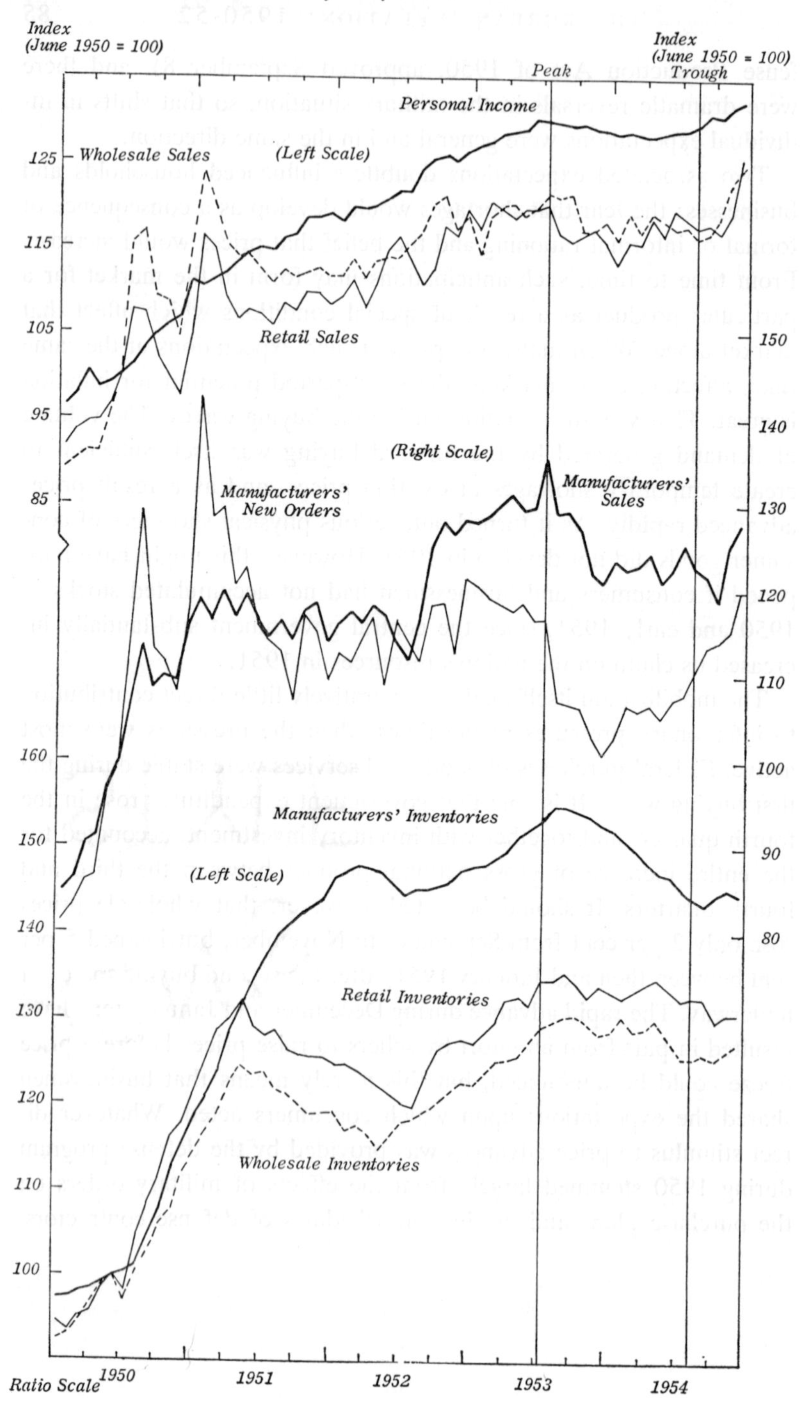

Source: Office of Business Economics, Department of Commerce.

It must be adjudged as secondary in comparison with the violent swings of civilian demand which characterized the period.[1]

By the same token, the fiscal and monetary actions taken to curb inflation were relatively ineffectual, partly because they were not especially restrictive before 1951, and also because general constraints on income and credit cannot prevent surges of speculative demand in a liquid economy. This is not to imply that government policy makers were complacent or inactive during 1950. The point is simply that many of the restraints initiated during the summer and fall of 1950 did not become fully operative for several months because of normal lags between actions and effects, whereas the direct controls which would have been necessary to prevent forward buying were unavailable during the first wave, and were unused for a time during the second because intervening events had suggested that the controls authorized in September might not be needed after all.

A bill to reduce tax rates was under consideration when the war began. In July 1950, the President recommended a tax increase of $5 billion, and approximately that amount was enacted in September. In the words of the Council of Economic Advisers, "A tax-reducing and adjusting measure was turned into a major tax-increasing measure, an unprecedented achievement made possible by the close cooperation of all concerned."[2] An Excess Profits Tax Act was subsequently enacted in January 1951, but with provisions effective July 1, 1950. Thus, higher tax rates account for part of the huge government surplus that

[1] New obligations (approximately, new orders) of the Department of Defense behaved as follows during the Korean period:

Year	Quarter			
	I	II	III	IV
	(In billions of dollars)			
1950	n.a.	n.a.	8.6	8.7
1951	16.1	16.2	13.0	13.0
1952	15.3	20.6	16.8	10.4
1953	10.8	8.5	6.5	6.0
1954	6.9	10.5	n.a.	n.a.

n.a. Not available.
Source: Murray L. Weidenbaum, *Government Spending: Process and Measurement* (Boeing Aircraft Co., September 1958), Table 19.

It will be seen that new defense orders did not rise substantially until the first quarter of 1951—that is, until after the second buying wave and the associated price increases had ended in January.

[2] Included in *Midyear Economic Report of the President* (July 1951), p. 41.

CHART 15. *Inventory-Sales Ratios, Monthly, Seasonally Adjusted, 1950-54*

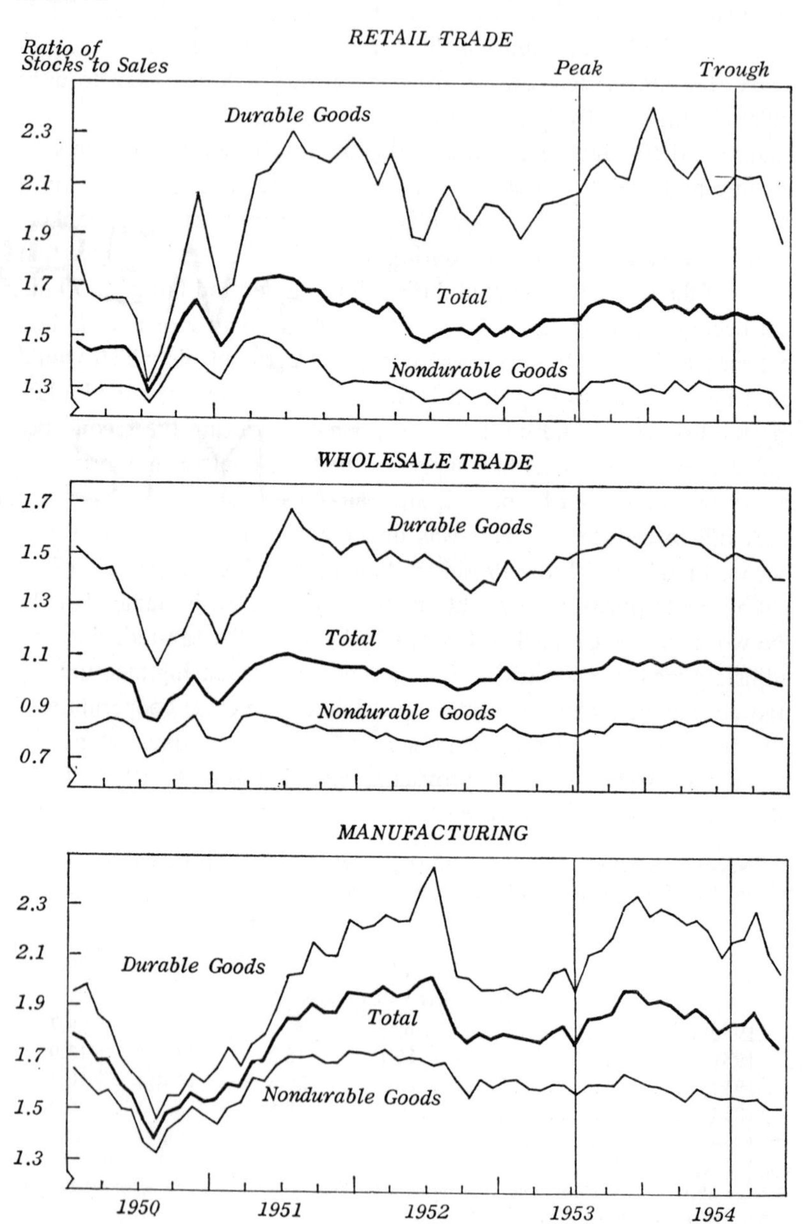

Source: Derived from data of the Office of Business Economics, Department of Commerce.

developed in 1950 and early 1951 (Chart 16). Roughly one-half of the increase in net taxes, however, was induced by the rise of income and employment. Increased rates of taxation restrained the growth of disposable personal income, especially in the first quarter of 1951, but this favorable development was offset by the renewed surge of consumer spending.

The Board of Governors of the Federal Reserve System remained committed to its postwar policy of support of bond prices until March 4, 1951. Because commercial banks, insurance companies, savings institutions, and other bondholders found it attractive to liquidate government securities in order to supply current demands for private credit, the central bank was obliged to acquire $3.5 billion of these securities between August 1950 and February 1951, thereby contributing to the expansion of bank reserves and the money supply. The privately held money supply increased about $4 billion or 3 per cent between the second quarter of 1950 and the first of 1951. This was not, however, the primary factor in the increase of money expenditure, since income velocity rose 12 per cent over the same interval—which indicates a substantial reduction in the proportion of the money supply held idle. A restrictive monetary policy might have mitigated the inflation, but it could scarcely have prevented substantial increments in current expenditures and prices.

Specific credit controls were invoked early in the inflation, but again with limited short-term success. The initial step to curb credit for residential construction was taken July 19, 1950, when mortgage terms on government-guaranteed loans were tightened. The restrictions were extended to other types of mortgage credit in October. Consumer credit controls were established in September and strengthened in October.

The real estate credit regulations had little effect on mortgage credit extended during late 1950 and early 1951 because they did not apply to buildings under construction or to credit already committed. The instalment credit curbs may have been partly responsible for the decline of durable goods purchases during the fourth quarter and their comparatively small increase in the following quarter. It is equally plausible, however, that the fourth quarter declines in sales of durables and nondurables alike reflected primarily improved expectations

CHART 16. *The Nation's Income, Expenditure, and Saving, Seasonally Adjusted Quarterly Totals at Annual Rates, 1950-54*

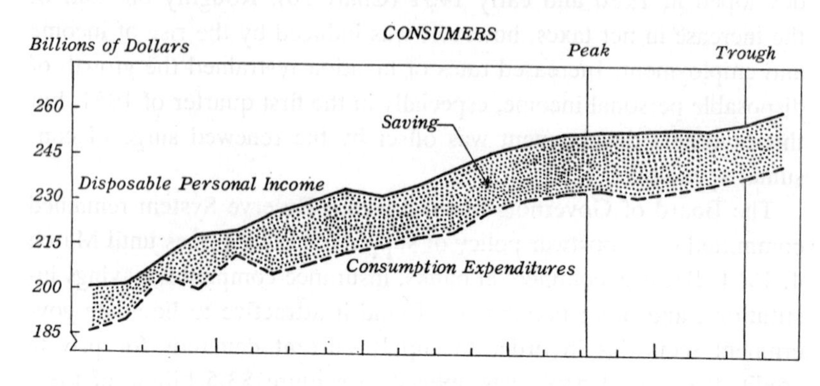

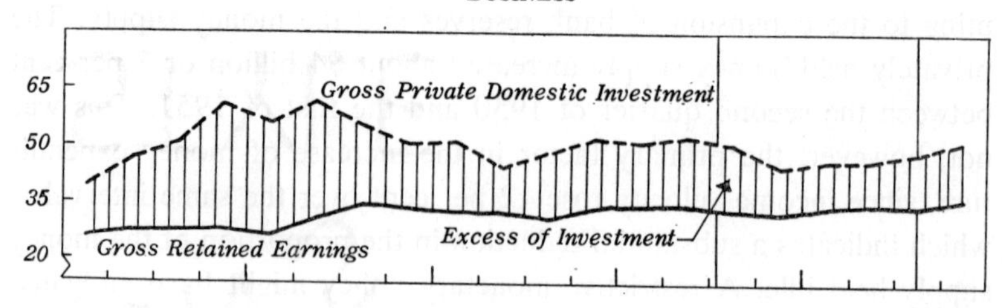

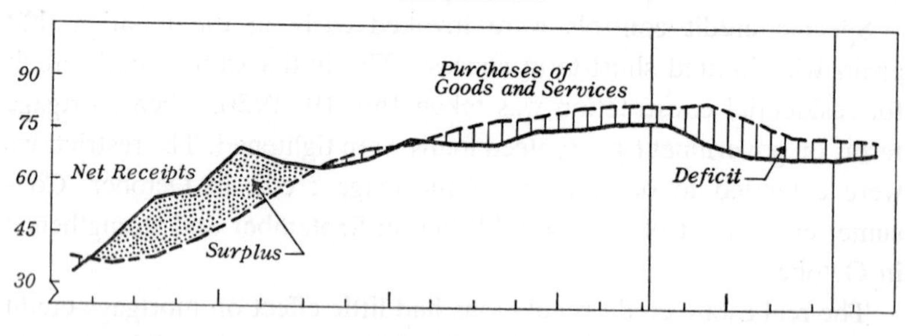

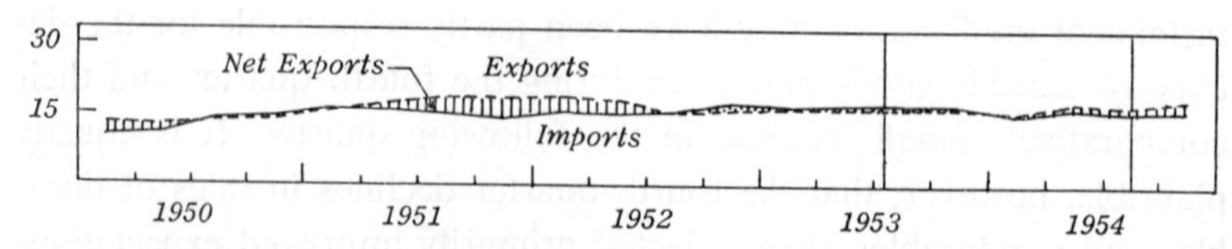

Source: Office of Business Economics, Department of Commerce.

stemming from military successes in Korea, and that sales of durables were relatively small during the second buying wave because speculative demands had been largely satisfied during the first wave. It is interesting to note, in any event, that it was durables which accelerated the most during the first wave and nondurables during the second (Chart 12). Whatever the success of the credit curbs as restraints on demand for durables during the second wave, they were obviously unable to reach nondurables and may even have diverted some purchasing power to the latter, perhaps leaving total consumer expenditure unaffected on balance.

Divided Economy: 1951 to Mid-1952

A general price and wage freeze was announced on January 26, 1951. Prices were under varying degrees of wartime control during the next two years, but it was a fascinating and unexpected feature of the times that average wholesale prices actually declined substantially and that prices of many commodities fell well below legal ceilings. This occurred, moreover, during a period of continuous full employment of labor (Chart 17) and while the government share of real gross national product was increasing from 6.8 per cent in 1950 to 15.2 per cent in 1952. What happened was that a decline of civilian demand in reaction from the early buying waves neatly offset the rise of defense spending.

As 1951 opened, the production of consumer goods was geared to high and rising retail sales, as a result of the forward buying induced by the developments in Korea. Retail sales fell suddenly and sharply beginning in February, however, causing an abrupt and unwanted increase of distributors' stocks during the next few months (Charts 14 and 15). The necessity subsequently to work off these excessive inventories magnified and prolonged the deflationary impact of the cutback of consumption expenditure well into 1952, despite a gradual recovery of retail sales after mid-1951.

For a time it was as though two economies existed side by side

CHART 17. *The Labor Force, Employment, and the Unemployment Ratio, Monthly, Seasonally Adjusted, 1950-55*

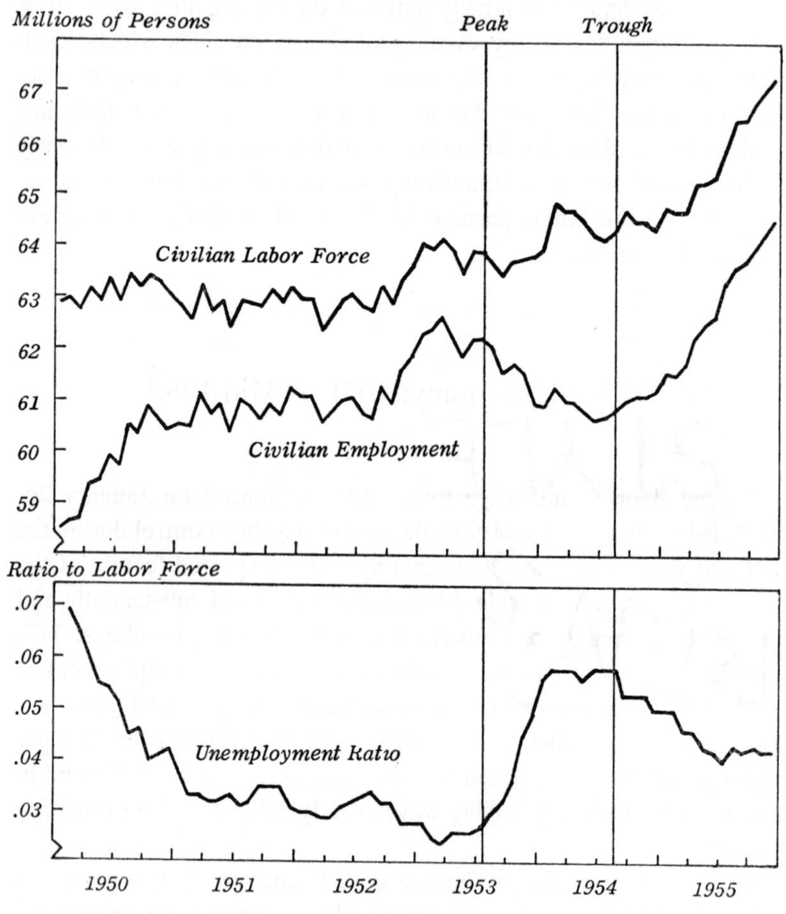

Source: Derived from data of Bureau of the Census.

without touching. The grand division was between consumption and nonconsumption goods. Reduced consumer and inventory demands depressed especially factory production and wholesale prices of textile, apparel, rubber, and leather products from early 1951 to mid-1952. Production of consumer durable goods also declined substantially, although prices remained at legal ceilings. The production cutbacks were required by defense restrictions on materials, but consumer demand had eased for durables as well as nondurables, and retailers' stocks remained above the 1949-50 levels, so that supplies were adequate at existing prices. Defense contracts and defense-oriented programs of facilities expansion replaced the business lost in the consumer sector, and average prices and production of durable goods were stable.

Because distributors and manufacturers of consumer goods were liquidating stocks, the aggregate rate of inventory investment declined $17 billion between the second quarters of 1951 and 1952 despite large accumulations in the defense industries. It was this decrease of inventory investment which freed resources to be channeled into defense production, since private expenditure for final goods and services was comparatively stable for a year or more following the second buying wave. This last was true not only of consumer expenditure but also of fixed investment (Charts 12 and 13).

Private fixed investment was closely controlled by the federal government. Residential construction declined during 1951 and recovered only partially in 1952. Business fixed investment changed little in the aggregate, but after mid-1951 only the defense industries were increasing their capital outlays. The capital-expansion programs of consumer goods industries were discouraged by materials allocations and by the softening of consumer demand. Fixed investment in the defense industries was encouraged directly by federal aid and indirectly by the continued high level of activity that was characteristic of those industries.

It is easy enough to understand the expansion of activity in the defense industries. The requirements of the defense program, moreover, dictated reductions in the output of consumer durable goods and nonessential private investment, and these reductions were implemented by various controls. But what factor or combination of factors was responsible for the decline in consumer spending following the second buying wave—the decline which in turn reacted on inventory demands and fixed investment in the consumer goods sector and permitted the transfer of resources to defense purposes without an upthrust to prices?

The explanation for the reduction of consumer expenditure must be sought on the side of demand, since it was not forced by a shortage of consumer goods. True, price controls were in effect, and restrictions on materials did require reductions in the output of important classes of consumer durable goods. However, at the very time that these restrictions began to limit the output of durables—that is, in the second quarter of 1951—the demand for such items eased. So also did the demand for soft goods. The declines in sales of soft goods cannot be traced to resource shortages, and the fact that they paralleled the reductions in durable goods strengthens my conviction that the latter reflected voluntary decreases of demand at existing (ceiling) prices. The inference that physical sales of durables would have decreased even in the absence of production controls is confirmed also by the failure of black markets to develop.

Finally, the most convincing evidence that the lull in retail trade resulted from a voluntary reduction of demand is provided by the data on inventories. The ratio of stocks to sales for all retail stores was far above the pre-Korea level when sales began their decline in early 1951 (Chart 15). Even by the summer of 1952, after the drastic reduction of retail stocks in the interim, the inventory-sales ratio was higher than before the outbreak of hostilities. These same statements can be made for durable goods taken separately. Thus the goods were available in 1951, and other factors must account for the decline of consumer spending.

A forward buying movement is intrinsically a short-period phenomenon. The consumer who purchases a car, refrigerator, or new suit a few months earlier than he intended is not likely to purchase another for some time to come, and the housewife who hoards sugar or coffee is not apt to lay in more than a six-month supply. Furthermore, the purchase of expensive commodities either reduces holdings of liquid assets or requires the assumption of new debt. The mortgage and consumer debt of individuals increased $11 billion in 1950. Since liquid assets in the form of currency and bank deposits, savings and loan shares, and securities increased only $6 billion, net liquid saving was *minus* $5 billion in a year when personal saving in all forms amounted to $12.5 billion.[3] This negative rate of aggregate

[3] In contrast, during 1951 personal saving was $18 billion and net liquid saving, $1 billion. The data are from *Economic Report of the President* (January 1959), Tables D-13 and D-15.

liquid saving must reflect financial dissaving by many individuals and smaller than customary saving on the part of others. Other things being equal, both the increase in household stocks of goods and the growing desire to replenish liquid assets or to diminish debt would tend to reduce consumer expenditures relative to current income after a buying wave had been underway for several weeks or months. Perhaps these factors are sufficient to explain the downturn of retail sales after January. On the other hand, advance buying might have persisted for a time had consumers continued to anticipate future shortages. There can be little doubt, however, that a new reversal of expectations removed the positive incentive to forward buying after the first few weeks of the year.

The decline in retail sales began immediately after the general price freeze was announced on January 26. Insofar as the forward buying of consumers had been for the purpose of anticipating price advances, the imposition of price controls may have removed one incentive for additional buying. One of the facts most clearly established by the 1951 Survey of Consumer Finances, however, was that a substantial majority of consumers expected price increases during 1951, and that few expected declines. Furthermore, the Survey, which was conducted in January and February, revealed that "imposition of price controls at the end of January 1951 had little immediate effect on consumer price expectations; opinions expressed in interviews taken before and after the date that controls went into effect showed no difference on this point."[4]

At about the same time that the price freeze was announced, it became apparent that retail stores were well stocked. Since businessmen as well as consumers had purchased heavily in late 1950, and since the mobilization had not interfered seriously with civilian production, an increased flow of goods matched the increase of final demand, and the anticipated shortages did not develop. This concrete evidence of plentiful supplies was probably the foremost reason for the shift in consumer expectations. It does not follow, however, that price anticipations played no part in the shift.

The major findings on the state of price expectations reported in the Survey were as follows:

[4] *Federal Reserve Bulletin* (June 1951), p. 632.

> Consumers were more generally agreed on the trend of prices in the coming year than at the time of any previous postwar survey. Approximately 7 of every 10 spending units thought that prices would rise. Very few believed that prices would fall. Despite the belief that prices would not fall, about one-half of all consumers said that this was a bad time to buy durable goods, principally because prices were too high. About one-third of all consumers thought that this was a good time to buy, before prices went higher or shortages developed.[5]

Why should consumers wish to defer purchases of durable goods because prices were "too high" if at the same time they expected prices to rise further? The last sentence in the quotation suggests an answer consistent with all the findings. Apparently only a minority expected shortages to develop, and it may therefore be inferred that only a minority expected rapidly advancing prices. Although consumers were asked to express an opinion about the probable trend of prices during 1951, they were not questioned on the magnitude of the change they expected. Even if consumers did not believe that price controls would stop the inflation, they surely believed that the controls would slow the rate of advance. But if this were the case, the penalty for postponed buying would not be severe, and there was no urgent reason to buy immediately—after all, goods were plentiful at current prices. Under the circumstances, some retrenchment from the abnormal rates of expenditure of recent months was desirable, and consumers acted accordingly.

It must not be inferred that the voluntary relaxation of private demand was exclusively responsible for the stability achieved after the second buying wave. Direct and indirect controls provided an economic environment in which the consumer lull could have maximum effect. The corrective forces inherent in forward-buying movements made inevitable a reduction of demand relative to income, but this need not have meant an actual decline of retail sales. Had money income continued to rise at a rapid pace, it is likely that consumers would have both saved more and spent more. Government actions slowed the growth of disposable personal income, however, so that the decision of consumers to save a larger portion of their incomes involved a decline of consumer expenditures.

[5] *Ibid.*, p. 628.

The expansion of money income was retarded in three main ways. First, a number of restrictions prevented private fixed investment from rising much. General monetary curbs were comparatively unrestrictive even after the famous Federal Reserve-Treasury Accord of March 1951 freed the central bank to pursue an anti-inflationary policy.[6] However, as the initial lags were overcome an increasing proportion of new real estate credit became subject to the selective restrictions instituted in 1950, and the restrictions were extended to additional categories of construction in February. Recall, also, that administrative allocations of materials constrained fixed investment in nondefense industries after mid-1951.

Second, higher taxes reduced the growth of spendable income relative to earned income. On balance, however, federal fiscal operations were expansionary after the first quarter of 1951, since defense expenditures increased more rapidly than tax receipts, and since the rise of tax receipts was largely induced by the increase of gross national product caused by the defense expenditures (Chart 16). It remains true, nonetheless, that federal fiscal activities were less expansionary than if higher tax rates had not been imposed in 1950 and raised again late in 1951. It is also relevant that the increase of defense expenditure tended more to raise production than prices, since much of it served as an offset to declines of demand elsewhere in the economy.

Third, direct controls over wages and prices prevented autonomous increases of money incomes at given levels of aggregate demand—a subject which is reserved for discussion in Chapter 14.

Thus, if consumers can claim a major share of the credit for promoting economic stability in 1951-52, they must in fairness admit that they had considerable help from government and business—and they must also accept a large share of responsibility for the preceding instability. Had government fiscal operations been more inflationary during 1951, and had private investment, wages, and profits been

[6] See Chapter 13. The money supply increased faster during the 15 months following the Accord than in the same interval preceding it. The increase between November 1949 and February 1951 was 6.2 per cent, as compared with 7.8 per cent between March 1951 and June 1952. (Based on seasonally adjusted data on demand deposits and currency from *Federal Reserve Bulletin,* July 1957, pp. 828-29.)

uncontrolled, consumers might not have been able to resist the lure of increased consumption expenditure made easy by rising money income. Had consumers not bought heavily during the months of inflation, they would not have saved as much later. Had businessmen not ordered and produced so heavily in 1950 and early 1951, the subsequent decline of inventory investment would not have occurred to moderate demand. The neat balance of inflationary and deflationary forces in 1951-52 was in no small part the consequence of developments growing out of the preceding inflation.

6 / *The Contraction of 1953-54*

THE 1953-54 CONTRACTION in United States economic activity was brief and mild. According to the business cycle chronology of the National Bureau of Economic Research it lasted 13 months, extending from a peak in July 1953 to a trough in August of the following year. Unemployment never reached 6 per cent of the civilian labor force. Measured in constant dollars, gross national product declined 4 per cent between the second quarters of 1953 and 1954. This decline in aggregate production reflected principally a 20 per cent reduction in the real volume of federal expenditures for final goods and services. The annual flow of consumer expenditures in 1954 prices was unchanged. Residential construction was up 7 per cent, while other private construction rose 2 per cent and expenditures of state and local governments 10 per cent. In fact, the only major component of final expenditure which declined along with federal spending was private purchases of producers' durable equipment, which dropped 6 per cent.

These figures suggest a somewhat cut-and-dried picture of a strongly buoyant economy depressed briefly by an autonomous reduction in government expenditures. There is a great deal of truth in this impression, for the cutback in federal spending was the major deflationary force acting throughout the contraction; and the private economy quickly absorbed the impact of this and other depressing influences and began an early and vigorous recovery—though not without the assistance of contracyclical actions in the tax and monetary fields. The experience merits closer examination, however, for a number of reasons.

To begin with, the processes by which the economy responds to external disturbances are an important part of the subject matter of cyclical analysis. The part played in the decline and recovery by induced changes in consumption and inventory investment will accordingly receive a good deal of attention.

As soon as the subject is approached in this manner, it becomes apparent that the contraction was more than a passive response to the decline in government demand. For example, the rate of growth of consumer spending diminished before the downturn, and there is evidence that this development led to an early independent decline in consumer goods production. This proposition is discussed in the first section of this chapter. The theme of consumer demand is pursued further in the two succeeding sections. It turns out that autonomous variations of consumer spending played an active and important role in both contraction and recovery. Again, developments in the consumer sector cannot be viewed merely as passive responses to autonomous changes in government expenditures or taxes, although these were certainly influential determinants of disposable personal income and, therefore, of consumption during this period.

Investment demand and fiscal and monetary developments are discussed in the concluding section, which is principally devoted to the changes in federal receipts and expenditures which figured so prominently in the contraction. These topics are of interest in their own right and because of the perspective they provide about the role of consumption in the contraction. The mildness of the contraction was partly due to the strength shown by fixed investment demand and to the fiscal and monetary actions which were taken to stimulate consumption and investment. Were it not for these favorable factors, it is unlikely that autonomous variations in consumer demand would have attained such eminence as determinants of the course of aggregate activity.

The Downturn

The downturn in mid-1953 had its origins in two main developments: the cutback in defense expenditures, and a deceleration in the rate of increase of retail sales. The importance of the former is obvious, but that of the latter cannot be appraised without a brief review of the events which preceded it.

The foregoing chapter showed how consumer goods expenditures were swelled by forward buying after the outbreak of the Korean War and how the markets for consumer goods subsequently softened, inducing a decline in production for sale and inventory which freed resources to be channeled into defense production at stable prices. The deflationary influence of reduced consumer demand, however, had largely run its course by the end of 1951 (Chart 16). Consumer expenditures rose absolutely and relative to disposable income during the first half of 1952, as the personal saving ratio dropped from 8.7 per cent in the fourth quarter of 1951 to 7.5 per cent in the two succeeding quarters. The improvement in final sales was reflected in a mild recovery of consumer goods production, though distributors' stocks still declined.

The developing recovery of the consumer sector was interrupted by the steel strike in the summer of 1952, with the eventual result that the defense expansion was capped by a vigorous boom in consumer goods production in the closing months of the year. The strike was settled late in July; and production, employment, and incomes expanded sharply as manufacturers and distributors rebuilt inventories and final expenditures mounted. Consumer expenditure, which had risen little relative to income in the third quarter, increased considerably more than income in the final quarter of the year (Table 11). This year-end bulge in expenditures occurred primarily because automobile production had been curtailed by steel shortages during the summer, so that purchases of automobiles dropped sharply in the third quarter and rebounded in the fourth. One effect of the strike, then, was to cause the short-term consumption function to shift downward in the third quarter and upward in the fourth—shifts that are reflected in the pronounced fluctuation in the average saving ratio and in the ratio of increments of consumption and income shown in the table.

The rate of increase of consumption expenditures diminished markedly during the first half of 1953. The absolute increments for the last quarter of 1952 and the first two quarters of 1953 were respectively \$7.6 billion, \$3.7 billion, and \$2.4 billion. It is natural to look to the behavior of income for an explanation of this tendency,

TABLE 11. *Behavior of Disposable Personal Income, Consumption, and Personal Saving, Quarterly, 1952-55*[a]
(Dollar items in billions)

Year and Quarter	Disposable Personal Income	Personal Consumption Expenditures	Personal Saving	*Personal Saving as Percentage of Disposable Income*	Change from Preceding Quarter in: Disposable Income	Change from Preceding Quarter in: Consumption Expenditures	Ratio of Change in Consumption to Change in Income
1952							
I.....	232.1	214.6	17.5	*7.5*	—	—	—
II.....	235.6	217.7	17.9	*7.6*	3.5	3.1	0.89
III.....	241.1	219.6	21.5	*8.9*	5.5	1.9	0.35
IV.....	245.6	227.2	18.4	*7.5*	4.5	7.6	1.69
1953							
I.....	250.0	230.9	19.0	*7.6*	4.4	3.7	0.84
II.....	252.8	233.3	19.6	*7.8*	2.8	2.4	0.86
III.....	253.8	234.1	19.7	*7.8*	1.0	0.8	0.80
IV.....	253.8	232.3	21.6	*8.5*	0.0	−1.8	—
1954							
I.....	254.6	233.7	21.0	*8.2*	0.8	1.4	1.75
II.....	254.8	236.5	18.3	*7.2*	0.2	2.8	14.00
III.....	256.8	238.7	18.0	*7.0*	2.0	2.2	1.10
IV.....	260.9	243.2	17.7	*6.8*	4.1	4.5	1.10
1955							
I.....	263.8	249.4	14.4	*5.5*	2.9	6.2	2.14
II.....	272.0	254.3	17.8	*6.5*	8.2	4.9	0.60
III.....	277.7	260.9	16.8	*6.0*	5.7	6.6	1.16
IV.....	283.0	263.3	19.8	*7.0*	5.3	2.4	0.45

[a] Quarterly totals are at seasonally adjusted annual rates. Source, *U. S. Income and Output*, a supplement to *Survey of Current Business* (November 1958), Table II-2.

and income retardation was of some importance during the spring. The major reason for the retardation in spending, however, was that expenditures had increased so much more rapidly than income in the last few months of 1952, owing largely to the spurt in automobile sales. In other words, with income rising at a relatively steady rate, the increase in expenditure associated with the upward shift of the short-term consumption function in late 1952 was much greater than

TABLE 12. *Personal Consumption Expenditures by Major Type and Share in Disposable Income, Quarterly, 1952-55*[a]
(Dollar items in billions)

Year and Quarter	Personal Consumption Expenditures					*Consumption Expenditures as Percentages of Disposable Income*				
	Total	Auto-mobiles and Parts	Other Durable Goods	Non-durable Goods	Services	*Total*	*Auto-mobiles and Parts*	*Other Durable Goods*	*Non-durable Goods*	*Services*
1952										
I........	214.6	10.1	17.6	113.3	73.6	92.5	4.4	7.6	48.8	31.7
II........	217.7	11.4	17.8	113.9	74.7	92.4	4.8	7.6	48.3	31.7
III........	219.6	9.3	18.2	115.9	76.2	91.1	3.9	7.5	48.1	31.6
IV........	227.2	13.4	18.8	117.2	77.9	92.5	5.5	7.7	47.7	31.7
1953										
I........	230.9	14.4	18.8	118.1	79.6	92.3	5.8	7.5	47.2	31.8
II........	233.3	14.5	19.0	118.6	81.2	92.3	5.7	7.5	46.9	32.1
III........	234.1	14.6	19.0	117.8	82.8	92.2	5.8	7.5	46.4	32.6
IV........	232.3	12.6	18.6	117.4	83.7	91.5	5.0	7.3	46.3	33.0
1954										
I........	233.7	12.4	18.8	117.9	84.6	91.8	4.9	7.4	46.3	33.2
II........	236.5	13.2	19.0	118.8	85.5	92.8	5.2	7.5	46.6	33.6
III........	238.7	13.3	19.0	119.6	86.9	93.0	5.2	7.4	46.6	33.8
IV........	243.2	14.5	19.4	121.0	88.3	93.2	5.6	7.4	46.4	33.8
1955										
I........	249.4	17.8	20.4	121.2	90.0	94.5	6.7	7.7	45.9	34.1
II........	254.3	18.1	21.0	123.7	91.6	93.5	6.7	7.7	45.5	33.7
III........	260.9	19.7	21.8	126.1	93.4	94.0	7.1	7.9	45.4	33.6
IV........	263.3	17.4	22.3	128.1	95.3	93.0	6.1	7.9	45.3	33.7

[a] Quarterly totals are at seasonally adjusted annual rates. Source, *U. S. Income and Output,* a supplement to *Survey of Current Business* (November 1958), Table II-6.

the increase associated with the movement along the stable function of the first half of 1953.

This is not the whole story, however. Small but significant shifts in the composition of expenditures were occurring at the same time that the rate of increase of aggregate consumption was tapering off. The shares of services and automobiles in disposable income increased, while those of other goods diminished (Table 12). This meant that sales of goods taken alone showed even greater retardation than did total expenditures for goods and services. It also meant that substantial retardations occurred not only in automobile sales but also in purchase of other goods.

CHART 18. *Indexes of Industrial Production, Monthly, Seasonally Adjusted, 1952-55*

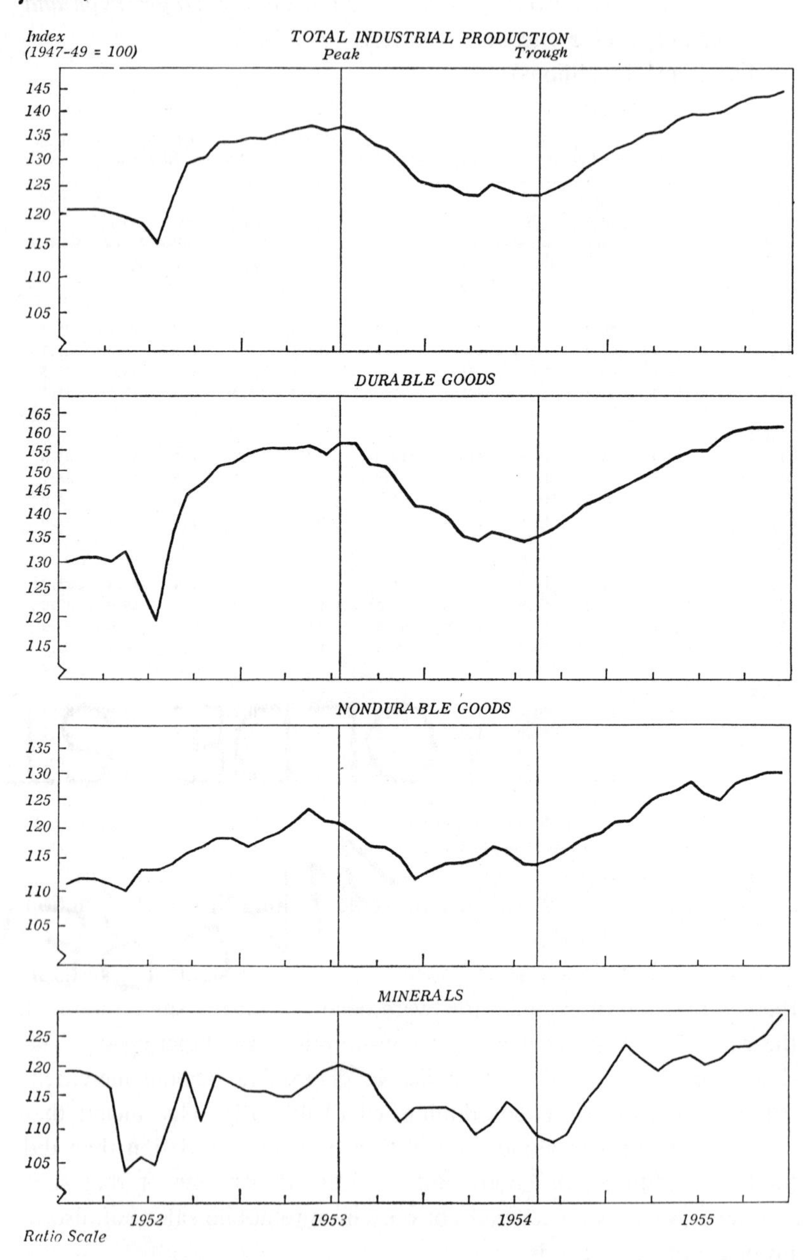

Source: Board of Governors of the Federal Reserve System.

So much for the causes of the retardation in the rate of increase of consumer expenditure on commodities prior to the business cycle downturn of mid-1953. The next thing to notice is that the retardation of retail sales was accompanied by an absolute decline of production of most consumer goods—and a decline, moreover, which preceded the downturn of total industrial production. Thus the output of major household durable goods reached its high in May, leading the peak in industrial production by two months and that of durable manufactures as a group by three months (Charts 18 and 19). May was also the peak month for production of foods and beverages, textiles and apparel, leather and rubber products, and the total index of nondurable manufactures. In fact, among the major industries engaged in the manufacture of consumer goods, only the automobile industry continued to increase output until July, which marks the peak in total industrial production and precedes by one month the peak in production of durable manufactures.

But why should a mere retardation in the rate of increase of retail sales cause an absolute decline of consumer goods production? Probably the principal reason is the fact that there is a close positive correlation between the rate of change of aggregate retail sales and the proportion of individual items for which sales are increasing.[1] A decrease in the rate of increase of aggregate sales usually means that sales are now falling for an increased percentage of individual items. Thus, the normal expectation during a plateau in aggregate sales would be widespread sales declines and production cutbacks, with the latter amplified by reduced or negative rates of inventory investment. An additional factor would be at work in those instances, if any, when despite rising sales retailers decreased their orders for incoming goods in an effort to adjust their inventory positions.[2]

[1] The economic rationale of this correlation and its implications for acceleration theory and for the behavior of inventory investment are discussed more extensively in my paper, "Diffusion, Acceleration, and Business Cycles," *American Economic Review* (September 1959), pp. 535-65.

[2] According to the acceleration principle, a decrease in the rate of growth of retail sales may be sufficient to cause a downturn in new orders by retailers, since reductions in orders for stock may more than offset the increase needed to supply current sales. This result depends on the assumption that retailers attempt to maintain a constant (average or marginal) ratio of stocks to sales. See

CHART 19. *Indexes of Production of Consumer Durable Goods, Monthly, Seasonally Adjusted, 1952-55*

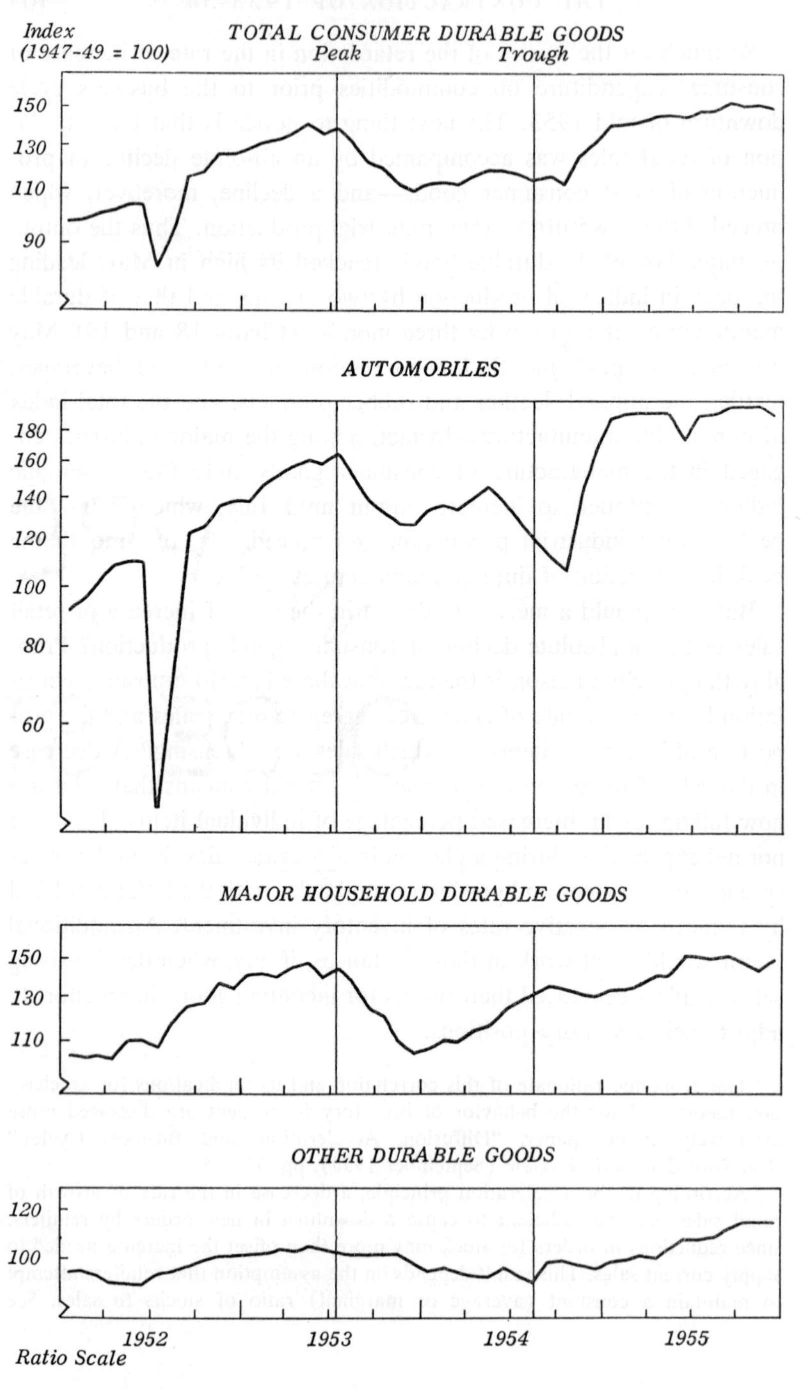

Source: Board of Governors of the Federal Reserve System.

Whatever the exact details of the early cutbacks in production of consumer goods, it is clear that those cutbacks played an important part in initiating the downturn, though they were not its sole cause. The flow of new defense contracts had begun to diminish before defense expenditures actually dropped in the third quarter of 1953, and this must have contributed to the decline in manufacturers' new orders which preceded the downturn. Some part of the early decline of manufacturers' orders may also reflect the behavior of purchases of producers' durable equipment, which showed a tendency toward retardation smiliar to that of consumer goods during the spring (Chart 13).

The Federal Reserve policy of monetary restraint may also have contributed to the downturn, but if so its influence was probably minor. Instalment credit continued to increase rapidly during the first half of 1953 and automobile purchases rose absolutely and relative to income. The increased tightness in the capital markets that developed abruptly in April and May with the flotation of a new long-term Treasury issue may have been partly responsible for the subsequent dip in residential construction, but the decline was small and short-lived. Similarly, some business investments may have been postponed because of credit stringency during the spring, but several of the most pronounced declines had begun earlier in industries which had participated heavily in the Korean defense facilities expansion program,[3] and, in any event, business fixed investment fell little during the contraction. Finally, the substantial cutback of federal spending was certainly unrelated to credit conditions.

Early Developments

I now turn to an examination of the behavior of consumer spending in the first half of the contraction—that is in the third and fourth quarters of 1953. Between the second and fourth quarters of that

Hickman, *op. cit.*, pp. 551-58 for an argument that such acceleration effects are secondary to the diffusion effects discussed in the present paragraph.

[3] *Ibid.*

year purchases of consumer goods fell $3.5 billion. Since expenditures for services increased, total consumption declined only $1 billion, but even so the personal saving ratio rose from 7.8 per cent in the second quarter to 8.5 per cent in the fourth (Tables 11 and 12). There was a $1 billion increase in disposable income between these quarters, since the decline of nearly $1 billion which occurred in wages and salaries was largely offset by increased transfers, and property incomes rose. Thus there was a small[4] downward shift of the consumption function, which was probably the result of increased caution on the part of consumers because of the deterioration in general economic conditions.[5]

The diminished flow of expenditures for consumer goods added to the deflationary impact of reduced defense expenditures and aggravated the inventory problems of businessmen. It should be noted in this connection that purchases of consumer goods fell more than defense expenditures during the last half of 1953, with the decrease for the two categories totaling $6.5 billion. There were offsetting increases in other major categories of final demand, however, leaving final expenditures unchanged in current dollars and down only $1.5 billion in real terms. Had production declined only in proportion to final sales, the drop would have been small indeed. This was not the case, however, for real inventory investment declined $8 billion, with the result that GNP fell not by $1.5 billion, but by $9.5 billion. In other words, the great bulk of the decline in national output during this period reflected a decline of production relative to final demand, and most of the decline in production must have stemmed from the sizable cutbacks in sales and the concomitant inventory adjustments in the defense and consumer sectors, since the demand for other final products was steady or increasing. It follows that a large proportion

[4] Note, however, that the decline of expenditures for goods relative to income was much greater than the decline of total consumption relative to income. This is likely to be true whenever there is a short-term downshift of the consumption function, since services cannot be stockpiled and it is therefore difficult for consumers to postpone their purchase.

[5] See F. Thomas Juster, "Consumers' Buying Plans," in *Thirty-ninth Annual Report* of the National Bureau of Economic Research (May 1959), pp. 35-38, for questionnaire evidence that buying plans are affected by changes in general business conditions.

of the 8 per cent drop of industrial production between July and December of 1953 was due to inventory disinvestment, and a large share of the latter was induced by the fall in consumption expenditures. The output of major consumer durable goods fell 25 per cent, while production cutbacks in the consumer nondurable goods industries generally rivaled those in durable goods manufacturing (Charts 18 and 19). Among the components of the index of industrial production, reductions of 10 per cent or more were recorded for textile, apparel, leather, and rubber products in the nondurables group and for primary and fabricated metals, electrical machinery, and furniture and fixtures in the durables group.

The Revival of Consumer Demand

The contraction entered a new phase at the beginning of 1954. The earlier decline of consumption expenditures was reversed and consumer demand became an expansionary force. Another consumer-oriented activity, residential construction, also figured prominently in the recovery. In concert with sustained rises in state and local expenditures, the early recovery of consumption and residential construction soon overcame the deflationary pressure exerted by falling federal expenditures (Charts 12 and 16).

Among the leading factors which strengthened the demand for consumer goods in the early months of 1954 was the rise of disposable income in the face of a fall in personal income from production. Automatic changes in tax receipts and transfer payments induced by the decline in earnings and employment served to offset part of the fall in production income, but the actual rise of disposable income was the result of reduced rates of personal income taxation that became effective January 1.[6] It was partly because of this tax

[6] Personal income taxes were reduced nearly $3 billion by the cut in tax rates, although the effect on disposable income was party offset by an increase of about $0.6 billion in personal contributions for old-age insurance, due to an increase in the rate at which covered earnings are taxed.

cut that the contraction failed to cumulate, for the cut helped to nullify the feedback effect of declining production income on consumer spending and consumption-related inventory investment.

The expansion of consumer spending was not, however, confined to the amounts induced by the growth of income. The stimulus of rising income during 1954 was augmented by an upward shift of the consumption function (Table 11). As a result, although disposable income increased $1 billion from the last quarter of 1953 through the second quarter of 1954, consumption expenditures rose $4 billion, and the percentage of income saved dropped from 8.5 to 7.2. While it is comparatively easy to assess the importance of this shift in the consumption function—on a conservative estimate it accounted for more than $3 billion of the increase in consumption expenditures[7]—it is not clear why the shift occurred. Doubtless it was partly induced by improved expectations resulting from the rise of disposable income itself, and perhaps would not have occurred but for the tax cuts. Other factors not directly related to the flow of current income may also have strengthened consumer demand, however, including capital

[7] If two reasonable assumptions are made—that the lag of induced expenditures behind income is brief enough to be neglected when using quarterly data and that the marginal propensity to consume disposable income is about .8-.9—it follows that no more than $0.2-$0.9 billion of the $4.2 billion increase in consumption was induced by the increase in disposable income. This is an estimate of induced versus autonomous changes in consumption from the standpoint of consumer decisions about the disposition of the income available to them for spending or saving. It is not an estimate of the importance of autonomous changes in consumption as a determinant of GNP, which would require a calculation of the multiplier effects of autonomous consumption. To make the latter calculation, account would need to be taken not only of the amount of the change in consumption in each production period which was accounted for by shifts in the function relating disposable income and consumption, but also of the effects of each such autonomous change on production in the following periods and hence upon GNP, disposable income, and induced consumption in those periods. Knowledge of these last effects would require information about the response of production to consumption and consumption-related inventory investment, about the marginal relationship between GNP and disposable income, and about the marginal propensity to consume disposable income. No such calculations are attempted here, although it will be shown below that the increase in total consumer spending was an important determinant of aggregate activity during 1954, and it is apparent that this increase in spending was to a very large extent autonomous.

gains arising from the brisk rise in stock market prices, intensified selling efforts, price reductions, and liberalized credit terms.

The importance of the early revival of consumer demand may be judged from an examination of the components of GNP. Federal purchases of goods and services fell $10.5 billion from the fourth quarter of 1953 to the second quarter of 1954. Most of this reduction and an additional drop of $1 billion in business fixed investment was offset by increases elsewhere in the economy. Consumption expenditures advanced $4 billion, and residential construction, net exports of goods and services, and state and local government expenditures together increased about $3.5 billion. As a result of these opposing movements, final expenditures fell only $4 billion. Gross national product declined even less, however—about $2 billion. This was because inventory investment, which had been such a pronounced deflationary influence during the first phase of the contraction now became an expansionary force with the recovery of consumer expenditures.

Inventory investment had dropped from an annual rate of $3 billion in the second quarter of 1953 to *minus* $4.5 billion in the fourth quarter. Inventory decumulation continued during the first half of 1954, but at a reduced rate which narrowed the gap between production and final sales. The increased flow of consumer expenditures induced lower rates of disinvestment or positive accumulations by distributors and manufacturers of consumer goods and counterbalanced the accelerated liquidation of defense-related stocks, thereby further stabilizing production. The production of building materials also turned upward as home building activity increased. Thus, the curve of industrial production flattened along with that of final expenditures during the first six or seven months of the year, with increases in the production of consumer goods and building materials largely offsetting reductions in defense production and the output of producer durable goods (Charts 18 and 19).

The balance of inflationary and deflationary forces shifted strongly to the side of expansion during the last half of 1954. The aggregate of final expenditures turned upward in the third quarter, as private spending mounted and the rate of decline of federal expenditures abated. It was during the last three or four months of the year that a vigorous expansion was set in motion by the rising tide of demand for consumer goods and new homes. Gross national product rose $9 billion in the fourth quarter, with one-third of the increase due to inventory investment. Distributors' stocks dropped as sales spurted during this period, but manufacturers were conscious of the strength of consumer demand and began to rebuild inventories in response to current and anticipated increases in orders and sales, giving a strong fillip to production and income.

The accelerated rise in consumer spending that began late in 1954 was in part a result of the very increase in production and earnings which consumer demand had itself induced, but the other factors mentioned in the paragraphs above worked in the same direction. Disposable income rose $7 billion from the third quarter of 1954 through the first quarter of 1955. The increase in consumption expenditures was a good deal larger—$10.5 billion—and the personal saving ratio fell from 7 to 5.5 per cent. Automobiles figured prominently in this expansion. The 1955 models met with immediate and enthusiastic public acceptance, and favorable credit terms enabled consumers to finance purchases of these and other expensive items while also increasing their outlays for other goods and services.

This surge of spending on new homes and consumer goods in late 1954 and early 1955 gave powerful impetus to the recovery. Industrial production increased 10 per cent between August and March. Durable manufactures gained 10 per cent, while the output of consumer durables as a class increased 25 per cent and that of automobiles alone 63 per cent. Increases of 9 and 11 per cent were recorded for nondurable manufactures and minerals production. Thus a strong recovery had been underway for half a year or more before business spending on plant and equipment belatedly joined in the advance during the spring of 1955.

Discretionary Public Policies

It is time to turn to an analysis of fiscal and monetary developments and of the role of investment demand in the contraction. It has been shown that fluctuation in consumer spending bulked large among the factors making for decline and recovery and that these fluctuations contained a sizable component of autonomous change. Consumption could not have become the expansionary force it proved to be, however, nor would the contraction have been so mild in the face of a 20 per cent reduction in federal expenditures, had it not been for the strength of fixed investment demand and for the stimulus imparted in investment and consumption by fiscal and monetary actions.

The deflationary impact of the post-Korean cutback in defense and other federal expenditures has been discussed, and note has also been taken of the favorable effect of the reduction in personal income taxes that served to raise disposable income during 1954. What was the net effect of these and other fiscal operations? As measured in the GNP accounts, federal purchases of goods and services fell $12 billion between the second quarters of 1953 and 1954 (Table 13). Federal receipts net of transfer items declined $10 billion, however, so that the deficit on income and product transactions diminished about $2 billion.

Further inspection of the table reveals that the reductions in receipts and expenditures were not balanced throughout the contraction. On the contrary, the deficit increased almost $5 billion during the last half of 1953. This increase was largely a reflection of the effect of reduced corporate earnings on corporate profits tax accruals, which accounted for $5 billion of the total drop of $6 billion in net government receipts. Federal purchases of goods and services fell little at that time, and even defense expenditures declined less than outlays for consumer goods. When account is taken of the inventory disinvestment which accompanied these reductions in final expenditures, however, it is clear that the cutback in federal spending contributed importantly to the decline in GNP and hence in corporate profits and taxes on those profits. The increase in the deficit is therefore far from being a sign of inflationary pressure; rather, it is a symptom of the deflationary force of the fall in defense expenditures, although it is not, of course, a measure of the magnitude of that force in isolation.

It is helpful to view these fiscal changes of the second half of 1953 in the perspective provided by Table 14, which shows the behavior of major components on both the income and expenditure sides of the

TABLE 13. *Federal Government Purchases, Receipts, and Deficit on Income and Product Transactions, Selected Quarters, 1953-54*[a]
(In billions of dollars)

Item	1953 II Q	1953 IV Q	1954 II Q	Change From: II Q 1953 to II Q 1954	Change From: II Q 1953 to IV Q 1953	Change From: IV Q 1953 to II Q 1954
Purchases of goods and services	58.9	57.8	47.1	−11.8	−1.1	−10.7
Receipts net of transfer items:						
Receipts[b]	72.3	66.3	63.3	− 9.0	−6.0	− 3.0
Less: transfer items[c]	20.4	20.3	21.5	+ 1.1	−0.1	+ 1.2
Equals:	51.9	46.0	41.8	−10.1	−5.9	− 4.2
Deficit on income and product transactions[d]	7.0	11.8	5.3	− 1.7	+4.8	− 6.5

[a] Quarterly totals at seasonally adjusted annual rates. Source, *U. S. Income and Output*, a supplement to *Survey of Current Business* (November 1958), Table III-3. These data are drawn from the national income accounts. Like the cash budget, they include the transactions of the trust accounts. In contrast to the conventional and cash budgets, they exclude certain capital and lending transactions. Corporate profits taxes are on an accrual rather than a cash basis, expenditures are timed with delivery rather than payment, and price support crop loans guaranteed by the Commodity Credit Corporation and financed by banks are counted as expenditures when the loans are made not when CCC redeems them.

[b] Personal tax and nontax receipts, corporate profits tax accruals, indirect business tax and nontax accruals, and contributions for social insurance.

[c] Transfer payments, grants-in-aid to state and local governments, net interest paid by government, and subsidies less current surplus of government enterprises.

[d] Purchases of goods and services less receipts net of transfer items.

GNP accounts. The offsetting changes in the components of final expenditure and the large share of inventory investment in the decline of GNP, of which so much has already been said, stand out on the expenditure side. With regard to the income side, it will be seen that the combined reduction in corporate profit tax accruals and undistributed corporate profits was sufficient to absorb the entire decline in expenditures. Put a little differently, corporate profits before taxes fell $10 billion, and since dividends were unchanged, the reduction was split between undistributed profits and corporate profits taxes. Net corporate savings was therefore an important automatic stabilizer during this period, as it has been historically. With so much of the decline in the value of national output absorbed by undistributed profits and taxes, personal income from production increased fractionally. Induced increases in transfer payments added enough to raise disposable income $1 billion.

Federal receipts and expenditures continued to decline during the first half of 1954, but the pace of the receipts diminished and that of the expenditures accelerated, with the result that the deficit was reduced $6.5 billion. Unlike the experience of the first phase of the contraction, the decline in receipts during 1954 was caused partly by changes in tax rates. Personal tax receipts of the federal government fell nearly $3 billion as a result of the cut in income tax rates alone, while the reductions in federal excises totaled another $1 billion. Corporate profits taxes increased slightly, however, owing to induced rises in corporate income taxes which more than offset the removal of the excess profits tax; and there was a rise of $1 billion in social insurance contributions. Federal tax receipts therefore on balance declined $3 billion.

Again it is useful to study these fiscal developments in the context of the behavior of the other major components of aggregate income and expenditure, and Table 15 has been prepared for the purpose. In the present case, however, the problem of interpretation is complicated by the fact that important autonomous changes occur on both sides of the table and almost every variable contains both autonomous and induced components. This contrasts with the preceding period, for which causation could be thought of as running primarily from the expenditure to the income side.

Federal expenditures dropped nearly $11 billion during the first half of 1954. Fortunately, the bulk of the decline was offset by increases in other sectors. The 1954 tax cuts were responsible for a portion of these counterbalancing increases, but the cuts were only about half as large as the decrease in federal purchases. Elimination of the excess profits tax probably strengthened investment demand, but insufficiently to prevent a decline of business expenditures for plant and equipment. Consumption expenditures rose substantially, however, in part because the $3 billion income tax reduction offset an equal fall in personal income from production.

The contributions of net exports and state and local expenditures, on the other hand, must have been largely independent of the changes in federal tax rates. Recall also, that consumption rose four times as much as disposable income. Clearly, then, if the influence of the tax reductions extended only to their direct income effects, federal fiscal

TABLE 14. *Changes in Gross National Product and Gross National Income, Second Quarter 1953 to Fourth Quarter 1953*[a]
(In billions of dollars)

Gross National Income			Gross National Product or Expenditure		
Federal receipts net of transfer items		−5.9	Government purchases of goods and services		+0.3
Receipts[b]	−6.0		Federal	−1.1	
Less: Increase in transfer items[b]	+0.1		State and local	+1.4	
Net state and local receipts		+0.1	Gross private domestic investment		−7.7
Gross business saving		−3.6	New construction and producers' durable equipment	0.0	
Capital consumption allowances	+1.2		Change in business inventories	−7.7	
Undistributed corporate profits[c]	−4.8		Net exports of goods and services		+0.7
Disposable personal income		+1.0	Personal consumption expenditures		−1.0
Other items		+0.8			
Corporate inventory valuation adjustment	+1.6				
Statistical discrepancy	−0.8				
Gross national income		−7.8	Gross national product or expenditure		−7.8

[a] Quarterly totals at seasonally adjusted annual rates. Source, *U. S. Income and Output*, a supplement to *Survey of Current Business* (November 1958), Tables I-3, I-9, I-18, II-2, and III-3.
[b] See footnotes b and c in Table 13.
[c] Corporate profits after taxes, less dividends.

operations were on balance deflationary during this period of rapid decline in federal expenditures. If the entire upward shift of the consumption function and the rise of inventory investment which it induced were also attributed to the tax changes—perhaps on the ground that the improvement of actual incomes raised expectations and caused the shift to occur—the net effect of fiscal actions would

TABLE 15. *Changes in Gross National Product and Gross National Income, Fourth Quarter 1953 to Second Quarter 1954*[a]
(In billions of dollars)

Gross National Income			Gross National Product or Expenditure		
Federal receipts net of transfer items		−4.2	Government purchases of goods and services		−9.1
Receipts[b]	−3.0		Federal	−10.7	
Less: Increase in transfer items[b]	+1.2		State and local	+ 1.6	
Net state and local receipts		+0.8	Gross private domestic investment		+2.0
Gross business saving		+2.7	New construction and producers' durable equipment	0.0	
Capital consumption allowances	+1.1		Change in business inventories	+ 1.9	
Undistributed corporate profits[c]	+1.6				
Disposable personal income		+1.0	Net foreign investment		+0.8
Other items		−2.0	Personal consumption expenditures		+4.2
Corporate inventory valuation adjustment	0.0				
Statistical discrepancy	−2.0				
Gross national income		−2.1	Gross national product or expenditure		−2.1

[a] Quarterly totals at seasonally adjusted annual rates. Same source as Table 14.
[b] See footnotes b and c in Table 13.
[c] Corporate profits after taxes, less dividends.

be judged more nearly neutral, though still on the deflationary side.

Public contracyclical actions were not limited to tax reductions. The Federal Reserve authorities pursued a policy of credit ease during the months of contraction and early recovery. Credit conditions eased generally and loanable funds were readily available at improved terms to borrowers. While commercial loans by banks declined along with industrial activity, and corporate security offerings for new

TABLE 16. *Gross Private Domestic Fixed Investment, 1952-55*[a]
(In billions of dollars)

Year and Quarter	Total	Residential Construction (Nonfarm)	Other Fixed Investment		
			Total	Construction	Producers' Durable Equipment
1952					
I..........	47.1	12.4	34.7	12.8	21.9
II..........	47.8	12.7	35.1	12.7	22.4
III..........	44.8	12.8	32.0	12.6	19.4
IV..........	47.3	13.4	33.9	12.7	21.2
1953					
I..........	49.4	13.7	35.7	13.2	22.5
II..........	49.8	14.0	35.8	13.8	22.0
III..........	50.4	13.8	36.6	14.0	22.6
IV..........	49.8	13.7	36.1	14.2	21.9
1954					
I..........	49.2	13.7	35.5	14.1	21.4
II..........	49.8	14.7	35.1	14.2	20.9
III..........	50.9	15.8	35.1	14.4	20.7
IV..........	51.5	17.0	34.5	14.6	19.9
1955					
I..........	54.4	18.5	35.9	15.4	20.5
II..........	57.0	18.9	38.1	16.0	22.1
III..........	59.8	18.9	40.9	16.5	24.4
IV..........	60.8	18.4	42.4	17.0	25.4

[a] Quarterly totals are at seasonally adjusted annual rates. Source, *U.S. Income and Output*, a supplement to *Survey of Current Business* (November 1958) Table I-3.

money were reduced, the demand for funds by state and local governments and home buyers remained high, and financial institutions and other investors proved eager to provide an increased flow of funds for these purposes. Mortgages insured or guaranteed by government became especially attractive to investors as yields on other investments declined relative to the fixed return on the mortgages.[8] Addi-

[8] See Chapter 13, section on structural changes in the demand for loanable funds, for further discussion of this point.

tionally, permissible credit terms on Federal Housing Administration and Veterans Administration mortgages had been liberalized in April 1953 and were further eased on FHA mortgages with the passage of a new Housing Act in August 1954.

The underlying demographic and economic factors which have supported a high level of residential construction in the postwar decade—population growth and migration and high and rising per capita real incomes are probably the most important—changed little during 1953-54. Thus, the primary stimulus for the early and vigorous recovery of home building doubtless came from the financial side and represented the major fruit of the policy of credit ease and the cyclical reduction in demand for external business funds.

The early revival of homebuilding and its salutary effect on total fixed investment stand out clearly in Table 16. Nonfarm residential construction fell only 2 per cent in the last half of 1953 and recovered strongly in the second quarter of 1954, carrying with it the aggregate of fixed investment. In contrast, the downswing in other fixed investment—primarily nonfarm producers' expenditures for plant and equipment—extended from the third quarter of 1953 to the fourth quarter of 1954. Note, however, that the total reduction amounted to only 5.5 per cent and that most of the fall occurred during the period of cyclical contraction, when it was definitely of secondary importance as a deflationary factor. Since business fixed investment lagged at both turning points and declined only moderately, it was not an active or important factor in the fluctuations of aggregate economic activity during 1953-54. In view of the potentially powerful destabilizing influence of such investment, however, it should be emphasized again that the contraction was mild in good part because long-term investment expectations remained favorable and business capital outlays sagged comparatively little.

Similarly, although business capital spending lagged the cyclical upturn by six months or more, it thereafter became a powerful force for expansion. This belated recovery was clearly induced by the prior improvement in new orders, sales, and production. According to the preliminary McGraw-Hill survey of investment plans for 1955, which was conducted in the fall of 1954, manufacturers planned to reduce capital outlays by 7 per cent from the 1954 level.[9] When surveyed again six months later, manufacturing companies were found to have revised their investment programs upward and now planned an increase of 4 per cent over 1954. Moreover: "Changes in plans of nonmanufacturing industries are less striking. But all these industries except petroleum and nonferrous metal mining have made some upward revisions since last fall in their plans for investing in new plants and equipment."[10] The upturn from the 1953-54 recession was by no means the result of purely endogenous forces—deliberate fiscal and monetary actions contributed to the recovery of residential construction and consumption, for example. Nevertheless, the upswing, once underway, was amplified by an induced revival of business investment.

[9] *Business Week* (November 6, 1954), pp. 30-32.

[10] McGraw-Hill Department of Economics, *Business' Plans for New Plant and Equipment, 1955-1958* (1955), p. 6.

7 / *The Cycle of 1954-58*

THE FIRST CYCLE after 1938 that was largely free of war influences came in 1954-58. It therefore presents the first opportunity to observe the workings of a peacetime business cycle in the new postwar environment. As noted in Chapter 2, the expansions of 1946-48 and 1949-53 were among the longest on record, spanning 37 and 45 months as compared with an average duration of 24 months for peacetime expansions between 1854 and 1938. But these two cases were exceptional, since the first was fed by abnormal demand backlogs and excess liquidity and the second was prolonged by the Korean War. Obviously, this is not true of the 1954-57 expansion, and yet it lasted 35 months. Not only that, the ensuing contraction was the briefest, although the deepest since the demobilization dip of 1945 and only three had been shorter in a hundred years (Table 6). Is this about what one should expect of a "normal" cycle in the postwar economy, or were the conditions of 1954-58 only somewhat less exceptional than those of 1946-54? An historical analysis of the cycle will help to distinguish its accidental properties from its systematic ones, thereby providing part of the answer to this question.

Rapid Expansion in 1955

The previous chapter traced the genesis of the expansion to the early revival of consumer demand and residential construction during 1954, and described how the expansion gained momentum from the enthusiastic response accorded the 1955 automobiles. With sales increasing over a broad front, business capital spending quickly fol-

CHART 20. *Indexes of Prices, Industrial Production, and Nonagricultural Employment, Monthly, and of Real Gross National Product, Quarterly, Seasonally Adjusted,*[a] *1954-58*

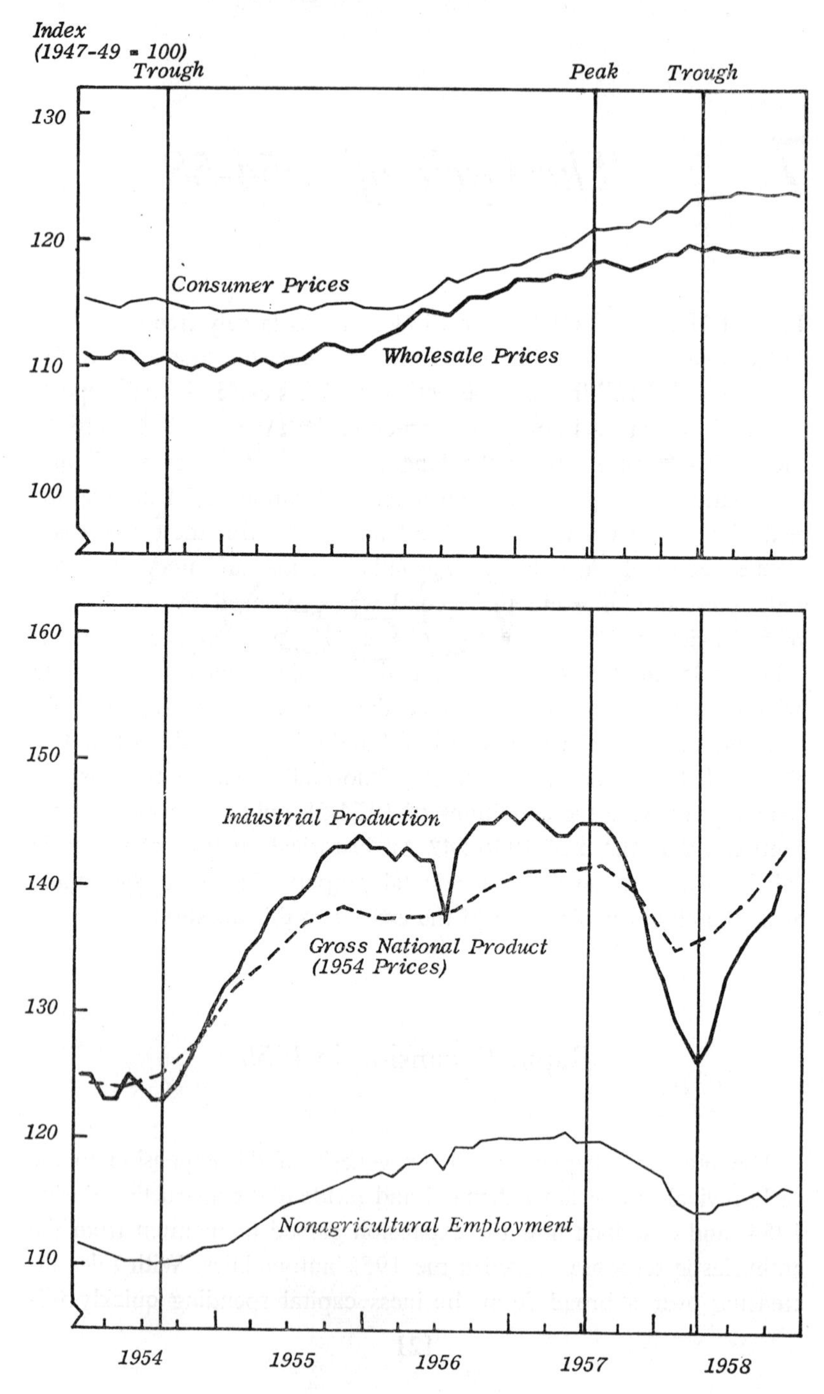

[a] Prices not adjusted for seasonal variation.

Sources: Bureau of Labor Statistics; Board of Governors of the Federal Reserve System; Office of Business Economics, Department of Commerce.

lowed suit; production and employment mounted swiftly (Chart 20). By the early months of 1955 every major component of gross national product save federal spending was on the rise (Charts 21, 22, and 23). Indeed, the pace of the expansion quickened so rapidly that, by mid-year, unemployment had fallen to 4 per cent of the labor force, industrial wholesale prices were rising, shortages were developing among metals and building materials, and the public authorities were seeking actively to restrain demand (Charts 24 and 20).[1]

The principal restrictive actions were in the field of money and credit. During the summer, the Board of Governors of the Federal Reserve System intensified the policy of general monetary restraint which it had initiated rather tentatively early in 1955. As a result, the seasonally adjusted money supply (demand deposits plus currency), which had increased nearly 2 per cent between December 1954 and June 1955, rose less than 1 per cent during the remainder of the year. Specific steps were also taken to curtail the increase of housing credit. In April, the Federal Housing Administration and the Veterans Administration ruled that closing costs could not be included in mortgage loans underwritten by the government. In July, these agencies raised minimum down-payment requirements and reduced maximum maturities on federally insured or guaranteed mortgages. No authority existed to regulate terms on consumer instalment credit, however, so that efforts to contain its rapid expansion were limited to moral suasion and the indirect effects of tight money.

Aggregate demand and production mounted rapidly during the last half of 1955 despite credit curbs. The rate of increase did diminish, however. Gross national expenditure increased 4 per cent from the second to the fourth quarters, as compared with a rise of 6 per cent during the two preceding quarters. The corresponding percentages for real GNP were 3 and 5. Industrial production also decelerated, with increases respectively of 7.3 and 4.1 per cent during the first and second halves of the year.

The deceleration of aggregate demand resulted only partly from

[1] See *Economic Report of the President* (January 1956), pp. 29-40, for a summary of policy actions during 1955. For a critical review of monetary policies, see Asher Achinstein, *Federal Reserve Policy and Economic Stability, 1951-57,* Senate Committee on Banking and Currency, Report No. 2500, 85 Cong. 2 sess. (1958), Chap. III.

CHART 21. *Government Purchases and Personal Consumption Expenditures, Seasonally Adjusted Quarterly Totals at Annual Rates, 1954-58*

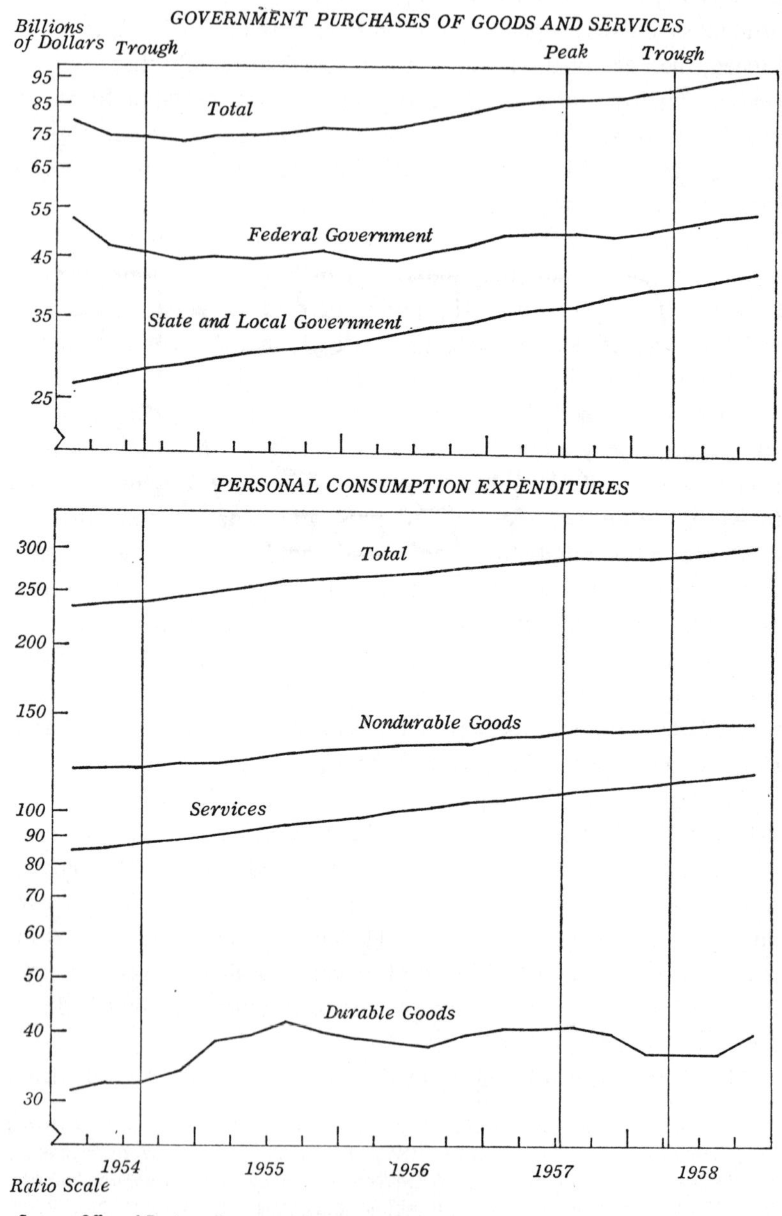

Source: Office of Business Economics, Department of Commerce.

credit restraints. The effects of the restraints were most notable in the field of residential construction. Home finance is especially susceptible to the waxing and waning of monetary stringency because of legislative and administrative limits on interest rates to be charged for VA and FHA loans. When yields on other investments rise, the fixed return on guaranteed or insured mortgages becomes less attractive to lenders and diminishes the supply of mortgage funds at the going rate.[2] Marginal home buyers may also be moved in or out of the market by administrative changes in down-payment requirements or permissible maturities on VA or FHA mortgages. Doubtless the 7.6 per cent decrease of nonfarm residential construction expenditure between July and December of 1955 was caused primarily by credit controls.

Automobile sales also declined, but not until the last three months of the year, and probably not because of credit conditions. The demand for instalment credit is little affected by interest charges as long as monthly payments can be kept low in relation to income. Both down payments and maturities on new automobile loans were liberalized considerably during 1955. Automobile sales and the volume of instalment credit extended on automobiles continued to rise until the new models were introduced in the closing months of the year. At that time, a sales decline set in which continued through most of 1956. Evidently the spectacular sales of 1955 models had satisfied the needs of many new-car buyers for at least two or three years ahead, producing a temporary saturation of segments of the new-car market and a corresponding decline of sales of 1956 models.

Business expenditure for plant and equipment was undeterred by tight money and increased more during the last half of 1955 than in the first half: $4.3 billion as compared with $3.6 billion. There were several reasons for this. Internal sources account for a large fraction of the funds invested by corporations[3] so that the deterrent effect of tight money is limited largely to the weak influence of higher interest rates on alternative earnings instead of the credit rationing which often

[2] Mortgage discounting provides only a partial escape from the squeeze on funds.

[3] In 1955, retained profits and depreciation allowances together were actually as large as plant and equipment outlays by nonfinancial corporations. See *Economic Report of the President* (January 1958), Table F-59.

CHART 22. *Gross Private Domestic Investment and its Components, Seasonally Adjusted Quarterly Totals at Annual Rates, 1954-58*

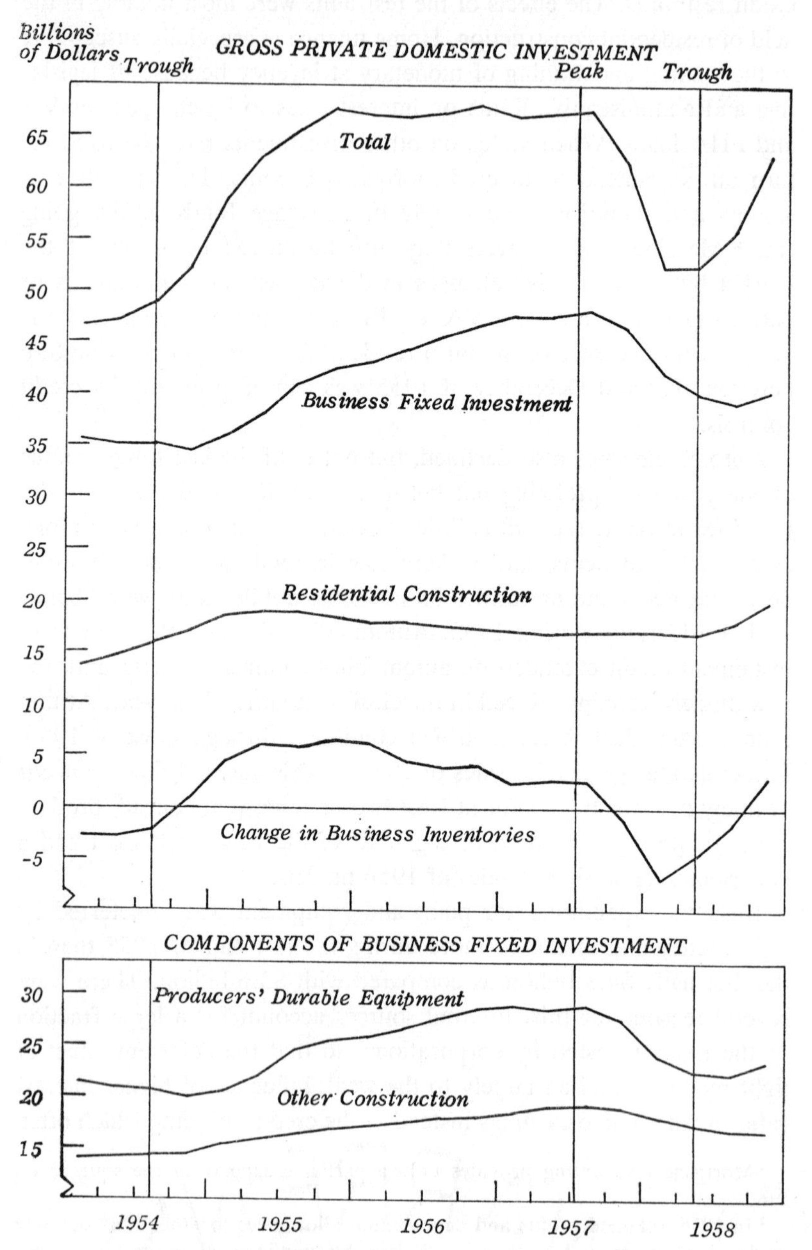

Source: Office of Business Economics, Department of Commerce.

restricts access to external funds. Moreover, the expansion of money and credit was merely retarded, and not halted, when the Federal Reserve authorities increased the pressure on bank reserves. Commercial banks borrowed more heavily from the Federal Reserve and continued to liquidate government securities in order to expand loans despite the pressure on reserves. Other lenders transferred idle funds to active investors either directly or through the medium of financial intermediaries. Thus both the money supply and the income velocity of money continued to rise after mid-year, although at reduced rates, and business enterprises secured a larger share of the expansion of loanable funds than when mortgage and consumer credit was rapidly increasing. Finally, the investment expenditure of the last half of 1955 was financed in part by funds raised earlier; and by the same token, the expenditure-restraining effects of credit stringency during the latter months of 1955, if any, would be partly delayed until 1956.

The deceleration of output growth during the latter months of 1955 was occasioned partly by supply limitations in bottleneck industries. According to the McGraw-Hill survey of business plans, manufacturing industry as a whole was operating at 92 per cent of capacity in December, or 2 per cent higher than the preferred rate. Most individual industries were either near 100 per cent of capacity, or above their preferred rate of utilization, or both (Table 17). Doubtless more could have been produced, but probably only at greater cost as marginal capacity was pressed into service. At the same time, it cannot be argued that the reduced rate of growth was forced on the economy as a whole by physical limitations of plant capacity. Perhaps that would have occurred had not aggregate demand been retarded by credit restrictions and other factors, but as it was, the economy did not reach a stage of highly inelastic aggregate supply. Additional demand would have meant additional production, although perhaps partly at the expense of higher prices.[4]

Nor was the expansion of production limited by inadequate growth of the labor supply. Employment had risen faster than the civilian

[4] The index of industrial wholesale prices did rise during the last half of 1955, but the increases were greatest in the bottleneck durable goods industries, and there is no evidence of generalized shortages in the over-all behavior of prices. See Chapter 14.

CHART 23. *The Nation's Income, Expenditure, and Saving, Seasonally Adjusted Quarterly Totals at Annual Rates, 1954-58*

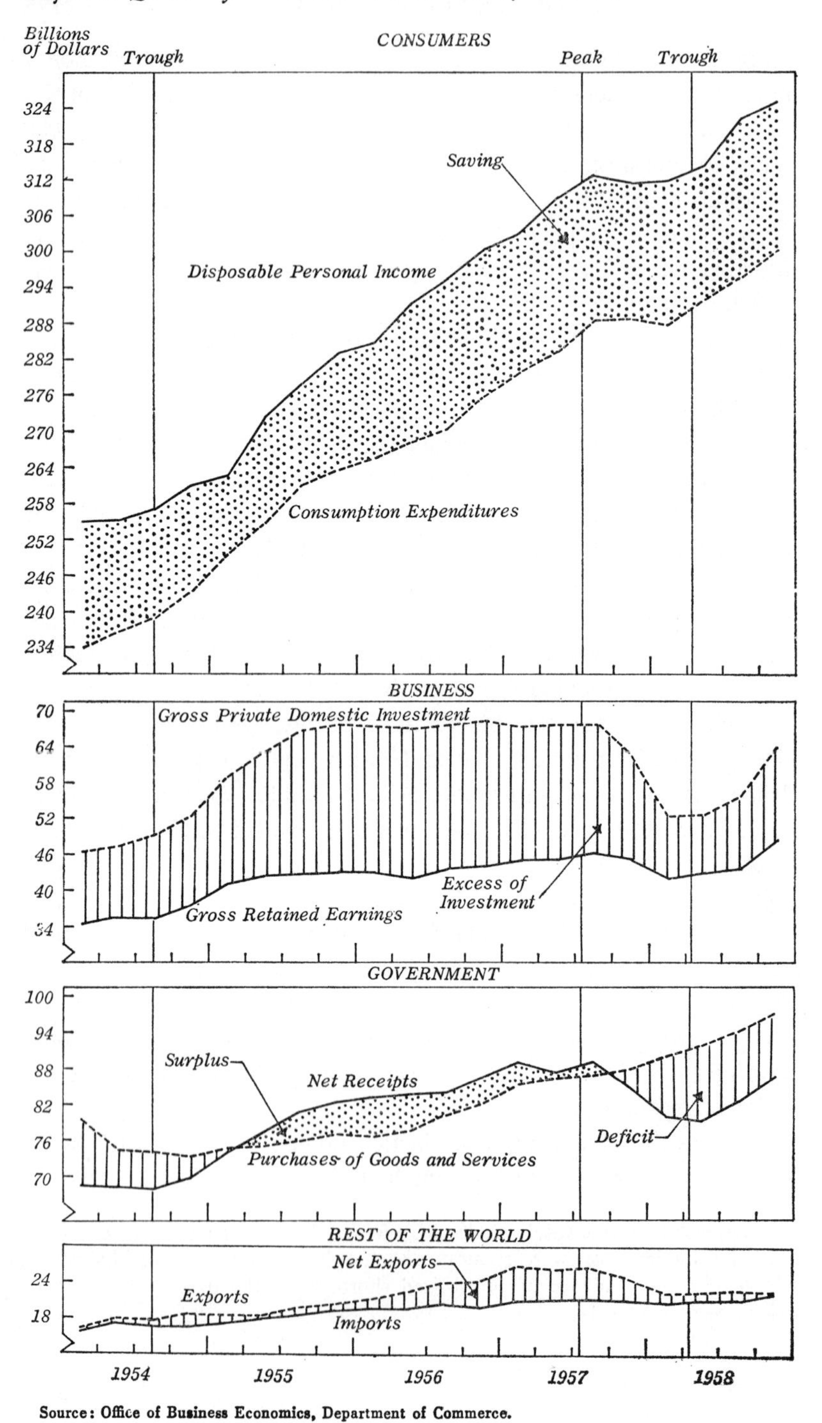

Source: Office of Business Economics, Department of Commerce.

CHART 24. *The Labor Force, Employment, and the Unemployment Ratio, Monthly, Seasonally Adjusted, 1954-58*

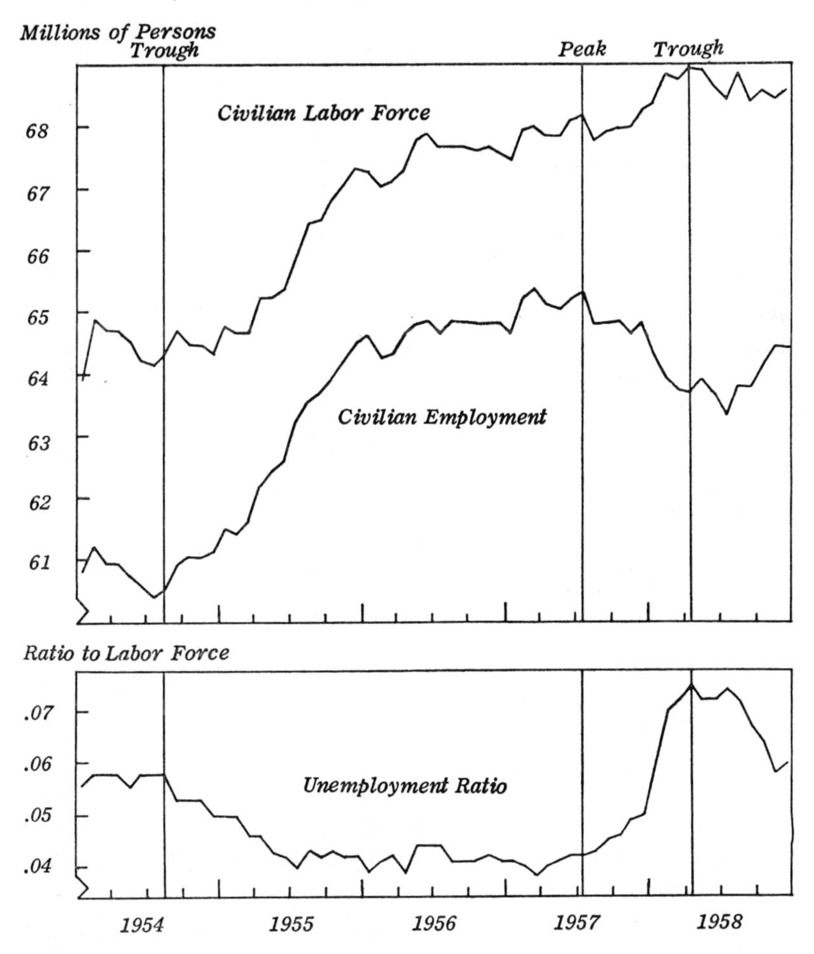

Source: Derived from data of the Bureau of the Census.

labor force between mid-1954 and mid-1955 (Chart 24), reducing the unemployment ratio from 6 to 4 per cent. A labor shortage appeared imminent at this point, and one would soon have developed had the labor force continued to increase at the same rate as before. Instead, its growth accelerated, so that it rose just as rapidly as employment during the last half of 1955, and the rate of unemployment stayed

TABLE 17. *Capacity Utilization in Manufacturing Industries*[a]
(In per cent)

Industry	Actual Operating Rate					Preferred Rate[b]
	1954	1955	1956	1957	1958	
Iron and steel	81	98	98	68	73	96
Nonferrous metals	87	95	92	74	77	89
Machinery (nonelectrical)	72	87	85	76	70	89
Electrical machinery	92	98	87	76	80	91
Autos, trucks, and parts	95	96	n.a.	76	78	n.a.
Transportation equipment	69	74	80	74	70	85
Other metalworking	81	94	83	80	80	88
Chemicals	79	90	83	81	80	92
Paper and pulp	97	100	96	88	87	95
Rubber	93	91	88	80	78	90
Stone, clay, and glass	87	94	90	74	79	86
Petroleum refining	90	96	96	90	87	95
Food and beverages	82	88	80	80	82	90
Textiles	88	93	90	80	87	93
Miscellaneous manufacturing	n.a.	n.a.	85	80	84	88
All manufacturing	84	92	86	78	80	90

n.a. Not available.

[a] All rates as of end of year. Physical capacity is measured by the reporting companies, according to their own definitions. However, companies in the same industry generally follow the same practice. Source, McGraw-Hill Department of Economics, *Business' Plans for New Plant and Equipment, 1959–1962* (1959).

[b] End of 1956.

near 4 per cent. On a seasonally adjusted basis, the civilian labor force increased nearly 2 million between June and December, or at an annual rate 4.6 times as great as the average annual increase between 1947 and 1958.

What happened was that with jobs easily available, women and youngsters entered the labor force in large numbers and in excess of their increase in the total population. To quote Ewan Clague, Commissioner of Labor Statistics,

> Growth in the labor force from year to year is very uneven. This uneven growth is closely related to changes in the demand for labor. When job opportunities are plentiful, the labor force expands rapidly, and it grows more slowly when jobs are harder to find. Women and young workers are the main groups which respond

quickly to changes in labor demand, and therefore account for most of the variation in the rate of labor force growth.[5]

Thus, during short periods the labor force is elastic to increases of labor demand, and is unlikely to impose an external constraint on the growth rate of production. This is partly because women refrain from entering the labor force during periods of slack demand, however, so that in such periods population growth adds more to the potential than to the actual labor supply. Presumably if demand continued to rise rapidly for several years, the pool of potential entrants would be emptied and the labor force would grow in line with population and secular changes in participation rates, imposing a supply check to the growth of production.

Precarious Balance in 1956

The expansion almost came to a halt during 1956. Gross national expenditure continued to rise throughout the year, but at a considerably diminished rate until the final quarter. Price increases were responsible for virtually all the rise in money expenditure until the fourth quarter spurt. Real gross national product and industrial production actually drifted downward until mid-year, and it was not until the fourth quarter that a production gain was recorded over the previous year (Chart 20).

The slowdown was due primarily to independent demand factors and money constraints rather than to physical limitations on aggregate supply. The civilian labor force did not increase much but it did keep up with employment, and doubtless would have increased more had jobs been available. Moreover, manufacturing capacity grew more rapidly than production during 1956 (Table 17).

As is normally the case, the retardation of aggregate demand during the first half of the year reflected actual declines in some sectors

[5] *Hearings on the January 1958 Economic Report of the President,* before the Joint Economic Committee, 85 Cong. 2 sess. (1958), p. 38. See also the statistical materials accompanying his testimony.

TABLE 18. *Changes in Gross National Product and Major Components, by Half-Year Intervals, 1955-57*[a]
(In billions of dollars)

Component	1955		1956		1957	
	I H	II H	I H	II H	I H	II H
Gross national product	+22.2	+15.9	+6.1	+15.0	+12.1	+0.2
Personal consumption expenditure	+11.1	+ 9.0	+4.9	+ 7.4	+ 7.7	+5.3
Durable goods	+ 5.2	+ 0.7	−1.6	+ 1.2	+ 1.0	−0.7
Nondurable goods	+ 2.7	+ 4.4	+2.9	+ 2.3	+ 3.5	+2.2
Services	+ 3.3	+ 3.7	+3.6	+ 3.9	+ 3.4	+3.7
Gross private domestic investment	+10.8	+ 4.5	−0.7	+ 1.2	− 0.8	−4.9
Residential nonfarm construction	+ 1.9	− 0.5	−0.4	− 0.7	− 0.4	+0.2
Business fixed investment	+ 3.6	+ 4.3	+2.0	+ 2.4	+ 0.9	−1.2
Change in business inventories	+ 5.3	+ 0.6	−2.3	− 0.4	− 1.3	−3.9
Net exports of goods and services	− 1.6	+ 0.2	+1.7	+ 1.7	+ 0.8	−1.6
Exports	− 0.1	+ 1.7	+2.3	+ 1.9	+ 1.9	−1.5
Imports	+ 1.4	+ 1.5	+0.6	+ 0.2	+ 1.1	0.0
Government purchases	+ 1.9	+ 2.2	+0.2	+ 4.7	+ 4.4	+1.3
Federal	+ 0.3	+ 1.4	−1.6	+ 3.0	+ 2.5	−0.6
State and local	+ 1.5	+ 0.8	+1.8	+ 1.7	+ 2.0	+1.9

[a] Half-year changes are measured between fourth and second quarters, and quarterly totals are at seasonally adjusted annual rates. Source, *U. S. Income and Output*, a supplement to *Survey of Current Business* (November 1958), Table I-3 and *Survey of Current Business* (July 1960), Table 1.

and slowed growth in others (Table 18). Substantial declines occurred in automobiles and homebuilding: the former in reaction to the extraordinary sales of 1955 models, the latter in response to the credit constraints which were imposed in 1955 and continued in 1956. Federal spending also dropped as a result of reduced purchases under agricultural price support programs. Meanwhile, the economy received a boost from the continued rise of state and local purchases and business fixed investment, and from an upsurge of exports, as well as from continued increases in consumer expenditures for nondurables and services.

The economy was on the brink of contraction during this period. The fall in automobile demand was a powerful deflationary shock. Consumer expenditures for autos and parts dropped at an annual rate of $4.2 billion dollars, or 21 per cent, between the third quarter of 1955 and the second of 1956. The peak of automobile production was delayed until the final quarter of 1955, but the decline during the first half of 1956 amounted to 31 per cent. The difference in timing and amplitude of sales and production reflects primarily the influence of inventory accumulation in the early months of the model year and decumulation later on.

The drop of automobile demand, and the gentler decline of residential construction which was occurring at the same time, caused production to fall not only in those sectors but in supplying industries as well. Among the production declines in closely related manufacturing industries during the first six months of 1956 were the following: primary metals, 9.3 per cent; fabricated metal products, 4.3 per cent; lumber and products, 2.4 per cent; and rubber products, 12.5 per cent. The decline in primary metals occurred despite increases of 3.7 per cent and 3.8 per cent for machinery and instruments and related products.

A diminished demand for materials is only the most obvious of the ways in which a decrease in some category of final expenditure may spread through the economy.[6] Consumer income and expenditure also may be adversely affected, as may business investment.

Employment and hours of factory workers did decline slightly during the early months of 1956, but the effect on personal income was minor. Factory wage increases partly compensated for reductions in man-hours of employment. Wage and salary disbursements in manufacturing, moreover, account for less than one-fourth of personal income, and income payments in most other sectors increased. Thus the rise of personal income was retarded, but by no means stopped, by the

[6] In fact, were it not that a decline of demand for a final product is usually amplified by inventory disinvestment as it is propagated to earlier stages of production, it would be a mere detail whether one or several industries was involved in producing the final product.

TABLE 19. *Quarterly Changes in Personal Income, Consumption, and Saving, 1955-58*[a]
(In billions of dollars)

Item	1955 Quarters				1956 Quarters				1957 Quarters				1958 Quarters			
	I	II	III	IV	I	II	III	IV	I	II	III	IV	I	II	III	IV
Personal income	4.3	9.0	6.3	5.9	4.1	7.1	4.5	5.7	4.0	6.3	4.2	−1.5	−0.9	2.7	8.8	3.4
Disposable personal income	2.9	8.2	5.7	5.3	1.6	6.5	4.1	5.1	2.7	5.8	3.9	−1.5	0.2	2.6	7.9	3.0
Personal consumption	6.2	4.9	6.6	2.4	2.3	2.6	2.2	5.2	4.5	3.2	5.4	−0.1	−0.9	3.5	3.6	5.4
Durable goods	4.3	0.9	2.3	−1.6	−1.0	−0.6	−0.5	1.7	1.0	0.0	0.5	−1.2	−3.2	−0.1	0.3	2.9
Nondurable goods	0.2	2.5	2.4	2.0	1.6	1.3	0.7	1.6	2.1	1.4	2.9	−0.7	0.7	1.7	1.6	0.8
Services	1.7	1.6	1.8	1.9	1.8	1.8	2.1	1.8	1.4	2.0	1.8	1.9	1.6	1.9	1.7	1.8
Personal saving	−3.3	3.4	−1.0	3.0	−0.8	3.9	1.9	−0.1	−1.8	2.5	−1.4	−1.4	0.9	−0.9	4.3	−2.4

[a] Quarterly totals are at seasonally adjusted annual rates. Source, *U. S. Income and Output*, supplement to *Survey of Current Business* (November 1958), Tables I-3 and II-2 and *Survey of Current Business* (July 1960), Tables 1 and 4.

weakness in manufacturing during the first quarter of 1956 (Table 19).

The rate of increase of disposable income was diminished even more by an increase in personal taxes. The combined effect of the retardation in earnings from production and the increase of taxes was to reduce the growth of disposable personal income from an annual rate of $5.3 billion in the fourth quarter of 1955 to $1.6 billion in the first quarter of 1956. Despite this retardation, however, personal consumption increased in the first quarter at about the same rate as before: $2.3 billion as compared with $2.4 billion in the preceding quarter.

Thus the deflationary impact of reduced activity in the heavy industries on aggregate consumption was mitigated by two main factors: income increases in other cyclically less sensitive sectors; and the fact that in the short run consumption expenditure is governed only loosely by income. Interestingly enough, however, the weakness in retail markets was not confined to automobiles: the point is simply that it was due less to induced income retardation than to increased saving by consumers and to a shift in the composition of expenditure from goods to services.

Probably there were good reasons for the higher level of personal saving in 1956. Consumers had saved less during every quarter except one from the beginning of 1954 through the third quarter of 1955, with the result that the personal saving ratio had decreased from 7.3 per cent in 1954 to an average of 6 per cent in the first three quarters of 1955. Evidently some retrenchment was called for thereafter, because the annual rate of increase of consumer expenditures dropped to $2.4 billion in the fourth quarter of 1955 and stayed at approximately that level through the next three quarters. Meanwhile, disposable income rose irregularly, but at a considerably higher average rate than $2.4 billion, and the saving ratio averaged 7.5 per cent.

Usually a retardation of consumer demand primarily affects goods instead of services,[7] and 1955-56 was no exception (Table 19). Dollar expenditures for automobiles actually declined, of course, while sales of other durables and of nondurables rose at retarded rates. Correction for price changes, moreover, reveals that sales even of non-

[7] See Chapter 10.

CHART 25. *Inventory-Sales Ratios, Monthly, Seasonally Adjusted, 1954-58*

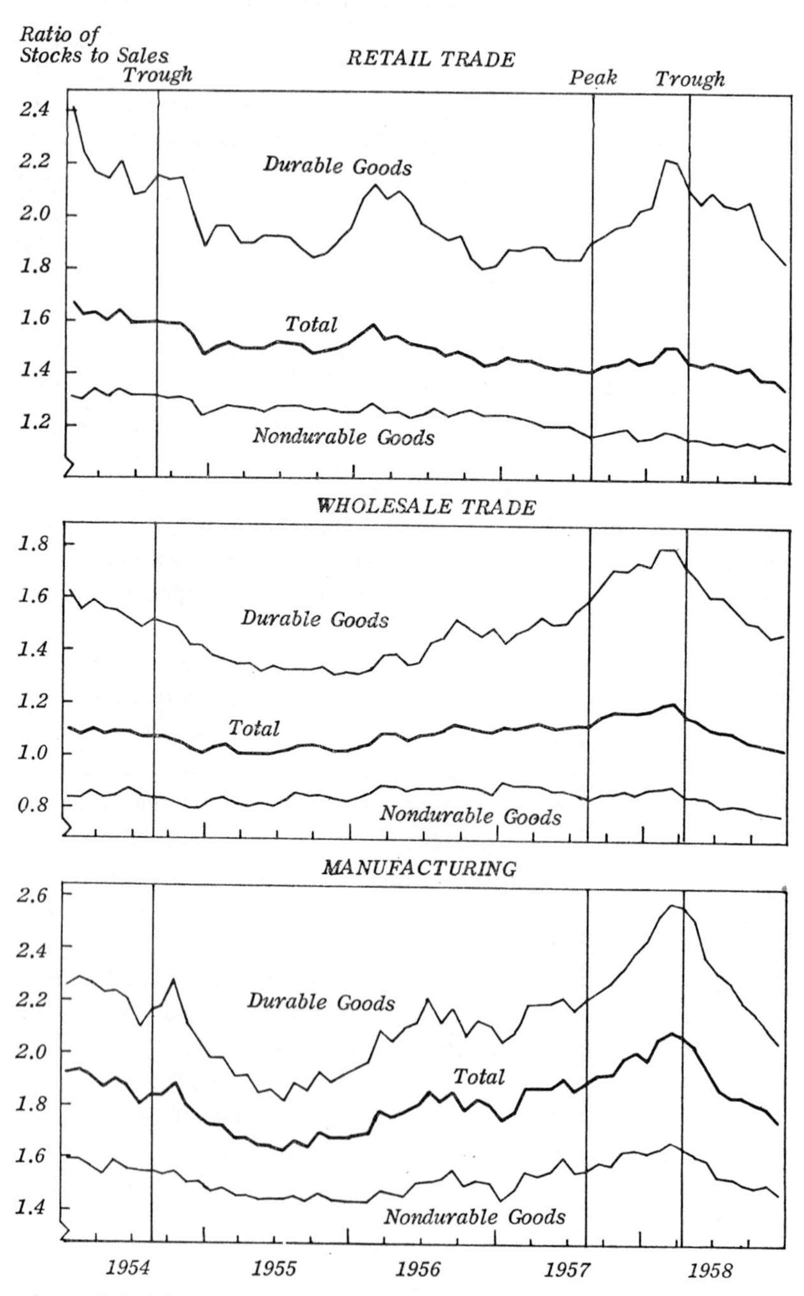

Source: Derived from data of the Office of Business Economics, Department of Commerce.

durables were virtually unchanged in real terms during the first three quarters of 1956.

Retail inventory investment diminished as sales slackened. With sales in individual lines stable or falling, distributors curtailed orders in an effort to keep inventories from rising relative to sales and in some instances actually to reduce them (Chart 25). Not only was automobile production hit especially hard, but production of furniture and floor coverings, radio and television sets, appliances and heaters, textiles and apparel, and leather products also decreased during the first half of 1956, by amounts ranging from 4 to 9 per cent.

We come now to one of the important factors that kept the downslide of 1956 from developing into a cumulative contraction. It might be thought that with production dropping in so many industries, businessmen would reduce outlays for plant and equipment, and yet business fixed investment continued upward throughout 1956 (Chart 22). This was partly because investment demands were strong in nonmanufacturing industries, but it is interesting to note that manufacturers accounted for two-thirds of the rise in business expenditures for plant and equipment during the year.

What helped to save the situation was that the downturns of early 1956 occurred primarily in industries in which investment lagged the production reversals by long intervals, presumably because of lengthy gestation periods. Table 20 shows the quarterly peaks of production and fixed investment in 16 industries—15 of them manufacturing industries—during the expansion of 1955-57. Notice that the peak levels of production for the entire period were reached late in 1955 or early in 1956 for motor vehicles and equipment, "other" durable goods, rubber products, primary nonferrous metals, primary iron and steel, and textiles. However, only in the case of textiles did investment expenditure fall within six months of the downturn of production; in all the other instances of early contraction the investment peak lagged the production peak by nine or more months. Thus the early production downturns did induce investment declines, but because of lags these industries continued to contribute—in several cases heavily—to the expansion of aggregate investment outlays until late-1956 or 1957.

Meanwhile, other developments put new life in the expansion. In-

TABLE 20. *Quarterly Dates of Peaks of Production and Fixed Investment Expenditure (Current Dollars) in 15 Manufacturing Industries and in Mining, 1955-57*[a]

Industry	Production Peak	Investment Peak
Motor vehicles and equipment	IV Q 55	III Q 56
Other durable goods	IV Q 55	III Q 56
Rubber products	IV Q 55	IV Q 56
Primary nonferrous metals	IV Q 55	III Q 57
Primary iron and steel	I Q 56	III Q 57
Textile mill products	I Q 56	III Q 56
Stone, clay, and glass products	II Q 56	III Q 56
Paper and allied products	III Q 56	IV Q 56
Electrical machinery	IV Q 56	IV Q 56
Nonelectrical machinery	IV Q 56	IV Q 57
Petroleum and coal products	I Q 57	I Q 57
Mining	I Q 57	I Q 57
Other nondurable goods	II Q 57	III Q 57
Other transportation equipment	II Q 57	II Q 57
Chemicals and allied products	III Q 57	III Q 57
Food and beverages	No peak	IV Q 57

[a] Seasonally adjusted indexes of production from Board of Governors of the Federal Reserve System. Current dollar estimates of new plant and equipment expenditures from Department of Commerce, Office of Business Economics, and Federal Trade Commission, adjusted for seasonal variation by the author. When corrected for price changes, the investment peaks come earlier in several industries. On this point, see Bert G. Hickman, "Diffusion, Acceleration, and Business Cycles," *American Economic Review* (September 1959), p. 544, Table 1.

dustrial production and prices moved upward on a broad front following the steel strike in July 1956. The prime movers were increased activity in the automobile and ancillary industries as the new models went into production, an upturn of federal defense expenditure after a year and a half of stability, and an upsurge of exports stimulated by economic expansion abroad and the Suez crises. (Charts 21 and 23). An added thrust was lent by restocking demand on the part of metal fabricators whose inventories had been drawn down during the steel strike.

The entire fourth quarter of 1956 was colored by the rebound of automobile production. As it turned out, sales increased less than had been hoped, but in the meantime production was augmented by the inventory accumulations of automotive manufacturers, their suppliers, and their distributors. The increase of automobile production was superimposed, moreover, on the gentler but steadier rise of machinery production as business expenditure for equipment continued its advance. Since total industrial production advanced, so also did manufacturing employment, hours, and earnings—the latter with an assist from wage increases. In this way, increased production consequent on expanded automobile output served to bolster personal income and helped to induce a part of the increased volume of retail sales which had been expected, and the expectation of which had started the process. Once again, however, it was a shift in saving rates, rather than income acceleration, which was primarily responsible for the fourth quarter acceleration of consumer expenditure (Table 19).

Downturn in 1957

As 1957 opened, the expansion was already more than two years old. It gradually lost momentum as the year progressed, and by late summer a downturn was underway.

Automobile sales reached a plateau in January which was sustained with moderate fluctuations until July. Residential construction continued to decline slightly until mid-year. The net effect of these movements was only mildly deflationary. The ominous depressant was the tapering off of business fixed investment which had begun early in the year (Chart 22). Money outlays for producers' durable equipment were virtually constant after the turn of the year, and since prices kept rising, the physical volume of sales drifted downward.

Thus, the year had scarcely begun before residential construction and the real demand for producers' durable equipment were sliding off. At that time, however, government purchases were rising slightly. Nonetheless, the balance was on the side of contraction in durable goods (Chart 26). Employment, hours, and payrolls of production workers declined in the affected industries, but gains among salaried employees and elsewhere in the economy kept personal income rising until August. With income rising, sales of food and soft goods moved

CHART 26. *Indexes of Industrial Production, Monthly, Seasonally Adjusted, 1954-58*

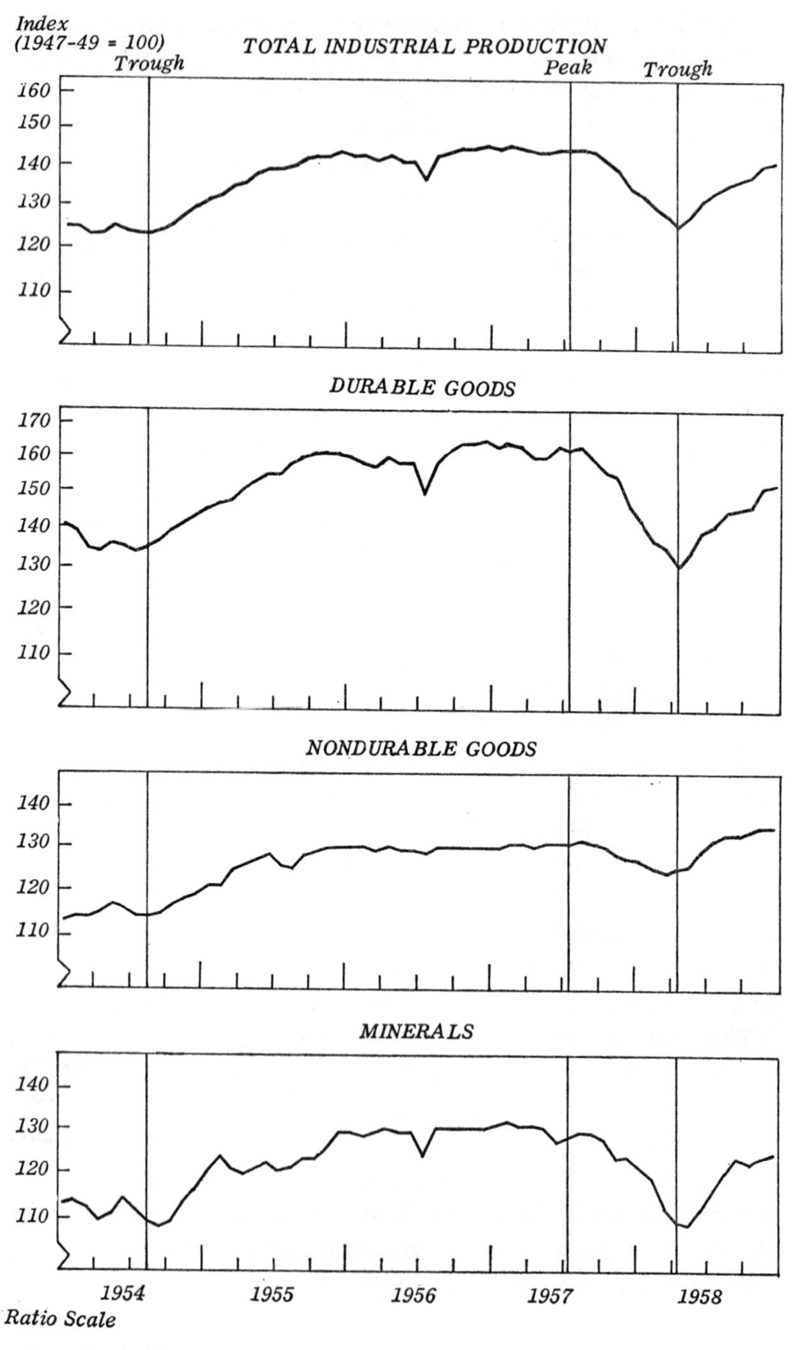

Source: Board of Governors of the Federal Reserve System.

strongly ahead during the spring and summer as consumers augmented their total expenditure and shifted its composition in favor of nondurables. Since distributors were watching inventories carefully, however (Chart 25), the incoming business of nondurable manufacturers did not rise much and the volume of production increased only slightly. After a slow second quarter, sales and production of consumer durables improved somewhat in the third, but insufficiently for durable goods output to regain the 1956 peak.

The final blows were dealt the expansion during the summer of 1957, when an economy already balanced on the edge of contraction because of internal developments in the private sector, was subjected to autonomous reductions in defense spending and exports. Neither decline was especially large (Table 18), but they occurred when the economy was vulnerable to disturbance and hastened a downturn which doubtless would have come soon anyway. Indeed, were it not for the previous increases of export demand and federal spending, the contraction might well have started six months or a year before it did.

Now industrial production dropped more swiftly, nonagricultural employment declined, and labor income turned downward and carried aggregate personal income with it. Retail sales decreased as personal income dropped, spreading the contraction to the consumer goods industries. The pace of contraction was speeded during the final quarter by induced declines of business investment in inventories and in plant and equipment.

It is apparent that one of the leading factors in the downturn was the decline of business fixed investment, but it is quite another and more complicated issue as to why that came about. It should be possible to distinguish some of the principal strands of causation, however. This is because the deceleration and eventual decline of aggregate investment resulted primarily from a growing accumulation of individual declines, and something is known about the causes of these individual declines.

A close relationship regularly exists between the proportion of industries in which investment is rising and the rate of increase of aggregate investment.[8] It is illustrated for 1954-58 in Chart 27. The

[8] The implications of this relationship are developed more fully in Chapter 11 and in my article, "Diffusion, Acceleration, and Business Cycles," *American Economic Review* (September 1959).

CHART 27. *Business Expenditures for Plant and Equipment: Total, Change, and Diffusion Index,*[a] *Quarterly Seasonally Adjusted, 1954-58*

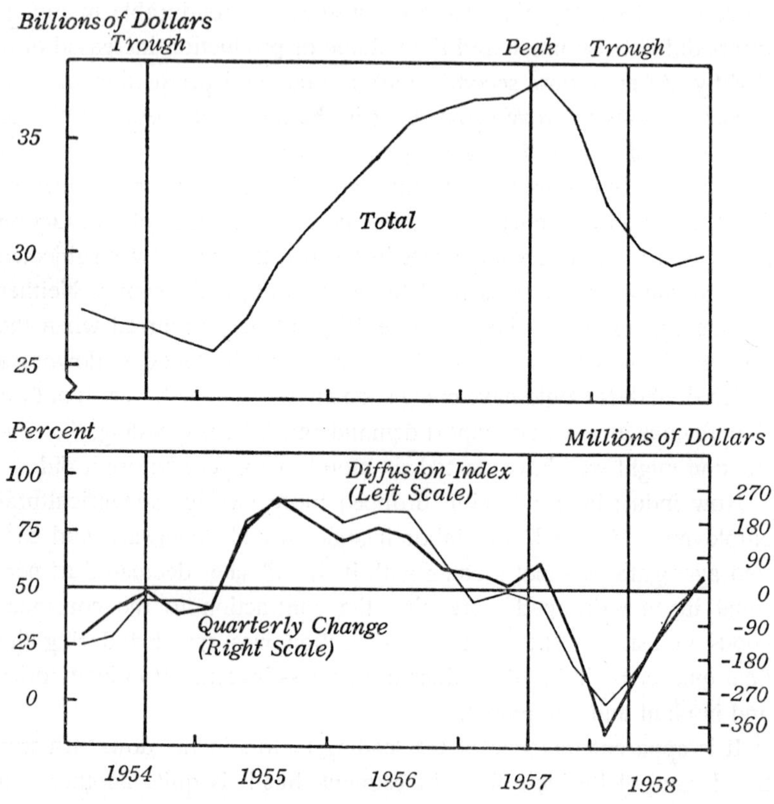

[a] The diffusion index shows the proportion of a group of 20 manufacturing and nonmanufacturing industries which increased investment expenditures in each quarter.

Source: Derived from data of the Office of Business Economics, Department of Commerce.

upper panel shows total business expenditure for plant and equipment. One of the curves plotted immediately below records the percentage of individual industries in which investment was increasing in each quarter, and the other curve depicts the absolute change of aggregate investment during the quarter. The correlation between the industrial scope and the pace of the investment expansion is readily apparent. Evidently, if the reason why investment declined in an increasing proportion of industries beginning in 1956—and especially after the third quarter of 1956—could be discovered, it would be possible to isolate at least some of the factors behind the downturn.

One possibility is that credit stringency caused the spread of investment declines, since the Federal Reserve pursued its tight money policy throughout 1956 and the first ten months of 1957. There are two major ways in which investment might be affected by tight credit.

First, high interest rates or credit rationing might deter investments which otherwise would have been undertaken, given the expected rates of return on the investments. This sort of reaction was clearly evident in the area of residential construction from mid-1955 to mid-1957. Imperfect access to credit markets may also have reduced investment expenditures by smaller businesses, since there is some, though admittedly inconclusive, statistical support for the a priori belief that "The recent credit restraints have had a greater impact on the availability of credit to small businesses than they have had on the large firms."[9] Perhaps this was one factor behind the early 1957 decline of investment expenditure in the "commercial and other" sector, which includes the trade, service, finance, and construction industries.

Second, financial constraints may induce investment declines indirectly, by depressing demands for final products and causing sales and profits to fall in (specialized) supplying industries. For example, the credit-induced decrease of residential building helps explain the early peaks of production (second quarter of 1956) and investment (third quarter of 1956) in stone, clay, and glass products (Table 20). Should credit constraints operate initially outside the sphere of investment and force reductions in, say, state and local construction or sales of consumer durables, this would tend also to reduce business investment demands in the affected supplying industries. With regard to 1956-57, however, it appears that the financing of state and local expenditure was little affected by credit stringency,[10] nor, for reasons discussed earlier, is it likely that credit conditions had much to do with the softness in the markets for automobiles, television sets, or household appliances during those years.

Rather, that softness was largely in reaction to the extraordinary

[9] Arthur F. Burns, *Prosperity Without Inflation* (1957), pp. 60-62.
[10] *Ibid.*, p. 59.

rates of purchase of consumer durables during 1955; purchases which added sharply to household stocks of durables and debt alike and either reduced demands for individual items, or stabilized them, in the face of income increases during 1956-57. Here is the primary factor behind the production declines which appeared early in 1956 among many of the durable goods industries and which induced subsequent investment declines beginning in the fourth quarter of the year (Table 20).

Other developments also may have diminished investment incentives somewhat in 1956-57. Profit margins per dollar of sales narrowed in a majority of manufacturing industries during 1956,[11] reinforcing the adverse effects of falling sales on profits in some industries and partly or wholly offsetting the favorable effects of sales increases in others. Rates of capacity utilization also decreased generally between the end of 1955 and that of 1956, and by the latter date were below preferred operating rates in a majority of reporting industries (Table 17). These depressants, however, were probably secondary to those discussed previously. The investment peaks of the last half of 1956 occurred primarily in industries in which production had already declined. The later investment peaks came primarily among industries in which production continued to increase for one or more quarters during 1957 (Table 20). This indirect evidence suggests strongly, though not conclusively, that business investment in the aggregate was little affected by instances in which profits declined because margins narrowed while sales were still increasing; or by instances in which capacity increased more rapidly than production but sales and production were still rising.

Contraction and Recovery, 1957-58

The 1957-58 recession, as already noted, was one of the briefest and also one of the sharpest of the minor contractions since the Civil War. The trough was reached in April 1958, only nine months from

[11] Geoffrey H. Moore, "The 1957-58 Business Contraction: New Model or Old?", Papers and Proceedings of the 71st Annual Meeting of the American Economic Association, *American Economic Review* (May 1959), p. 300.

the peak as dated by the National Bureau of Economic Research, but the declines of production and employment were considerably greater than during the longer contractions of 1948-49 and 1953-54 (Table 21). The peak rate of unemployment was 7.5 per cent, as compared with figures of 6.9 and 5.8 per cent for the two earlier recessions. The swiftness of the decline, and the fact that it was prompted partly by a downturn of real business fixed investment, aroused fears among contemporary observers that a classical business contraction was underway and might get out of hand if not arrested at an early date. Nor were these fears ungrounded, for the downswing did show signs

TABLE 21. *Amplitudes of Production and Employment During Three Recent Business Contractions*[a]
(In per cent)

Item	Contraction of:		
	1948–49	1953–54	1957–58
Real gross national product (Quarterly, 1954 dollars)...	2.4	3.6	4.7
Industrial production (Monthly, 1947–49=100)......	10.5	10.2	13.7
Nonagricultural employment (Monthly)............	3.8	3.5	4.6

[a] Based on individual peaks and troughs of seasonally adjusted series. Source, Department of Commerce, Office of Business Economics; Board of Governors of the Federal Reserve System; and Bureau of Labor Statistics.

of increasing momentum for a time, and the rebound was so sharp when it came as to surprise even those persons who had anticipated some improvement in the near future (Chart 20).

The contraction spread rapidly through the economy during the closing months of 1957. To summarize briefly—Exports and federal expenditures were dropping for autonomous reasons. Retail sales had improved during the summer, but they, too, declined once personal income turned down in September (Chart 28 and Table 19). Investment plans were revised downward as business conditions deteriorated generally and sales and orders fell in an increasing number of industries.[12] The annual rate of inventory investment decreased $3.3 billion during the fourth quarter despite involuntary accumulations in some

[12] As mentioned earlier, tight money contributed somewhat to the downshift of business investment, both directly and by depressing sales of some industries.

CHART 28. *Indexes of Personal Income, Sales, Inventories, and New Orders, Monthly, Seasonally Adjusted, 1954-58*

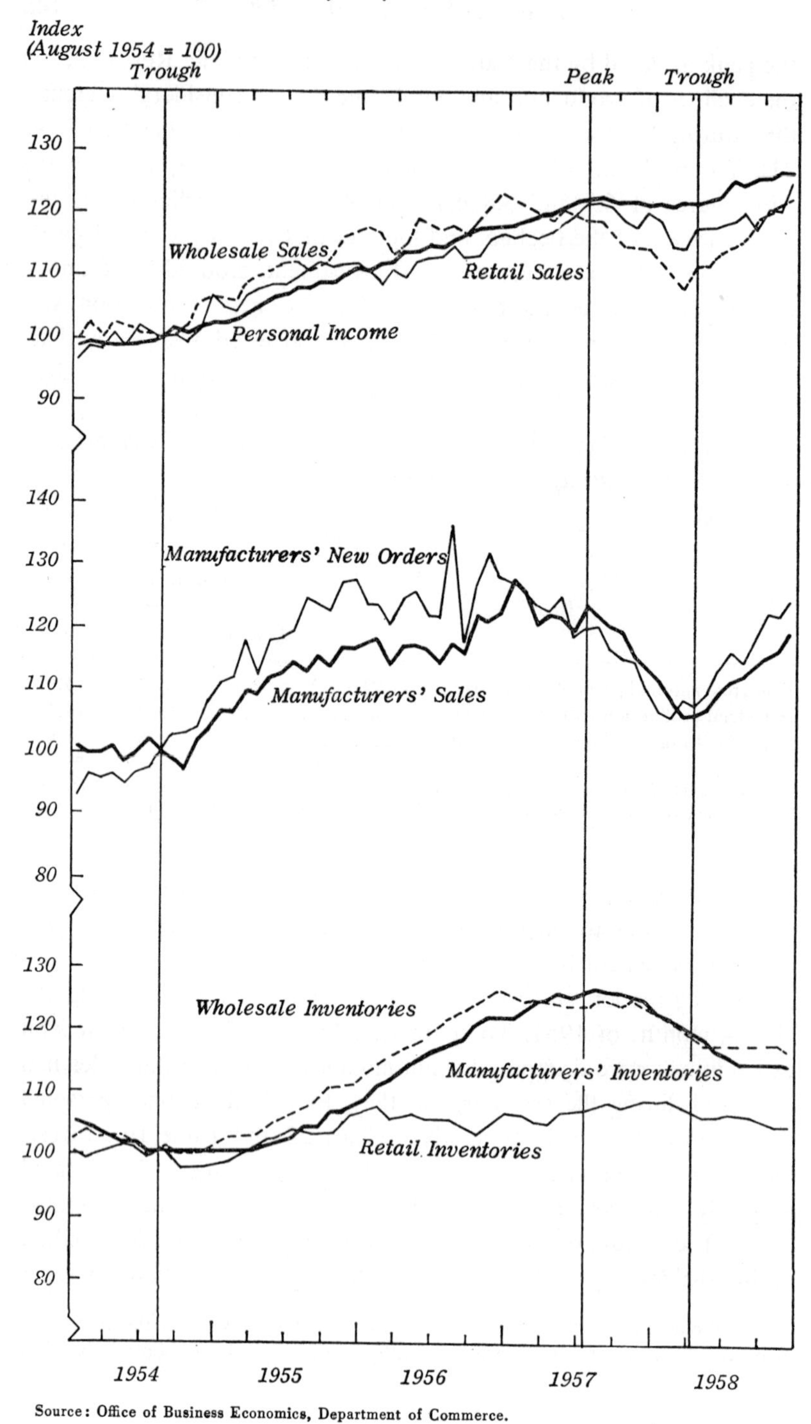

Source: Office of Business Economics, Department of Commerce.

lines of production and distribution. Much of the decline of business fixed investment during the fourth quarter must be traced to decisions made earlier, but there is no doubt that additional reductions were induced by the contraction itself—although in many cases the planned expenditure cuts were not realized until 1958. Even so, business expenditure on new plant and equipment dropped about $1.5 billion during the fourth quarter, or considerably more than the $250 million reduction which had been anticipated when firms reported their investment plans as late as October or November of 1957.[13]

Thus the contraction diffused through the economy, and by January 1958 production was dropping in 80 per cent of a comprehensive sample of 146 manufacturing industries, as compared with less than 50 per cent in the last month preceding the downturn. January marks the nadir in this respect, however. The percentage of production increases rose from 20 in January to about 30 in February and March and to more than 40 in April. By May, a majority (60 per cent) of the industries were experiencing increases, the index of aggregate manufacturing production had turned upward, and the recession was over (Chart 35). What were the principal factors which stopped and reversed the cumulative spread of contractive forces during the early months of 1958?

Part of the answer to this question can be read from Table 22, which shows the quarter-to-quarter changes in the major components of gross national product during the contraction and recovery. As usual, state and local spending rose throughout the period. Home building was another source of strength, although it did not repeat the prominent role which it had played in the upturns of 1949 and 1954, when residential construction expenditure had risen well before the recovery of general business. (Compare Charts 6, 13, and 22.) Aggregate consumption expenditure did not fall much during the contraction, and expenditures for nondurables recovered quickly after an initial loss. Another early upturn was recorded for federal purchases of goods and services.

These favorable developments were offset at first by accelerated reductions in purchases of producer and consumer durable goods and

[13] U.S. Department of Commerce, *Survey of Current Business* (December 1957), p. 6, and *ibid.* (March 1958), p. 12.

TABLE 22. *Quarterly Changes in Gross National Product and Major Components, 1957-58*[a]
(In billions of dollars)

Component	1957		1958			
	III Q	IV Q	I Q	II Q	III Q	IV Q
Gross national product	6.2	−6.0	−10.3	4.8	10.2	14.0
Personal consumption expenditures	5.4	−0.1	− 0.9	3.5	3.6	5.4
Durable goods	0.5	−1.2	− 3.2	−0.1	0.3	2.9
Nondurable goods	2.9	−0.7	0.7	1.7	1.6	0.8
Services	1.8	1.9	1.6	1.9	1.7	1.8
Gross private domestic investment	0.3	−5.2	−10.0	0.1	3.3	7.4
Residential nonfarm construction	0.1	0.1	0.0	−0.2	1.1	1.9
Business fixed investment	0.5	−1.7	− 4.3	−2.1	−1.2	1.1
Construction	0.2	−0.3	− 0.9	−0.7	−0.4	−0.1
Producers' durable equipment	0.3	−1.4	− 3.4	−1.4	−0.8	1.2
Change in business inventories	−0.2	−3.7	− 5.7	2.4	2.9	4.5
Net exports of goods and services	0.0	−1.6	− 1.8	−0.4	0.3	−1.2
Exports	0.2	−1.7	− 2.4	0.1	0.8	−0.4
Imports	0.2	−0.2	− 0.5	0.6	0.0	0.9
Government purchases of goods and services	0.5	0.8	2.4	1.8	2.9	2.3
Federal	0.0	−0.6	1.2	1.2	1.9	0.6
State and local	0.5	1.4	1.2	0.6	1.1	1.6
Addendum: Final expenditures (GNP less inventory changes)	6.4	−2.3	− 4.6	2.4	7.3	9.5

[a] Quarterly totals are at seasonally adjusted annual rates. Source, *Survey of Current Business* (July 1960), Table 8.

by a continued decline in net exports. As a result, final expenditures dropped at an accelerated rate in the first quarter of 1958 and inventory investment responded in kind, considerably amplifying the drop of national output in the process. However, during the second quarter the declines abated in the falling sectors and the rises came to predominate, so that final expenditure increased in the aggregate and carried with it inventory investment.

These observations are instructive, but only as a first step. What lay behind the expenditure shifts, and how did they interact?

Consider first the behavior of aggregate consumption expenditure. It comes as no surprise to observe that it was stable primarily because disposable personal income declined less than 0.5 per cent during the contraction. The automatic stabilizers did their work well, with corporate profits, as usual, absorbing the bulk of the decline in national income. Thus national income decreased $14 billion between the third quarter of 1957 and the first of 1958, whereas corporate profits after adjustment for inventory valuation dropped $9.9 billion. Again, as usual during recent mild contractions, dividends were maintained and the reduction of profits was split about equally between undistributed profits and corporate profits taxes. Personal income from production fell $5 billion despite the decline of corporate profits, but meanwhile government transfer payments increased $2.6 billion and personal taxes decreased $1.2 billion. The net result of all these changes, plus other minor ones, was that disposable personal income decreased only $1.3 billion over the period.

Wage advances may also have bolstered personal income during the contraction. There is no doubt that wage rates increased (Chart 47), but the effect on the total wage bill is uncertain because employment decisions may have been modified by the pay increases. (This question, and other aspects of the problem of the total response to wage increases, is discussed in Chapters 8 and 14.)

An unusual aspect of the behavior of personal income during this period was an increase of about $2 billion in farm proprietors' net income from the average for the last half of 1957 to the first half of 1958. This contracyclical rise was caused by a combination of autonomous factors: reduced supplies of price-inelastic meats, fruits, and vegetables; and increased production of price-supported crops.[14] The effects on the economy were mixed, though probably favorable on balance.

To some extent the rise of meat and produce prices merely shifted income from the nonagricultural sector to farmers. However, part of any decrease of expenditure for nonfood consumer items that was induced by higher food prices would diminish corporate profits instead of nonagricultural personal income, so that total personal income

[14] *Economic Report of the President* (January 1959), pp. 100-101.

would rise.[15] Aggregate consumption expenditure might not increase, however, since the marginal saving propensities of farmers are considerably higher than those of others whose incomes would be partly displaced. Similarly, although higher farm incomes probably induced the early upturn of farm equipment expenditures during 1958,[16] this rise may have been offset by an induced decline of nonagricultural investment resulting from the diversion of consumption expenditure from other items to food.

Thus, that part of the rise of farm earnings which resulted from diminished supplies and increased prices of certain foods, may have been approximately neutralized in its effects on aggregate demand by induced shifts in other sectors. This is not true of that portion of the rise of incomes resulting from increased government purchases under the agricultural price support programs, however, since those purchases provided a net injection into the income stream. Nor was the injection small. In fact, the great bulk of the $2.4 billion increase of federal purchases of goods and services during the first half of 1958 reflects government operations for stabilization of farm prices and income.[17] Here, then, is the principal cause of the early upturn of federal expenditure during the contraction: it was the autonomous result of bountiful harvests and inflexible price supports. While not inspired by contracyclical considerations, it nonetheless had a salutary effect on income and expenditure. Indeed, it would be difficult to exaggerate the importance of the early recovery of personal income from this and other sources.

It is sometimes said that the automatic income stabilizers can mitigate a contraction but cannot reverse one, since they depend for their operation on prior, and larger, losses of income from sales and

[15] The squeeze on profits would be enhanced by escalated wage increases resulting from the effects of higher food prices on the consumer price index, assuming that the short-run demand for labor was inelastic to wage increases.

[16] Expenditures on farm equipment increased from an annual rate of $2 billion in the first quarter of 1958 to an average of $2.25 billion in the second and third quarters. The corresponding figures for nonfarm producers equipment show a decline from $20.8 to $20.1 billion. See *Economic Report of the President* (January 1959), Table D-8.

[17] *Survey of Current Business* (July 1960), Table 23, shows the breakdown of government expenditures by type of function on an annual basis.

production. However, induced changes in profits, taxes, and transfers —by narrowing the response of disposable personal income and consumption demand to a decrease of national income—can provide opportunity for an upturn of personal income prompted by comparatively small increases from cyclically autonomous sources of demand. Thus, during 1958, the trough of personal income was reached in February, two months before the low point of industrial production, nonagricultural employment, and wage and salary disbursements. Industrial wages and salaries declined more slowly after February; there were small increases of labor income in cyclically insensitive employments like service and government; business and professional proprietors' income and property incomes were steady; and transfer payments increased sharply. The net result was an increase of aggregate personal income of $1.7 billion at an annual rate between February and April (Table 23).

The upturn of personal income led quickly to an increase of retail sales (Chart 28). March marks the trough of retail and wholesale trade, and by a smaller margin, also of manufacturers' sales. Notice how much larger was the fluctuation of retail sales than personal income during the contraction and recovery. This disparity appeared also during the contraction of 1953-54 and reflects the fact that consumers curtail expenditures for goods instead of services when income falls only for brief periods. Thus a reversal of personal income is apt to prompt a considerably larger reversal of retail sales, although the latter may still lag relative to the recovery of income and total consumption because of continued increases in purchases of services. Moreover, the favorable effect of the income recovery on demand will be further amplified by induced increases in inventory investment at the various stages of production and distribution. Evidently, then, the early upturn of personal income, and the increases of sales and production which it induced, were among the principal causes of the business revival.

Federal expenditure for purposes other than agricultural stabilization advanced comparatively little during the recovery. Defense expenditure had been a significant deflationary factor when it dropped from an annual rate of $45 billion in the third quarter of 1957 to $44 billion in the fourth. It recovered subsequently, but only to $44.4

TABLE 23. *Personal Income and Major Components, July 1957-June 1958*[a]
(In billions of dollars)

Item	1957						1958					
	July	Aug.	Sept.	Oct.	Nov.	Dec.	Jan.	Feb.	March	April	May	June
Personal Income	355.3	356.2	355.4	354.7	354.6	352.8	353.4	352.4	353.7	354.1	355.6	358.1
Wage and salary disbursements:												
All industries	240.8	241.2	240.6	239.1	239.0	238.1	236.2	234.3	233.6	233.5	235.1	238.1
Commodity producing	103.2	103.1	102.4	101.5	101.1	100.0	98.1	95.7	95.4	95.2	95.7	96.9
Distributive	64.1	64.4	64.3	63.6	63.8	63.8	63.6	63.5	62.9	62.5	63.1	63.5
Services	33.0	33.1	33.1	33.2	33.3	33.5	33.6	33.8	33.9	34.1	34.3	34.7
Government	40.5	40.7	40.8	40.7	40.7	40.8	40.9	41.2	41.5	41.7	41.9	43.1
Other labor income	9.2	9.3	9.4	9.4	9.5	9.5	9.5	9.4	9.3	9.3	9.3	9.3
Proprietors' income:												
Business and professional	33.0	33.0	32.7	32.7	32.2	32.2	31.9	31.3	31.4	31.9	32.0	32.1
Farm	12.2	12.5	12.2	12.0	12.0	12.3	13.3	14.9	15.8	14.4	13.8	13.3
Rental income of persons	12.0	12.1	12.2	12.3	12.2	12.2	12.1	12.1	12.1	12.1	12.1	12.1
Dividends	13.0	13.0	12.9	12.9	12.8	11.1	12.7	12.7	12.6	12.6	12.6	12.6
Personal interest income	19.8	20.0	20.1	20.2	20.2	20.3	20.2	20.2	20.2	20.3	20.4	20.6
Transfer payments	22.1	21.9	21.9	23.0	23.4	23.8	24.3	24.2	25.3	26.7	27.1	26.6
Less: Personal contributions for social insurance	6.8	6.8	6.7	6.8	6.7	6.7	6.8	6.7	6.7	6.7	6.7	6.8

[a] Seasonally adjusted monthly totals at annual rates. Source, *Survey of Current Business* (July 1960), Table 15.

billion in the first quarter of 1958 and $44.6 billion in the second. It would appear, then, that the contracyclical contribution of fiscal policy on the expenditure side was limited largely to the removal of a deflationary tendency in government purchases. Nevertheless, this was a significant contribution for two main reasons.

First, a change of final expenditure for the entire economy is the net outcome of pluses and minuses in the various sectors. At a minimum, the removal of a minus will slow the aggregate decline, and if it occurs when other items are rising sufficiently, it may tip the balance toward aggregate expansion. But were the 1957-58 changes in defense expenditure sizable enough to have much effect? Decidedly so. The billion dollar (annual rate) reduction during the fourth quarter of 1957 accounts for nearly one-half of the decrease of final expenditure at that time. A decline of the same amount during the first quarter of 1958 would have added 20 per cent to the observed reduction of final expenditure, everything else the same.

Second, the economic impact of the budgetary pinch on the defense program during 1957 is inadequately reflected in the figures for defense expenditure. The pinch, which was considerably aggravated by an imminent collision with the statutory federal debt ceiling, resulted not only in smaller current expenditures for finished defense goods but also in deferred progress payments and sharply reduced orders to defense contractors.[18] Similarly, the gradual 1958 rise of defense spending was preceded by a considerably larger increase in new orders during the early months of the year.[19] Thus a much larger swing of orders accompanied and briefly foreshadowed the moderate swing of defense expenditures during 1957-58, presumably accentuating the production and inventory fluctuations of defense contractors and their suppliers.

Apart from the 1958 acceleration of defense procurement, discretionary contracyclical actions were concentrated largely in the financial area. The Federal Reserve authorities began a belated and tentative shift in the direction of credit ease when they lowered the

[18] Marshall A. Robinson, *The National Debt Ceiling, An Experiment in Fiscal Policy* (1959), pp. 38-46; *Economic Report of the President* (January 1958), pp. 14-15, and *ibid.* (January 1959), p. 13.

[19] *Economic Report of the President* (January 1959), pp. 22 and 40-41.

discount rate in November 1957. After January 1958, they moved more actively to increase the availability of bank credit through open market operations and reductions in member bank reserve requirements. Thus monetary policy, like fiscal policy, shifted from a deflationary factor to an expansionary force about midway through the contraction.

Interest rates dropped from the October 1957 peaks as business activity diminished and credit became more readily available (Chart 39). A six-month decline in the seasonally adjusted volume of demand deposits and currency was arrested in January, and the money supply increased $5.4 billion during the next six months. Other evidences of monetary ease during the first half of 1958 were a sharp expansion of time deposits and an increase of $10 billion in the loans and investments of commercial banks, most of it in the form of increased holdings of government securities. Business loans by banks decreased about $1.5 billion, although the ready availability of credit may have prevented investment declines which might otherwise have occurred.

As in other recent years, however, the investment activity most notably affected by changes in credit conditions was residential building. Not only were mortgage yields made more attractive to lenders by the cyclical fall in other rates of return, but a series of specific administrative actions during the early months of 1958 served to augment the supply of mortgage funds and to reduce down-payment requirements on government-backed loans.[20] In response to these financial stimuli, the seasonally adjusted annual rate of private nonfarm housing starts increased from 915,000 in February to 918,000 in March and shot upward thereafter, reaching 1,432,000 by the end of 1958. Although residential construction expenditure did not begin to rise until several months after starts because of the normal construction time lag, the springtime upturn of starts was reflected immediately in sales and production of building materials. It remains true, nonetheless, that during the contraction itself residential construction was largely a neutral factor, neither rising nor falling significantly (Table 22), in contrast to its active contracyclical role during the previous postwar recessions.

[20] *Ibid.*, pp. 38-39.

In the aggregate, business fixed investment was a deflationary force throughout the contraction. A breakdown of business expenditure for new plant and equipment reveals, however, that the over-all decrease was due principally to declines in investment by the manufacturing, mining, and transportation industries (Table 24). Investment expenditure by public utilities and by commercial and "other" enterprises fell little in either absolute or percentage terms. Hence the decline of total business expenditure for plant and equipment was on the order

TABLE 24. *Business Expenditure for New Plant and Equipment, By Industry, Third Quarters 1957 and 1958*[a]
(Dollar items in billions)

Industry	Expenditure		Decreases between IIIQ 1957 and IIIQ 1958	
	IIIQ 1957	IIIQ 1958	Billions	*Per Cent*
Manufacturing	16.37	10.86	5.51	34
Mining	1.24	.88	.36	29
Railroads	1.54	.63	.91	59
Nonrail transport	1.81	1.29	.52	29
Public utilities	6.64	6.10	.54	8
Commercial and other[b]	10.15	9.85	.30	3
Total	37.75	29.61	8.14	22

[a] Quarterly totals at seasonally adjusted annual rates. Source, *Economic Report of the President* (January 1960), Table D-30.
[b] Includes trade, service, finance, communications, and construction.

of 20 per cent instead of the 30 per cent and more which was characteristic of the volatile industries. Just as in the case of residential construction, then, the stability of investment by public utilities and commercial enterprises served to moderate the business contraction without becoming an active factor in the recovery. In Part III, I shall have more to say about the variety of investment behavior among industrial sectors, its causes, and its implications for growth and stability.

As I have just observed, the mere cessation of a deflationary influence can foster aggregative recovery by diminishing the drag on expansive forces elsewhere in the economy. In addition to the favorable internal developments already discussed, the economy benefited significantly when exports leveled off during the second quarter of 1958, since the dollar magnitude of their total decline during the preceding two quarters had equalled that of consumer durables and had been exceeded only by the decreases in business investment in productive facilities and inventories (Table 22). Conditions also improved in the markets for consumer durable goods and producers' durable equipment during the second quarter, in the sense that the pace of decline decelerated markedly. These last developments, and also the rebound of inventory investment beginning in the same quarter, were largely the consequence and not the cause of the aggregative upturn, but they did increase its vigor. By midsummer, sales had improved sufficiently, and in a sufficient number of industries, to cause an upward revision of business investment plans,[21] and by the fourth quarter, investment expenditure for plant and equipment was rising once more (Chart 27).

In summary, the contraction of 1957-58 was halted and reversed by a growing accumulation of favorable developments in various parts of the economy. Some of these developments—principally the cessation of the fall of exports and the rise of federal expenditure for stabilization of farm prices and income—were accidental from the cyclical point of view. Others resulted from discretionary contracyclical actions affecting residential building and the defense program. The most pervasive influence of all—the early recovery of personal income and retail sales—reflected a combination of factors. The automatic stabilizers kept personal income from falling much in the depressed sectors of the economy, whereas income increases from other sources, including some resulting from the favorable developments mentioned above, tipped the balance toward expansion of aggregate personal income. The entire experience is an instructive example of how moderate shifts in fiscal and monetary policy can act in concert with propitious autonomous factors to reverse a vigorous business decline.

[21] "Plant and Equipment Programs, Second Half 1958," *Survey of Current Business* (September 1958), pp. 5-9.

PART III / Key Factors in the Postwar Cycles

8 / *A Profile of the Postwar Economy*

THE PURPOSE of Part III is to appraise the significance for growth and stability of some of the principal changes which have occurred in the economy during the past quarter century or more. To what extent have structural changes insulated the economy against severe depression? What has been the contribution of autonomous factors to the maintenance of growth and stability? Has the economy developed an inflationary bias? Conclusive answers to these questions probably cannot be attained by scientific criteria, but an informed judgment is certainly possible, and the questions are useful guideposts for analysis.

This chapter undertakes a broad survey of features of the postwar economy which bear on these questions, with special reference to similarities and differences as compared with prewar days. The treatment is not exhaustive, and in some instances I can do little more than comment on the issues and caution the reader about the hasty generalizations which abound in this field. Later chapters deal more intensively with certain crucial determinants of aggregate activity and their interrelationships. Thus one chapter is devoted to the influence of federal spending, and one to consumer demand, in the postwar economy. Another chapter contains a discussion of factors affecting the creation and exploitation of business investment opportunities, and yet another is concerned with the behavior of residential construction. Financial reforms and monetary policies are discussed next, and finally the causes and implications of postwar price behavior are analyzed.

War, Population Growth, and Technological Change

Three powerful forces—war, population growth, and technological change—pervade many aspects of economic life and do much to determine the course of aggregate activity yet they themselves are determined only partly by economic factors.

War Influences

During the years between 1939 and 1954, unlike many prolonged epochs in our history, war must be placed high on the list of significant forces at work on the American economy. And, even today, its shadow remains in the form of a substantial defense program. World War II left as part of its heritage to the 1940's an abundance of investment opportunities and the psychological and financial conditions favorable to their implementation. The early 1950's were markedly affected by the Korean War. The importance of federal expenditure in the present day economy springs largely from security needs, and on several occasions since 1945 the economy has been subjected to potent inflationary or deflationary shocks from variations in defense spending caused by military or political events. Big government has also meant high taxes, so that induced changes in tax yields have diminished the response of disposable income and consumption to changes in national income.

Because of this all-pervasive character, the analysis of war effects merges with those of growth forces and structural change. The war-created investment opportunities which were exploited in the forties resulted in part from the influence of the war on population and technology—both of them basic growth determinants and partly autonomous in respect to short-term fluctuations. They stemmed also from the shift from a wartime to a peacetime economic structure, an example of short-term structural change which was nonetheless a powerful force during the period of transition. Its power derived from the extra leverage given to consumer demand by the removal of wartime depressants and to investment demand by the technical need to increase capital stock from the abnormally low wartime ratio to output and, in the instance of housing, the low ratio to population.

The financial counterpart of the "real" backlogs of consumption and investment demand at war's end was an abnormally high ratio of money supply and other liquid assets to income. Excess liquidity and the continuation of the wartime policy of stabilizing interest rates were factors favorable to the creation and exploitation of investment opportunities during the late 1940's, albeit partly at the expense of price inflation.

Postwar psychological attitudes also fostered prosperity. Successful prosecution of the war, and the production feats which contributed so much to that success, had swept away the prewar pessimism about the vitality of the economy. Consumers wanted goods and were eager to spend idle funds to get them. Businessmen expected a postwar boom and invested to prepare for it. These were short-term effects, although the several years of prosperity to which they contributed confirmed the viability of the economy. In the process, the foundation for continuing prosperity was strengthened by focusing attention on the underlying real prospects for expansion instead of the latent potential for depression.

By early 1950, the direct effects of World War II had largely run their course, although important indirect effects persist even today in the financial sphere and in connection with certain aspects of population growth.

At this important juncture, the outbreak of hostilities in Korea again brought active war influences to the forefront and kept them there until the 1954 readjustment to a cold war economy. Since then, fluctuations in defense spending have been comparatively small, though not insignificant, as noted in Chapter 7. The effects of the high level of federal spending on the stability of the postwar economy will be discussed in Chapter 9.

Population Growth

Perhaps the most unexpected and remarkable social feature of the times is the resurgence of population growth which developed during

TABLE 25. *Population Change, 1940-58*[a]
(Thousands of Persons)

Year	Net Change	Births	Deaths	Net Civilian Immigration
1940.....	1,210	2,559	1,428	73
1941.....	1,367	2,703	1,408	63
1942.....	1,704	2,989	1,402	96
1943.....	1,791	3,104	1,498	160
1944.....	1,581	2,939	1,577	208
1945.....	1,452	2,858	1,545	169
1946.....	2,145	3,411	1,404	171
1947.....	2,638	3,817	1,451	275
1948.....	2,530	3,637	1,449	329
1949.....	2,551	3,649	1,448	354
1950.....	2,520	3,627	1,464	350
1951.....	2,718	3,826	1,497	379
1952.....	2,644	3,912	1,508	240
1953.....	2,681	3,965	1,527	239
1954.....	2,841	4,078	1,485	249
1955.....	2,862	4,104	1,532	295
1956.....	2,984	4,218	1,568	335
1957.....	2,936	4,301	1,638	275[b]
1958.....	2,864	4,249	1,648	264[b]

[a] Source, Bureau of the Census, *Current Population Reports*, Series P-25, No. 195, Table 1. Net change ncludes change due to admissions into, and discharges from, Armed Forces overseas, mostly on the part of residents of the outlying areas of the United States. Figures are not shown separately. Births are adjusted for underregistration. Deaths are those occurring in the United States, adjusted for underregistration of infant deaths, plus estimated deaths occurring to Armed Forces overseas. Figures on net civilian immigration for 1940 to 1950 include slight adjustments for "error of closure"; see *Current Population Reports, op. cit.*, No. 71, page 3, for detailed explanation.

[b] Preliminary.

and after World War II. It began with a wartime increase in marriages and births, accelerated during the postwar marriage and baby boom of the late 1940's, and persisted during the 1950's as the annual number of births set new records each year until 1958 (Table 25). The average annual increase of population during 1950-58 was about 2.8 million persons, as compared with averages for the 1920's, 1930's and 1940's of 1.7 million, 0.9 million and 1.9 million.[1] The moderate up-

[1] Bureau of the Census, *Statistical Abstract of the United States, 1959*, Table No. 1, and *Current Population Reports,* Series P-25, No. 195.

trend during the 1950's, moreover, contrasts sharply with the downturn of population increase after 1924 (Chart 2).

There can be no doubt that the change of social attitudes which prompted the recent demographic revolution was itself partly induced by postwar prosperity. Marriage and birth rates are sensitive to income and employment levels. At the same time, the high rate of population increase doubtless stimulated income and employment by creating investment opportunities in important sectors of the economy.

The influence of population growth on demand is most marked in the fields of housing and community facilities. These demands are inelastic with respect to income.[2] For a given rate of increase of aggregate income, the more rapidly does population grow the smaller is the rate of increase of income per capita, and hence the more rapidly does the demand for income-inelastic goods increase, everything else being the same.[3] Thus population growth narrows the differences among growth rates of individual demands by raising those of income-inelastic goods and services and lowering those of income-elastic ones. The result is a shift in the composition of demand toward such income-inelastic items as housing services.

This is not the whole story, of course. Housing demand has increased considerably more rapidly than the average of all consumer items during the postwar years (Chapter 11). The influence of population growth is to raise the growth rate of income-inelastic demands relative to income-elastic ones, but not to make the former grow faster than the latter. Other influences which have stimulated housing demand during the postwar years include the postwar housing shortage, internal migration, and a rapid growth of single-person households. The latter development, which is partly a reflection of demographic

[2] H. S. Houthakker, "An International Comparison of Household Expenditure Patterns, Commemorating the Centenary of Engel's Law," *Econometrica* (October 1957), pp. 532-52, presents income (or more exactly, expenditure) elasticities for food, clothing, housing, and a miscellaneous group comprised of all other items. The estimated elasticities of food and housing are less than one and those of clothing and miscellaneous are greater than one. My statement that the demand for community facilities is income-inelastic is an a priori assumption.

[3] James S. Duesenberry, *Business Cycles and Economic Growth* (1958), pp. 227, 263.

factors and partly of high incomes, has greatly mitigated the decline during the 1950's in the rate of new family formation resulting from the small number of persons born in the 1930's and reaching marriageable age in the 1950's.[4]

The results of population-induced demand shifts are favorable for over-all growth because many of these population-linked services, especially housing, are highly capital-intensive in production. The large investments necessary to increase the flow of such services considerably outweigh the loss of investment opportunities in other, less capital-intensive, areas resulting from the substitution of final demands. Some rough quantitative estimates of the extent to which demand shifts have augmented aggregate investment demand during the postwar period are presented in Chapter 11.

Stability also has been favored by the demand shifts because residential construction has not only bulked large in total investment and grown rapidly during the postwar years, but has often moved contracyclically. The compensatory pattern is a reflection of the industry's sensitivity to credit conditions. Given the underlying housing demand created by demographic factors and high incomes, the rate of residential construction has varied with changes in the cost, terms, and availability of mortgage credit, and has accounted for much of the success of monetary policy during recent recessions.

In past periods, residential building has sometimes become a powerful deflationary force. If reversed, the characteristics which have made it a favorable influence in the postwar economy could operate with considerable leverage on the downside. Since houses depreciate very slowly, replacement demand at any time is a small fraction of the existing stock. Hence the demand for additional houses induced by population increase is a large portion of total new construction, and moderate fluctuations in the rate of household formation may cause wide swings in gross construction. The causes of the prolonged

[4] L. J. Atkinson, "Factors in the Housing Market," *Survey of Current Business* (April 1960), p. 17. As Atkinson points out, the high birth rate of the 1950's was of smaller significance for housing demand during that decade than it will be for housing demand during the 1970's. This is because larger families do not spend more on housing than smaller ones at any given income level, whereas the number of people reaching marriageable age is an important determinant of new housing demand.

building downswings of the past, and the extent to which structural changes have diminished them as a threat to the future, are discussed in Chapter 12.

Among the demands which are sensitive to population increase are many which are publicly financed, such as primary and secondary education, roads, and recreational facilities. The rapid growth of population during the postwar years has put constant pressure on the stock of public facilities despite substantial efforts to remedy the deficiencies which existed at war's end. Largely as a result of backlog demands and population growth, state and local government expenditure has increased at a faster average rate than any other major component of gross national product during 1947-58. Since it is unresponsive to brief business declines, moreover, state and local spending has been a major expansionary force during each of the postwar recessions.

The foregoing relationships are merely the most direct of those which exist between population growth, investment opportunities, and aggregate economic activity. To some measure, population growth enlarges virtually all markets, just as it also enlarges the labor force.

A common method of expressing the relationship between aggregate investment demand and population growth is to refer to the need to equip entrants into the labor force with capital goods. It is preferable, however, to emphasize the dependence of investment on expected sales and, hence, on total population and its increase. Unless businessmen expect demand to rise because of population growth or for independent reasons, they have little incentive to increase capital stock merely because the increase of numbers enlarges the labor force. If they do act in anticipation of demand, of course, they provide part of the investment necessary to generate the demand to justify their expectations.

Since investment demand is geared to total population increase instead of growth of the labor force, the recent population upsurge was the more favorable because it followed a period of slow increase, and hence reversed a long-standing tendency for total population to increase less rapidly than that in the working ages. Between 1900 and 1940, the declining rate of population growth reduced the proportion of children by more than it increased the percentage of persons 65 years old or over (Table 26). The proportion of the population in the principal working ages (14-64 years) therefore increased. Since 1940, the resurgence of population growth has caused a substantial increase in the proportion of children and a corresponding decrease in the intermediate age group from which the labor force is largely drawn.

Thus, in recent years, demographic factors have augmented the

TABLE 26. *Age Distribution of the Population of Continental United States, Selected Years*[a]
(In per cent)

Year	Age Groups		
	13 and Under	14–64	65 and Over
1900	32.3	63.6	4.1
1910	30.1	65.6	4.3
1920	29.8	65.5	4.6
1930	27.3	67.2	5.4
1940	23.1	70.0	6.8
1950	25.5	66.3	8.1
1958	29.2	62.1	8.7

[a] Excludes Armed Forces overseas. Source, Bureau of the Census, *Current Population Reports*, Series P-25, Nos. 98, 114, 146, 193.

number of dependent consumers, and hence the demand for labor, more than they have increased the supply of labor.[5] Both children and retired people are dissavers. Children consume but do not earn. Although older persons consume more than children, they also earn more from current production, so that the net dissaving per person in the two age groups is perhaps about equal.[6] But this implies that the net result of the conflicting trends in the two age groups from 1900 to 1940 was to reduce the ratio of consumption to earned income, since

[5] One important symptom of the relative shortage of population in the "productive" age groups is the increased participation of women in the labor force. The percentage of females in the civilian labor force increased from 25.4 in 1940 to 29.6 in 1950 and 32.7 in 1958. *Statistical Abstract of the United States, 1959, op. cit.,* Table 263.

[6] That this is so is suggested by a comparison of the "productive" and "consumption" weights assigned to various age groups by Warren S. Thompson and P. K. Whelpton in *Population Trends in the United States* (1933), p. 169.

the proportion of children fell more rapidly than that of oldsters increased, whereas the increase in the relative importance of both groups since 1940 has tended to raise consumption at any given level of earned income.

Population growth acts like an automatic stabilizer during contractions—but not expansions—since it causes parents to save less and retards the fall of consumption for a given decline of disposable personal income. The magnitude of the effect depends on the amount of population increase and the amplitude of the income decline. According to a careful recent study, the population effect could increase consumption expenditure by as much as $2 billion or $3 billion per year, at a constant level of personal income approximating that of 1957 and with population growth at about the 1957-58 rate.[7] During a severe contraction of personal income, however, the population effect would be swamped by the income reduction. (If the contraction was prolonged as well as severe, moreover, population growth itself would diminish.) For example, between 1929 and 1933, real disposable personal income declined 27 per cent, whereas disposable income per capita fell 29 per cent.[8] The small difference must have had negligible effects on the aggregate consumption ratio. The difference was also small in 1937-38, when the declines were respectively 5.8 and 6.6 per cent.

Technological Change

Technological change probably enlarges the reservoir of investment opportunities, although for a number of reasons the net increase is likely to be considerably smaller than first thought would suggest.[9]

[7] James S. Duesenberry, Otto Eckstein, and Gary Fromm, *Stability and Instability in the American Economy,* Harvard University (multilithed, 1958), p. 46. Most of the calculated consumption increase is due to the effect of population growth on personal saving propensities, although part of its reflects the income tax savings resulting from the increased number of personal exemptions.

[8] *Economic Report of the President* (January 1959), Table D-14.

[9] Howard R. Bowen, "Technological Change and Aggregate Demand," *American Economic Review* (December 1954), pp. 917-21; Robert Eisner, "Technological Change, Obsolescence and Aggregate Demand," *American*

What matters, of course, is the extent of innovation; that is, the application in practice of new techniques of production or the introduction of new products. The rate of innovation will depend on the existence of opportunities and also upon the intensity of prevailing desires to exploit them, but this last factor will be disregarded for the present.

Technological change may alter the demand for capital in several ways. If innovations tend preponderantly to increase capital-output ratios, for example, more capital will be required for a given expansion of output capacity than if capital intensities were unchanged. New methods of production may also shorten the economic life of existing capital goods and thereby enlarge replacement demand. The favorable effect of speedier obsolescence will be partly nullified if it comes to be expected and enters calculations of anticipated investment yields, however, or if depreciation charges are correspondingly accelerated, augmenting gross business saving.[10]

New product innovation perhaps raises the ratio of consumption to income, because it broadens the range of consumer choice with tempting new additions and speeds the obsolescence of durable consumer goods. Quite possibly, however, new products simply alter the composition of consumption demand while leaving unaffected its total relative to income.[11]

With regard to the influence of shifts in the composition of demand and output, the role of technology merges with the other factors making for change, most of them autonomous. Population growth and spontaneous changes of taste are leading examples. In most cases, a gain of sales in one sector induces sales losses elsewhere, so that differential rates of industry growth need not necessarily increase aggregate investment and conceivably could depress it. On balance, the net effect has been favorable in the postwar economy, for reasons to be discussed in Chapter 11.

The implications of the secular growth of organized business programs of research and development are difficult to assess. And yet the

---

Economic Review (March 1956), pp. 92-105; Duesenberry, *Business Cycles and Economic Growth, op. cit.*, pp. 225-35.

[10] Bowen, *op. cit.;* Eisner, *op. cit.*

[11] Bowen, *op. cit.*

issues raised go to the heart of the unresolved problem of the past and present importance of technological change as a determinant of trends and cycles in economic activity. It is certain that hasty generalizations abound among comments on the subject, but it is much less certain what the actual effects may be.

According to rough estimates collected by John W. Kendrick, expenditures for scientific research and development (R and D) as a percentage of net national product increased from .08 in 1920 to .21 in 1930 and .41 in 1940.[12] A new and more reliable series of estimates begins in 1941 and rises from .82 in that year to 1.20 in 1950 and 1.66 in 1955. Both series cover estimated expenditures by government, industry, and nonprofit institutions for basic and applied research in the sciences and engineering. In 1953, about seven-tenths of the total research was performed in private industry, although the federal government financed more than half of the industrial share.[13] Apparently, the tendency for R and D to expand more rapidly than national product is of long standing, dating back at least to the first world war. If any change has been introduced in the past decade, it must be because of the size, rather than a break in trend, of organized research efforts.

It is significant that R and D is rising more rapidly than national product.[14] Unless the average investment required per innovation increased over time, a constant stream of inventions would merely sustain, instead of increase, investment demand. Given the plausible assumption that inventive output rises with research inputs, the more than proportional increase in R and D provides some grounds for the belief that the flow of investment opportunities from technological change may be expanding as much or more than national income.

[12] Kendrick, *Productivity Trends in the United States,* National Bureau of Economic Research (mimeographed, June 1959), Table IV-19.

[13] *Economic Report of the President* (January 1954), Appendix F.

[14] Notice, however, that the ratio of research and development outlays to national product has not increased at an accelerating rate. As Kendrick points out (*op. cit.,* p. IV-53): "The ratio more than doubled during the 'twenties, doubled in the 'thirties, and increased by one-half in the 'forties. Based on a McGraw-Hill survey of business intentions to spend for research and development in 1960, it appears that the ratio will again increase by more than one-half in the 'fifties."

Whether the opportunities will be exploited, and how smoothly over time, is another, equally vital, question; as is the relative importance of innovational investment in total investment demand.

In view of the fact that rapid technological change has been a leading feature of United States economic development for a century or more, it is certainly premature to conclude that a significant change in growth or stability has occurred because of the recent spread of organized research. Productivity indexes show little sign of postwar acceleration in the pace of technological change, although they are imperfect indicators of such change. Thus Kendrick's index of output per weighted unit of labor and tangible capital combined rose at an average annual rate of 1.7 per cent between 1889 and 1957. The rate of increase accelerated after World War I, rising from 1.3 per cent before 1919 to 2.1 per cent thereafter. The average rate from 1945-48 to 1953-57 was also 2.1 per cent.[15]

Private research expenditures tend to be maintained in the face of moderate business contraction, although they did drop from 1931 to 1933. Perhaps this adds stability to the flow of inventions, but it does not follow that innovation and investment are thereby stabilized. The timing of innovational investment is subject to the same general forces as any investment decision, including swings in investment costs and expected yields induced by general business fluctuations. And, of course, bunching of investments is encouraged by imitative innovation forced upon lagging firms by aggressive competitors. Finally, it is past, rather than current, research which is crucial for investment demand at any given time. This is partly because of the technical lag between initiation of research and economic fruition of the process or product, which is commonly estimated at several years.

Another reason for the lag is especially significant for product innovations. The expenditure on capital goods required to launch a new product often is small. Accordingly, the maximum contribution to investment demand is apt to come midway in the life of an industry when its output has become sufficiently large to be quantitatively important but is still growing fairly rapidly. Stimulation of complementary investment demands, if any, is also likely to occur with a lag and

[15] Solomon Fabricant, "Basic Facts on Productivity Change," National Bureau of Economic Research, Occasional Paper 63 (1959), Tables 2 and 7.

to assume importance some time after the first phase of introduction of the product.

Institutions, Attitudes, and Market Structures

A number of organizational and attitudinal changes may have affected postwar economic performance. Among those that merit attention are the government's postwar commitment to an active stabilization policy, the climate of business and consumer expectations, various types of financial reforms, and the effects of market structures on aggregate economic activity.

Government Commitment to Stabilization

The Employment Act of 1946 was a tangible expression of the nation's determination that depression could and would be avoided in the future—if necessary, through the positive intervention of the federal government. The Act declared that the continuing policy and responsibility of the government would be to use all practicable means, consistent with the promotion of free competitive enterprise and the general welfare, to promote maximum employment, production, and purchasing power. A Council of Economic Advisers to the President and a congressional Joint Committee on the Economic Report[16] were established to advise their respective branches on the economic situation and outlook and on programs and legislation to meet the objectives of the Act.

The goals of the Act have been abetted by the many stabilizing structural changes of the past 25 years, but to a considerable extent they depend for their achievement on the use made of discretionary policy instruments. On the whole, the postwar record has been encouraging in this respect. It is perhaps less than satisfactory when it comes to the containment of inflationary pressures, although even here

[16] Now called the Joint Economic Committee.

it should be recognized that in good part the inflationary bias of the economy is another aspect of its expansionary bias (Chapter 14).

One vital gain is that we have learned to avoid the cyclically perverse fiscal and monetary actions which studded our previous history. It is now widely recognized, largely because of the theoretical developments of Keynesian economics, that federal expenditure should not be slashed when tax revenues fall off during business declines, and that if tax rates are to be altered, cuts instead of increases are the proper step during contractions.[17] Similarly, it is unlikely that severe deflationary actions will be taken by the monetary authorities during business contractions, as they were in 1920-21 and again in 1931, even should a conflict arise between the goals of domestic economic stability and international monetary stability.

Another notable advance has been made in the sphere of information about current economic developments. More data are available than ever before, and with briefer lags behind the events which they record. The policy maker of today is markedly better informed than his prewar counterpart about current expectations, plans, orders, sales, inventories, production, employment, prices, credit, incomes, and other significant variables. Moreover, bodies like the Council of Economic Advisers, Joint Economic Committee, and the Office of Statistical Standards are continually seeking ways to augment the coverage and speed the flow of information, and further improvement may confidently be expected. This flood of data has not completely solved the problem of short-term forecasting—despite substantial advances, knowledge of the relevant economic relationships is still too primitive for that—but it has certainly decreased the time required for policy makers to recognize that a change calling for corrective action has occurred in the economic situation.

All this is not to imply that the postwar record of stability has been due exclusively to wise employment of contracyclical tools. Even apart from the question of the weight of discretionary correctives in comparison with other autonomous factors and the self-reversing proper-

[17] Lewis H. Kimmel of the Brookings staff has given a stimulating account of the radical change in American attitudes toward government taxing, spending, and borrowing since the early 1930's in *Federal Budget and Fiscal Policy, 1789-1958* (1959).

ties of the economy, there were several instances of adverse timing. The premature tax reduction in 1948, the excessive financial stringency during the spring of 1953, and the defense cutbacks and delayed shift of monetary policy in the latter months of 1957 come readily to mind (Part II and Chapter 13). At other times, favorable actions were taken for reasons largely unrelated to stabilization objectives. Among these were the housing legislation and defense spending of 1948-49; the tax cuts of 1953-54, legislated before the downturn and heavily influenced as they were by a reduction in the defense budget and by the desire for tax relief; and the autonomous increase of farm price support expenditure in 1957-58. These reservations are entered more for the sake of perspective than criticism. On the one hand, the adverse actions of 1953 and 1957 were recognized and reversed rather promptly; on the other, there is every reason to take advantage of autonomous factors when they are favorable to a contracyclical strategy.

Confidence and Postwar Expectations

The weight one gives to the factor of confidence as an independent determinant of business activity is largely a matter of personal judgment, since confidence itself is intangible. None will deny that a favorable climate of expectations is essential to the maintenance of full employment in an enterprise economy, but opinions differ widely as to the relative importance of conditions fostering such a climate.

Government attitudes and actions are important. The Employment Act of 1946 must be reckoned among the factors strengthening confidence in the postwar years. Its very existence has probably eased the task of avoiding depression by inhibiting the spread of pessimism when aggregate demand declines. By the same token, however, it may have augmented the inflationary bias of the economy. And it is imperative to recognize that the confidence inspired by the Employment Act arises from the conviction that government can and will prevent excessive instability. As long as that conviction holds, it will cushion induced reductions of demand. Should sales and production deteriorate for more than a few months, however, or should the impression develop that government is not acting with sufficient vigor, confidence will be quickly undermined. It is not a mystical entity with independent existence, but the creation of favorable economic conditions and of deeds instead of words.

Thus, in its stabilization policy the federal government cannot be content merely with fostering an atmosphere congenial to private enterprise. For one thing, the government itself is much too large a factor in the economy to remain aloof, especially since its own activity may often be destabilizing and require corrective action (Chapter 9). Moreover, although a congenial governmental attitude toward private enterprise is one of the significant favorable determinants of business decisions, it is one determinant among many, and is insufficient in itself to inspire stability in business investment. These facts are now generally recognized, of course, and have been reflected in active contracyclical actions during the 1950's, particularly in the field of money and credit and to a lesser extent in the conduct of fiscal affairs.

Similar comments apply when it comes to certain other determinants of business plans and expectations. For example, it is often suggested that business investment is less responsive than formerly to sales declines, because businessmen are looking farther into the future and expect growth to continue, as evidenced by the increased use of capital budgeting techniques and long-term projections in the formation of investment programs.

Formal arrangements for budgeting and controlling capital expenditures have become increasingly popular in recent years.[18] It is important, however, not to misunderstand the purposes of these devices. They are not firm commitments to spend for long spans into the future. Rather, they compel staff and operating personnel to think about investment opportunities as a means of diminishing the chances that profitable ones will be overlooked, providing the data for comparison of alternative projects, and assisting management in its forecasts of needed funds. The typical capital budget is prepared only for the coming fiscal year, although periods varying from six months to five years are not unusual. Since conditions may change between the

[18] National Industrial Conference Board, *Controlling Capital Expenditures,* Studies in Business Policy, No. 62 (1953).

preparation of the budget and the initiation of projects, moreover, authority to disburse funds is not ordinarily provided in the budget itself. Instead, specific authorizations are required when the time comes to commit or disburse funds, and these authorizations are subject to frequent review, often on a quarterly basis.

A principal reason for these provisions for frequent review is precisely to facilitate prompt cutbacks of capital expenditures when business conditions deteriorate. The National Industrial Conference Board capital appropriations data for 500 large manufacturing corporations are instructive in this connection. Manufacturing production reached a cyclical peak in the first quarter of 1957. Between that time and the second quarter of 1958, the seasonally adjusted quarterly volume of new approvals by the 500 companies fell 47 per cent, and appropriations outstanding at the end of the quarter declined 37 per cent.[19] Cancellations quadrupled over the same period. The ratio of cancellations to new approvals rose from 8 per cent in the second and third quarters of 1957 to a high of 23 per cent in the first quarter of 1958.[20]

Evidently the use of formal administrative techniques to plan and control capital expenditures in large enterprise does little in itself to stabilize investment. It may even destabilize it, by providing the means for quick adjustment to changing conditions. Nor does the experience of 1957-58 offer much hope that manufacturing companies are so growth conscious, and so certain of the ability of government to limit economic fluctuations, that they will confirm the following opinion:

> In the future, businessmen will probably feel more assurance about the size of their markets. They will make definite plans for building or purchasing necessary plant and equipment farther into the future; and they will carry out capital expansion plans in the face of temporarily declining sales.[21]

Consumer confidence is also significantly affected by current busi-

[19] My seasonal adjustment.

[20] *Conference Board Business Record* (December 1958), p. 520.

[21] Neil H. Jacoby, "The Interdependence Between An Effective Stabilization Policy of Government and Business Spending and Investment Policies," *The Employment Act Past and Future,* Gerhard Colm, ed., National Planning Association, Special Report No. 41 (February 1956), p. 111. Similar views by other authors appear on pp. 53 and 81 of the volume.

ness conditions. The relationship for long-term commitments is clearly revealed in the co-cyclical variations of marriages and births.[22] Short-term commitments also vary cyclically, as shown by the large cutbacks in purchases of consumer durable goods and in the use of instalment credit during contractions. Survey measures of expectations and attitudes confirm the sensitive response of consumers' confidence to changes in general business conditions.[23] Even consumers whose incomes are unaffected, tend to become cautious and to curtail buying plans for durables during periods of depressed activity.[24]

Again, these remarks are not intended to belittle the importance of attitudes and expectations, but merely to emphasize that they are strongly affected by economic conditions. Nor do I wish to deny any independent weight to expectational factors. Evidently the influence of continuing prosperity on attitudes toward early marriage and large families was undervalued by observers who regarded the initial postwar baby boom as a transitory reaction to wartime dislocations. But, even so, the population upsurge, in its turn, has contributed to continuing prosperity. The background of growth expectations engendered by the prolonged postwar prosperity is also favorable to business investment, even though insufficiently favorable to prevent sizable induced declines during contractions. Moreover, builders would not start homes and buyers would not purchase them during depressed periods, despite basic needs, if either group were pessimistic about the economic outlook. Nor should it be overlooked that the threat that liquidity crises will be induced by business declines has been diminished by knowledge of the cushioning effects of automatic stabilizers, of the favorable discretionary actions of monetary and fiscal authorities, and of the financial reforms to be discussed next.

[22] Births may not actually decline unless the contraction is long or severe. The mild contractions of the postwar years have induced (lagged) plateaus in births instead of declines.

[23] Thus, the index of consumer attitudes of the Survey Research Center, University of Michigan, dropped sharply during the contractions of 1953-54 and 1957-58, as reported in *Business Week* (December 6, 1958), p. 19.

[24] F. Thomas Juster, "Consumers' Buying Plans," *Thirty-ninth Annual Report* of the National Bureau of Economic Research (May 1959), pp. 35-38.

Financial Reforms

Many different types of financial reforms have been put into effect since the early 1930's. One group is designed to curb disequilibrating financial activities through regulatory devices. It includes the regulation of security exchanges under the Securities Exchange Act of 1934, the disclosure provisions of the Securities Act of 1933 with regard to new issues, the control of new utility issues under the Public Utility Holding Company Act of 1935, and the restrictions on margin trading provided by the Securities Exchange Act and administered by the Board of Governors of the Federal Reserve System. From the point of view of this study, these reforms are important to the extent that they inhibit speculative developments during upswings which might cause or aggravate the subsequent contractions.

Another set of reforms dating from the 1930's clusters about residential mortgage finance. The fully amortized home mortgage came into widespread use during the late 1930's under the influence of the Home Owners' Loan Corporation and the Federal Housing Administration. Provision for regular amortization has diminished the risk of demoralizing foreclosures during economic contractions, although this improvement may have been partly offset by the associated trend toward low down payments and, hence, thin equities during the early years of ownership. The insurance and guarantee programs under FHA and Veterans Administration legislation also have reduced the potential for secondary deflation in the markets for real estate and in the assets and liabilities of financial institutions holding residential mortgages. In addition to these structural influences, the FHA and VA programs, and the participation of the Federal National Mortgage Association in the secondary market for FHA and VA loans, have provided instruments for discretionary action to affect the volume of residential building—and these instruments have seen frequent use in the postwar period.

The bank failures of the early 1930's prompted the development of safeguards to prevent their mass recurrence. Outstanding among these is insurance of bank deposits, and the promotion of sound management, by the Federal Deposit Insurance Corporation. Deposit insurance was later extended to savings and loan associations.

Basic modifications of the monetary system were spawned by the tumultuous events of the depression decade and the second World War. The breakdown of the international gold standard during the early 1930's led to its abandonment by the United States and the substitution of a managed standard. The world economy is less vulnerable than formerly to autonomous disturbances arising from gold discoveries or to epochs of chronic deflationary pressure because of inadequate physical supplies of the monetary metal. It is now possible for the nation to pursue domestic stabilization objectives within wider limits of international tolerance, moreover, since it need not deliberately deflate in the interests of exchange stability, nor witness defeat of independent expansionary efforts because of loss of international currency reserves.[25] Domestic flexibility in these respects was augmented by postwar creation of the International Monetary Fund, which provides machinery for short-term stabilization of exchange rates and for cooperation in the correction of fundamental disequilibria in the world balance of payments.

Some of these recent financial changes provide automatic safeguards against liquidity panics during business contractions. Others, however, have enhanced the discretionary power of the monetary authorities, and depend for their effectiveness both on the wisdom with which the power is used and its impact on the economy. The role of financial factors in past depressions and the scope and efficiency of postwar monetary policy, are discussed in Chapter 13.

Market Structures

Imperfect competition in the markets for products, capital, or labor may affect aggregate economic activity in several ways. Since labor and business monopolies[26] resist wage or price reductions during pe-

[25] Thus the current (1959) concern about the United States gold outflow possibly may stiffen the anti-inflationary policy of the Federal Reserve authorities, but it is unlikely to persuade them to repeat the monetary deflation of 1920-21.

[26] For the purposes of this discussion, a business or union is monopolistic if it has some degree of monopoly power in the sense of discretionary control over its own selling price. The firm or union may be part of a monopolistically competitive or oligopolistic industry or market, and will seldom or never be a single seller with complete control in its field.

riods of falling demand, they hamstring the classical mechanism of cost-price adjustment to eliminate unemployment. There are strong grounds to question the efficiency of the mechanism in the real world, however, especially since price adjustments which would be equilibrating in a hypothetical frictionless world of perfect foresight, may in actuality become destabilizing because the process of adjustment encourages speculation on further changes in the same direction.[27] Thus downward rigidity of the wage-price level is probably more blessing than curse as far as resistance to contractions is concerned. But it is not an unmixed blessing, since prices are less resistant to upward pressures, and the combination of stability during contractions and increases in expansions adds up to secular inflation (Chapter 14).

Monopolistic practices and other market imperfections may delay offsetting adjustments to deflationary impulses originating in specific sectors. This suggests that the greater the degree of imperfection, the more likely that developments in particular industries will initiate general movements. In contrast, this sort of inertia may diminish the amplitude of responses to disturbances even if it increases their frequency, because of the tendency for price adjustments sometimes to become disequilibrating because of adverse expectational effects.

Apart from the question of cyclical price flexibility, will monopolistic market structures tend to augment or diminish private investment and economic growth? The answer depends upon the net resolution of opposing forces. Given the rate of invention and freedom of access to capital markets, the purely competitive firm will innovate before the monopolistic one if the latter has sunk investment costs which it wishes to recoup, and is able to recoup because of its ability to block entry of new competition and to control price. Thus, monopolization may introduce a lag between invention and innovation which at times could cause a temporary dearth of investment.

Conversely, it has been trenchantly argued that monopolistic restrictions are a necessary element in secular progress.[28] Innovation

[27] John Maynard Keynes, *The General Theory of Employment, Interest, and Money* (1936), Chap. 19; John H. Power, "Price Expectations, Money Illusion and the Real Balance Effect," *Journal of Political Economy* (April 1959), pp. 131-43.

[28] Joseph A. Schumpeter, *Capitalism, Socialism, and Democracy,* 2nd ed. (1947), especially Chap. VIII.

will be fostered by the lure of abnormal short-term profits resulting from monopoly power—a presumption which has been institutionalized in the United States patent system. Emphasis on nonprice competition in imperfect markets may induce a higher rate of product innovation than in purely competitive industries. Moreover, large firms can afford expensive research facilities which could not be supported by the small firms typical of competitive industries and yet which are essential for technical progress in the modern world.

A considerable body of evidence has accumulated in recent years to indicate that this second set of arguments, while undoubtedly containing a substantial core of truth, is by no means universally valid.[29] A study of 61 important inventions made since 1900 revealed that more than half resulted from work done by individual inventors outside of industrial research laboratories and usually with limited resources and assistance.[30] As noted earlier, nowadays the federal government finances more than half the research performed by private industry. Many outside sources of research activity are available to the small firm—individual inventors, equipment suppliers, nonprofit research institutions, universities, and independent profit-seeking research firms are among the more important. Thus, research need not be done—and quite commonly is not done—by the firms which will ultimately produce a new product or use a new process or type of equipment. The impressive postwar growth of agricultural productivity, for example, reflects largely the application by small firms in a competitive industry of technological opportunities developed externally.

The uncertainties regarding the influence of monopolistic markets on the growth and stability of the economy are no greater than those concerning trends in monopoly power. There was a small decline in the extent of concentration of manufacturing industry between 1935 and 1947, as measured by a weighted average of the percentages of

[29] For a summary of the evidence on invention and innovation and a vigorous analytical critique of Schumpeter's position, see D. Hamberg, "Size of Firm, Monopoly, and Economic Growth," statement for Hearings on *Employment, Growth, and Price Levels,* Part 7, Joint Economic Committee, 86 Cong. 1 sess. (1959), pp. 2337-53.

[30] John Jewkes, David Sawers, and Richard Stillerman, *The Sources of Invention* (1958), pp. 82 ff.

output produced by the four leading firms in each of 129 industries.[31] On the basis of later statistics, it appears that changes in concentration indexes among 367 manufacturing industries were approximately offsetting between 1947 and 1954.[32] Certainly there is no suggestion in these data either of substantial increase or decrease of over-all concentration after World War II. This does not, of course, prove that monopoly power has remained unchanged. Because of technical deficiencies, the published concentration ratios may not be accurate measures of market dominance by the "large" firms in each "industry," and market shares in themselves are an imperfect, though not irrelevant, index of the possession and exercise of monopoly power.

Whatever its trend, however, there is no doubt that the level of concentration is high in several parts of the economy—especially in manufactures, public utilities, and some branches of mining—and has been high for half a century or more. Although there is little promise in a hypothesis that the depression of the 1930's and the prosperity of the 1950's resulted from an historical trend toward monopoly and its reversal, it is well to recognize that important markets are sufficiently imperfect to modify crucially the behavior of aggregate activity at some junctures.

The potential for destabilizing actions of big business has probably been enhanced by the growth of labor unions in the mass production industries since the late 1930's. Whatever the trend of business monopoly, control over money wages from the supply side is greater now than in the prosperous 1920's.[33] Bilateral monopoly in labor markets, coupled with oligopoly in the sale of products, can lead to autono-

[31] Gideon Rosenbluth, "Measures of Concentration," *Business Concentration and Price Policy* (1955), pp. 79-83. Other measures confirm this finding: see Edward S. Mason, *Economic Concentration and the Monopoly Problem* (1957), Chaps. 1-2.

[32] *Concentration in American Industry,* Report of the Subcommittee on Antitrust and Monopoly of the Committee on the Judiciary, United States Senate, 85 Cong. 1 sess. (1957), Table 19.

[33] The following figures, given by Irving Bernstein in "The Growth of American Unions," *American Economic Review* (June 1954), p. 303, Table I, on union membership as a percentage of the civilian labor force are instructive:

Year	Per cent	Year	Per cent	Year	Per cent
1900	3.0	1929	7.0	1945	23.6
1914	6.8	1933	5.8	1950	22.1
1920	12.0	1939	14.0	1953	26.8

mous wage-price decisions which pose serious problems of adjustment for the entire economy, especially during cyclical expansions (Chapter 14). It bears reiteration that union resistance to wage cuts during contractions, however, may well be stabilizing insofar as employment and production are concerned.

Efforts to organize small units into effective aggregates for market control were not confined to the labor movement during the depression decade. The state intervened to organize such units in some sectors where the aim could not be achieved by private means. Thus, federal programs have made farm prices less responsive to fluctuations of market demand, although there is still relatively little concentration in agriculture. The waxing and waning of fair trade legislation has also influenced retail prices perceptibly since the 1930's.

Secular Shifts in the Composition of Output and Employment

Between one historical epoch and another, long-term shifts in the relative importance of major economic sectors may alter cyclical behavior if they affect the economy's exposure to disturbances or its response to them. Detailed analysis must await later chapters, but it may be noted at the outset that two characteristics of product demand are especially relevant: type of purchaser and durability of product. The first will affect the degree of cyclical independence and the inherent stability of demand—federal spending is largely autonomous but not necessarily stable, for example. The second is an important determinant of the sensitivity of demand to fluctuations of current income, whether the demands be final (for example, food or shelter) or derived (farm equipment or new houses).

The broad sweep of changes among the four major components of gross national product since the turn of the century is shown in Table 27. The outstanding feature, of course, is the growth in the share of government. The increase was comparatively moderate between the opening of the century and the 1920's, and was entirely at the ex-

TABLE 27. *Distribution of Components of Gross National Product, Selected Periods*[a]
(In per cent)

Expenditure Category	Constant (1929) Dollars			Current Dollars		
	1899–1908	1920–29	1947–55	1899–1908	1920–29	1947–55
A. Components of Gross National Product						
Government purchases of goods and services	6.8	8.0	15.8	6.2	7.8	18.7
Gross private domestic investment	19.3	15.7	12.4	18.4	15.8	14.9
Personal consumption expenditure	73.0	75.2	71.3	74.5	75.3	66.1
Net foreign investment	0.9	1.1	0.5	0.9	1.1	0.2
Total	100.0	100.0	100.0	100.0	100.0	100.0
B. Components of Gross Private Domestic Investment						
Business fixed investment	13.5	10.0	9.0	12.8	9.9	10.5
Producers' durable equipment	4.5	5.0	6.3	4.4	5.0	6.8
Construction	9.0	5.0	2.8	8.5	4.9	3.8
Residential nonfarm construction	4.3	4.5	2.5	3.8	4.3	3.5
Change in business inventories	1.5	1.2	0.9	1.8	1.7	0.8
Total	19.3	15.7	12.4	18.4	15.8	14.9
C. Components of Personal Consumption Expenditures						
Perishable goods	30.4	27.5	27.2	31.7	27.1	27.4
Semidurable goods	10.7	9.6	6.6	10.3	10.6	7.5
Durable goods	6.9	8.4	9.1	6.2	8.4	8.7
Services	25.0	29.6	28.3	26.3	29.1	22.6
Total	73.0	75.2	71.3	74.5	75.3	66.1

[a] Sources, Department of Commerce and unpublished estimates prepared for the National Bureau of Economic Research by Simon Kuznets and John W. Kendrick.

pense of the share of private investment. Since the end of the 1920's, however, the government share has doubled or more, and both investment and consumption have diminished in relative importance.

These shifts are present whether the shares are calculated from GNP in real or money terms, but they differ in magnitude on the two bases. Because average prices of capital goods have risen more than those of consumer goods, the share of investment has diminished more and that of consumption has fallen less in real than in money terms. Similarly, the relative increase of government is smaller in constant than in current dollars.

The shares in real product are the more meaningful for present purposes, since they better reflect the relative importance of the various sectors in physical activity. Thus, a complete collapse of investment expenditure would have meant a direct loss of about 16 per cent of the national output in the 1920's and about 12.5 per cent in the early 1950's. At the same time, it should be remembered that because of relative price changes, a given amount of real investment (or government expenditure) today is equivalent to a larger quantity of consumer goods than in prewar years. This implies that the change of consumption induced by a one-dollar change of investment is larger when the changes are measured in constant instead of current dollars, partly offsetting the fact that the investment share is now smaller in constant than in current dollars.[34]

Growth of Government Expenditure

The government share of real national product increased from 6.8 per cent in 1899-1908 to 8 per cent in the 1920's and 15.8 per cent in 1947-55. State and local purchases of goods and services accounted for approximately four-fifths of the government total in the early years of the century. The federal and state and local branches grew roughly apace between then and the 1920's, preserving about the same division of total expenditure but together taking a larger fraction of the nation's production. In contrast, the doubling of the government proportion since the 1920's has been due entirely to the

[34] I am indebted to R. A. Gordon for this point. For the period 1947-55, the marginal relationship between consumption and gross national product in current dollars is .526, whereas the same relationship in 1929 dollars is .556 (calculated from least-squares regressions). These marginal propensities imply multipliers of 2.11 and 2.25 respectively. Thus, the difference between the multipliers is smaller than the difference between the investment shares in current and 1929 dollars. Needless to say, these multiplier estimates are crude even for expansions, and are quite inaccurate for contractions because of asymmetries in the operation of personal income stabilizers (Chapter 9), but they will suffice to illustrate the point.

federal sector. State and local purchases slipped from 6.5 to 6 per cent of national product and amounted to only two-fifths of government expenditure in the recent period.

This is not the place for an analysis of the factors behind the rapid growth of government.[35] My interest lies rather in its effect on the growth and stability of the postwar economy. The ramifications of the increase in federal spending are so widespread and its influence so substantial as to require separate treatment in Chapter 9. As for state and local expenditure, it has been a favorable factor throughout the postwar period.

The state and local claim on the national product was drastically reduced during World War II and has risen sharply ever since under the impetus of war-created backlogs, population growth and urbanization, and the rise of per capita income. Nor is that all. The postwar uptrend of state and local expenditure was not only exceptionally rapid but quite stable. As Part II revealed, the postwar recessions have been kept mild in good part by the substantial increase of state and local spending which occurred during each. There has been no recurrence of the sort of cyclically perverse decline which appeared during the 1930's, partly because the postwar needs for government services were pressing and partly because none of the recent contractions was long enough or deep enough to have much effect on the tax revenues or borrowing propensities of states and municipalities.

Diminished Relative Importance of Private Investment

Both residential construction and business fixed investment have participated in the relative decline of real gross private domestic investment since the 1920's. Before dealing extensively with both types of capital formation in later chapters, it is convenient at this point to

[35] Defense requirements are responsible for most of the increase in the federal sector, of course. For a summary statement of the manifold forces affecting the growth of government activity, see Solomon Fabricant, "Government in Economic Life," *Thirty-fifth Annual Report* of the National Bureau of Economic Research (May 1955), pp. 1-15. A more extended treatment is contained in the same author's *The Trend of Government Activity in the United States Since 1900* (1952).

discuss certain implications of the decline in business fixed investment, which comprises business construction and producers' durable equipment.

The reduced share of business fixed investment has diminished its potential range of fluctuation relative to GNP, but insufficiently to prevent a substantial deflationary shock should investment collapse, as evidenced by the calculations in Table 28. Thus, business fixed invest-

TABLE 28. *Hypothetical Decline of Real Business Fixed Investment (1954 Dollars) Relative to Peak GNP During Five Contractions*[a]

Contraction of:	Actual Decline of Investment (Per cent)	Actual Ratio of Investment to GNP in Peak Year (Per cent)	Hypothetical Investment Decline (Per cent of peak GNP)				
			1929–33	1937–38	1948–49	1953–54	1957–58
	(1)	(2)	(3)	(4)	(5)	(6)	(7)
1929–33.....	71.2	12.8	9.1[b]	6.6	8.3	7.0	7.2
1937–38.....	26.8	9.2	3.4	2.5[b]	3.1	2.7	2.7
1948–49.....	9.1	11.6	1.2	0.8	1.1[b]	0.9	0.9
1953–54.....	3.8	9.9	0.5	0.3	0.4	0.4[b]	0.4
1957–58.....	16.5	10.1	2.1	1.5	1.9	1.6	1.7[b]

[a] The hypothetical declines are shown under alternative assumptions about the amplitude of the investment decline and the share of investment in peak GNP. Each decline shown in columns 3 through 7 is the product of the investment amplitude listed in column (1) for the given row, and the actual ratio of investment to GNP in the peak year of the given contraction (column 2). Source, *U. S. Income and Output*, a supplement to *Survey of Current Business* (November 1958), Table I-2 and *Survey of Current Business* (July 1960), Table 4. Business fixed investment is the sum of nonresidential construction and producer's durable equipment.

[b] Actual declines.

ment (in 1954 dollars) fell 71 per cent between 1929 and 1933. Measured relative to the 1929 GNP, this was a decline of 9.1 per cent. Now in 1957, business investment was only 10.1 per cent of GNP, so that a 71 per cent reduction of investment as in 1929 would have been 7.2 per cent of peak GNP. This hypothetical decline is a good deal smaller than the 1929-33 drop of 9.1 per cent, but it is nonetheless a substantial figure, and far exceeds the actual reduction of 2.5 per cent during the major contraction of 1937-38.

Similar calculations have been prepared for other contractions. Each line of Table 28 shows how much investment would have declined relative to peak GNP during two prewar and three postwar contractions, had it fallen by the same percentage as in the contraction listed in column 1, but had each contraction begun with the actual ratio of investment to GNP. It will be seen that the actual postwar investment declines of 1948-49, 1953-54, and 1957-58 were considerably smaller relative to peak GNP than were those of 1929-33 or 1937-38. The contrast with 1929-33 is due both to the huge amplitude of contraction of investment at that time and to the diminished postwar importance of business fixed investment. With regard to 1937-38, however, the difference lies in the relative amplitudes of the prewar and postwar investment declines and not in the share of investment in total income.

Thus business fixed investment is a smaller fraction of total demand than in the 1920's, but it is still large enough to exert a sizable deflationary force unless its inherent instability has diminished markedly because of structural change.

SECULAR SHIFTS IN CAPITAL STOCK. The capital-output ratio has fallen along with the share of investment in gross national product. According to the estimates of the Machinery and Allied Products Institute, the ratio of privately owned plant and equipment to privately produced GNP dropped 22 per cent between 1923-29 and 1947-59 (Chart 29).[36] It is doubtful that an over-all capital-output ratio has much quantitative meaning as a determinant of the short-term response of net investment to a change of real national income, since the capital intensities and production trends of individual industries differ widely and individual responses are not narrowly circumscribed by technological factors. The decline of the over-all ratio does show that the weighted average of individual ratios has diminished, however, and it is clear from other evidence that the decline

[36] Machinery and Allied Products Institute, *Capital Goods Review,* No. 39 (September 1959). The capital stock estimates were derived by applying survival curves to estimates of past installations. "Since these curves give the estimated percentages of original installations surviving after given intervals, it is possible to compute the survival at any point from all prior installations, and to trace the movement of the survival over time" (p. 1). Capital goods owned by government, nonprofit institutions, and consumers (including residences) are excluded from the figures.

CHART 29. *Ratio of Privately Owned Stock of Plant and Equipment to Privately Produced Gross National Product, Annually, 1959 Prices, 1915-59*

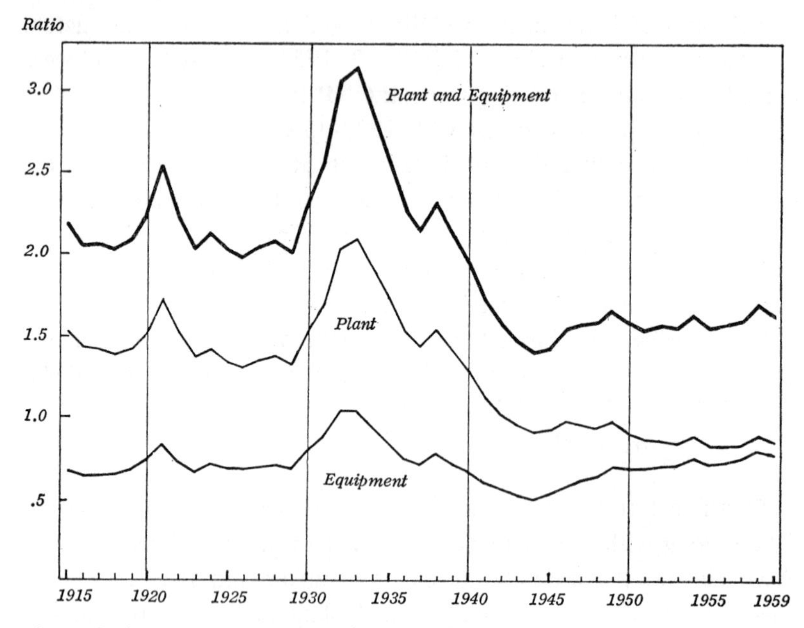

Source: Machinery and Allied Products Institute, *Capital Goods Review*, No. 39 (September 1959).

was general, at least within manufacturing and mining.[37] In a rough and ready way, this implies that a given increase of real national income will induce (create the opportunity for) a smaller amount of net investment than in prewar years, since capacity will increase more per dollar of investment with a lower capital-output ratio.[38]

There has also occurred a relative substitution of equipment for plant, which makes for quicker as well as less capital-intensive ad-

[37] Daniel Creamer, "Capital and Output Trends in Manufacturing Industries, 1880-1948," National Bureau of Economic Research, Occasional Paper 41 (1954); Israel Borenstein, "Capital and Output Trends in Mining Industries, 1870-1948," National Bureau of Economic Research, Occasional Paper 45 (1954).

[38] Assuming that the marginal ratio has declined along with the average. This appears reasonable even if the average ratio is not an accurate measure of the size of the marginal ratio.

justment of capacity to actual or expected sales. (Production and installation of equipment takes less time than construction of new plant.) The figures of the Machinery and Allied Products Institute show a decline of 34 per cent in the ratio of plant to output, but a rise of 3 per cent in the equipment-output ratio, between 1923-29 and 1947-59.[39]

The fact that total investment can fall faster when it becomes more equipment-intensive has positive and negative aspects, corresponding to the capacity and income effects of investment. On the one hand, quick responses diminish overshooting, so that for a given production decline extending over a given period, the more rapidly is investment reduced, the smaller will be the increase (or the larger the decrease) of excess capacity by the end of the period. The reduction of investment, on the other hand, will itself depress demand and augment excess capacity at any given level of capacity. Now suppose the lower limit to income contraction were set by some constraint which was independent of the speed of decline—for example, by the requirement that gross investment cannot fall below zero, as in the models of Hicks and Goodwin.[40] Then the result of a briefer investment lag would be to drive the economy downward more rapidly, but to reduce the duration of the contraction, since the floor would be reached sooner and less disinvestment would be required thereafter. Another influence working in the same direction is the fact that the maximum time-rate of disinvestment is positively correlated with the share of equipment in the stock of fixed capital.

A rapid downshift of business investment demand may not be an unmixed evil even in situations far less serious than the preceding case of large-scale disinvestment. Assume, for instance, that a sharp

[39] The uptrend in the ratio of equipment to plant has been going on since World War I. For a discussion of this and other aspects of structural change in the composition of investment expenditure, see Robert A. Gordon, "Investment Opportunities in the United States Before and After World War II," *The Business Cycle in the Post-War World,* Erik Lundberg, ed. (1955), pp. 283-310.

[40] J. R. Hicks, *A Contribution to the Theory of the Trade Cycle* (1950); R. M. Goodwin, "A Model of Cyclical Growth," in Lundberg, *op. cit.,* pp. 203-21.

decline of business investment induced largely compensating increases in other categories of demand at a given income level—perhaps because it released capital funds for the purchase of homes or consumer durables, or because government expenditure was increased deliberately to offset the investment decline. The unfavorable income effects of the reduction of business investment then would be largely neutralized, especially since the multiplier is also small during contractions, and the favorable capacity effects would come to the fore. This combination of circumstances presupposes, of course, that excess capacity was not an existing or emerging problem in the other sectors, as it might be at times except for the federal government.

BUSINESS INVENTORIES. Businessmen have learned to economize inventories as well as plant. The manufacturers' inventory-output ratio fell about one-fourth between 1920-29 and 1947-58, and approximately the same decline occurred in retailing.[41] Just as in the case of fixed capital, this appears to imply a diminished response of investment to fluctuations in final demand. As the historical analysis of Part II repeatedly revealed, however, inventory investment is still substantial enough and volatile enough to contribute conspicuously to economic instability. Indeed, there is little or nothing to choose between its prewar and postwar behavior in this respect.

T. M. Stanback, Jr. has uncovered what is probably the principal reason for the largely undiminished instability of inventory investment.[42] Although the ratio of manufacturers' stocks to sales is lower than in prewar years, the proportion of stocks held by durable goods producers is larger than before. But fluctuations in inventory investment are wider for durables than nondurables, so that the cyclical sensitivity of total inventory investment has increased relative to the size of stocks. The larger amplitude of durable goods inventory investment is due both to the greater cyclical conformity and amplitude of sales in those industries and to technical conditions which make for a more sensitive response of inventories to changes in sales.

The destabilizing role of inventory investment should be kept in

[41] *Survey of Current Business* (April 1959), p. 8.

[42] The relevant results of his as yet unfinished study are summarized in the *Thirty-ninth Annual Report* of the National Bureau of Economic Research (May 1959), pp. 43-44.

perspective. It has always been important in minor fluctuations but has never played a dominant role in major cycles. Inventory change may foster major expansions or contractions by initiating them or amplifying their early phases, but further developments depend on the stability of final demands rather than on inventory phenomena.

THE VARIETY OF INVESTMENT BEHAVIOR. Trends and cycles in gross fixed capital formation differ widely among industrial sectors,

TABLE 29. *Percentage Distribution of Gross Private Fixed Investment by Industrial Sector, at Postwar Business Peaks*[a]

Industrial Sector	1948	1953	1957
Public utilities	7.0	9.8	10.7
Durable goods manufacturing	9.6	12.1	13.9
Residential nonfarm construction	27.9	29.6	29.4
Commercial and other (trade, service, finance, construction, and communications)	19.0	17.2	18.0
Mining	2.4	2.1	2.1
Transportation other than rail	3.5	3.3	3.1
Nondurable goods manufacturing	15.6	13.4	13.7
Railroads	3.6	2.8	2.4
Farms	11.3	9.7	6.7
Total	100.0	100.0	100.0

[a] Expenditures on new plant and equipment by business (excluding expenditures of agricultural business and outlays charged to current account) are from the Department of Commerce, Office of Business Economics, and Securities and Exchange Commission. Farm investment and residential construction are from Department of Commerce, National Income Division. See *Economic Report of the President* (January 1960), Tables D-8 and D-30. The Commerce-SEC data on business expenditures for plant and equipment are not strictly comparable to the corresponding figures for nonfarm business investment included in the national income accounts, although the differences are unimportant in the present context. Farm investment is omitted from Chart 30 because quarterly estimates are not available throughout the period.

as Chart 30 and Table 29 illustrate vividly for the postwar period. The divergent trends reflect primarily the differential impact of growth factors like population, technology, and the secular increase of income per capita, but defense programs also affected industry unevenly during the period. The investment uptrends were pronounced for public utilities, durable goods manufacturing, and residential construction, all of which increased relative to aggregate fixed capital formation between 1948 and 1957. The relative declines of

CHART 30. *Trends and Cycles of Gross Fixed Investment in Selected*

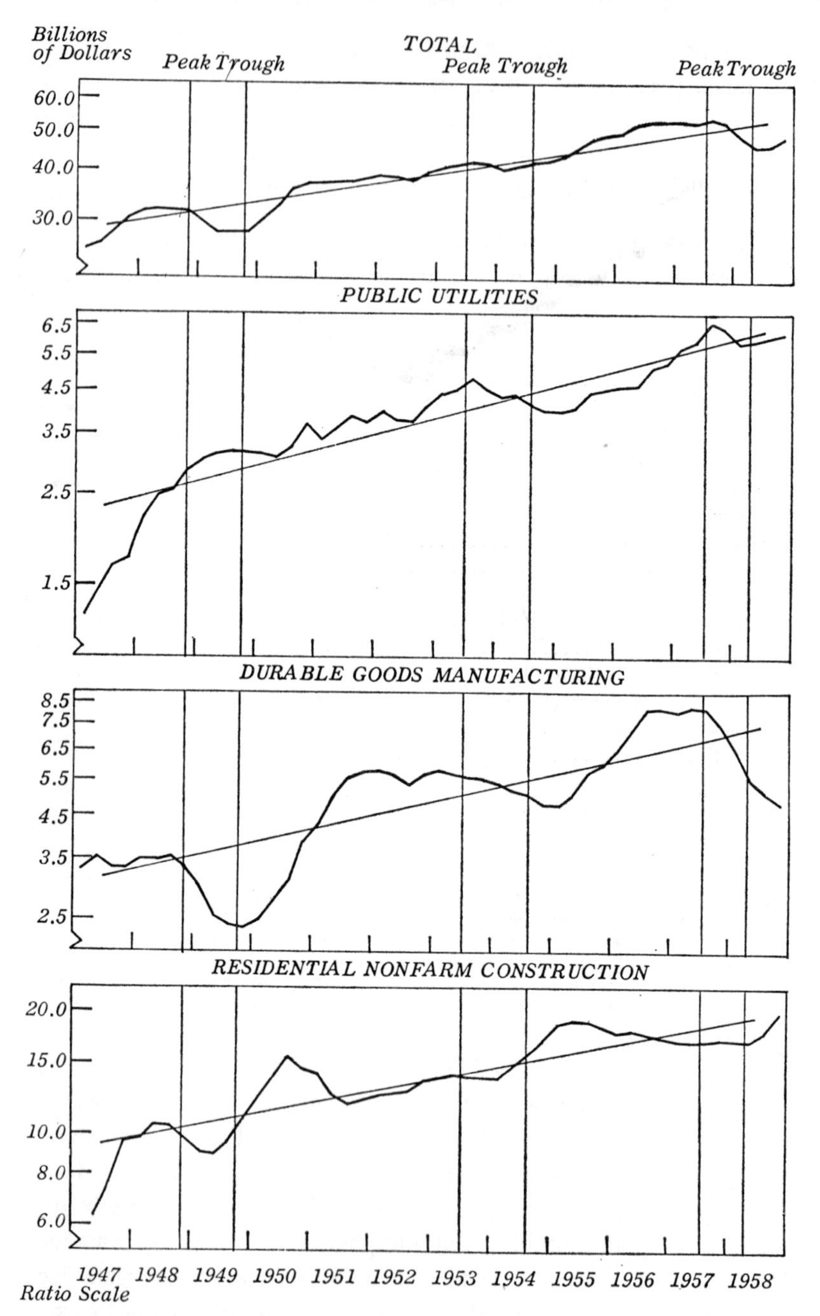

[a] The exponential trends are fitted to the annual data for 1947 to 1958 by the method described in footnote c of Table 34.

Source: Office of Business Economics, Department of Commerce.

Industries, Seasonally Adjusted Quarterly Totals at Annual Rates, 1947-58[a]

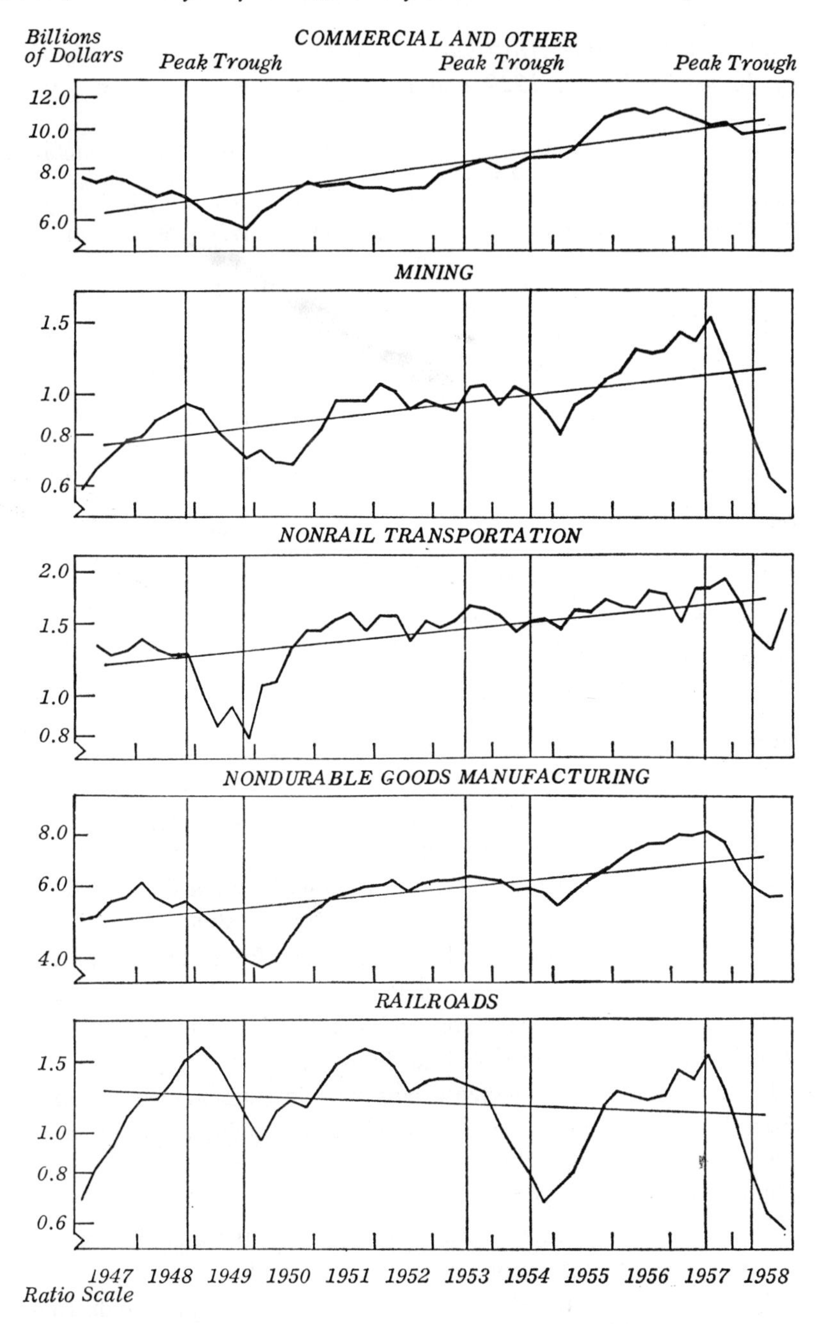

TABLE 30. *Percentage Distribution of Income by Industrial Sector, 1929 and at Postwar Business Peaks*[a]

Industrial Sector	1929	1948	1953	1957
Public utilities	2.1	1.6	2.0	2.2
Durable goods manufacturing	13.8	17.5	22.3	21.5
Housing (net rent and interest from rental and owner-occupied nonfarm housing)	7.3	3.6	4.4	5.1
Commercial and other (trade, service, finance, construction, and communications)	43.3	42.4	42.9	45.5
Mining	2.5	2.6	1.9	1.9
Transportation other than rail	2.5	2.7	3.0	3.0
Nondurable goods manufacturing	13.0	15.5	14.2	13.6
Railroads	5.6	3.5	2.9	2.3
Farms	9.9	10.6	6.2	4.8
Total	100.0	100.0	100.0	100.0

[a] Source, *U. S. Income and Output*, a supplement to *Survey of Current Business* (November 1958), Tables I-10 and II-4, *Survey of Current Business* (July 1960), Tables 8 and 15 and *op. cit.* (June 1953), pp. 20–22, Tables 2–4. The total income originating in the nine sectors is smaller than national income by the amounts originating in agricultural services, forestry, and fisheries; government and government enterprises; and the rest of the world.

railroad and farm investment were especially large, whereas the remaining sectors experienced comparatively minor reductions.

These postwar investment trends are broadly consistent with the corresponding changes of national income by industrial origin (Table 30). That is, they reflect in good part the link between the growth of demand for a given product and the trend of investment in facilities required for its production. Clearly revealed, for instance, are the investment counterparts to the relative production declines for farm products and rail transportation and the relative gains of utilities, durable manufactures, and nonfarm housing.

Production shifts will increase aggregate investment demand at a given level of national income provided the gainers invest more heavily than the losers. Because of the high capital-output ratios for utilities and housing, the rapid growth of these sectors has augmented postwar investment demand. Rough estimates of the quantitative importance of this factor are presented in Chapter 11.

As for stability, it may be affected in three main ways by industrial differences in investment behavior. First, investment opportunities in the growth sectors may inhibit the fall of investment demand during business contractions, since favorable long-term expectations will tend to diminish investment cutbacks in response to declines of sales and profits in such industries. Moreover, sales and profits themselves will tend to decline less in growth industries, everything else being the same, and this factor will also be favorable to aggregate investment demand if the industries are capital-intensive. (In Chapter 11, I discuss the hypothesis that past severe contractions were caused by growth retardation in those industries which had sparked the preceding major cycle expansion.)

Second, growth forces may interact with other investment determinants to modify individual fluctuations in either a stabilizing or destabilizing direction. For example, should one of the growth industries be particularly sensitive to monetary constraints, it might well be forced into an early investment cutback even though demand for its product was still rising. But this would diminish the likelihood that excess capacity would develop in that industry before or during the subsequent general contraction, and hence would leave intact a ready source of investment expenditure to be tapped by easy money policies. This combination of industry characteristics certainly underlies the contracyclical tendencies of residential building during the past decade. It may—or may not—also explain the lead of investment in the "commercial and other" sector on both the downturn of 1957 and recovery of 1958.[43]

Third, some industries are inherently more unstable than others in response to cyclical changes in aggregate demand. The wide fluctuations which occur in the production and transportation of industrial commodities during business cycles tend to induce correspondingly

[43] That is, the recent investment leads in this sector—which includes trade, service, finance, construction, and communications—may reflect the preponderance of small firms in several of its divisions. Small firms are more dependent than large ones on external sources of investment funds, and hence should be more responsive to changes in credit conditions. I have not tested either this hypothesis or another, namely, that commercial and other investment was responding to fluctuations in urban and suburban housing development. However, on this last relationship, see the discussion of residential-service investment in Chapter 12.

wide fluctuations in investment by railroads, manufacturers, and mining companies. Investment in these industries has therefore conformed closely and with considerable amplitude to the postwar business cycles, whereas the other sectors showed greater independence (Chart 30). Nor are these new tendencies, for similar disparities were to be found during the mild cycles of the 1920's, only to be narrowed considerably by the catastrophic collapse of the 1930's.[44]

Manufacturing has increased substantially as a proportion of production (value added) in the private sector of the economy since 1929 (Table 30). Rail transportation and mining have lost some ground, but on net balance the proportion of income originating in the cyclically more sensitive group of industries rose from 35 per cent in 1929 to 39.5 in 1957. This development has worked against the investment-stabilizing effect of lower postwar capital-output ratios. The net resolution of these and other forces affecting the behavior of induced investment is problematical, although it is clear from recent experience that business fixed investment still responds quickly and substantially to business declines. It must be kept in mind, moreover, that those investment sectors which are relatively insensitive to brief or mild fluctuations in aggregate demand, have not always performed as favorably as during the past decade. Residential construction is a case in point, for in prewar years it experienced prolonged downswings as well as extended booms. Thus, the fact that it is a much smaller factor in the present-day economy has diminished the chances that prolonged or severe contractions will occur (Chapter 12).

International Trade

Foreign trade today is a relatively unimportant, though by no means insignificant, determinant of the over-all level of United States economic activity, just as it was in the interwar period. Net exports of goods and services averaged only 0.4 per cent of gross national

[44] Millard Hastay, "The Cyclical Behavior of Investment," *Regularization of Business Investment,* Conference of the Universities-National Bureau Committee for Economic Research (1954), pp. 3-34.

product (1954 prices) during 1948-58. (The percentage was 0.1 in 1929.) However, this small net contribution to national output was the difference between considerably larger flows of exports and imports, averaging respectively 5.1 and 4.7 per cent of GNP. Thus exports are large enough to induce a significant change in aggregate demand if, as occasionally may happen, they rise or fall sharply during a brief interval and leave imports lagging far behind. This occurred quite recently, when the wide swing of export demand helped first to prolong the business expansion during 1956-57 and then to induce the subsequent contraction (Chapter 7).

The export swing of 1956-58 was unusually large, however, primarily because it was amplified by the Suez crisis. Although exports have conformed positively to United States business cycles since 1921, the amplitude of the swing during 1956-58 was far above the average and proceeded at a rate unprecedented except for the major cycle of 1929-37.[45] Evidently there is little to fear on this score except during international political or military crises.

Personal Consumption Expenditure

The outstanding fact about personal consumption today is that it is a much smaller share of the gross national product than in the 1920's. Consumers are spending nearly as high a proportion of their after-tax income as before, but increased taxes have reduced the ratio of disposable personal income to national income. The increased tax bite also diminished the amount of change in consumption expenditure which is induced by a change of one dollar in gross national income, since a large fraction of federal taxation is on personal and corporate income. The automatic tax and transfer stabilizers are discussed in Chapter 9. Notable shifts in the distribution of personal income by type and by size have also occurred since prewar years, and may have modified the response of consumer demand to changes in disposable income. The effects appear to be small, however, for reasons discussed in Chapter 10.

[45] Ilse Mintz, "Foreign Trade and Business Cycles," *Thirty-ninth Annual Report* of the National Bureau of Economic Research (May 1959), pp. 76-78.

TABLE 31. *Percentage Distribution of Gross National Product by Expenditure Category and by Major Type of Product and Purchaser, 1929 and 1957*[a]

Item	Constant (1954) Dollars		Current Dollars	
	1929	1957	1929	1957
A. By Expenditure Category				
Personal consumption expenditures	70.5	66.4	75.6	64.4
Gross private domestic investment	19.3	14.2	15.5	14.9
Net exports of goods and services	0.1	0.9	0.7	1.1
Government purchases of goods and services	10.2	18.5	8.1	19.5
Total	100.0	100.0	100.0	100.0
B. By Major Type of Product and Purchaser				
Durable goods	16.9	20.9	17.2	21.3
Personal consumption expenditures	8.2	9.4	8.8	9.1
Producers' durable equipment	6.1	6.0	5.6	6.4
Government purchases	0.4	4.2	0.4	4.4
Net exports of goods and services	0.8	1.1	1.2	1.1
Change in business inventories	1.4	0.2	1.3	0.2
Nondurable goods	35.6	33.7	36.5	32.5
Personal consumption expenditures	35.9	32.5	36.1	31.1
Government purchases	0.6	1.0	0.6	1.1
Net exports of goods and services	− 1.1	0.1	− 0.4	0.2
Change in business inventories	0.2	0.2	0.3	0.1
Services	33.2	34.6	35.4	34.8
Personal consumption expenditures	26.4	24.5	30.7	24.1
Government purchases	6.3	10.3	4.8	10.9
Net foreign investment	0.5	− 0.2	− 0.1	− 0.2
Construction	14.4	10.8	10.7	11.3
Private construction	11.5	7.8	8.3	8.2
Government construction	2.9	3.0	2.4	3.2
Total	100.0	100.0	100.0	100.0

[a] Source, *U. S. Income and Output*, a supplement to *Survey of Current Business* (November 1958) Tables I-1, I-2, VII-5, VII-6 and *Survey of Current Business* (July 1960), Tables 1, 5 and 66.

Not all components of consumption expenditure have diminished relative to national product (Table 27). The brunt of the over-all reduction was borne by semidurables and services. Durable goods have actually increased as a percentage of total output. How economic stability has been affected by the growth in importance of consumer durables and instalment credit is analyzed in Chapter 10. That chapter also examines the destabilizing role of autonomous variations of consumer demand in the postwar cycles and the extent to which offsetting changes in the various categories of expenditure affect the stability of aggregate consumption.

Shifts in the Composition of Output by Durability of Product

Thus far, shifts in the composition of output have been examined primarily from the viewpoint of the shares going to government expenditure, investment, and consumption. In Table 31, the components of these broad expenditure categories are rearranged to highlight changes in the relative importance of durables, nondurables, and services in total production. Since this detailed breakdown is available only for years since 1929, that year is used as a prewar bench mark for comparison with 1957, a recent year of like cyclical position.

The figures in panel A confirm the general trends in the shares of capital formation, consumption, and government which were revealed by the previous estimates.[46] The new breakdown by type of product and purchaser adds some interesting information, moreover. Production of durable goods for all purposes accounted for a larger share of real gross national product in 1957 than in 1929, whereas the reverse was true of construction activity. Since construction fell less than durables rose, the share of heavy industry in final product increased from 31.2 to 31.7 per cent (1954 prices).

Similar though smaller counterbalancing movements left the aggregate of nondurables and services slightly lower while decreasing the share of the former and increasing that of the latter. Inspection of the

[46] The fact that the constant dollar estimates are based on 1954 instead of 1929 prices is responsible for the sizable differences between the "real" shares shown here for 1929 and the average real shares for 1920-29 presented in Table 27.

TABLE 32. *Percentage Distribution of National Income and of Persons Engaged in Production, by Industry, 1929 and 1957*[a]

Industry or Group	National Income by Industrial Origin		Number of Persons Engaged in Production[b]	
	1929	1957	1929	1957
A. By Industry				
1. Agriculture, forestry, and fishing	9.4	4.5	19.9	8.2
2. Mining	2.3	1.7	2.2	1.3
3. Contract construction	4.3	5.5	5.0	6.2
4. Manufacturing	24.9	30.7	22.8	25.6
5. Wholesale and retail trade	15.2	16.4	16.9	19.5
6. Transportation	7.6	4.7	6.6	4.3
7. Communications and public utilities	3.3	3.7	2.2	2.3
8. Finance and insurance	4.7	3.5	2.6	3.1
9. Real estate	9.8	6.2	0.8	1.0
10. Services	11.8	10.9	14.0	13.6
11. Government and government enterprises	5.8	11.8	6.9	14.9
12. Rest of world	0.9	0.6	0.0	0.0
Total	100.0	100.0	100.0	100.0
B. Special Groupings				
13. Goods-producing industries, total (lines 1–4)	40.9	42.4	49.9	41.3
14. Nonagricultural (lines 2–4)	31.5	37.9	30.0	33.1
15. Agricultural	9.4	4.5	19.9	8.2
16. Services, total (lines 5–12)	59.1	57.8	50.0	58.7
17. Private service industries, total (lines 5–10, 12)	53.3	46.0	43.1	43.8
18. Goods-handling industries (lines 5–6)	22.8	21.1	23.5	23.8
19. Other private services (lines 7–10, 12)	30.5	24.9	19.6	20.0
20. Government and government enterprises	5.8	11.8	6.9	14.9
Total	100.0	100.0	100.0	100.0

[a] Source, *National Income, 1954 Ed.*, a supplement to *Survey of Current Business*, Table 28; *U. S. Income and Output*, a supplement to *Survey of Current Business* (November 1958) Tables I-10 and VI-16; and *Survey of Current Business* (July 1960), Tables 8 and 55.

[b] This series measures man-years of full-time employment by persons working for wages or salaries and by active proprietors of unincorporated enterprises devoting the major portion of their time to the business. Excludes unpaid family workers.

product detail by type of purchaser discloses that the increases for durables and services were due primarily to the concentration of government spending in those categories. Private purchases of consumer durable goods also increased considerably more than GNP, however, while expenditures for consumer services underwent relative decline.

It is somewhat surprising that the share of services in GNP is merely one-third and has increased only moderately since 1929, in view of the widespread impression that ours has recently become an economy dominated by services. In a sense the impression is valid, for the service industries accounted for one-half of all employment as long as three decades ago, and by 1957 their share was nearly three-fifths (Table 32). These industries also earned considerably more than one-half the national income in both 1929 and 1957, although by this measure their relative importance diminished between the earlier and later year.

If one starts from a premise that demands for services are inherently more stable than those for goods, or that employment in service industries is steadier than in other pursuits, it is easy to jump from the belief that services are more important in the present-day economy to the conclusion that economic stability must have increased in consequence. This is a possible but not necessary result. The distinction between final and intermediate services must be emphasized in this connection.

FINAL SERVICES. As was just observed, services which are final from the standpoint of the purchaser, amount to only one-third of national product. The fact that government purchases of services—primarily representing direct employment of government workers—have increased substantially is probably favorable to stability of final demand, national emergencies excepted. This is because government demands are less sensitive than private ones to changes of national income, however, and not because services bulk large in government purchases.

Private purchases of final services, on the other hand, have diminished somewhat in importance since 1929. Three points should be kept in mind in appraising the significance of this development. First, personal consumption expenditures for services are merely less sensitive to income declines than those for goods, and are by no means absolutely inflexible. Thus, from 1929 to 1933, expenditures on durable goods dropped 50 per cent, on nondurables, 15 per cent, and expenditures on services also 15 per cent. For this period the drop in total consumer expenditures was 19 per cent.

Second, the very steadiness of service expenditure can be destabilizing during contractions. If consumers wish to decrease total consumption expenditure by a given amount because income has fallen or for other reasons, but do not wish to curtail spending on services, more of the reduction will fall on goods than would occur if all expenditures were cut proportionally. But this means that production will decline more than otherwise, since inventories are held primarily in connection with goods, and the amplified decline of sales of goods will therefore amplify the fall of inventory investment (Chapter 10).

Third, the derived demands for goods to produce final services may vary widely even if the services themselves are relatively stable. Important consumer services like shelter, household utilities, and telegraph and telephone communications are far above average in capital-intensity, so that comparatively small reductions or even mere retardations of final demand could induce substantial declines of investment in the supplying industries (Chapters 11 and 12). These three categories accounted for 44 per cent of consumer service expenditure in 1957.

INTERMEDIATE SERVICES. Intermediate services are those which enter into the production of further goods and services. All persons engaged in production contribute labor services, but in the commodity-producing sector these are embodied in tangible goods. Service industries produce intangible values which may either become embodied in physical products, or be sold directly as services to final users. This last category comprises the final services which are a component of gross national product. Stability of demand for an intermediate service (or product) depends upon both the stability of the final demand from which it is derived and the nature—technological and economic—of the derived relationship itself. Stability of employment depends partly on the same factors and partly on the technological and institutional relationships between production and employment in the industry. These considerations suggest that valid inferences about stability cannot be drawn solely or even primarily from data on the industrial distribution of income or employment.

What is needed in principle is knowledge, first, of how observed shifts in the internal structure of final demand would affect the stability of the total and its parts; second, about relationships and changes in relationships between final and intermediate demands; and third, of how the foregoing factors would modify the response of employment to fluctuations of production. The first sort of effect will be examined in subsequent chapters. The others will not, however, since a systematic investigation of them would be a formidable research project in itself. It is worth noting, nevertheless, that the outstanding shifts described by Table 32 are the decline of agriculture and the rise of government. These changes are roughly offsetting insofar as direct effects on employment during contractions is concerned, though for different reasons: agriculture because reduced demands diminish income instead of employment, and government because demands themselves are depression-resistant. For the rest, changes among private nonagricultural industries are comparatively small and unlikely to have altered the response mechanism appreciably.

9 / *Federal Spending*

FEDERAL EXPENDITURES for newly produced goods and services have averaged 11 per cent of the gross national product annually since the end of World War II, as compared with shares of 1 per cent and 4 per cent in 1921-29 and 1930-40. It is commonly supposed that one major result of the growth in the size of government has been to increase the stability of the postwar economy. Examination of this proposition in the present chapter is confined to a discussion of the structural effects of big government as a factor influencing the exposure of the economy to disturbing forces, and the manner in which it reacts to those forces. Discretionary fiscal actions to offset unwanted fluctuations in private demand were discussed in the historical chapters of Part II.

Autonomy of Federal Expenditure

The first question to be decided is the degree of independence of federal expenditure. A distinction also must be drawn between government expenditures which represent an outright demand for newly produced goods and services and those which do not. Since our interest lies in the role of government as it actually exists in the postwar economy, these matters may be discussed with reference to the prevailing pattern of federal outlays.

Federal expenditures in 1958, as measured in the national income accounts, are shown in Table 33. About three-fifths of the total was devoted to the purchase of goods and services, while the remainder consisted of various items which transferred income from taxpayers to one or another sector of the economy. In 1958, the direct federal

TABLE 33. *Federal Expenditures as Shown in the National Income Accounts, Calendar Year 1958*[a]
(In billions of dollars)

Purchases of goods and services	52.6
Transfer payments	21.3
Grants-in-aid to state and local governments	5.4
Net interest paid	5.6
Subsidies less current surplus of government enterprises	3.0
Total expenditures	87.9

[a] These figures differ somewhat from those contained in the conventional and cash budgets, in that they exclude certain capital and lending transactions, expenditures for goods and services are timed with delivery instead of payment, and nonrecourse loans guaranteed by the Commodity Credit Corporation are recorded as expenditures when the loans are made rather than when they are redeemed by the CCC. Also, they include the transactions of the trust accounts, which are omitted from the conventional budget although counted in the cash statement. In addition to these conceptual differences, the expenditures are given for the calendar year rather than for the fiscal year. The figures may appear unfamiliar to persons accustomed to the cash or conventional budgets, but they are conceptually the most desirable for present purposes. Source, *Survey of Current Business* (July 1960), Table 20.

purchases of goods and services consisted of $44.5 billion for national defense and $7.7 billion for all other purposes.

How might these expenditures for goods and services be expected to change in response to movements of aggregate economic activity? The answer to this question will depend partly on the period of time allowed for the occurrence of induced responses. A certain amount of short-term built-in flexibility exists since changes may be made within previously defined and budgeted programs. According to recent careful estimates, however, such expenditure changes are likely to be comparatively unimportant, both absolutely and relative to the much larger induced movements of tax receipts and transfer payments.[1]

[1] See David W. Lusher, "The Stabilizing Effectiveness of Budget Flexibility," and Comment by Samuel M. Cohn in *Policies to Combat Depression,* Conference of the Universities—National Bureau Committee for Economic Research (1956), pp. 77-100. Much of the flexibility which does exist is due to the price changes which accompany movements of national output. Price-induced expenditure fluctuations are cyclically perverse in monetary terms, although neutral in real terms, unless administration officials take discretionary steps to use the resulting monetary savings to accelerate real expenditures during contractions, or act to absorb price increases by curtailing real operations during expansions. Apart from the uncertain area of price effects which might or might not alter real expenditures, sizable automatic or quasi-automatic variations may occur in such activities as the agricultural price support and stockpile programs. The potential

If sufficient time elapses so that programs can be altered by congressional action, induced responses of another sort become possible. The character of these responses would depend upon the fiscal attitudes of administration officials and legislators. Thus at given tax rates, tax receipts will rise and fall in conformity with national income. If actual or expected increases in revenue were viewed as favorable opportunities to augment expenditures, and decreases were regarded as signals that retrenchment was necessary, much of the potential stabilizing influence of federal spending would be dissipated. While deliberate contracyclical changes in expenditures or receipts have been excluded from discussion in this chapter, it is relevant and important to emphasize that one premise of the view that large-scale federal expenditures are stabilizing per se, is that they are determined independently of induced fluctuations in revenue. This thought may be clarified by three hypothetical situations.

In the first situation, it is assumed that when national income declines, the entire brunt falls upon disposable personal income. Thus, a decline in gross national product of $10 billion produces an equal fall in disposable income, which in turn induces a reduction of, say, $8 billion in personal consumption expenditures. In the second situation, account is taken of induced changes in tax receipts. When gross national product falls by $10 billion, personal and corporate income taxes decrease by $4 billion, and disposable income falls by only $6 billion, rather than the $10 billion of the preceding example. If the relative response of consumption to disposable income remains the same as before, the induced reduction in consumption expenditures is only $4.8 billion, or 60 per cent as much as in the first situation. Automatically induced changes in tax receipts cushion the decline of income after taxes and therefore of consumption expenditures, adding to the stability of the economy. But this conclusion will not necessarily hold in situation three, in which a behavioral response of government spending to changes in revenue is postulated. If a successful effort were made to keep the budget balanced at all times, for instance, the net effect of government fiscal operations would be destabilizing. Thus in situation two, the $4 billion fall in tax receipts

contribution of such variations to changes in federal spending, however, is limited by the small size of the programs in the total budget, although in some years they have accounted for a substantial fraction of the total change.

prevented a decline of $3.2 billion in consumption which otherwise would have occurred. If the fall in tax receipts induces an equal reduction in government expenditures, however, the $4 billion decline in expenditures more than offsets the $3.2 billion cushion to consumption expenditures. The combined reduction in expenditures by consumers and the government per $10 billion drop of gross national product is $8.8 billion, or more than the $8 billion drop in consumption which would have resulted if there were no change in tax receipts at all.[2]

I do not mean to assert that this last situation is especially likely. For one thing, the adjustment of expenditures to receipts would not be exact even if a continuously balanced budget were the goal; or perhaps something less than an exact adjustment would be sought. In these circumstances, expenditures might not change as much as receipts. If the proportional response of government expenditure to a change in tax receipts were the same as the response of consumption expenditure to a change in disposable income, the government fiscal operations would leave national income unaffected. But if government spending changed less per dollar of tax change than consumption spending did per dollar of income change, the net effect would be stabilizing, although less so than if government spending did not change at all. Again, it may be that advocates of a balanced budget would behave differently; that they would react to increases or decreases in tax receipts by seeking decreases or increases in tax rates rather than changes in expenditure. The important thing to notice in this connection, however, is that such actions would also be destabilizing. Yet, again, possible effects on private investment have been neglected in the example. These could go either way, since the ad-

[2] The potential extent to which these situations differ may not be immediately apparent to the nontechnical reader. Taking the three cases in order, the total maximum change in gross national product per $1 initial change in, say, investment, would be $5.0, $1.9, and $8.3. The comparatively small differences in the amount of induced expenditure per dollar of change in gross national product during any one period add up to sizable amounts when successive rounds of income and expenditure are considered, since each drop of income reduces expenditure in this period and therefore leads to a further decline of production, income, and expenditure in the next period. The reader should also note that the figures I have used are illustrative only and are not to be taken as estimates of actual relationships in the economy, and that no allowance was made in the example for changes in business saving.

verse effects of unstable government expenditures on business sales might be augmented or diminished by psychological reactions of the business community to the policy of continuously balanced federal budgets; reactions which are uncertain in direction and strength and may change with the attending circumstances. Finally, federal expenditures in the present economy may in fact be largely autonomous with respect to induced fluctuations in tax receipts, so that instability does not arise from that source. My concern has simply been to emphasize that any conclusion that a large volume of federal spending is inherently stabilizing implies, among other things, an expenditure policy which if not actively contracyclical, at least is not of the cocyclical balanced-budget variety.

It will be assumed in the remainder of the discussion that income-induced changes in federal purchases of goods and services are comparatively unimportant, and that postwar variations in government expenditures have been due primarily to autonomous factors. This is a reasonable assumption, if for no other reason than the fact that expenditures for national defense bulk large in the total.

Granted that federal spending is a largely autonomous source of demand for output, is it a stabilizing or destabilizing source? To ask this question is to raise several others. Is it subject to frequent or wide fluctuations? Do its fluctuations tend to counteract or to augment the ebb and flow of private expenditures? How has the growth of federal expenditure affected the potential variability of the autonomous component of aggregate demand? How has it affected the response of induced expenditures to changes in gross national income? I will deal with each of these queries in turn and in the light of experience since World War II.

The Instability of Federal Spending

The major components of domestic demand for final goods and services are shown annually for the period 1946-58 in Chart 31. Foremost among the features revealed by the chart is that in most meanings of the term, federal expenditures have shown the least short-term stability of all major categories of final domestic demand during the postwar years. To mention the exception first, if stability be defined in terms of the number of reversals of direction during a given period, the federal sector was more stable than consumer durable goods or residential construction. Frequency of change of direction is not the only criterion of stability, however. It is surely necessary to distinguish between what may be called instability in the small and in the large. The postwar history of durable goods—either producer or consumer —exemplifies instability in the small, in the combination of frequent but moderate oscillations. In contrast, the swings of federal expenditure occurred less often but were considerably larger.

Stability measures which reflect relative amplitudes are readily constructed. Two types are presented in Table 34. In the first column, the average annual percentage change is shown for each of the series displayed on Chart 31. The increase or decrease from one year to the next is expressed as a percentage of the average level in the two years, and an average of the resulting annual percentage changes is struck without regard to sign for the entire interval from 1947 to 1958. The outcome is a measure of average year-to-year variability, in which account is taken of the size of the economy at the time of the change, but not of its growth throughout the period. In effect, the position of the economy in a given year is accepted, and we ask how much each category of expenditure expanded or contracted from that year to the next. A glance at the table will demonstrate that by this test, federal spending out-ranked all subcategories in degree of instability, and that only residential construction ran a close second.

A drawback to the foregoing measure of variability is that it makes no allowance for smoothness or regularity of change. This disadvantage largely disappears when the measure is supplemented by a chart, but it may be preferable to handle the difficulty more directly. Suppose that the fitted exponential "trend" lines shown in Chart 31 are taken to be representative of the prevailing growth tendency of each series during 1947-58.[3] A movement along the line would then signify stable growth at a constant percentage rate, and fluctuations

[3] Since 1946 was a disturbed year of postwar transition, it has been eliminated from the computations. The method by which the exponential curves were fitted is described in footnote c of Table 34.

CHART 31. *The Growth and Fluctuations of Gross National Product*

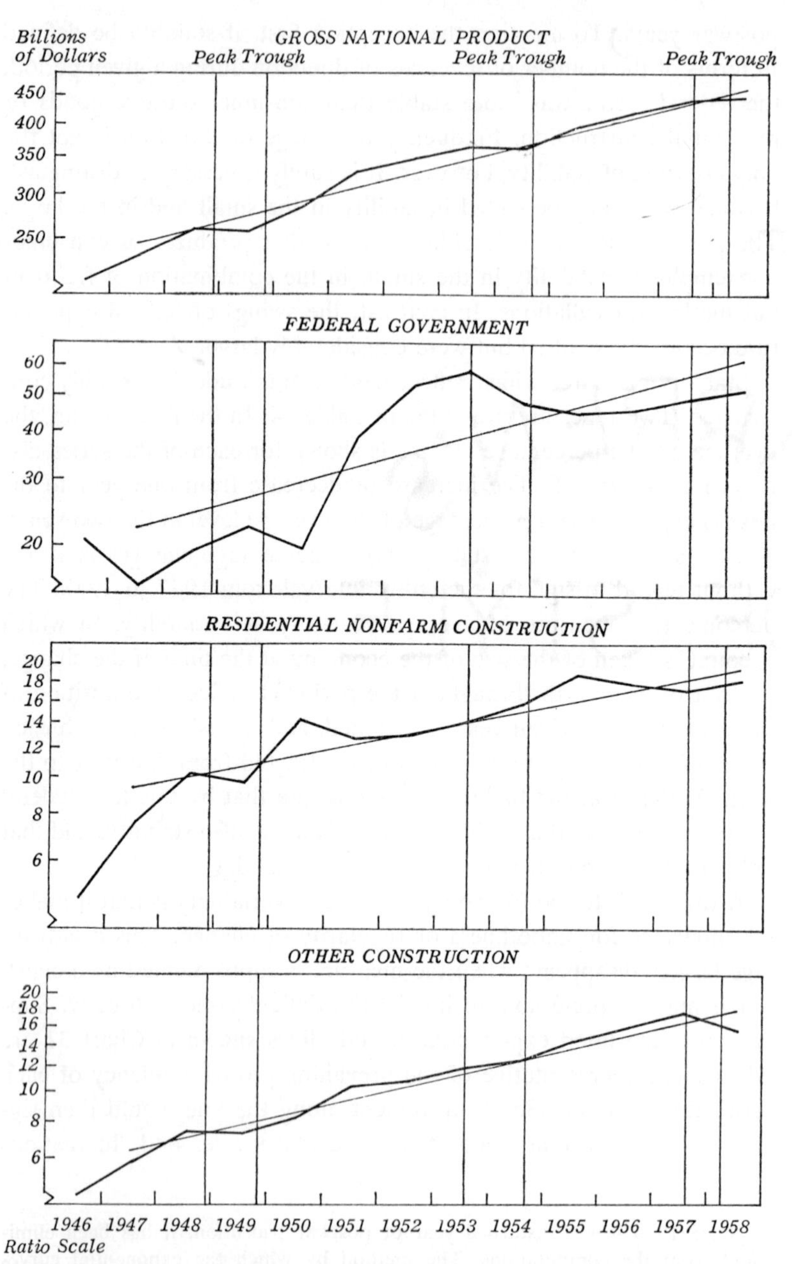

[a] The exponential trends are fitted to the annual data for 1947 to 1958 by the method described in footnote c of Table 34. The trend line has not been drawn for consumer services since it would be scarcely distinguishable from the actual data.

Source: Office of Business Economics, Department of Commerce.

and Selected Components, 1946-58[a]

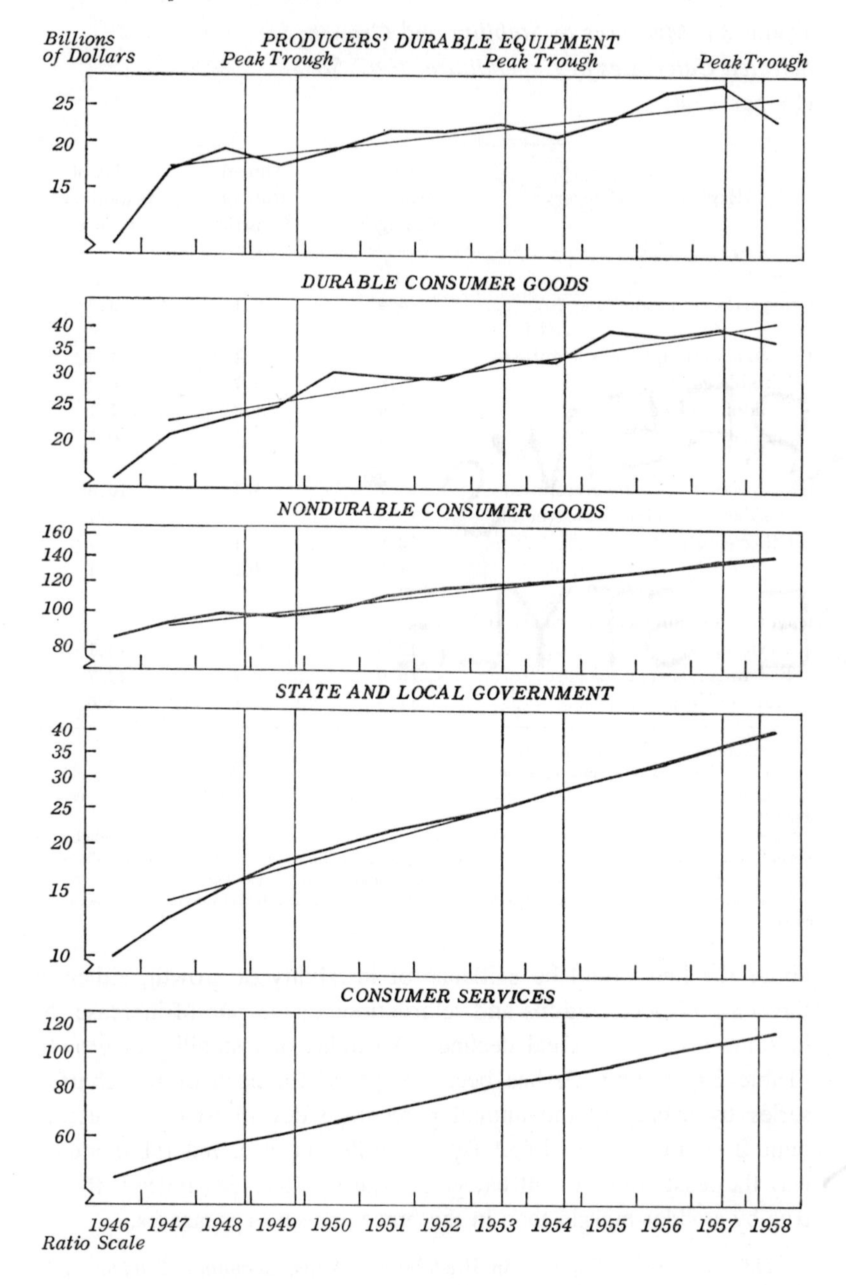

TABLE 34. *Measures of Stability and Growth, Selected Categories of Expenditure, 1947-58*[a]
(In per cent)

Expenditure Category	Average Annual Change[b]	Annual Rate of Growth[c]	Index of Instability of Growth[d]
	(1)	(2)	(3)
Gross national product	6.4	6.1	3.2
Personal consumption expenditures	5.8	5.4	1.2
Durable goods	9.8	5.7	6.2
Nondurable goods	4.6	4.0	1.7
Services	7.5	7.4	0.7
Gross private domestic investment	15.7	5.4	10.6
Residential nonfarm construction	15.3	7.0	8.1
Other construction	10.3	8.1	5.1
Producers' durable equipment	12.6	4.1	6.1
Government purchases of goods and services	12.5	9.8	14.1
Federal	16.0	9.7	22.7
State and local	11.8	10.1	2.6

[a] From *Survey of Current Business* (July 1960), Table 1.

[b] The arithmetic mean of annual percentage changes, signs disregarded. Each annual percentage change is computed as the ratio of the absolute change from the previous year to the average level in the previous and current year.

[c] Annual compound interest growth rate as computed from an exponential curve fitted to the data by the use of Glover's mean value table (J. W. Glover, *Tables of Applied Mathematics* [1923], pp. 468 ff.). The average rate of growth is the slope of a straight line drawn on a ratio scale, as in Chart 31.

[d] An arithmetic mean of the percentage deviations of the annual observations from the fitted exponential curve.

about the line would be evidence of instability of growth, either in the sense of accelerations and retardations of the rate of increase, or in some instances, actual declines. An index of instability of growth (Table 34, column 3) has been computed for each of the charted series by averaging the annual percentage deviations of the actual data from the growth line.[4] By this criterion also, federal spending was the least stable of all categories during 1947-58; indeed, this is true by a wider margin than in the preceding set of measures.

[4] This measure is discussed in Frederick C. Mills, *Economic Tendencies in the United States* (1932), pp. 46-49.

The reader, at this point, may be tempted to enter a mental reservation to the effect that the postwar swings in federal spending have been caused by the unusual conditions of World War II and its aftermath. It should be remembered, however, that my present concern is with the structural effects of big government on the inherent stability of the postwar economy. Throughout the postwar years and at the present time, the great bulk of federal expenditure has been for purposes of national security. Under the circumstances, the built-in sensitivity of defense expenditures to changes in the international situation is a property which cannot be left out of account.

Instability of individual components of aggregate expenditure is not intrinsically undesirable, since the fluctuations may be offsetting rather than reinforcing. The retardations or declines of expenditures for privately purchased durable goods and residential construction during the Korean War, for example, provided stabilizing offsets to rising federal expenditure. Counterbalancing fluctuations may at times result from essentially accidental causes, at others from the self-adjusting properties of the economic system, and at still others, from deliberate governmental actions. These reflections suggest two further questions about the postwar record of federal spending: From the point of view of its contribution to economic stability, were its fluctuations accidental, deliberate, or induced; and did they augment or diminish over-all stability?

A look back reveals that the postwar oscillations in federal outlays were largely accidental in the sense used here, and that—as would be expected of accidental movements—they were sometimes stabilizing and sometimes not. The initial, huge postwar cutback in defense expenditures was accomplished between mid-1945 and mid-1947 (Chart 32). For the first six to nine months of this period the cutback was a powerful deflationary force, to which, however, the economy adjusted rapidly and successfully. Thereafter, until mid-1947, federal expenditures fell as private spending mounted, moderating the inflationary influence of the latter rise. The downward course of federal expenditure was reversed during the summer of 1947 and it rose during 1948 and most of 1949. Again defense outlays led the movement, and again the movement first strengthened and later weakened the prevailing tendency of the economy, helping to prolong the expan-

CHART 32. *Federal Government Receipts, Expenditures, and Surplus or Deficit, Seasonally Adjusted Quarterly Totals at Annual Rates, 1946-58*

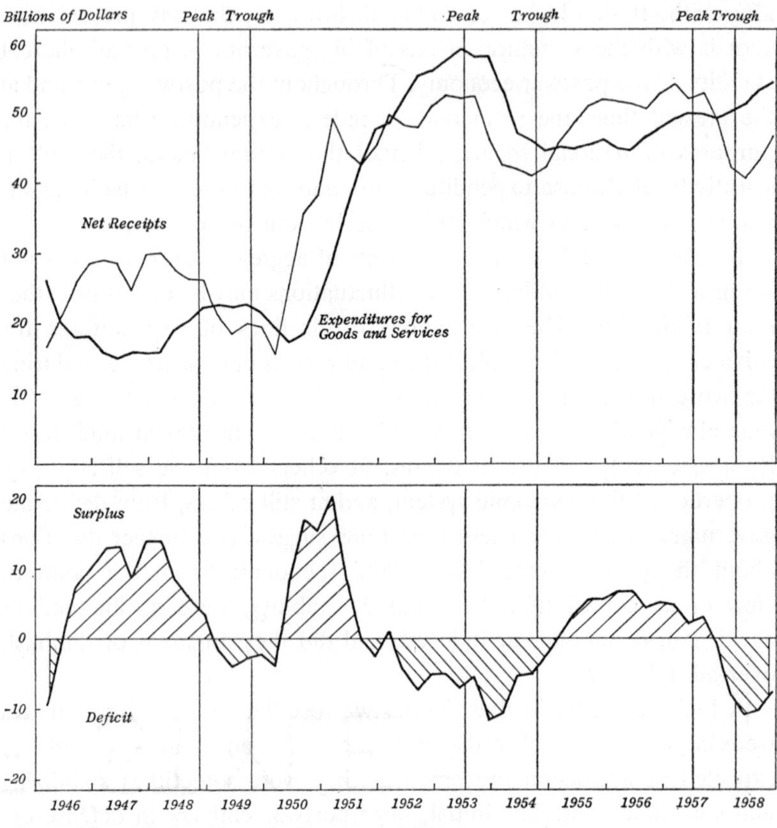

Source: Office of Business Economics, Department of Commerce.

sion and inflation in 1948 and providing an important offset to deflationary declines in private demands during 1949. The economy also received an assist during the contraction of 1948-49 from a substantial induced increase in government outlays under the agricultural price support program.

Federal expenditure did not lead on the upswing in late 1949, although the previously mentioned support during the preceding months had helped to foster conditions making for prompt recovery. In fact, government purchases of goods and services decreased notably during the latter part of 1949 and the first eight to nine months of 1950, owing to reductions under the national defense and agricultural price support programs. This situation was altered radically by the outbreak of hostilities in Korea, of course, and for the next three years the economy was driven upward under the impetus of defense expenditures. That the subsequent decline of defense spending was a major cause of the contraction of 1953-54 is a matter of history. The decline abated about the middle of 1954, however, and for two years thereafter, federal expenditure was stable as the private economy expanded.

Variations in federal spending during 1956-58 were small in comparison with the swings of the previous decade. Nevertheless, a $6 billion increase in the annual rate of defense outlays between the second quarters of 1956 and 1957 was a principal factor in the mild expansion of the period, especially after private investment declined at the turn of the year. Similarly, the small decline in defense expenditures (and the larger drop in commitments for future military spending) between the third and fourth quarters of 1957 was a significant deflationary force during the contraction. The cutback, of course, was due largely to the autonomous federal debt ceiling. Finally, the renewed expansion of federal expenditures during 1958—which was partly the consequence of deliberate contracyclical actions and partly a reaction to the Sputniks and a result of increased agricultural price support payments—contributed prominently to the recovery of business in that year.

The principal conclusions of this brief survey of the postwar behavior of federal expenditure may be summarized as follows: It has been the least stable of the major components of domestic expenditure for final goods and services. This instability was primarily a reflection of changes in the climate of international relations, which several times exposed the economy to potent inflationary or deflationary shocks. In some instances, these shocks acted to initiate or to quicken the prevailing tendencies toward expansion or contraction, and in others to mitigate them. It is evident that federal expenditure cannot be counted among the inherently stable components of aggregate demand so long as it consists predominantly of outlays for national defense.

Federal Expenditure and the New Composition of Demand

The stabilizing potential of federal spending is affected by its own stability, but is not fully determined by it. The share of federal expenditure in the gross national product has risen many times since 1929, yet this development will not have increased over-all stability unless it has decreased the variability of total demand in at least one of two ways: By reducing the range of fluctuation of autonomous expenditure, or by moderating the response of induced expenditure to changes in income. Whether this has occurred depends in good part on the characteristics of the demands which have declined in relative importance as federal expenditure has grown.

At first thought, the only relevant characteristic would appear to be the inherent stability of the displaced demands. If federal expenditure is steadier than the demands which have diminished in importance, then stability has increased, and vice versa. This is substantially true, but it conceals two difficulties. The most important from the present point of view is that the very growth of the government share may have affected the stability of other demands, so that a simple before-and-after comparison does not suffice to settle the issue. The other difficulty has already been touched upon: suppose that federal expenditure were highly variable but always moved against the tide. It could then be stabilizing even if less stable itself than any other component of expenditure. But, accidental fluctuations cannot be relied upon to be compensating. Deliberate changes could always be compensating if properly timed, but that subject falls outside the scope of this discussion of stability in the absence of discretionary fiscal actions.

For the moment, I will blink the first difficulty as well, and proceed as if the growth of the central government had not influenced the variability of any other category of demand. This would mean that other autonomous demands were as stable as before, and that induced demands responded to fluctuations of income in the same way and to the same degree as in former years. With the latter assumption consideration of induced expenditures can be deferred until the next section of this chapter.

That is, induced expenditures can be temporarily disregarded if they can be identified. A complete specification is conceivable in principle but probably impossible in practice. Theoretical and empirical considerations suggest, however, that investment demands may fluctuate widely with changes in technology, population, degree of unutilized capacity, terms of finance, expectations, and the like, whereas consumption demands are more closely dependent on income alone. As a first approximation, then, all investment may be classified as autonomous and all consumption as induced. State and local expenditures may also be treated as autonomous demands. This overlooks the possibility that state and local expenditures may vary co-cyclically during severe and prolonged contractions—as in 1931-33—but the response is slow and has not appeared in the mild postwar contractions. Net export demand is comparatively unimportant in the economy and will be ignored.

The shares of the various categories of expenditure in gross national product are shown for 1929 and three postwar years in Table 35. All comparisons are for years of full employment. The lowest point of postwar federal expenditure came in 1947 and its maximum in 1953. The figures for 1957 are representative of the position of the economy during the late 1950's.

The first thing to be noticed is that autonomous demands as defined above have increased as a percentage of postwar gross national product. When gross national product is measured in current dollars, the share of consumption is found to have decreased nearly as much as the proportion of federal expenditure increased between 1929 and 1957. The picture is altered somewhat when account is taken of price changes, but consumption still remains a considerably smaller proportion of gross national product than in 1929, though this is also true of investment.

The enhanced importance of autonomous demands could work in either direction. If government expenditures prove to be stable elements of demand in the future, the fact that real private investment is now relatively less important is favorable to stability, even though taken altogether autonomous expenditures are larger than before.

TABLE 35. *Percentage Distribution of Components of Gross National Product, Selected Years*[a]

	Constant (1954) Dollars				Current Dollars			
	1929	1947	1953	1957	1929	1947	1953	1957
A. Major Components of Gross National Product								
Government purchases of goods and services	10.2	13.2	22.8	18.5	8.1	12.1	22.7	19.5
Gross private domestic investment	19.3	14.7	13.7	14.2	15.5	13.4	13.8	14.9
Personal consumption expenditures	70.5	69.3	63.7	66.4	75.6	70.6	63.7	64.4
Net exports of goods and services	0.1	2.8	−0.2	0.9	0.7	3.9	−0.1	1.1
Total	100.0	100.0	100.0	100.0	100.0	100.0	100.0	100.0
B. Subcomponents of Gross National Product								
Government purchases of goods and services:								1.2
Federal[b]	1.6	6.9	15.9	10.6	1.2	6.7	15.9	10.0
National defense	n.a.	n.a.	n.a.	n.a.	n.a.	4.8	13.5	11.3
Other	n.a.	n.a.	n.a.	n.a.	n.a.	2.3	2.5	1.3
State and local	8.6	6.3	6.9	7.9	6.9	5.4	6.8	8.3
Total	10.2	13.2	22.8	18.5	8.1	12.1	22.7	19.5
Gross private domestic investment:								
Fixed investment	17.6	14.7	13.6	13.8	13.9	13.6	13.7	14.6
Residential nonfarm construction	4.8	3.4	3.7	3.7	3.5	3.2	3.8	3.8
Other construction	6.7	3.6	3.8	4.0	4.9	3.3	3.8	4.3
Producers' durable equipment	6.1	7.7	6.1	6.0	5.6	7.1	6.1	6.4
Change in business inventories	1.7	0.0	0.1	0.4	1.6	−0.2	0.1	0.4
Total	19.3	14.7	13.7	14.2	15.5	13.4	13.8	14.9
Personal consumption expenditures:								
Durable goods	8.2	8.3	9.0	9.4	8.8	8.8	9.0	9.1
Nondurable goods	35.9	37.3	32.1	32.5	36.1	39.9	32.3	31.1
Services	26.4	23.7	22.7	24.5	30.7	22.0	22.4	24.2
Total	70.5	69.3	63.7	66.4	75.6	70.6	63.7	64.4

n.a. Not available.

[a] From *Survey of Current Business* (July 1960), Tables 1 and 5.

[b] Excludes government sales.

Historically, investment demand has been a highly variable factor, and its diminished share has restricted its maximum potential range of fluctuation. Lest this make us overly complacent, however, it is well to recall that real fixed investment still bulks large enough to decline as far relative to gross national product at full employment as it did between 1929 and 1933.[5] Its maximum range then was 17.6

[5] The comparison excludes inventory investment. Since the latter can (and usually does) become negative during business contractions, its downward range

per cent of peak gross national product (1954 prices), and its actual decline amounted to 13 per cent of peak (1929) gross national product. The 1957 peak share was 13.8 per cent. Clearly, there is still room for a marked reduction of fixed investment. It is not as if stable government expenditure had been completely substituted for unstable investment expenditure and had reduced the latter to insignificance. Incidentally, the same inferences hold if the autonomous demand category is broadened to include durable consumer goods, since expenditures of this type are a larger percentage of real gross national product than in 1929 and have a correspondingly larger maximum range.

It cannot be maintained, then, that the potential range of private autonomous demand has been radically diminished by the growth of federal expenditure. In the language of multiplier analysis, the multiplicand may still undergo substantial decline. The next question to consider is the extent to which the growth of federal expenditure has affected the size of the multiplier, or in other words, the extent to which it has diminished income-induced fluctuations in private demand. It is sometimes said that the growth of federal spending since the 1920's has augmented the resistance of the economy to contraction because the central government need not reduce its purchases of goods and services when tax revenues decline. In itself this is not a significant change, however, since federal spending was too small and too unresponsive to revenues to be an important factor in induced fluctuations of demand in prewar years. (Federal purchases of goods and services, moreover, actually rose during 1929-33 and 1937-38.) Insofar as the stability of induced demand is concerned, a far more important change is to be found in the effects of expanded programs of taxation and social security on induced movements of personal income and consumption.

---

is not limited to its share of GNP at cyclical peaks. It is worth noting also that the destabilizing potential of private fixed investment should be measured relative to full-employment GNP and not, as is commonly done, relative to total autonomous expenditure. If it is assumed that government expenditure is apt to be stable during contractions, the relevant question is how much private autonomous expenditure could decrease as a percentage of full-employment GNP, and not how much it could decrease as a percentage of total (public and private) autonomous expenditure.

TABLE 36. *Government Expenditures and Receipts as Percentages of Gross National Product Selected Years*[a]

Item	1929	1947	1953	1957
Federal expenditures:				
Purchases of goods and services	1.2	6.7	15.9	11.2
Transfer items	1.3	6.6	5.4	6.8
Transfer payments	.7	3.8	3.1	3.9
Grants-in-aid to state and local governments	.1	.7	.8	.9
Net interest paid	.4	1.8	1.3	1.3
Subsidies less current surplus of government enterprises	.1	.2	.2	.6
Total	2.5	13.3	21.3	18.0
Federal receipts:				
Personal tax and nontax receipts	1.2	8.4	8.9	8.4
Corporate profits tax accruals	1.2	4.6	5.3	4.5
Indirect business tax and nontax accruals	1.1	3.4	3.1	2.8
Contributions for social insurance	.1	2.2	2.0	2.8
Total	3.6	18.5	19.3	18.5
State and local expenditures:				
Purchases of goods and services	6.9	5.4	6.8	8.3
Transfer items	.5	.7	.6	.6
Total	7.4	6.1	7.4	9.0
State and local receipts:				
Taxes	7.1	5.9	6.7	7.8
Federal grants-in-aid	.1	.7	.8	.9
Total	7.2	6.6	7.5	8.7
Government expenditures:				
Purchases of goods and services	8.1	12.1	22.7	19.5
Transfer items	1.8	7.3	6.0	7.4
Total	9.9	19.4	28.7	26.9
Government receipts, total[b]	10.8	24.4	26.0	27.2

[a] From *Survey of Current Business* (July 1960), Tables 20 and 21.
[b] Excluding federal grants-in-aid.

The Federal Government and Automatic Stabilizers

The stabilizing properties of induced changes in tax revenues and transfer payments are among the most analyzed and best publicized features of the postwar economy. This is partly because there has been a notable expansion of federal transfers along with purchases of goods and services by the central government, and tax revenues have kept pace with the total of both types of expenditure (Table 36). From the standpoint of stabilization, however, the particular forms taken by the expansion of transfers and taxes are just as important as the expansion itself. This is because—deliberate alterations in payments or tax rates aside—the stabilization potential of these items depends upon their responsiveness to changes of income, rather than their size at a given income. No matter how large they were, if they were steady over time neither transfers nor taxes would tend automatically to mitigate fluctuations of income.[6] What has actually occurred, of course, is that the total tax take has increased quite substantially and that most of it has been levied in the form of the cyclically sensitive corporate and personal income taxes. The situation differs somewhat with regard to transfer items. Unemployment insurance benefits account for a minor fraction of all transfer items but do most of the stabilization work in the category.

Automatic stabilizers reduce the amplitude of cyclical fluctuations to the extent that they diminish the response of induced expenditures to prior changes of income and inhibit the spread of expansionary or contractionary impulses from one sector of the economy to another. This result is accomplished by affecting the relationship between changes of gross and net income. Again it is assumed that consumption is the major category of induced demand, and that it depends upon the amount of disposable personal income available to

[6] In technical terms, the stabilizing potential of net taxes is determined by their effect on the marginal relationship between consumption and gross national product. It is not the downshift of the consumption function but the change in its slope which affects the value of the multiplier.

CHART 33. *Some Relationships Among Gross National Product, Disposable*

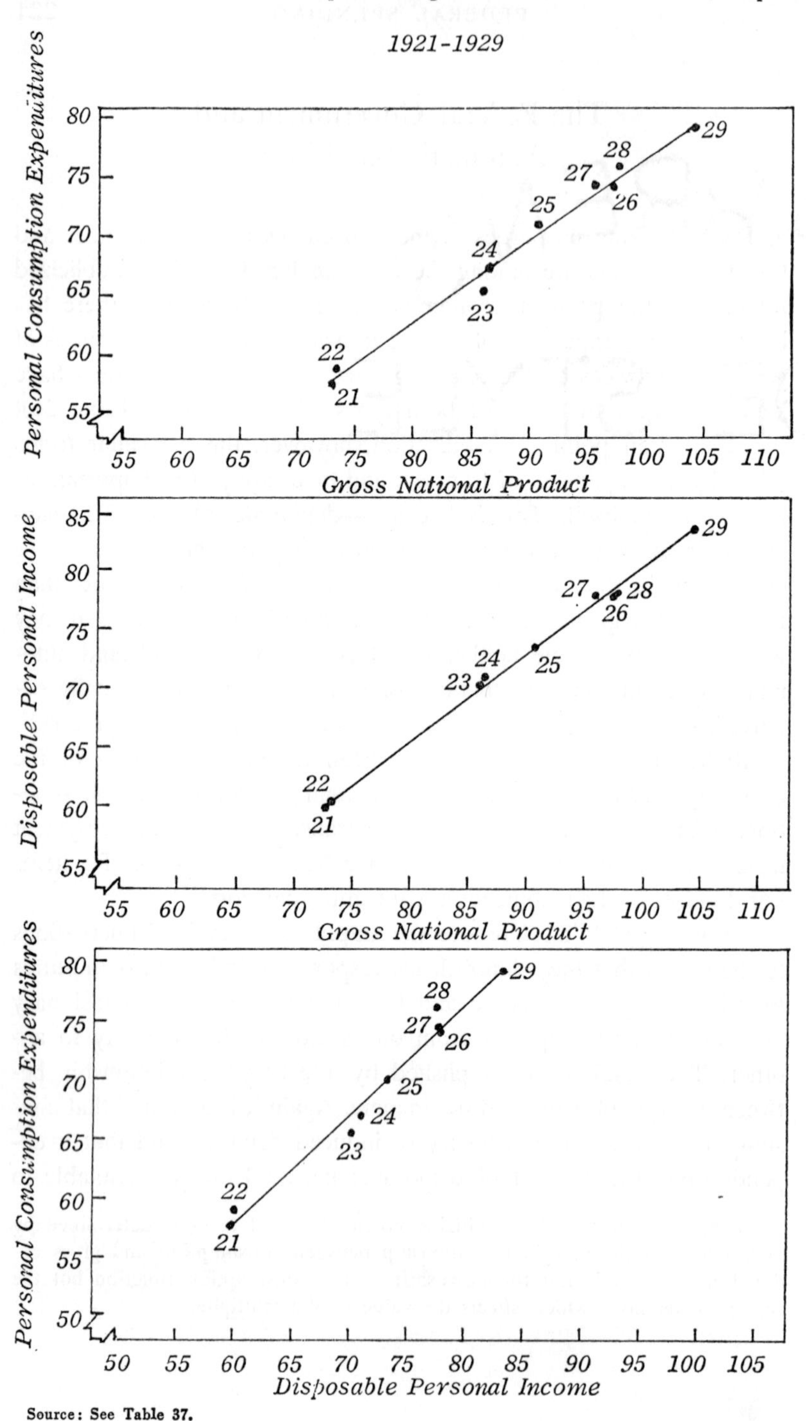

Source: See Table 37.

Personal Income, and Consumption Expenditure, 1921-29 and 1947-58

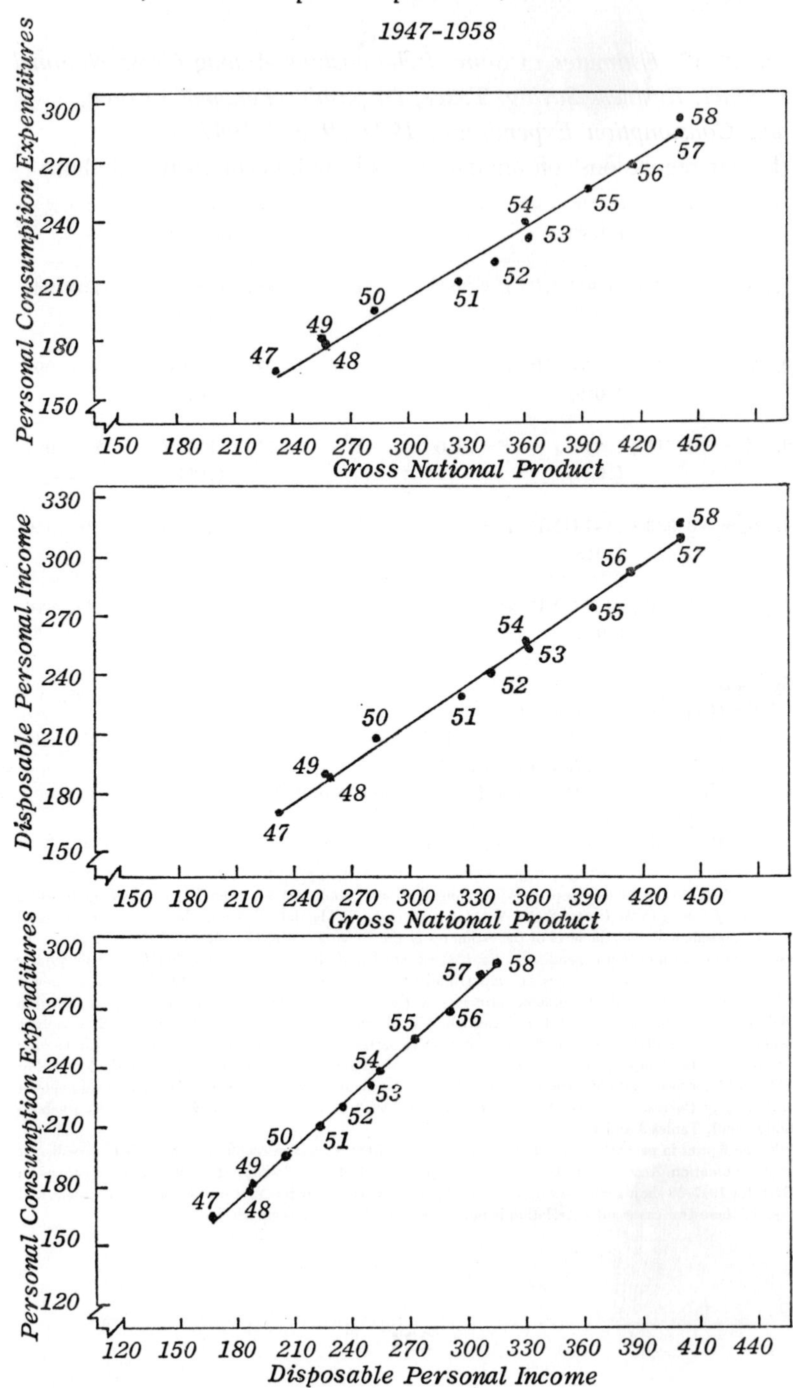

TABLE 37. *Estimates of Some Relationships Among Gross National Product, Business Saving, Taxes, Disposable Personal Income, and Consumption Expenditure, 1921-29 and 1947-58*[a]
(Linear regressions[b] on annual values in billions of current dollars)

	1921–29		1947–58	
1.	$C = 7.894 + .686\ GNP$ $(.029)$	$r^2 = .987$	$C = 26.467 + .581\ GNP$ $(.021)$	$r^2 = .987$
2.	$Y_d = 6.413 + .736\ GNP$ $(.019)$	$r^2 = .995$	$Y_d = 15.225 + .662\ GNP$ $(.018)$	$r^2 = .992$
3.	$C = 2.311 + .927\ Y_d$ $(.050)$	$r^2 = .980$	$C = 12.775 + .879\ Y_d$ $(.014)$	$r^2 = .997$
4.	$S_b = -0.936 + .121\ GNP$ $(.018)$	$r^2 = .860$	$S_b = -4.108 + .111\ GNP$ $(.008)$	$r^2 = .956$
5.	$T_n = -4.989 + .137\ GNP$ $(.012)$	$r^2 = .951$	$T_n = -19.358 + .246\ GNP$ $(.019)$	$r^2 = .946$

Symbols:
GNP = Gross national product.
S_b = Gross business saving (depreciation *plus* undistributed corporate profits after inventory valuation adjustment).
T_n = Net tax receipts (tax receipts *minus* transfer items).
Y_d = Disposable personal income.
C = Personal consumption expenditure.

[a] For 1921–28, all items except personal consumption expenditures are from Raymond W. Goldsmith, *A Study of Saving in the United States*, Vol. III (1956), Pt. V. The data shown in the source were adjusted by the present writer to the level of the estimates of the Department of Commerce for the year 1929. The estimates of consumption expenditures for 1921–28 are based on Simon Kuznets, *National Product Since 1869* (1946), Tables I 4B (services, column 1) and I-5 (goods, columns 1–3). Each consumption series was adjusted to the level of the Commerce estimates for the year 1929 and the resulting series were summed to yield the annual estimates of total consumption. The alternative series on services (Table I 4B) was used because "there is little question that the alternative series gives a more reliable picture of year to year variations in the flow of services to consumers than the present or the old series. . . . " (*ibid.*, p. 11). For 1929 and later years, all data are from Department of Commerce, *U. S. Income and Output*, a supplement to *Survey of Current Business* (November 1958), Tables I-17 and II-1 and *Survey of Current Business* (July 1960), Tables 3 and 4.

[b] The figures in parentheses are the standard errors of the regression coefficients and r^2 is the coefficient of determination. According to the von Neumann test, only the regressions of consumption and taxes on GNP for 1947–58 show significant autocorrelation in the residuals at the 5 per cent level of significance, and even in these two cases autocorrelation is not significant at the 1 per cent level.

the public for spending or saving. This means that the smaller the change in disposable income for a given change of gross national product, the smaller is the secondary fluctuation of consumption and hence, of gross national product in response to an initial change in autonomous expenditure. It is because induced movements of taxes and transfers diminish the reaction of disposable income to changes of gross national product that they have come to be called automatic stabilizers. But there are also sizable private leakages between gross national product and disposable personal income—depreciation charges and undistributed corporate profits—and these private deductions fluctuated cyclically before the government stabilizers became important. Thus we need to ask whether the increase in the strength of the governmental stabilizers has been at the expense of the private stabilizers or whether it represents a net gain.

To answer this question, I compare the postwar economy with that of the 1920's, when government stabilizers were unimportant. Moreover, the period 1921-29 is similar to 1947-58 in regard to freedom from protracted depression, so that the comparison will not be distorted by the pronounced differences in saving behavior which are known to exist between periods of prolonged depression and sustained prosperity.

Three relationships are diagrammed side by side for the two postwar periods in Chart 33. The top panel shows the relationship of consumption to gross national product. This, in turn, is resolved into two components in the middle and third panels: one relating disposable personal income and gross national product; the other personal consumption expenditures and disposable personal income. Straight lines have been fitted to the data in all panels by the method of least squares. The figures for the 1920's are based on incomplete source data and are less reliable than the estimates for recent years. The regression equations are shown in Table 37.

Comparison of the two lines relating consumption and gross national product discloses that the one for the 1920's is steeper than that for the recent period. The line for the 1920's implies an increase of 69 cents in consumption expenditures for an increment of $1.00

in gross national product, whereas that for 1947-58 places the increase at 58 cents.

Further inspection of the diagrams reveals that the diminished response of consumption is due primarily to the fact that disposable income increases less for a given change of gross national product than in former years; that is, to the fact that the growth of taxes and transfers has added to, rather than replaced, the stabilization potential of induced changes of business saving. The increment of disposable income per dollar increase of gross national product may be estimated from the fitted lines at 74 and 66 per cent, respectively, in the earlier and later periods. The corresponding values for the ratio of changes of consumption and disposable income are 93 and 88 per cent, a smaller though substantial difference.[7] With the earlier relationship between consumption and disposable income and the present one between disposable income and gross national product, it is easily calculated that the ratio of increments of consumption and gross national product would now be 61 per cent (93 multiplied by 66), or only three points higher than the actual postwar estimate of 58 per cent. The same tax leakages and corporate saving as formerly in combination with the present behavior of personal saving, on the other hand, would yield a marginal ratio of consumption to gross national product of 65 per cent, or seven points above the present ratio.

The regressions of gross business saving and of net taxes on gross national product are given separately in Table 37. The estimated relationship between a change in gross national product and a change in gross business saving is about the same in the two periods, whereas

[7] Notice that for each period the estimated marginal relationship between consumption and gross national product is equal to the product of the two underlying marginal relationships. Thus, let

(1) $C = a + b(Yd)$,
(2) $Yd = g + h(GNP)$ and
(3) $C = m + n(GNP)$,

where the symbols have the same meaning as in Table 37. Then, substituting (2) into (1),

(4) $C = (a + bg) + bh(GNP)$.

Therefore, $n = bh$.

the corresponding marginal ratio for net taxes and gross national product is much larger nowadays than in the 1920's.[8] Thus, it appears that the great bulk of the increase in the strength of the governmental stabilizers since the 1920's represents a net addition to the stabilizing potential of gross business saving.

Although the foregoing comparisons are probably of the correct order of magnitude, little weight should be given to the precise numerical results. Neither the data nor the techniques employed in the calculations permit more than a first approximation to the relevant relationships. Even apart from inaccuracies in the data on income and consumption (especially troublesome for the 1920's), the variables themselves are subject to autonomous disturbances[9] and random variations, and the estimated relationships could not be more than approximations to the average strength of the induced responses. Chart 32 shows that the changes from one year to the next do not always parallel the lines of average change even during expansions, and that vertical movements of consumption relative to gross national product were the rule for the years of mild contraction covered by the charts (1924, 1927, 1949, 1954, and 1958).

It is particularly important to recognize that the regression coefficients tell nothing about consumption-income relationships during cyclical contractions. Thus the multiplier values implied by the regressions of consumption on gross national product are respectively $1/1 - .69 = 3.2$ and $1/1 - .58 = 2.4$ for 1921-29 and 1947-58.[10] These values are much too high for brief contractions. Even if they were the correct limiting values for a period multiplier sequence of infinite duration, the values reached in the three or four multiplier

[8] Since gross business saving and net taxes are the principal leakages between gross national income and disposable personal income, the sum of these two marginal "saving" propensities should be nearly equal to the marginal gap between gross national income and disposable personal income. Comparison of equations 2, 4, and 5 in Table 37 discloses that the expected approximate relationship holds for both periods of estimation.

[9] For example, although the level of taxation was much higher throughout the period since 1947 than in the 1920's, substantial changes in tax rates occurred in 1948, 1951, and 1954.

[10] The differences between the multiplier values would be smaller if the calculations were made at constant prices, for reasons discussed in the section on secular shifts in the composition of output and employment in Chapter 8.

time periods contained in a one-year contraction would be smaller—about 2.5 and 2.1 respectively for 1921-29 and 1947-58 if the multiplier period were three months.[11] But even the corrected values would require that consumption expenditure accounts for half or more of the decline of gross national product during a business contraction, whereas consumption has been much more stable than that during the recent recessions and was probably quite stable during the mild contractions of the 1920's.[12]

Measured on a quarterly basis and in current dollars, consumption expenditure actually rose during the contractions of 1948-49 and 1953-54 and was virtually constant during that of 1957-58.[13] When measured in constant dollars, consumption still increased during the first two contractions, and although it fell substantially during the last one, it accounted for only one-fifth of the reduction in gross national product. A recent econometric investigation yielded a multiplier estimate of 1.34 under recession conditions like those of 1957-58, implying that only 25 per cent of the reduction of gross national product would be directly due to a fall of consumption expenditure.[14] The estimates of income and consumption for the 1920's are available only on an annual basis and, in any case, are of dubious reliability

[11] Notice that the difference between the one-year values is considerably smaller than the difference between the theoretical limiting values. As Fritz Machlup has demonstrated, the proportion of the theoretical limit which will be reached at the end of a finite number of multiplier time periods varies inversely with the size of the theoretical limit. See his "Period Analysis and Multiplier Theory," *Quarterly Journal of Economics* (November 1939), pp. 1-27, reprinted in American Economic Association, *Readings in Business Cycle Theory* (1944), pp. 203-34.

[12] If account is taken of the induced decline of inventory investment as well as that of consumption expenditure, however, the "super-multiplier" which includes both effects might well approximate a value of 2.5 during mild contractions even though the consumption multiplier alone would be much smaller. See footnote 14 below.

[13] The consumption rise during the first two recessions was due partly to autonomous increases of consumption and not just to multiplier effects. See Chapter 10.

[14] James S. Duesenberry, Otto Eckstein, and Gary Fromm, *Stability and Instability in the American Economy,* Harvard University (multilithed, 1958), pp. 36-37. The estimated value of the super-multiplier (including inventory reaction) under the same conditions was 2.72.

for year-to-year comparisons. But, for what they are worth, they also suggest great consumption stability during mild contractions even in those days (Chart 33 and Table 38). It is worth noting also that the monthly Federal Reserve index of department store sales declined scarcely at all during the contractions of 1923-24 and 1926-27, whereas it fell moderately during each of the recessions since 1948.[15]

One of the principal reasons for cyclical variations in the value of the multiplier is the fact that changes in before-tax corporate profits account for a larger share of the decrease of gross national income during a mild contraction than they do of the increase of gross national income during periods of expansion. As a result, corporate profits taxes and after-tax corporate profits tend to absorb relatively more of a fall than of a rise of gross national income. Moreover, the average response of dividends to a decline of after-tax profits appears to be smaller than the response to an increase, so that the cyclical swings of undistributed profits relative to gross national income are for that reason also accentuated more for contractions than for expansions.[16]

This is not the place for an investigation of the causes of asymmetry in the cyclical fluctuations of the share of before-tax corporate profits in gross national income. As far as contractions alone are concerned, the tendency for the profit share to fall sharply is caused in the first instance by short-term rigidities in overhead costs and wage rates, and the tendency will accordingly weaken if the contraction becomes severe or prolonged. At first sight, however, at least one of the short-term cost rigidities appears to be a destabilizing influence during contractions. Depreciation charges are primarily a function of past investment decisions and continue to increase during mild contractions. Notice, however, that with dividends relatively constant, the net effect of a rise of depreciation allowances at the expense of profits is a shift in the composition, but little change in the size, of total

[15] See *Historical Supplement to the Federal Reserve Chartbook on Financial and Business Statistics* (September 1959), pp. 102-03.

[16] See John Lintner, "Distribution of Incomes of Corporations Among Dividends, Retained Earnings, and Taxes," *American Economic Review* (May 1956), pp. 107, 109.

TABLE 38. *Relationship Between Changes of Gross National Product and Disposable Personal Income, Selected Business Cycle Contractions*[a]
(In millions of dollars)

Item	Change between Initial and Terminal Year of Contraction				
	1923–24	1926–27	1948–49	1953–54	1957–58
Decrease of gross national product	− 451	1,562	1,372	2,273	−1,455
Less: Decrease of taxes	− 185	− 329	2,829	4,932	1,031
Indirect business taxes	− 327	− 324	−1,232	52	−1,164
Corporate profits taxes	51	90	2,108	3,002	2,308
Personal taxes	102	− 74	2,470	2,845	192
Social security contributions	− 11	− 21	− 517	− 967	− 305
Less: Increase of transfer items	− 133	21	1,223	2,310	4,358
Government transfer payments	− 9	55	1,080	2,074	4,428
Net Government interest	− 124	− 34	143	236	− 29
Less: Decrease of business saving	662	1,816	−1,059	−1,100	993
Capital consumption allowances	− 224	− 281	−1,803	−2,283	− 696
Undistributed corporate profits after inventory valuation adjustment	886	2,097	744	1,183	1,689
Less: Decrease of other items	n.a.	n.a.	−1,267	542	1,203
Statistical discrepancy	n.a.	n.a.	−1,357	430	1,060
Excess of wage accruals over disbursements	n.a.	n.a.	81	− 76	0.0
Surplus minus subsidies of Government enterprises	n.a.	n.a.	9	188	143
Equals: Decrease of disposable personal income	− 795	54	− 354	−4,411	−9,081
Addendum: Decrease of personal consumption expenditures	−1,600	− 300	−2,845	−5,376	−8,331

n.a. Not available
[a] See Table 37 for sources. Negative signs indicate changes opposite in direction to those described in the caption for each category.

leakages (depreciation plus taxes plus undistributed profits) from corporate income.

This brief investigation of personal income stabilizers concludes with a closer look at recession behavior than is provided in Chart 33. Five business contractions are covered by the data for the 1920's and the present period (Table 38). All were mild and, in the first and last of the contractions, gross national product actually increased slightly when measured in the crude unit of annual observations. During the contractions of 1923-24 and 1926-27, net taxes increased and, of course, depreciation allowances also increased. Large reductions in undistributed corporate profits more than compensated for these increases, however, so that disposable income rose substantially relative to gross national product during both recessions.

Stabilizing decreases in undistributed corporate profits (after inventory valuation adjustment) also occurred during each of the recent recessions. Gross business saving increased on balance during the contractions of 1948-49 and 1953-54, however, owing to large increases in capital consumption allowances (including depreciation on owner-occupied houses).

The contribution of changes in tax receipts to income stability was positive and substantial during the three postwar recessions. Reduced rates of personal income taxation account for most of the decline of personal tax receipts between 1948 and 1949 and for all of it between 1953 and 1954, however. Moreover, during 1953-54 about one-fifth of the fall in corporate income tax accruals was due to rate reductions, and reduced federal excise tax rates more than compensated for the rise of indirect state and local taxes. Thus, the contributions to income stability of induced reductions in tax receipts during 1948-49 and 1953-54 is greatly overstated by the unadjusted changes in tax receipts shown in Table 38.

Government transfer payments rose substantially during 1948-49 and by successively larger amounts in the subsequent contractions. Personal income is raised during recessions by the secular growth of pension and retirement benefits as well as by induced increases in unemployment benefits. During 1957-58, the contribution of transfer payments to income stability was considerably greater than the combined influence of decreases in tax receipts and gross business saving.

The foremost conclusion which emerges from this brief review of five contractions is that net corporate saving not only acted as a personal income stabilizer before the government stabilizers became important, but that it was sufficiently effective to raise disposable personal income substantially relative to gross national product during the two mild contractions of the 1920's. As for the government stabilizers themselves, it is interesting to observe that contrary to a widely held impression, the induced changes in personal income tax receipts during the recent recessions have been quite unimportant when compared with the induced changes in corporate income tax receipts and with the substantial and growing influence of transfer payments.

Federal Spending and Stability in a Growing Economy

The discussion thus far has been limited to problems of short-term fluctuation. The implicit bench mark of perfect stability was a constant level of gross national product in money terms, and increases and decreases from that level were regarded as evidence of instability. What modifications of previous conclusions become appropriate when it is recognized that the goal is not merely stability for a year or two but stable growth over the long run, including the avoidance of chronic unemployment or inflation?

The first fact to be stressed is that the historical analysis has dealt with certain characteristics of the actual postwar economy; that is, of an economy unmarked by severe contraction and experiencing more than a decade of high-level activity. Federal expenditure was shown to be the least stable of the major components of final demand during the period, and the conclusion was reached that on several occasions it contributed importantly to over-all instability. The dominant impulse was toward expansion, however, so that federal expenditure increased more rapidly on the average than other components (except state and local spending) and after each retrenchment remained a larger share of gross national product than before. Does this mean that the net effect of the autonomous demands of national security was to foster expansion and to prevent severe contraction, albeit at the cost of a moderate degree of short-run instability?

There are really two issues raised by this last question: What was the actual effect of large-scale government spending, and what would have occurred in its absence? It is idle to speculate about the second issue, but something may be said on the first.

Suppose that an autonomous increase of federal expenditure occurs at a time when unemployed resources are available to expand national output. Will an expansion actually develop, and, if so, how vigorous will it be? Clearly, more information is needed before an answer can be given. Will the additional expenditure raise autonomous demand? And, if it does so, by how much will induced expenditures rise in consequence?

If other demands remain unchanged at the time of the increase, autonomous expenditure will rise by the amount of the additional federal outlay, and further gains will result from the subsequent rise of induced expenditure. The direction of the impulse is plainly evident in this simple case, and a tolerably good estimate of its strength is possible. But will other demands be initially unchanged? In general, no. In the first place, the private sector may respond directly to the same stimulus that spurs federal spending. There were dramatic instances of this in the forward-buying waves during the early months of the war in Korea. Less startling than this sort of simultaneous reaction to an outside stimulus is the regular tendency for private investment to be made in inventory and plant in anticipation of subsequent federal purchases for which orders have been placed. This is an important problem for short-term analysis of the impact of federal spending, but is not the concern here. I also leave aside the case in which the new expenditure is directly competitive with private investment and causes an offsetting reduction in the latter.

What is needed is consideration of the method by which the new government expenditure is financed. If tax rates are increased in order to raise the additional revenue, private demands will be diminished, and at least part of the stimulus of the added expenditure will be lost. Just how much will be lost depends upon the amount and type of the tax increase and the effect of the resultant reduction in private disposable income upon private expenditure. The possibilities are manifold, but a simple example will suffice to illustrate the basic point.

Assume that an increase of $10 billion in spending is contemplated, and that personal income tax rates are adjusted upward to raise an equal amount of additional revenue at the same level of national income as prevailed before the new expenditure is made.[17] Since the initial effect of the tax increase is a $10 billion reduction of disposable personal income, consumption expenditures will fall by, say, $8 billion, offsetting that much of the increase of government expenditures. A net gain of $2 billion of autonomous expenditure still results, however, and, when transformed into earned incomes, will induce further increases of aggregate demand. Notice that, although the initial effect of these fiscal operations was a balanced-budget increase of federal expenditure, the induced rise of taxes due to the secondary expansion of incomes and demand will yield a surplus on government account. The emergence of this surplus (or diminished deficit, if the initial position was one of deficit) is a sign of the restraining or deflationary influence of the automatic tax stabilizers, but it is a restraining influence that was called into being by the initial net expansionary increase of federal spending. A before-and-after comparison would show an increase in the surplus, yet the end result of the entire fiscal operation would be expansionary. The expansion would be smaller than if their increase of expenditure were financed by loans, but it is not necessary that a deficit be incurred in order to raise gross national product by raising government expenditures.

What the foregoing example means when translated into practice is that an observed increase of federal expenditure may have a net expansionary effect even if matched by an approximately equal rise of receipts. It is not enough to observe whether a deficit or surplus exists or is developing in order to gauge the expansionary or contrac-

[17] See W. J. Baumol and M. H. Peston, "More on the Multiplier Effects of a Balanced Budget," *American Economic Review* (March 1955), pp. 140-48; Alvin H. Hansen, "More on the Multiplier Effects of a Balanced Budget: Comment," *op. cit.* (March 1956), pp. 157-60; William A. Salant, "Taxes, Income Determination, and the Balanced Budget Theorem," *Review of Economics and Statistics* (May 1957), pp. 152-61.

tionary influence of government fiscal operations. A further complication results from the fact that the effect on private expenditure depends upon the type, as well as the amount, of the additional taxes. For instance, because part of the incidence of a given increase in corporate-income taxes will probably fall upon undistributed profits, dividends—and hence disposable personal income—will fall by less than if the same amount of tax revenue were raised by an increase in taxes on personal income. The smaller reduction of consumption per dollar of tax increase may or may not be compensated by a tax-inspired reduction of corporate-investment demand, but, in any event, a direct comparison of total tax revenue with total government expenditure will not settle the question. With these strictures in mind, I turn to a brief assessment of the impact of postwar changes in federal expenditures and revenues on aggregate economic activity.

Federal purchases of goods and services, net tax receipts, and the excess of receipts over expenditures are shown quarterly for 1946 through 1958 in Chart 32. There is no need to discuss the year-to-year changes in detail. It is sufficient to note that the generalizations offered earlier about the expansionary or contractionary effects of the postwar swings in federal expenditures remain valid when cognizance is taken of the concomitant changes in revenues. Thus, during 1948 and 1949, the expansionary stimulus of expenditure increases was strengthened by the tax cuts which diminished receipts in the former year and by the induced decline of receipts in the latter. The rise in expenditure during the Korean War was less expansionary than if automatic and discretionary increases in revenues had not also occurred; nonetheless, that it was expansionary can scarcely be doubted in view of the history of the upswing. Again, the deliberate and induced reductions of receipts in 1953-54 helped to cushion the impact of the cutback in federal expenditure, but did not prevent it from exerting a net deflationary pressure on the economy.

Fiscal operations were contracyclical during 1955-56, when expenditures were relatively stable and tax receipts increased because of the rise of national income. Expenditures accelerated and the federal surplus declined beginning in mid-1956, however, probably prolonging the business expansion in the process. The expansion was ended partly because defense contracts were sharply reduced, but federal expenditures dropped only slightly and were quickly reversed by discretionary actions. Meanwhile, induced declines in net tax receipts mitigated the contraction.

Viewing the postwar era as a whole, then, the effect of the autonomous demands of national security has been to foster expansion, notwithstanding the instability of growth of federal expenditure. Federal spending was an expansionary factor in 1948-49, 1950-53, and except for a few months, in 1956-58. Even the 22 per cent drop from 1953 to 1955 left federal spending a much higher percentage of gross national product than before Korea, and did not lead to a major contraction. These facts stand out despite the short-term shifts in the balance of receipts and expenditures and despite their rough correspondence in level throughout the period.

Modification of another previous conclusion is indicated when stability is considered in the context of growth. This was the conclusion that federal spending would become a destabilizing factor if it were altered to keep pace with induced movements of tax receipts. This still holds unreservedly for declines. When it comes to stable growth, however, it may be desirable that federal outlays rise along with revenues, lest the expansion of income be restrained unduly by an uncompensated increase in tax collections. Whether increased federal expenditures (or tax cuts) would in fact be desirable from the standpoint of stability would depend upon the degree of prevailing inflationary pressure—upon whether the effect would be primarily to raise prices or real income—and also upon the probable expansion of private autonomous expenditure.

Summary

The growth in relative importance of the federal government has augmented economic stability in some respects and diminished it in others. Federal expenditure on goods and services was the least stable of the major components of final demand during 1947-58. Its fluctuations were due largely to autonomous causes and hence were sometimes stabilizing and sometimes not. Despite substantial short-term variability, however, its pronounced uptrend after World War II fostered expansion over the period as a whole.

The share of private fixed investment in gross national product has remained about the same in current dollars but has declined somewhat in constant dollars as federal expenditure has grown. Even in real terms, however, fixed investment is still large enough to decline as far relative to gross national product at full employment as it did between 1929 and 1933, so that it cannot be maintained that the potential range of private autonomous expenditure has been radically diminished by the growth of federal expenditure.

The stability of consumption demand has been augmented by the growth in strength of government tax and transfer stabilizers. It would be easy to exaggerate the extent to which the multiplier has been diminished by these developments, however, since business saving exerted a substantial stabilizing influence over personal income before the government stabilizers became important. Thus, to judge from the imperfect empirical data and from theoretical considerations, the value of the multiplier was already quite small for mild contractions during the 1920's. A larger reduction has probably occurred since then in the value of the multiplier during business expansions. This is a favorable development should inflation threaten, but it has the disadvantage that it also retards the growth of demand for real output when unemployed resources exist.

The principal over-all conclusion to which I am led is that future prosperity will depend more on the wisdom with which discretionary public policies are pursued than on the structural effects which big government has wrought on the economy. Because the federal share of national income has grown so much, autonomous variations of taxes and expenditures nowadays provide powerful tools for economic stabilization, if only they are properly used.

10 / *Consumer Demand*

HOW DOES CONSUMER DEMAND affect, and how is it affected by, aggregate economic activity? This chapter seeks an answer by treating, first, the influence of shifts in the distribution of personal income on the cyclical behavior of consumption expenditures. Next, the consequences for economic stability of the secular increase in the relative importance of consumer durable goods and the associated uptrend in the use of instalment credit are explored. And, then, the active role of consumer spending in the postwar business fluctuations is systematically reviewed and analyzed.

Income Distribution and Consumer Demand

Notable shifts have occurred in the distribution of national income since prewar days; the question is how these changes have influenced the cyclical behavior of consumer demand. The effects of the dramatic rise in the share of taxes on the relationship of personal to national income were discussed in the preceding chapter. Here, the implications of the secular shifts in the distribution of personal income by type and by size are considered.

Distribution by Type

Trends in the shares of the various functional forms of personal income between 1913 and 1957 may be examined with the assistance of Table 39. The top panel shows how personal income was

TABLE 39. *Percentage Distribution of Personal Income and Personal Income From Production, by Type of Income, Selected Years*[a]

Income Category	Years				
	1913	1929	1948	1953	1957
A. Personal Income					
Wages and salaries, private	48.0	52.9	54.8	56.2	55.3
Wages and salaries, government	4.6	5.6	8.4	11.3	10.8
Other labor income and transfer payments	.9	2.4	6.7	7.0	8.8
Farm proprietors' net income	10.1	7.0	8.5	4.6	3.4
Nonfarm proprietors' net income	15.2	10.3	10.6	9.4	9.1
Dividends	6.0	6.8	3.4	3.2	3.6
Interest	4.0	8.7	4.1	4.6	5.6
Rent	11.2	6.3	3.5	3.7	3.4
Total	100.0	100.0	100.0	100.0	100.0
B. Personal Income From Production[b]					
Wages and salaries, private	48.0	54.6	59.2	60.2	60.1
Wages and salaries, government	4.6	5.8	9.1	12.1	11.7
Other labor income[c]	.9	.7	1.4	2.2	2.8
Farm proprietors' net income	10.1	7.2	9.1	4.9	3.6
Nonfarm proprietors' net income	15.2	10.6	11.5	10.1	9.9
Dividends	6.0	7.0	3.7	3.4	3.9
Interest[d]	4.0	7.7	2.1	3.0	4.2
Rent	11.2	6.5	3.7	3.9	3.7
Total	100.0	100.0	100.0	100.0	100.0

[a] Data for 1913 are from Daniel Creamer, *Personal Income During Business Cycles* (1956), p. xxix. All other years from *U. S. Income and Output*, a supplement to *Survey of Current Business* (November 1958), Tables I-17, II-1 and III-6, and *Survey of Current Business* (July 1960), Tables 3, 4 and 25. Detail may not add to totals because of rounding.

[b] Personal income excluding transfer payments and interest received from government.

[c] Excludes transfer payments.

[d] Excludes interest received from government, except in the year 1913.

divided in each of several years, when government transfer payments are allocated to labor income, and government interest payments are included in the interest component. The distribution of personal income from production, which excludes transfer payments and government interest, is presented in the bottom panel. A comparison of recent postwar years with 1913 and 1929 shows that the share of labor income has increased while that of property income—dividends, interest and rent—has diminished. The net income of farm proprietors has fallen sharply from the unusually large share of 1948, and in 1953

TABLE 40. *Actual and Hypothetical Changes in Personal Income During the 1953-54 Contraction, Assuming Alternative Distributions*[a]
(Dollar items in millions)

Income Category	Actual 1953 Distribution			Assumed 1929 Distribution		Assumed 1948 Distribution		Assumed 1957 Distribution	
	1953 Total (1)	*1953–54 Change (Per cent)* (2)	1953–54 Change (3)	1953 Total (4)	1953–54 Change (5)	1953 Total (6)	1953–54 Change (7)	1953 Total (8)	1953–54 Change (9)
Wages and salaries, private	161,949	*− 1.8*	−2,847	152,489	−2,745	157,966	−2,843	159,407	−2,869
Wages and salaries, government	32,436	*+ 1.1*	+ 371	16,142	+ 178	24,214	+ 266	31,132	+ 342
Other labor income and transfer payments	20,250	*+10.8*	+2,187	6,918	+ 747	19,313	+2,086	25,367	+2,740
Farm proprietors' net income	13,278	*− 4.4*	− 587	20,178	− 888	24,502	−1,078	9,801	− 431
Nonfarm proprietors' net income	27,226	*+ 1.1*	+ 302	29,691	+ 327	30,555	+ 336	26,232	+ 289
Dividends	9,225	*+ 6.7*	+ 614	19,602	+1,313	9,801	+ 657	10,377	+ 695
Interest	13,367	*+ 8.9*	+1,185	25,079	+2,232	11,819	+1,052	16,142	+1,437
Rent	10,528	*+ 3.2*	+ 341	18,160	+ 581	10,089	+ 323	9,801	+ 314
Total	288,259	*+ 0.5*	+1,566	288,259	+1,745	288,259	+ 799	288,259	+2,517

[a] Each hypothetical change is calculated on the assumption that the several components of income changed by the same percentages as they actually did during the 1953–54 contraction (column 2), but that the actual 1953 income of $288,259,000,000 was distributed as in 1929, 1948, and 1957 (columns 4, 6, and 8). The sources of the data and the percentage distributions for the various years are given in Table 39.

and 1957 was much smaller than in 1913 or 1929. That of nonfarm proprietors diminished substantially between 1913 and 1929, but was comparatively stable thereafter.

How might these income shifts have affected the cyclical stability of consumption demand? First, personal income itself may have become more, or less, stable relative to national income because of them. Second, the shifts may have altered the marginal relationship between personal income and consumption expenditures. These possibilities will be discussed in turn.

As Geoffrey H. Moore emphasized in his foreword to Daniel Creamer's study of personal income,[1] the several forms of income exhibit typical differences in timing and amplitude during business contractions. Pronounced secular increases have occurred in two of the more stable components—transfer payments and government payrolls. Property income has diminished in importance, and two of its elements—interest and rent—typically also are stable. Even dividends, the third element, are rather stable during mild contractions. Finally, a substantial decline is to be noted in the share of farm income, historically an unstable type. How may one determine whether these conflicting trends have augmented or diminished the stability of personal income?

Moore's method is to calculate how much total personal income would have declined if each type of income had decreased by the same percentage that it actually did during a given contraction, but total income had been distributed differently than it actually was when the contraction began. The method is illustrated in Table 40 for the contraction of 1953-54 and with three assumed alternative income distributions.

Personal income actually rose on an annual basis during the mild contraction of 1953-54. If the assumptions underlying the estimates are accepted, the increase would have been smaller under the 1948 distribution but larger under that of 1957. The unfavorable showing of the 1948 distribution is due principally to the considerably larger share of farm income in 1948 than in 1953. The improvement under the 1957 distribution may be traced to the diminished share of farm income and the augmented importance of transfer and interest in-

[1] Creamer, *Personal Income During Business Cycles* (1956).

comes as compared with 1953. Interestingly enough, the actual increase of personal income in 1953-54 was smaller than would have occurred with the 1929 distribution, despite the lesser importance of government payrolls and of transfer payments in 1929. What happened was that property incomes fared especially well in 1953-54, and these incomes were relatively much larger in 1929 than in 1953.

Though interesting, these results cannot be accepted at face value because they rest on a faulty assumption—namely that the amplitudes of all individual components can be independent of their relative importance in personal income. They assume, in other words, that if a given component were relatively more important, and therefore changed more in absolute amount for the same percentage amplitude, no other incomes would be induced on that account to change differently in percentage terms. The flaw in this assumption is that aggregate income must decline by an amount equal to the reduction of aggregate expenditure, so that it is not free to change by just any sum of independently determined component changes.[2] Thus, if a change in the distribution of personal income by type is to stabilize the total from the income side, it must do so by diminishing the change of personal income for a given change of gross national product.

This is not to say that the implications of Table 40 are entirely spurious. In the first place, several of the components can change at a given level of gross national product without directly affecting any of the others. An autonomous increase of government payrolls will itself increase gross national product and personal income by the same amount, so that it does not force a compensating adjustment elsewhere. Government transfers and government interest merely redistribute a portion of gross national income and do not impose any reduction on before-tax production incomes. But this was already known—evidently the subject of automatic stabilizers merely has been approached in a different way from that in Chapter 9.

One new question is implicit in the present approach, however. Will changes in the relative importance of the various forms of personal

[2] Notice that I am abstracting temporarily from the possibility that income redistribution may alter the response of consumption expenditure to a given change of income. This is certainly a legitimate procedure, since Moore deals neither with the relation of consumption to personal income nor of the latter to GNP, and since his calculations can reveal nothing about such relationships.

income earned in private production affect the relationship of total personal income to gross national income? Given the 1953-54 decline of gross national product, would personal income really have increased more under the 1929 distribution than it actually did and despite the lesser importance of transfers and government payrolls, as Table 40 suggests? Probably not. Rather, a reasonable assumption appears to be that property incomes would actually have changed by the 1953-54 percentages even if they were proportionately as large to begin with as in 1929.[3] Suppose, also, for the sake of argument, that private wages and salaries would have decreased by the same percentage even though smaller at the onset of contraction—certainly a more questionable assumption. Assume finally, the same 1953-54 dollar changes as actually occurred in depreciation allowances, indirect business taxes, and corporate taxes and saving, so that personal production income could not change more or less for the given change of gross national income on their account—which means that it could not do so at all.[4] All this leaves two shares of national and personal income still unaccounted for—the incomes of farm and nonfarm proprietors. But these are profit incomes, calculated as the residual between sales receipts and all other costs of production, and they therefore could not remain unaffected in percentage amplitude under the stipulated conditions. On the contrary, their amplitudes would adjust so that private personal income from production would change by the same amount as it actually did under the 1953 distribution.[5]

[3] Private interest payments and rents are fairly rigid for short periods. Dividends depend partly on their own past level and not just on current profits. Hence all three components of property income might well change by the same percentages during a brief contraction, no matter what their initial size.

[4] The assumption that corporate taxes and saving would remain unaltered under the changed conditions is both unrealistic—corporate profits are no less a residual than are proprietors' incomes—and logically inconsistent—if before-tax profits and tax rates are unchanged, larger dividends mean less saving. It is necessary to make the assumption, nevertheless, in order to isolate the effect of the distribution of private personal production income on its own stability, as contrasted with the effect of the distribution of gross national income on the stability of private personal production income. However, if the same estimating technique were used to analyze the latter effect, the same objection would apply; namely, that the several income shares are not independent.

[5] Notice, however, that one response to the actual secular decline of farm

Once again, then, I may conclude that the increased importance of government payrolls, government interest, and government transfers has damped the response of personal income for a unit decrease of aggregate demand. The first is because an autonomous increase of government payrolls offsets part of the decrease of aggregate demand and makes gross national product and personal production income fall less than otherwise; and the others, because they add to the income payments received by some individuals without altering anyone's before-tax earned income. Whether shifts in the relative importance of the various types of private personal production income have affected the marginal relationship between gross national product and personal income depends essentially on their effect on corporate profits and corporate saving, and cannot be discovered by looking at the distribution of personal income alone. In view of the finding in Chapter 9 that changes of gross business saving are about as large relative to changes in gross national product nowadays as in the 1920's, however, it appears that such effects were minor or offsetting insofar as their influence on the cyclical behavior of personal income is concerned.

So much for the relationship between the distribution of personal income and its stability relative to gross national product. What of the relationship between the distribution of personal income and the response of consumption to a change in personal income? In analyzing the influence of distributional shifts on consumer demand, the usual procedure is to assume that total income is not affected by the redistribution. Given that assumption, redistribution would alter consumption only to the extent that the spending habits of income receivers differed. A shift from spending groups with low marginal propensities to consume to those with high propensities, for example, would raise the ratio of aggregate consumption to disposable personal income—and also, be it noted, would increase the over-all marginal propensity to consume. It would tend, in other words, to raise national income for a given amount of nonconsumption expenditure, but it would also increase the multiplier response of national income to

---

income has been public assistance to farmers. To the extent that the assistance has taken the form of commodity purchases, it has made government purchases and hence gross national product and net farm income higher than it otherwise would be.

changes in such expenditure, in the direction of automatic destabilization.

Lawrence Klein has found significant differences among three groups in the marginal propensities to consume, with the propensities of farmers, businessmen, and others rising in that order.[6] Since the distribution has shifted toward labor income, the effect is to raise the ratio of consumption to disposable personal income at a given level of the latter, but also to offset part of the cyclical damping due to automatic personal income stabilizers.

The amount of the offset to the damping effect of the personal income stabilizers appears to be small, however. For one thing, the Klein-Goldberger consumption equation implies a private redistributional effect which is small relative to the influence of the enlarged share of net taxes in national income and changes in national income.[7] Second, although the divergent consumption propensities of the three occupational groups may partly reflect differences in their concentration along the income scale from poor to rich, or in the variability of their incomes, another influence is also at work. Owners of unincorporated enterprises, both farm and nonfarm, typically save in order to invest directly in their own businesses. Their household and business accounts, moreover, are merged in their own financial records and in the official statistics on personal income and saving. Hence, both their way of life and prevailing accounting procedures make for relatively large personal saving ratios. To the extent that the extra saving takes the form of direct investment, however, a change of income will induce a

[6] Klein's earlier estimates are reproduced in L. R. Klein and A. S. Goldberger, *An Econometric Model of the United States 1929-1952* (1955), pp. 51, 90.

[7] The equation yields an estimated ratio of consumption to disposable personal income of 97.2 per cent for 1950. Assuming the same level of income, but a distribution as in 1929, and all other variables unchanged, the estimated ratio becomes 95.7 per cent. Notice that a small gain of 1.5 points in the consumption ratio due to redistribution means a large decline in the personal saving ratio, and thus in the amount of investment needed to offset personal saving. The implied decline in the ratio of gross private saving (including undistributed corporate profits and depreciation allowances) to gross national income, however, is again small, since that ratio has averaged about 17 per cent in the postwar years. And, of course, the implied drop in the ratio of saving plus net taxes to gross national income is smaller still, since that ratio has averaged about one-third.

change not only of consumption expenditure, but also of investment. When account is taken of the induced investment demand, the differences among the three groups in total spending propensities—as contrasted with consumption propensities alone—will be narrowed.

Shifts in Size Distribution

Family personal income is distributed more evenly than in prewar years. The decline in the relative importance of upper-bracket incomes is especially striking, and although all other brackets shared in the redistribution, the gains were largest in the lower brackets (Table 41). One warning: these data may overstate the decline of inequality, since they omit from "income" some items which are unequally distributed and which increase personal command over goods—such as business expense accounts and capital gains—and since they do not take fully

TABLE 41. *Distribution of Family Personal Income Among Fifths, and by Top 5 Per Cent, of Consumer Units, Selected Years*[a]
(In Per Cent)

Fifths Ranked by Size of Income	1929	1935–36	1941	1947	1956	*Percentage Change, 1935–36 to 1956*
Lowest	n.a.	4.1	4.1	5.0	5.0	*22*
Second	n.a.	9.2	9.5	11.0	11.3	*23*
Third	n.a.	14.1	15.3	16.0	16.5	*17*
Fourth	n.a.	20.9	22.3	22.0	22.3	*7*
Highest	n.a.	51.7	48.8	46.0	44.9	*−13*
Total	100.0	100.0	100.0	100.0	100.0	
Top 5 per cent	30.0	26.5	24.0	20.9	n.a.	—

n.a. Not available

[a] Family personal income represents the current income received by families and unattached individuals from all sources, including wage and salary receipts (net of social insurance contributions), other labor income, proprietors' and rental income, dividends, personal interest income, and transfer payments. In addition to monetary income flows, family personal income includes certain nonmoney items such as wages in kind, the value of food and fuel produced and consumed on farms, the net imputed rental value of owner-occupied homes, and imputed interest. Sources, Selma Goldsmith *et al.*, "Size Distribution of Income Since the Mid-Thirties," *Review of Economics and Statistics* (February 1954), Tables 4 and 9; and Selma Goldsmith, "Size Distribution of Personal Income," *Survey of Current Business* (April 1958), Table 3.

into account the decline of home production and the associated shift of housewives into the labor market.[8] These conceptual omissions from income are assumed here to be relatively unimportant in their influence on aggregate consumer behavior.

Has the redistribution of income by size significantly affected the average and marginal propensities to consume? The answer depends on three factors: the amount of the redistribution, the differences in the marginal propensities to consume of the various income classes, and whether the propensities remain unaltered when the distribution shifts. The redistribution of after-tax family incomes between 1941 and 1950, as measured by the decrease in the Gini concentration ratio, was on the order of 10 per cent.[9] Estimates based upon observed consumption propensities at various family income levels in a given year indicate a maximum increase in consumption of 2 per cent for a 10 per cent decrease of inequality, and a minimum effect of little more than zero.[10] The estimated increases would probably be smaller if allowance could be made for the damping effect of the decrease of emulative consumption which would follow from the reduced disparity between upper and middle incomes. This judgment, however, rests on the unverified assumption that the competitive urge to "stay ahead of the Smiths," which would be enhanced by the diminished gap between the middle and lower groups, is weaker than the emulative motive to "keep up with the Joneses."[11] All this is distressingly problematical. But it appears safe to conclude that the redistribution

[8] Robert J. Lampman, "Recent Changes in Income Inequality Reconsidered," *American Economic Review* (June 1954), pp. 251-68.

[9] Thomas R. Atkinson, "Some Frontiers of Size-Distribution Research," *An Appraisal of the 1950 Census Income Data,* National Bureau of Economic Research Studies in Income and Wealth, Vol. 23 (1958), p. 31. Atkinson's estimate is derived from Selma Goldsmith *et al.,* "Size Distribution of Income Since the Mid-Thirties," *Review of Economics and Statistics* (February 1954), Tables 4 and 9. For a discussion of the properties of the Gini concentration ratio, see Mary Jean Bowman, "A Graphical Analysis of the Personal Income Distribution in the United States," *American Economic Review* (September 1945), pp. 607-28, reprinted in American Economic Association, *Readings in the Theory of Income Distribution* (1946), pp. 72-99.

[10] M. Bronfenbrenner, Taro Yamane, and C. H. Lee, "A Study in Redistribution and Consumption," *Review of Economics and Statistics* (May 1955), pp. 1949-59.

[11] *Ibid.*

of personal income since 1929 has had only minor effects on the cyclical stability of consumption expenditure or its share in national income.

Consumer Durables and Instability

The long-term growth in the relative importance of durable goods in total consumption expenditure has been noted. This section explores the direct consequences of this trend for the cyclical behavior of consumer demand. Before reaching a final judgment about over-all stability, however, it will be necessary in Chapter 11 to consider the effects which shifts in the composition of consumer demand may have on investment as well as on consumption, especially since stability of final consumption demands does not necessarily imply stability of derived investment demands.[12]

Does the fact that, as a class, consumer durables rank high in short-term instability (Chart 31) mean that as durables become more important cyclical swings in consumption and income will be larger? Not necessarily, for the wider swings of durables might result merely in compensating variations in other goods, leaving total consumption and saving unaffected. If the proportion of durable goods is to have an independent effect on total consumption, it must be because expenditures for durables are prone to uncompensated variations at a given level of income.

Is there anything in the nature of durable goods which makes them especially susceptible to uncompensated variations? Their very durability works in that direction, for two related reasons which hinge on the fact that it is really the services of the goods, rather than the goods themselves, which are in demand. Since existing household stocks will yield services for some time, replacement may be postponed when income falls and bunched when it recovers. The market for a given durable can be saturated in the sense that household stocks are sufficiently large to yield the services desired at the current income level.

[12] See the section on Shifts in the Composition of Output by Durability of Product in Chapter 8.

Once this saturation point is reached, demand for the durable good will not exceed replacement needs unless income grows—and it will then exceed replacement in proportion to the rate of increase, and not the level, of income. (Market saturation may be delayed if successful efforts are made to speed replacement by making existing units obsolete in the eyes of consumers.) Taken together, these factors imply that market demands for durables will fall below normal replacement needs when income declines, and will be swollen by deferred replacements and by the net additions required to increase the stock of goods if income rises enough during the next upswing to eliminate the "excess capacity" from existing household stocks.

To repeat, the factor of durability explains why these demands are especially sensitive to income change. Nevertheless, it is insufficient in itself to make consumer durables an independent cyclical force. Thus, were durable goods inexpensive, cyclical fluctuations in demand could easily be absorbed in the household's total expenditure from current income. Many items of consumer's capital are quite costly, however. This means that purchase of a major durable good usually cannot be financed from a given month's income merely by curbing other expenditures. The act of purchase will require dissaving in that month, since expenditures for nondurables and services plus the outlay for the durable will ordinarily total more than monthly income.

Again, this fact in itself need not necessarily result in independent changes in aggregate expenditure for durable goods. While it is true that in a given period some households will be dissaving to acquire a new durable, it is also true that others will be saving in anticipation of later acquisition. If aggregate income were undergoing steady secular growth, it is conceivable that the dissaving of the first group would be offset by the saving of the second, so that aggregate saving would be unaffected, and total consumption would increase functionally with income.

When the attributes of durability and costliness are joined together, however, it is probable that durables will exert a positive influence on income and cause it to fluctuate more than otherwise. This is because durability will foster bunching of expenditure and dissaving on the upswing, and a corresponding deficiency of expenditure and surplus of saving during the downswing, although neither tendency need persist throughout long cyclical phases. If income is fluctuating because of developments in the investment or government sectors, consumer durables may amplify the movement; and if not, they are a potential first cause of fluctuations, because of replacement waves, the acceleration effect, or autonomous factors.

To this point, the discussion—while establishing the partial independence of durables from income—has implied more regularity within the business cycle than is justified by the historical record. The disturbances introduced by independent variations need not always be destabilizing. Consider, for example, the postwar fluctuations in automobiles, by all odds the most important of consumer durables. The early upturn of automobile sales under the spur of unsatisfied war-deferred demands was a major factor in the recovery of 1949-50. The reaction from the forward buying of the Korean War helped relieve inflationary pressures in 1951. The automotive boom of 1955 amplified the cyclical upswing of that year, but the subsequent relapse in 1956 moved against the cycle and probably mitigated inflationary pressures. The continued softness of 1957, on the other hand, was one among several causes of the contraction that began late in the year.

The Role of Instalment Credit

Since autonomous increases of consumption expenditure must be financed from outside the current income stream, instalment credit may add to instability by facilitating such increases. This is not to argue that availability of instalment credit is a necessary condition for instability, of course, since autonomous purchases may also be financed from previously accumulated assets. To the extent that consumer credit encourages greater expenditures than would otherwise occur, however, it is an independent force in itself. That it does do so, seems to be established by its popularity, since people are willing to pay high effective interest rates in order to buy now, rather than pursue the alternative of saving each month an amount equivalent to the instalment payment (less interest) and purchasing the item when enough has been accumulated to pay for it. Perhaps the major reason for this preference is that young married persons may use credit to equip their households with durables several years earlier than if they attempted to accumulate a capital fund.

Evidently, then, in a going credit economy new credit usually finances purchases which otherwise would not be made currently. But this is only half the story.[13] The credit must be repaid in subsequent periods, and it is likely that the repayments will be partly at the expense of consumption instead of saving, since so much saving nowadays is in fixed contractual forms. If all new extensions represented additional dissaving due purely to the use of credit, and all repayments additional saving, then the net autonomous contribution of instalment credit to consumption during a given income period would be measured by the excess of extensions over repayments. It appears likely that these assumptions are more nearly correct than incorrect. The deficit or surplus of extensions over repayments is probably a good index of the direction of the autonomous contribution, although probably overstating its magnitude.[14] It leaves out of account, of course, the multiplier effects of past autonomous contributions to current income and consumption.

Consumer instalment credit has doubtless contributed to the secular increase in the relative importance of durable goods in total consumption. Credit-financed purchases are concentrated among durables, whereas repayments depress consumption generally. The net effect is to encourage durables as against nondurables and services. In a sense, then, the observation that durables have increased in relative importance, and thereby made the economy less stable, subsumes under it the proposition that consumer credit is destabilizing, since the latter is a condition for both the growth and instability of the former.

At times, credit may be more than an enabling condition, however,

[13] See the classic analysis in Gottfried Haberler, *Consumer Instalment Credit and Economic Fluctuations* (1942).

[14] There could be a net expansionary effect even if extensions equaled repayments. Assume that the proportion of extensions which represents net additional dissaving is larger than the proportion of repayments which is at the expense of consumption instead of other saving. Then new extensions would increase consumption expenditure by more than the reduction caused by an equal volume of repayments. The reader will recognize that this proposition is analogous to the application of the balanced-budget multiplier theorem to government finance.

because the terms on which credit is available will affect its use. Autonomous variations in terms may be invoked by the government as a stabilization instrument when the authority exists, as it did during the early postwar years and the Korean War. Private discretionary changes may augment or diminish the demand for durables, moreover. A substantial lengthening of the duration of instalment contracts appears to have been partly responsible for the flood of automobile sales in 1955, for example. By the same token, it helped weaken the car market in 1956 and 1957, indirectly because the stock of cars on the road spurted abnormally during 1955, and directly because the new car buyers of 1955 did not emerge from automotive debt for two or three years, and they tend to form the group which buys the new when the "old" becomes obsolete.

Another corollary of credit availability should be mentioned. If there is a monetary constraint on the expansion of total credit, as when the economy is at or near full employment, the supply of instalment credit will not be perfectly elastic at going interest rates and for going qualities (maturities, down payments, etc.). Since consumers must then bid credit away from other uses, the expansionary effect on consumption demand will be wholly or partly offset by a reduction of investment or government spending. This would be beneficial to over-all stability during inflationary periods, leaving questions of resource allocation aside. The analogous proposition for an economy without instalment credit would be that household dissaving to finance current consumption reduces the flow of net personal saving which is available to finance current investment.

Postwar Behavior of Instalment Credit

The volume of newly extended instalment credit exceeded the flow of repayments in each postwar year until 1958. But the margin of excess, and with it the absolute and percentage additions to the stock of credit, fluctuated considerably from year to year (Table 42). Certain regularities stand out despite these annual variations, however.

First, the volume of net credit extensions (gross extensions *minus* repayments, column 3) tends to rise and fall cyclically, serving to

TABLE 42. *Relation of Consumer Instalment Credit to Disposable Personal Income, 1945-58*[a]

	Instalment Credit (Billions of dollars)					*Ratio of Instalment Credit to Disposable Income (Per cent)*				*Annual Increase of Outstanding Credit (Per cent)*
	Extended (1)	Repaid (2)	Net Increase (3)	Outstanding (4)	Disposable Personal Income (5)	*Extended (6)*	*Repaid (7)*	*Net Increase (8)*	*Outstanding (9)*	*(10)*
1945....	n.a.	n.a.	n.a.	2.5	150.4	*n.a.*	*n.a.*	*n.a.*	*1.6*	*n.a.*
1946....	8.5	6.8	1.7	4.2	160.6	*5.3*	*4.2*	*1.1*	*2.6*	*68.0*
1947....	12.7	10.2	2.5	6.7	170.1	*7.5*	*6.0*	*1.5*	*3.9*	*59.5*
1948....	15.6	13.3	2.3	9.0	189.3	*8.2*	*7.0*	*1.2*	*4.7*	*34.3*
1949....	18.1	15.5	2.6	11.6	189.7	*9.5*	*8.2*	*1.4*	*6.1*	*28.9*
1950....	21.6	18.4	3.2	14.7	207.7	*10.4*	*8.9*	*1.5*	*7.1*	*26.7*
1951....	23.6	23.0	0.6	15.3	227.5	*10.4*	*10.1*	*0.3*	*6.7*	*4.1*
1952....	29.5	25.4	4.1	19.4	238.7	*12.4*	*10.6*	*1.7*	*8.1*	*26.8*
1953....	31.6	28.0	3.6	23.0	252.5	*12.5*	*11.1*	*1.4*	*9.1*	*18.6*
1954....	31.0	30.5	0.6	23.6	256.9	*12.1*	*11.9*	*0.2*	*9.2*	*2.6*
1955....	39.0	33.6	5.4	29.0	274.4	*14.2*	*12.2*	*2.0*	*10.6*	*22.9*
1956....	40.1	37.2	2.9	31.8	292.9	*13.7*	*12.7*	*1.0*	*10.9*	*9.6*
1957....	42.4	40.2	2.3	34.1	308.8	*13.7*	*13.0*	*0.7*	*11.0*	*7.2*
1958....	40.5	40.7	−0.2	33.9	317.9	*12.8*	*12.9*	*−0.1*	*10.7*	*− 0.6*

n.a. Not available.

[a] Sources, *Federal Reserve Bulletin* (June 1959), pp. 630 and 632; *Economic Report of the President* (January 1959), Tables D-44 and 45; and *U. S. Income and Output*, a supplement to *Survey of Current Business* (November 1958), Table II-1, and *Survey of Current Business* (July 1960), Table 4.

augment short-term instability. Yet there are numerous exceptions to exact cyclical conformity. Thus, although net extensions declined during the contractions of 1953-54 and 1957-58, they rose in 1948-49 under the spur of deferred automobile demand and with beneficial results for economic stability. Again, the declines in 1951 and 1956-57 helped relieve inflationary pressures, although in the latter instance not without contributing to the eventual downturn.

Second, the ratio of repayments to disposable personal income rose steadily until 1957 and declined only slightly in 1958 (column 7). It is true, of course, that repayments were exceptionally low after World War II, so that much of the rise in the repayment ratio represents a return to prewar behavior. The 1939 ratio, which was 8.6 per cent, was not exceeded until 1950. But what of the subsequent pronounced increase? Does it mean that consumers are becoming increasingly burdened with fixed obligations and will eventually be forced to reduce the percentage of income which they devote to current purchases of goods and services, perhaps touching off a serious depression?

This is a possible result, but by no means a necessary one. For one thing, the repayment ratio may not continue to rise. Although importantly affected by credit terms and the proportion of expenditure which is financed on credit, repayments are basically a function of the volume of durable goods sold in the preceding two or three years. The share of durable goods in disposable income averaged almost the same during 1955-58 as in the business cycle of 1950-54. Contract durations on new car loans have lengthened substantially since the 1920's, but they may not go much further because each increase of duration prolongs the interval during which the depreciated value of the automobile declines more rapidly than the lender's equity, exposing him to greater risk.

Should the repayment burden continue to grow, moreover, its deflationary influence could be offset or more than offset by a concomitant rise of new extensions. Extensions exceeded repayments even during the recession years 1949 and 1954, and were only fractionally below them in 1958. Consumer credit probably made a positive net contribution to effective demand during 1949 and 1954 and was probably about neutral in 1958.

The question remains, however, whether extensions will continue to exceed repayments indefinitely, since each year in which net extensions are positive adds to the stock of debt and to the flow of future repayments (unless more than offset by changes in credit terms). Alain Enthoven has shown that this question of debt burden and its effects cannot be settled by comparison of the percentage increases of instalment credit and aggregate personal income over short periods.[15]

His reasons are as follows. Assume that net extensions are a constant percentage of income each year, and that the initial position of the economy is one in which outstanding debt is small. Then if income grows at a constant percentage rate, the absolute increments to debt will get larger in each successive year. The percentage increments will become progressively smaller, however, since the larger absolute increments of the later years will be smaller percentages of

[15] "The Growth of Instalment Credit and the Future of Prosperity," *American Economic Review* (December 1957), pp. 913-29.

the growing stock of debt. The ratio of debt to income will increase over time, but at a diminishing rate as the annual percentage increase of debt approaches the growth rate of income.

These assumptions correspond fairly well to postwar reality, if cyclical fluctuations in income and credit are ignored. Thus, net credit extensions averaged 1.3 per cent of disposable personal income during 1946-49, 1 per cent in 1950-54, and 0.9 per cent in 1955-58. The corresponding average annual absolute increments of debt were respectively $2.3 billion, $2.4 billion, and $2.6 billion. The debt outstanding at the end of 1945 was only $2.5 billion, moreover, so that the early debt increments were large in percentage terms. Over the years, however, the annual percentage increment declined irregularly, and with it, the rate of increase of the ratio of outstanding debt to income (Table 42, columns 9 and 10).

Enthoven is on firm theoretical ground in his demonstration that a rising ratio of debt to income is compatible with a constant ratio of net extensions to income and with convergence to a stable equilibrium between the growth rates of debt and income. Notice, however, that the actual ratio of repayments to income rose threefold between 1946 and 1957. This is important because the same ratio of net extensions to income, and hence the same secular behavior of debt and the debt-income ratio, is consistent with either a constant or a rising ratio of repayments (and extensions) to income, and yet it is the repayments ratio which best measures the burden of instalment debt on consumption demand.

It should be emphasized that Enthoven does not argue that the postwar rise of the debt-income ratio was unalarming despite the rise of the repayments ratio. Instead, he bases his empirical conclusions on a model which assumes a constant repayments ratio, and does not raise the question of the causes and implications of the actual postwar rise of the latter.

His basic premise is that the ratio of gross extensions to income is independent of the outstanding debt or debt-income ratio. He rightly rejects the implicit assumption of many economists that a rising ratio of aggregate debt to aggregate income is indicative of a rising ratio of debt to income in most households. Instead, he argues convincingly that the use of instalment credit varies with the life cycle of families.

Borrowing is concentrated in the first years of marriage, and is relatively unimportant in later years. Assume for simplicity that all new borrowing in a given year is done by couples in their first year of marriage. Suppose also that the number of married couples increases at the same rate as total population, that the distribution of income with respect to age is stationary, and that the ratio of borrowing to income of the newly married couples is constant. Then gross credit extensions to the new borrowers will be a constant proportion of aggregate income,[16] and the repayments of old borrowers will also be a constant proportion of aggregate income under conditions of steady growth. The new borrowers have no outstanding debt to deter them, and the old ones are completely deterred, yet net extensions can continue to increase indefinitely in proportion to aggregate income, and if the initial position was one of little outstanding debt, the aggregate debt-income ratio can rise indefinitely toward its ultimate stable equilibrium.

It is this model which Enthoven believes fits postwar experience sufficiently well to serve as a basis for conclusions about the 1957 burden of consumer debt. However, the model is a poor fit in one vital respect: the striking uptrend in the ratio of gross extensions to income, and hence—with a lag and allowing for changes in credit terms—in the ratio of repayments to income. Now, this is not necessarily damaging to Enthoven's main point. For instance, the rise in the ratio of extensions to income could be caused by a more rapid increase of new borrowers than aggregate income. Enthoven rejects this as an important factor during 1946-56, since the number of married couples grew little faster than the total population over the decade.[17] Perhaps this was overhasty.

During the first few postwar years practically all borrowers were new borrowers, in the relevant sense that few of them were making instalment payments on outstanding loans at war's end. Not only that—a considerable, though in the aggregate a progressively diminishing,

[16] It is at this point that Enthoven's basic premise is given the specific—and for the present period, at least, the empirically incorrect—form that gross extensions are not only independent of outstanding debt but are also a constant proportion of income.

[17] *Ibid.*, p. 916.

fraction of durable goods expenditure was probably financed from household liquid balances during the early years. Finally, the growth of households and married couples was twice as rapid as that of population in those early years. Thus, the rapid rise in the ratio of gross extensions to income between, say, 1946 and 1950 may primarily reflect an increasing ratio of new borrowers and not much change in individual debt-income ratios. Like the 1939 repayment ratio, the prewar ratios of aggregate extensions and debt to disposable personal income were not surpassed until 1950.

It is not implausible, moreover, that individual debt limits have risen during the 1950's. Since per capita disposable income is much above prewar levels, it is reasonable to suppose that a higher portion of income can now be devoted to purchases of consumer durables, and to instalment payments on them, simply because food and other necessities require a smaller fraction of the consumer's dollar. A lower repayment ratio is now consistent with any given ratio of debt to income, furthermore, since instalment contract durations have lengthened considerably since the 1920's—and even since 1954.

In summary, the postwar rise of the aggregate repayment ratio may well have reflected both a return to the prewar proportion of borrowers in the population and an increase in tolerable debt-income limits for individual spending units. If so, the uptrend of the repayment ratio, and a fortiori of the debt-income ratio, has not yet posed a serious threat to stability. More relevant to the future is the further course of repayments relative to income. As long as new borrowers increase as rapidly as total population, a constant ratio of gross extensions (and repayments) to income is compatible with stability, notwithstanding the attendant growth of outstanding debt if net extensions are positive. A rising ratio of gross extensions (and repayments) would also be unalarming if it were caused by a growth of new borrowers relative to population, or by an increase in tolerable debt-income ratios.

Comparison With the Prewar Economy

Granted that consumer durables introduce an element of instability which is roughly proportional to their relative importance, the question remains whether the economy is substantially more vulnerable to disturbances from this source than in prewar days. In my judgment, the answer is no. In the first place, although the proportion of consumer durables in consumption has risen appreciably since the 1920's, the increase relative to gross national product has been much smaller, owing to the fact that total consumption has declined relative to national product. Thus, even if consumer durables are fully as autonomous with respect to income as private investment or government expenditure, the proportion of autonomous demand in national product has not risen much on their account (Tables 27 and 35).

Second, with regard to short-term instability in the absence of severe contraction, the fluctuations of consumer durables during the 1920's were on the same order as those since World War II, so there probably has been no increase in inherent instability within durables themselves.[18]

Third, when it comes to major fluctuations, the severity of the contraction of 1929-33 can scarcely be attributed to the growth of consumer durables before and after World War I. Depressions of comparable magnitude occurred long before consumer durables increased in importance. Moreover, as Haberler showed, "The cyclical importance of instalment credit during the period 1929-1940, while not negligible, was not very great: instalment credit tended to accentuate the cycle but cannot well be regarded as a major factor in the cyclical fluctuations of general economic activity in these years."[19] This conclusion rested on a comparison of annual net changes of instalment credit (excess of extensions over repayments) with annual figures on national income, consumer expenditure, government deficit or surplus, and the like. Since the accelerated growth of consumer durables after World War I was bound up with the growth of instalment credit, any additional instability resulting from the augmented importance of durable goods, would be largely reflected in the credit element, and if this was comparatively unimportant, so also was the added instability.

[18] Table 34 showed that for the period 1947-58, consumer durables had an average annual fluctuation of 9.8 per cent, an average growth rate of 5.7 per cent, and an index of instability of growth of 6.2 per cent. The comparable figures for 1919-29, based on Kuznets' data, are 9.9, 5.3, and 4.7 per cent.

[19] *Op. cit.*, p. 149.

Active Role of Consumer Spending in Postwar Fluctuations

Keynes argued that real consumption demand was an essentially stable function of real national income.[20] He recognized that consumption expenditure is influenced by other factors than income—indeed, his pioneering discussion of them was remarkably complete in view of what has been written on the subject since then. But he thought that most of the factors were unlikely to be important in ordinary circumstances, apart from occasional large-scale capital gains or substantial changes of interest rates or government fiscal policies. It followed that fluctuations of national income are caused primarily by fluctuations of investment demand, with consumption demand adapting passively to prior income changes and amplifying, but not initiating, the movements of income.

Has postwar experience proven Keynes to be right or wrong? Let us enquire briefly into the recent history of consumer spending before reaching a judgment on this question.

The top panel in the upper section of Chart 34 shows the quarterly changes of real disposable personal income from 1947 through 1958. Thus disposable income in 1954 dollars fell from $202.3 billion in the first quarter of 1947 to $197.1 billion in the second, and the decline of $5.2 billion is plotted below the zero line and in the second quarter of the year. Similarly, an entry above the zero line indicates that disposable income increased by the indicated amount from the preceding quarter.

With the help of the vertical lines on the chart dividing the period into business expansions and contractions, it will be observed that income generally rose during expansions and leveled off or declined during contractions. The quarterly changes of income were decidedly irregular in amplitude, however. If consumption expenditure in a given quarter were a stable function of income in that quarter and of nothing

[20] John Maynard Keynes, *The General Theory of Employment, Interest, and Money* (1936), Book III.

CHART 34. *Quarterly Changes in Real Income and Consumption and in Consumption-Income Ratios, Seasonally Adjusted Annual Rates, 1947-58*

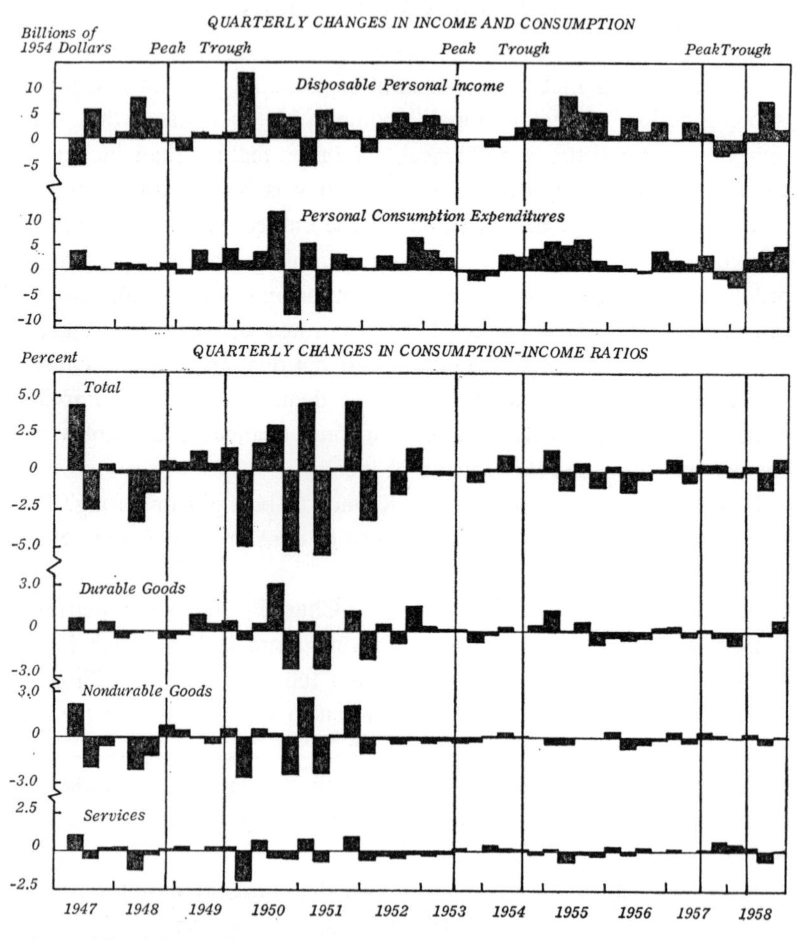

Source: Office of Business Economics, Department of Commerce.

else, the quarterly changes of consumption would also be decidedly irregular.

A glance at the second panel in that section of the chart reveals that the quarterly consumption changes were uneven, but that the irregularities do not correspond closely to those of income. It is true that with few exceptions consumption increased whenever income did. Consumption often increased when income decreased, however. More important, the amplitudes of the changes of consumption often differed markedly from those of income even when the two moved in the same direction.

These differences in relative amplitude emerge forcibly when consumption and income are compared in the lower section of the chart, which shows the quarter-to-quarter changes in the average consumption ratio. That is, if consumption was 93 per cent of income in one quarter and 95 in the next, the quarterly increase of 2 percentage points is plotted in the second quarter. Thus, a positive entry means that consumption rose relative to income during the quarter, and a negative one, that it fell relatively. As an empirical matter, fluctuations of the consumption ratio are usually evidence of autonomous changes of consumption relative to current income.[21]

One point must be clarified before going on to a detailed inspection of the fluctuations of the consumption ratio. Some part of current consumption expenditure may be autonomous with regard to current income and yet induced with respect to previous income. If lagged responses to income change were the only source of variation in the current consumption ratio, little could be learned from an examination of the current ratios. That is not the case, however. Lagged responses would produce a smooth and regular pattern of change in the current ratios instead of the frequent and erratic variations actually observed.[22] Many of the observed variations, moreover, can be related

[21] The average ratio of consumption to income would change even with a constant marginal ratio if the consumption function were linear but had a positive intercept. The average ratio would also change if the consumption function were curvilinear and concave downward. In either event, however, the pattern of change would be more regular than the one observed, since the average ratio would fall continuously as income rose and rise continuously as income fell. When income is rising, moreover, an increase in the observed average ratio usually means that the absolute increase of consumption was greater than that of income (compare the three top panels of the chart). With the average ratio in the neighborhood of .92 to .95 most of the time, a quarter-to-quarter marginal ratio greater than the average ratio, and hence capable of raising the latter, will itself usually be greater than one. And, of course, if consumption rises when income falls, the autonomous nature of the change relative to current income is even clearer.

[22] Support of this conclusion may be found in a recent statistical investigation in which the ratio of this quarter's consumption to last quarter's income depended on the ratio of last quarter's income to previous peak income and on the ratio of last quarter's consumption to the income of the preceding

to particular events and connected plausibly and convincingly with particular causes, as was done in the historical chapters of Part II.

Perhaps the most striking feature of the chart is the greater variability of the consumption ratio before than after 1953. The earlier variations were the result of disturbances created by war or its aftermath. As I wrote in 1954, these episodes in no way demonstrated that peacetime business cycles are regularly affected by independent fluctuations of consumer spending.[23] On the surface, the smaller fluctuations of the post-Korea years appear to confirm my caution, and it is certainly true that they represent significantly smaller disturbances than in wartime. However it should not be overlooked that a "small" change of one point in the percentage of income consumed means an absolute change of consumption of about $3 billion at current levels of disposable income.[24] Thus, the comparatively mild independent shifts of consumer demand during and after 1953 substantially affected aggregate activity at several junctures (Chapters 6 and 7).

The lower section of Chart 34 not only shows changes in the total consumption ratio, but also shows separately the changes in the ratios to income of durables, nondurables, and services, which make up the total. Interestingly enough, although it is frequently assumed that independent variations of consumer demand occur principally among durable goods, the Chart indicates considerable variability in the other classes of consumption expenditure. Notice that even services fluctuate considerably relative to income. This does not mean that the demand for services is itself unsteady. To the contrary, it is income which is unsteady. That is, the ratio of service expenditure to income usually rises when income retards or falls, and usually falls when income accelerates or rises (compare the top and bottom

---

quarter. The standard error of estimate was about 1.7 per cent of income, so that random variation could produce a change of consumption of about $5 billion at recent income levels and without any change of income. James S. Duesenberry, Otto Eckstein, and Gary Fromm, *Stability and Instability in the American Economy,* Harvard University (Multilithed, 1958), p. 12.

[23] *The Korean War and United States Economic Activity, 1950-52,* National Bureau of Economic Research, Occasional Paper 49 (1955), p. 61.

[24] It would require a change of 3.5 per cent in government expenditure or one of 4.5 per cent in private investment (1957 levels) to produce a $3 billion change of expenditure.

panels). The demand for services, then, is relatively immune to current fluctuations of income and rises steadily over time—presumably because services cannot be stockpiled by consumers during prosperous periods and also because of the inertia involved in shifting one's residence when income improves or deteriorates.

Unfortunately, the very steadiness of service demands can be destabilizing during contractions. If consumers wish to decrease total expenditure because income has declined or because they wish to consume less relative to income, the brunt of the reduction will be borne by goods instead of services. But this means that production will fall further than if all categories of consumer expenditure were cut proportionally, since business inventories are held primarily in connection with goods, and reduced demands for goods will induce amplifying declines of inventory investment. A shift of this sort against goods occurred in the last few months of 1953 and accounted for a large part of the decline of production at that time. A similar shift, largely against durable goods, was repeated with similar results during the 1957-58 contraction.

It was emphasized earlier that instability of demand for durable goods relative to income would be comparatively unimportant if compensating variations usually occurred among other consumer demands. Total consumption would still be fully determined by income, and only its components would vary independently.[25] Such neat offsetting is unlikely to occur during short periods in individual households because of the costly nature of many durable goods. And in a fluctuating economy it would be surprising indeed if current dissaving for durables by some households were consistently offset by saving for durables in others. Nor should the possibility that nondurables may also fluctuate independently of income be neglected. Still, offsetting movements could certainly arise now and then, and partial compensation is likely to be the rule even in individual households.

The first thing observed in examining the postwar record is that nondurables were considerably more variable in relation to income

[25] However, shifts in the composition of consumption expenditure could affect aggregate inventory investment because of industrial differences in product characteristics, inventory-sales ratios, market structures, and other determinants of inventory demands. Exactly the same possibility arises in connection with fixed investment, to be discussed in Chapter 11.

than were durables during 1947-48. Consumption itself grew steadily after mid-1947, so that the wide fluctuations in the consumption ratio reflect the uneven rate of increase of disposable income. What happened was that expenditures for nondurables leveled off while durables continued to rise along with income. Pent-up demands had been satisfied for nondurables but still persisted for durables. Notice particularly the abrupt decline of the consumption ratio when disposable income spurted during the second and third quarters of 1948. The income spurt was largely caused by a cut in personal income taxes, but consumers failed to respond by increasing consumption and were especially uninterested in nondurables. As explained in Chapter 4, because of its adverse effects on inventory demand and on sales of individual products, the soft market for nondurables was one of the precipitating factors in the downturn of 1948. Hence, a downshift of the consumption function in the face of accelerated income growth caused a retardation of consumer expenditure which was confined primarily to nondurables and reacted adversely on inventory demand.

Along with residential construction and government expenditure, consumer demand was one of the principal autonomous factors in the recovery from the 1948-49 contraction. Indeed, the consumption ratio rose continuously throughout the contraction. During the last quarter of 1948 and the first of 1949, the rise was in nondurables and services as durables fell absolutely and relative to income, in good part because of restrictive instalment credit regulations. Thereafter, it was durables which rose strongly relative to income, with partial offsetting from nondurables during one quarter. Thus, the upshift of the consumption function occurred first in nondurables and services and later in durables and services, with incomplete compensation against the dominant category of goods during several of the quarters.

The Korean period was the most unstable of all,[26] and nondurables

[26] There was a substantial decline of the consumption ratio in the first quarter of 1950, or several months before the war began. It was due to a once-for-all flood of transfer payments (the dividend to veterans on National Service Life Insurance) which caused the largest quarterly increment of disposable personal income in the entire period. Apparently this windfall was not spent immediately, although some part of the expenditures of subsequent quarters is doubtless attributable to it.

were, if anything, less stable than durables until early 1952.[27] From the start of the Korean War in mid-1950 to early 1952, the fluctuations in the ratios for durables and nondurables were in the same direction in every quarter, but now the one and then the other was the larger. Through most of the period, these reinforcing movements represent common reactions to the same expectational stimuli (Chapter 5). Their differential magnitudes reflect the fact that consumers concentrated on durables during the first Korean buying wave but switched to potentially scarce nondurables during the second one. Interestingly enough, however, the downshifts in both categories were about equal after each buying wave. This suggests that the size of each reaction of total consumption was governed more by the amount of the preceding consumption upshift than by its composition.

Nondurables became a largely stable element of consumption demand during the last year or so of the Korean expansion, but this was not true of durables, primarily because of the steel strike in the summer of 1952. Disposable income increased at a fairly steady absolute rate, but the consumption ratio fell sharply in the third quarter of 1952 and rebounded in the fourth because of fluctuations in automobile production and purchases. After that, durables rose only slightly relative to income and nondurables continued to decline relatively. In combination, these developments caused a sharp retardation in the rate of increase of aggregate consumption expenditure which was felt by a broad range of industries and which was one of the causes of the downturn of mid-1953. The major reason for the expenditure retardation was that with income rising at a relatively steady rate, the increase in expenditure associated with the upward shift of the consumption function in late 1952 was much greater than the increase associated with the movement along the stable function of the first half of 1953.

[27] That is, they were less stable relative to income, which is the important consideration. Expenditures on nondurables are ordinarily three to four times as large as those on durables, so that an equal absolute change in either category, and hence an equal change of either relative to income, means a smaller percentage fluctuation in nondurables than in durables. The parallel to my earlier observation about the relative amplitudes of investment and consumption required to produce a given absolute change of expenditure will be obvious.

The prominent role played by "small" fluctuations of the consumption ratio during the contraction of 1953-54 was stressed at length in Chapter 6. It is necessary to repeat at this point only that nondurables as well as durables participated in the consumption downshift of the latter months of 1953 and the subsequent upshift during the first half of 1954, and that, indeed, nondurables led both movements, with considerable offsetting from durables during the third quarter of 1953 and the first quarter of 1954.

A striking saw-tooth pattern with frequent quarterly reversals characterizes the aggregate consumption ratio during the expansion of 1954-57. The separate patterns for durables and nondurables are considerably smoother, however, and so is the contour of absolute consumption increments, so that the uneven pace of income increase is responsible for much of the quarter-to-quarter variability of the consumption ratio.

Concentrating on the systematic tendencies, we observe that with the exception of a single quarter of rapid income advance, expenditures for durables increased more rapidly than income during the first year of the expansion. This autonomous upsurge was the result primarily of the favorable reception accorded the 1955 automobile models and was assisted by easy credit. Expenditures on nondurables decreased as a percentage of income during the first half of 1955, partly offsetting the upsurge of durables during the first quarter and more than compensating for it in the second.

Automobile demand ebbed with the introduction of the new models in the fourth quarter of 1955, and (until the last quarter of 1956) sales of durable goods declined relative to income. At first, nondurables were neutral or offsetting, but they too, sagged during the spring and summer of 1956. Thus there was a substantial progressive retardation of absolute consumption expenditure and a corresponding, though less regular, downshift of the aggregate consumption ratio from the fourth quarter of 1955 through the third of 1956. Meanwhile, demand increases occurred elsewhere and especially in business fixed investment, offsetting the deflationary influence of weak consumption demand.

New automobile models were introduced once again in the fourth quarter of 1956, and once again durable goods sales moved ahead more rapidly than income and were incompletely offset by relative reductions among nondurables. The increase in the consumption ratio understates the expansionary stimulus of the new models, incidentally, since the increased production undertaken in anticipation of automobile sales provided an important part of the sizable increase of disposable income during the fall of 1956 and itself helped induce the expansion of automobile sales.

Consumer demand slackened generally during the second quarter of 1957 because expenditures on goods failed to keep pace with income, but a closing spurt of retail sales climaxed the business expansion during the third quarter. The spurt was largest in nondurables, but automobiles also moved ahead after having fallen in the preceding period. These increases were insufficient to counteract decreases in other demands and prevent a business downturn, but it is apparent that consumption demand was not an active deflationary factor in the downturn (Chapter 7), and this for the first time in ten years.

Consumption continued to play a passive role in the contraction and recovery during 1957-58, and again for the first time in the postwar era. During the contraction itself, consumption declined $4.4 billion in real terms (1954 prices), but the decline was induced by a $5.1 billion drop in real disposable income. Nor did consumption increase autonomously on the recovery. Except for a slight edge in the second quarter, which was more than wiped out in the third, consumption increased less rapidly than income until the final quarter of 1958, when the new expansion had already been underway for several months.

To recapitulate, autonomous variations of consumer demand significantly affected the course of aggregate economic activity during 1947-57. They helped precipitate the downturns of 1948 and 1953 by retarding the growth of consumption—in the first instance, because consumption failed to respond to a tax-induced increase of disposable income; in the second, because a prior upshift of the consumption function had fostered an unsustainable rate of increase of durable goods expenditure and because nondurables were losing relative to income. Autonomous upshifts of consumer demand made important contributions to the recoveries of 1949 and 1954, although in the latter case, not without first having aggravated the initial phase of contraction. Finally, the contours of the long expansions of 1949-53 and 1954-57 were modified at several points by autonomous variations of consumption expenditure, which did not, however, cause corresponding cyclical movements of national income. Consumer demand was, however, a largely passive influence in the contraction and recovery of 1957-58.

Whether postwar experience has proved Keynes to be right or wrong in his proposition that consumption demand is an essentially stable function of national income depends on one's criteria with respect to three factors. First, what is to be included in the concept of consumption demand? It is often suggested that the acquisition of a consumer durable good is really an investment decision, and that only the imputed value of the services of durables should be included in current consumption. As we have seen, under peacetime conditions current expenditures for durable goods are somewhat more variable in relation to income than are expenditures for nondurables and services.[28] Elimination of durable goods purchases would therefore improve the stability of the income-consumption relationship.[29]

The improvement would be smaller than is commonly implied, however. Nondurables can and do fluctuate substantially relative to income. As a class, their intrinsic variability is smaller than that of durables, but they are so much more important in total consumption expenditure that their absolute fluctuations can easily attain the size of those of durables. Nor are their fluctuations always in a direction to counteract durables: though sometimes offsetting, they are often reinforcing. Recall also that nondurables contributed as much or more than durables to fluctuations of the consumption-income ratio during 1947-52 when normal relationships were admittedly disturbed.

[28] The data for services include some imputed items, but purchased services are also stable.

[29] Incidentally, the same logic would indicate that many items currently classified as nondurables, because normally scrapped within three years or less of use, should be included in investment when purchased and represented in quarterly or annual consumption estimates only by their current use value. The major items affected would be household textiles, clothing, and footwear. In quarterly data, even storable "perishables" may be affected on occasion, as when hoarding of food occurs because of a war scare.

The next question to arise is this: How rigid must a relationship between two economic variables be before it can be called stable? Keynes' proposition was after all a question of degree. He did not argue that consumption was determined exclusively by income, but only that other determinants were comparatively unimportant; and conversely, that current income was relatively much less important as a determinant of investment demand. In my opinion, postwar experience has demonstrated that within the context of business fluctuations as mild as those actually experienced, independent variations of consumer expenditure can substantially influence the level of income and employment and are not sufficiently different from investment or government demands in that respect to be neglected in short-term analysis or forecasting.

Keynes, however, was writing during the 1930's and had in mind income changes on the order of those experienced during severe contractions or over the entire course of major upswings. Under such conditions, the sort of mild independent fluctuations of consumer demand considered in this chapter would be swamped by the influence of income change on consumption expenditure.

These remarks still leave unresolved one important question. To what extent were the postwar business contractions mild because of autonomous consumption increases? Such increases were certainly significant in 1949 and 1954, though not in 1958. Their major bearing on the present issue is this: perhaps Keynes overemphasized not so much the dependence of consumption on income as the independence of investment from income.[30] In other words, to the extent that autonomous increases of consumption demand inhibit the fall of national income, they diminish induced declines of investment and may prevent disposable income from falling enough actually to swamp the autonomous changes in consumption. The same result, of course, could be accomplished by income-autonomous increases of other categories of demand.

The final point is this: Thus far I have dealt with the relation of consumption to disposable personal income and neglected the relation

[30] The major step taken in the neo-Keynesian cycle models was to make investment a function of income change or of the relation of capital stock to income.

of the latter to national income. Now it is upon disposable personal income that consumers base their spending decisions, but as Keynes emphasized, the share of disposable personal income in national income depends on government fiscal policies and on business practices with regard to retained earnings and depreciation allowances. Two propositions follow from this observation:

1) The response of consumption demand to a given change of national income will be altered if tax relationships or business practices are altered.

2) Discretionary changes in tax rates or transfer incomes may be used to affect current consumption demand by altering disposable personal income at any given level of national income.

Chapter 9 showed that, on the average, consumption has increased less per dollar increase of national income in recent years than in the 1920's, and that this has been due more to the increased importance of taxes and transfers than to a change in the response of consumption to disposable personal income. This finding is in itself perhaps sufficient justification of Keynes' emphasis on disposable income as the basic determinant of consumption. It is noteworthy also that wage cuts or reductions of government spending are no longer widely advocated to combat recessions, because it is recognized that they would depress income and consumption, and that the most widely advocated discretionary fiscal action during the 1957-58 recession was a cut in personal income taxes to stimulate consumption demand.

11 / *Growth Industries and Investment Demand*

THE RELATIONSHIP between the changing fortunes of individual industries and cyclical fluctuations in aggregate activity is examined in this Chapter. Since the influence of the diversity of industrial experience on the behavior of aggregate investment is of principal interest in this connection, I begin with some general considerations about the determinants of investment decisions.

Creation and Exploitation of Investment Opportunities

In the most general terms, an investment will be undertaken whenever the expected rate of return over the productive life of the asset at least equals the cost of the funds to be invested.[1] This bald formulation emphasizes several key facts about investment decisions. First, an investment opportunity must exist—that is, there must be some reason why a new asset might be expected to yield a positive return on its contribution to production. Second, since the profits will be earned in the future and cannot be known with certainty, it is the expected return after discount for uncertainty which counts. Third, given the opportunity and its expected return, the investment will be made only if investment funds are available on sufficiently favorable terms.

[1] John Maynard Keynes, *The General Theory of Employment, Interest, and Money* (1936), Chap. 11.

It is useful to distinguish several ways in which investment opportunities are created: replacement requirements; demand for additional capacity induced by income growth; opportunities arising because a new composition of output becomes appropriate owing to changing tastes or new products; alterations in the composition of the capital stock made profitable by changes in technology or relative factor prices; and new opportunities in the field of housing stemming chiefly from population growth and migration.[2]

A crucial point is that investment opportunities may be created by factors which are to an important degree autonomous with respect to the level or rate of change of national income, though this is not to deny that business cycles also affect the stock of opportunities. Population growth and the development of innovational opportunities may be augmented or diminished by cyclical expansion or contraction, and cyclical changes in the supply prices of capital goods affect investment yields. And, of course, the stock of opportunities may be diminished if the rate of exploitation exceeds the rate of creation of new opportunities during an investment boom. Thus the stock of opportunities at any time is a function of secular growth forces as modified by cyclical factors and such sporadic or other special influences as may be currently important.

Although fixed investment demands depend on expected long-term yields and the factors which underlie them, the timing of investment expenditures is influenced by current and prospective near-term movements of profits, sales, prices, and interest rates. This is partly because such changes may directly swell or diminish investment opportunities by altering expected yields, and partly because the cost and availability of funds will respond to changes in aggregate activity.

The income-autonomous factors which create investment opportunities will appear in specific firms and industries. The time-path of investment in a given industry will therefore depend partly on such factors and partly on the general influences which bear on all industries. Conversely, the path of aggregate investment and national income will be determined not only by general influences, but also by

[2] This classification is from Robert A. Gordon, "Investment Behavior and Business Cycles," *Review of Economics and Statistics* (February 1955), pp. 23-34.

the factors specific to individual industries. What is needed, therefore, is a conceptual apparatus to deal with the mutual interaction of components and aggregates.[3]

The first element of the framework is the "law of industrial growth" which says that individual industries pass through a life cycle of several stages: introduction of the product and a period of vigorous expansion as it wins general acceptance, then slower growth as it nears market saturation, and eventual decline.[4] These phases would occur, I assume, even if national income were stationary, and would have obvious consequences for the composition of demand and production. Since national income itself has a rising trend, however, each industry growth curve will be tilted upward to reflect the increase which would occur even with constant output composition. Now, since the life span of an industry is usually long—at least if it is not defined too narrowly in terms of product—a given segment of its growth curve during a period of, say, five or ten years, may be approximated by a straight line of constant percentage increase. The line may tilt up or down depending upon the growth stage, and represents the prevailing tendency of output due to the combination of specific growth factors affecting the industry and the secular uptrend of national income.

Next, make gross investment a positive function of level of output. This means that industries with strongly rising production tendencies during the five to ten years, will have correspondingly rapid investment uptrends. It may be objected that rapid production growth could be achieved with a constant, though large, annual flow of net investment. If "steady growth" is taken to mean growth at a constant percentage rate, however, it would require an increasing amount of net investment per year: increasing, in fact, at the same percentage rate as production if capacity were always adjusted optimally to output.[5]

[3] The one with which I will work is merely a restatement of propositions made familiar by a long line of students of the cycle, including Schumpeter, Mitchell, Robertson, Burns, Hansen, Haberler, Fellner, and Gordon.

[4] See especially Arthur F. Burns, *Production Trends in the United States Since 1870* (1934).

[5] The postulated relation between production and investment "trends" amounts to a loose application of the acceleration principle to the case of long-term adjustment of capacity to output, but without the implication that investment fluctuates with the rate of change of output in the short run. Notice that, under the assumed trend conditions, net investment would always be in fixed propor-

Additionally, replacement demand will increase over time in growing industries, although not in constant proportion to output if growth occurred at different rates in previous decades. These are not rigid relationships which are being assumed, but merely positive correlations between average growth rates of production and gross investment.

Actual growth will not, of course, occur steadily. National income will fluctuate, and with it production in each industry, according to its price and income elasticities. Another source of instability will be found in factors which foster independent fluctuations specific to certain industries. Nor will investment proceed steadily, for it varies with output during the short run as well as over the decade, although often with a lag. Notice that this formulation simultaneously embraces those autonomous investment determinants which underlie industry growth curves, and the tendency for movements of national income to induce fluctuations of investment by influencing individual outputs. These two aspects correspond to the distinction between autonomous factors which create investment opportunities and cyclical factors which augment or diminish them or influence the rate at which they are exploited. Several important investment determinants have to be handled independently, however, including changes in desired capital—output ratios, sporadic shocks due to war, and the influence of cost and availability of external funds.

How Industrial Shifts May Augment Aggregate Demand

Aggregate demand may be increased by output shifts at a given level of national income, despite the fact that the increases in some sectors are at the expense, at least virtually, of decreases elsewhere.[6]

---

tion to both the level of output and its absolute change. The factor of proportionality in the latter case would be the accelerator coefficient, and in the former, the product of the accelerator coefficient and the growth rate of output.

[6] Notice the implicit assumption that an increase of sales of commodity A occurs because buyers shift from B to A at the same level of total expenditure.

This can occur for several reasons.[7] First, if investment lags output growth, aggregate investment demand will be augmented by the output shift if A is more capital intensive than B; or if, with capital intensities equal, the maximum time rate of disinvestment in B (set by the level of replacement demand before the fall of output occurred) is smaller than the increased rate of net investment in A; or if gross investment lags behind production by a longer period in B than in A.

Second, if the growth industry invests in anticipation of demand and has a long gestation period, the resulting output will be delayed and with it the depressive effect on production and investment in B, provided this was not anticipated by B before the event. The reader will observe that this case differs from the others in that investment leads expected output in the growth industry (although it may lag cyclical fluctuations in the industry's actual output), so that the secular shift in the composition of output is imminent rather than actual. It differs also from instances of "building ahead of demand" in the sense of adding a margin of unused capacity which is expected to persist for several years. Such industries merely have higher capital intensities per unit of actual output than per unit of full capacity output. To the extent that vigorous growth encourages this practice, however, it will tend to raise actual capital intensities in growing industries relative to others, even if technological relationships alone would make for equality of capital intensities per unit of capacity on the average in the two groups.

Finally, a net stimulus to aggregate demand will result only if the industrial shifts raise planned investment relative to planned saving. This will occur if growth industries finance an average, or less than average, share of gross investment from depreciation allowances and retained earnings. And it may occur if self-financing is of more than

---

This differs from situations where the demand for B falls because buyers initially reduce total expenditure at the given income level. In the latter event, there may or may not follow an induced increase in the demand for commodity A. If lags delay the latter increase, or if the preference of buyers for liquidity instead of goods is other than temporary, a generalized contraction may develop instead of the generalized expansion discussed in the text. See William Fellner, *Monetary Policies and Full Employment* (1946), Chap. 4.

[7] *Ibid.* Also see James S. Duesenberry, *Business Cycles and Economic Growth* (1958), pp. 225-35.

average importance in growth industries, but not enough more to offset completely the rise of investment demand.[8]

If autonomous demand has increased for one of the foregoing reasons and unemployed resources are available, the result will be a generalized expansion of income which will raise the demand for most products at given prices. Thus, instead of declining, the "losers" may merely rise more slowly than national income.

Why Must Expansion End?

The literature abounds with answers to this question, and it is not my intention to select or invent a particular one as the cause, or even the main cause, of downturns. Contractions can and have resulted from a variety of causes in the past and will do so in the future. This is not to deny any regularity in business cycles, however. First, there are regularities in the processes by which expansionary and contractionary forces become diffused through the economy. Second, the differences among past business cycles, and especially between major and minor cycles, may be systematically related to particular sets of causal factors.

The first sort of regularity is well illustrated by the fact that the industrial scope of business expansions consistently diminishes before the downturn.[9] As the proportion of expanding industries diminishes, aggregate production decelerates correspondingly, and when the proportion falls below one-half, the aggregate declines (Chart 35). As I have shown elsewhere,[10] this correlation between the scope and pace

[8] Duesenberry, *op. cit.*

[9] See Wesley C. Mitchell, *Business Cycles* (1913), Part III; Arthur F. Burns, "New Facts on Business Cycles," *Thirtieth Annual Report* of the National Bureau of Economic Research (1950); Geoffrey H. Moore, *Statistical Indicators of Cyclical Revivals and Recessions*, National Bureau of Economic Research, Occasional Paper 31 (1950); and Moore, "The Diffusion of Business Cycles," *Economics and the Public Interest*, Robert A. Solo, ed. (1955), pp. 35-64.

[10] Hickman, "Diffusion, Acceleration, and Business Cycles," *American Economic Review* (September 1959), pp. 535-65. This paper contains a negative

CHART 35. *Manufacturing Production: Total, Absolute Change, and Diffusion Index,*[a] *Monthly, Seasonally Adjusted, 1947-58*

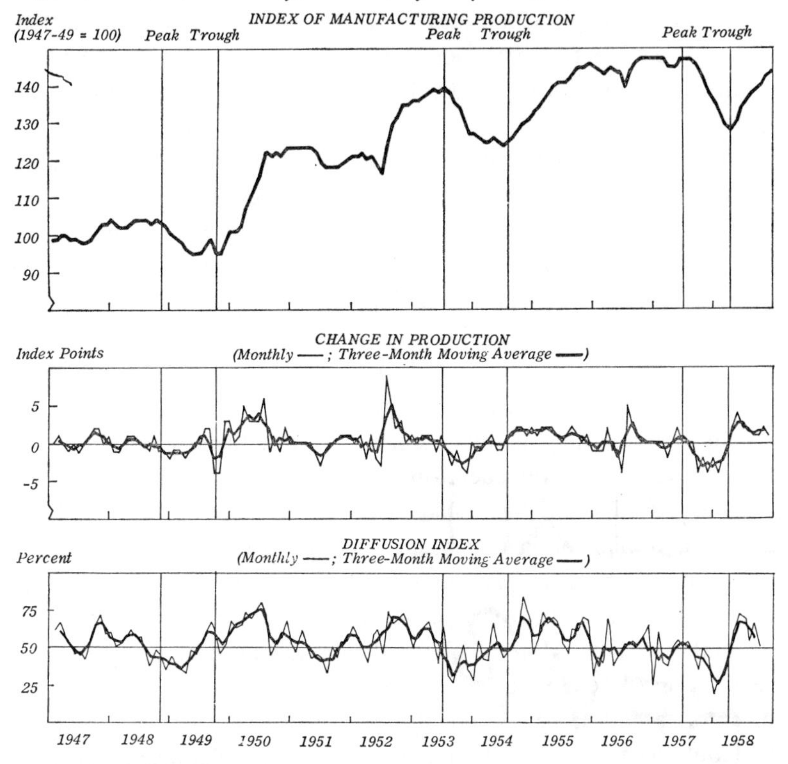

[a] The diffusion index shows what proportion of a group of 146 industries increased production in each month.

Source: Derived from data of the Board of Governors of the Federal Reserve System.

of a business expansion is to be expected no matter what the cause of the slowdown of aggregate activity. In particular, it will be observed whether the rate of increase of national income is retarded by some over-all constraint—such as a real or monetary ceiling on resources—or, conversely, whether aggregative deceleration occurs because of an accumulation of uncompensated autonomous declines in individual industries. It does not follow, however, that the course of

---

test of the acceleration principle, together with a demonstration that the adverse effects of aggregative deceleration on aggregate investment are probably due more to individual declines than to individual decelerations of production.

the subsequent contraction will be the same under all circumstances.

This brings us to the second type of possible regularity—that the severity of the contraction may depend partly on the factors responsible for ending the expansion.[11] I will consider some of the possibilities, dealing with each case in turn and altering the assumptions as I proceed.

At first, I assume that the underlying growth tendencies of the various industries remain unaltered during a business expansion: that is, that the set of constant-percentage lines which approximate the prevailing production growth rates of the several industries does not shift. I abstract also from sporadic changes of taste or other special short-term influences affecting specific industries. Finally, I assume that fixed investment is a lagged or synchronous function of current output in each industry, and interpret this to mean that firms do not err by overinvesting in new capacity before their outputs decline. Why should a downturn develop under these circumstances?

One possibility is that imbalances between stocks and sales may induce a decline of inventory investment. Such imbalances can develop at any time in particular markets, but generalized instances may sometimes result from speculative episodes grounded in political or military events. More regularly, they may be caused by aggregative retardation (deceleration). In the latter event, the mechanism relating inventories and sales is probably much like that relating fixed plant and output, except for shorter lags. That is, deflationary efforts to adjust inventories to sales of specific products are probably motivated more by the sales declines which accompany aggregative retardation than by individual sales retardations.[12] Be that as it may, a contraction induced by inventory maladjustments alone is unlikely to develop severe proportions when underlying opportunities for fixed investment remain strong, as under the present assumption. The combination of relatively stable fixed investment and the small consumption multiplier, which is typical of downswings, will narrowly limit the contraction of final sales, and hence the induced decline of inventory investment. Production will soon fall below sales, facilitating a prompt

[11] See Gordon, *op. cit.,* and his "Types of Depressions and Programs to Combat Them," *Policies to Combat Depression* (1956), pp. 7-25.

[12] Hickman, *op. cit.*

reduction of excess stocks and an early revival of production.

Next, suppose that business expansion is slowed because the economy has reached full employment, limiting the advance of real national income to the rate made possible by growth of the labor force and of man-hour productivity. Now, rapid advances in the growth industries will induce production declines among others less favored in the competition for labor and materials.[13] The early decliners will tend to be the slow growers, forced to adapt to the new pattern of resource usage dictated by innovations and other dynamic factors.[14] Investment will also decline in these industries, but total capital formation need not fall so long as compensating increases occur in the growth sectors. Given the present assumption that investment does not lead production in any industry, a downturn might nonetheless develop endogenously if the average capital intensity of the declining group came to exceed that of the expanding one, and if the average lag of investment behind output were not especially long in the declining group.[15] Notice, however, that excess capacity at the time of the downturn would be confined largely to the secularly retarded industries.[16] Of course, the growth industries might develop surplus capacity during the ensuing contraction, but, even so, the induced investment declines would tend to be smaller than if capacity had

[13] Notice that a full-employment ceiling rather than a full-capacity ceiling is postulated. The case where investment reductions are induced from the cost side of the investment decision because of advancing prices in the capital goods industries will be discussed later.

[14] The classic analysis of the processes of innovation and adaption is that of Joseph A. Schumpeter. See, for example, his *Business Cycles,* Vol. 1 (1939), especially Chap. 4. The actual innovations may have occurred during preceding cycles, of course. The maximum stimulus to production and investment may lag the introduction of a new product or process by many years and even decades.

[15] Hickman, *op. cit.* An endogenous downturn could also occur if the average internal saving ratio of the declining group came to exceed that of the expanding group. In the cited paper, I overlooked this possibility of an endogenous decline of consumption caused by an induced increase of business saving.

[16] "Largely," because of my initial assumption that the average capital intensity of the group of growth industries was higher than that of the secularly retarded ones, and some of the growth industries must therefore be admitted into the group of early declines if the average capital intensity of the latter group is to rise sufficiently to cause a decline of aggregate investment under these simplified conditions.

been excessive before the downturn. This factor would favor early recovery, as would the continued strength of underlying investment opportunities.

Now, I permit investment to lead production in some industries, although not yet as a result of excess capacity. Instead, allowance is made for changes in supply prices of capital goods, in interest rates (regarded as indexes of availability as well as cost of external funds), or in expectations about future values of these variables. A general downturn may be caused under these circumstances by advancing investment costs, which curb investment in some industries even though product demand is still rising and capacity is being utilized at optimum rates or better. Again, the prospects are good for prompt recovery, since the long-term potential of the growth industries is unimpaired and investment costs will fall during the contraction.

The form of the foregoing investment curbs is not a matter of indifference. First, the industrial impacts will differ. A given increase in prices of capital goods will reduce the prospective rate of return over cost of a short-lived investment relatively more than one with a longer period of amortization. The shorter the investment horizon, the larger is the proportion of the income stream which represents capital recovery at any given percentage rate of return, and therefore the tighter is the squeeze on the profit rate when the costs of physical capital increase.[17] Conversely, an increase in the price of capital funds will be a stronger deterrent to long-lived investments because of the greater weight of interest charges in the income stream. Thus, a rise in construction and equipment costs will hit sectors like manufacturing and farming the hardest, whereas higher interest rates will restrict investment relatively more in areas like housing, utilities, and state and local construction, with their long horizons. Capital rationing works in the same direction, since internal financing is less important in the

[17] This statement assumes that the prospective income stream is not affected by the rise in prices of capital goods. A current increase in these prices might, however, be caused by general inflationary pressures which engendered expectations that all prices would rise for a considerable period into the future. If so, expected sales revenues from investments with short pay-off periods might rise relatively more than others (since prices might be expected to rise for five years but not for 25), and thus offset the differential impact of current increases in costs of plant and equipment.

latter industries. Because capital intensities also vary among these sectors, the question whether aggregate investment was curbed more during the expansion by advancing prices than by financial constraints is a matter of considerable importance in explaining the behavior of investment after the downturn. It is the combination of rapid growth of demand, a high capital-output ratio, and a sensitive response to changes in credit conditions which has made of residential construction such a prominent contracyclical force in the postwar economy.

Another reason why the relative importance of the two investment deterrents is of some moment is that interest rates are more likely to fall during a contraction than are prices, at least in the postwar economy with its inflationary bias and contracyclical monetary policy (see Chapter 14). Under these conditions, cyclically induced changes in prices of capital goods lose much of their influence over investment decisions. Endogenous price reductions cannot be relied upon to raise investment demand during contractions, although expectations of future increases may augment investment after the upturn—or even earlier, if businessmen become convinced for other reasons that an upturn is imminent. Similarly, the restraining influence of induced price increases during expansions has probably been diminished in the present-day economy because there is little reason to expect that plant and equipment will cost less in the near future.

Individual leads of investment over output which result from excess capacity may now be admitted to the analysis. This is the case elucidated by capital-stock adjustment theories, in which, for one reason or another, capacity eventually overtakes current production, even though the latter has not yet started to decline. The "overshoot" of capacity usually occurs because the firm's output is retarded in some way, especially in models based on a fixed technical coefficient between capital and output. However, the case also embraces error models based on psychological premises (overoptimism generated by improved business conditions) or imperfect knowledge of the actions of existing and potential competitors. It is not, in other words, necessarily restricted to a technological rationale as in the acceleration principle, nor does it require that industry output be retarded in order for overshooting to occur. Capacity might outrun unretarded industry demand because the several firms had overestimated their prospective market shares. Overshooting is apt to aggravate the investment cutbacks which accompany specific production declines, but the over-all situation will not be especially serious unless a substantial proportion, in terms of relative importance, of the growth industries develops excess capacity prior to the general contraction.

Finally, an expansion might end partly because underlying investment opportunities had weakened in the growth industries. This would mean a break in the prevailing production trends of the various industries and a new set of growth lines. The industries which had been growing rapidly would slow down, and this would tend both to slow the over-all rate of growth and to reduce the dispersion of individual rates around the average, so that the entire set of growth lines would draw closer together. Autonomous investment demand would be smaller than before at a given level of national income, and the economy would have lost some of the upthrust which had been provided by the growth sectors. (The condition might or might not be aggravated by the development of excess capacity in the growth industries prior to the downturn: this depends on whether the growth retardation was anticipated.) A contraction occurring under such circumstances is apt to be severe, since the autonomous downshift of investment demand may swamp the favorable influence of reductions in capital costs. A weak recovery may also follow, because there will be fewer industries in which secular growth tends rapidly to eliminate excess capacity.

It is possible, of course, for one set of investment opportunities to succeed another without an intervening period of severe contraction. This is particularly likely where war stimuli are concerned.

The hypothesis that past major contractions were partly the result of a temporary exhaustion of long-term autonomous investment opportunities is not new. Nor is the specific form of the hypothesis as presented here in terms of the dispersion of production growth rates among industries. Fellner found that the relative importance of manufacturing industries growing substantially in excess of the average rate decreased in 1923-29 as compared with 1909-23.[18]

[18] This was due principally to a slowdown of motor vehicles and petroleum refining. See *op. cit.;* Tables 5 and 8. Subsequent unpublished work by Gordon,

He concluded:

> The hypothesis that substantial shifts in the composition of output may give rise to over-all growth and that the cessation of significant shifts may contribute to stagnant over-all trends is broadly supported by these data. More is not claimed. The significance of other causal factors should not be denied or minimized. It is very likely, for example, that the temporary saturation in the field of residential construction belonged among the circumstances that, in the 1930's and also in the earlier "protracted depressions," aggravated the situation considerably.[19]

The housing market is, of course, a specific industry in which investment opportunities may diminish because of slowed growth, but it deserves separate attention (see Chapter 12) because of its great size and because of the long swings, instead of steady growth or decline, which residential construction has exhibited in the past.

Burns also investigated the relation between dispersion of industrial growth rates and severe business contractions. Working with measures of exponential production trends for overlapping decades, he established:

> When the trends of production have on the whole moved steeply upward, the degree of divergence of production trends has also been high; and that when the trends of production have on the whole moved only moderately upward, the degree of divergence of production trends has also been only moderate.[20]

An examination of American experience between 1870 and 1933 led to the following conclusion, advanced tentatively because based on a limited range of experience and imperfect statistical measures:

> First, that periods of sharp advance in the trend of general production, which are characterized invariably by considerable divergence in production trends, have been followed invariably by severe business depressions; second, that most of the business depressions of marked severity have been preceded by a sharp advance in the

---

using another set of production data and a different statistical technique, substantiates the conclusion that shifts in the composition of output diminished in importance during the late 1920's.

[19] *Ibid.*, pp. 132-33.

[20] Burns, *Production Trends in the United States Since 1870, op. cit.*, p. 243.

> trend of general production and considerable divergence in the trends of individual industries.[21]

This correlation is attributed to "the strain and loss of industrial balance" which accompanies rapid secular advance and which may "culminate in a general economic crisis serving to terminate the upward movement."[22]

The contradiction between Burns' hypothesis that severe contractions are often caused by the industrial divergencies which develop during prolonged periods of vigorous expansion and Fellner's hypothesis that they result from a prior diminution of the dispersion of growth rates, is perhaps more apparent than real. Burns' statistical measures of growth rates were based on overlapping calendar decades; hence, as Fellner points out, they are ambiguous as to whether the dispersion of growth rates was increasing or decreasing immediately prior to severe contractions. As for interpretations of the empirical evidence, Burns' "loss of industrial balance" is a symptom of the imperfect adjustment of the economy to those same changes in technical relations and consumer habits which Fellner emphasizes in his theory of generalized expansion from production shifts. Fellner's explanation is the more attractive, however, in that it allows for interaction between production shifts and the rate of growth of aggregate activity. It can, therefore, explain why the favorable effects of rapid growth in some sectors can for a time outweigh the unfavorable influences on investment demand in those industries which are forced into retardations or declines, and conversely, how aggregative decline may result from a slowdown of the growth industries. In a sense, it is also less pessimistic than Burns' hypothesis, for if autonomous factors continue to foster rapid growth, there is no implication that the economy must necessarily pass through a period of retarded growth or severe cyclical contraction, or both, in order to restore industrial balance. Thus, the reduced dispersion of industrial growth rates during periods of slow aggregative growth, need not reflect an inevitable adjustment process. It may simply be evidence of a lack of vigorous growth in some sectors, and hence of diminished displacement of others, which explains

[21] *Ibid.*, p. 251.
[22] *Ibid.*, p. 248.

both the reduced over-all growth rate and the diminished dispersion of individual rates.

Shifts in Consumer Demand

My study of industrial shifts and investment activity in the postwar economy begins with annual estimates of 13 categories of real consumption expenditure during 1947-57 (Table 43). Together, these products accounted for about 71 per cent of the nation's consumption expenditure in 1947. Their postwar growth rates ranged from a decline of 1 per cent per year to an increase of 7 per cent, with an over-all average increase of 3 per cent. Whether these growth divergencies tended to augment or diminish aggregate investment demand depends (if lags are ignored) on the balance of capital intensities between the relative gainers and losers and the size of the increment or decrement to investment depends also on the amount of the shift in output composition. These points may be clarified by a numerical example.

Suppose that industries A and B each produce $1,000 of output and that it takes $2.00 of fixed capital in A and $1.00 in B to produce $1.00 of output under optimal conditions. Let the sales of both industries increase 10 per cent and investment rise accordingly. The output of each industry will rise by $100 and net investment will be $200 in A and $100 in B. Contrast this with a situation where A gains relative to B within the same over-all production increase. If A's sales rise $150 and B's $50, aggregate net investment will become $350 instead of $300. The output shift of $50 has increased A's investment by $100 and lowered B's by only $50. Given the initial size distribution of industries, the larger will be the effect on investment of shifts in the composition of output, the greater is the disparity between either the growth rates or the capital intensities of the gaining and losing sectors. Whether total investment is increased or decreased depends, of course, on the direction of the shift in composition.

The illustrative calculations shown in Table 43 suggest that investment demand was probably augmented by consumption shifts

TABLE 43. *Hypothetical Effects of Shifts of Consumption Expenditure on Investment Demand, 1947-57*[a]
(Dollar items in billions at 1947-49 prices)

Expenditure Item	*Expenditure Growth Rate (Per cent per annum)* (1)	*Index of Instability of Growth (Per cent)* (2)	Estimated Consumption Expenditure, 1947 (3)	Estimated Change of Consumption Expenditure, 1947–57		Estimated Gain or Loss of Expenditure from Changed Composition (6)	Capital Requirements per $ Final Expenditure (7)	Estimated Investment Gain or Loss from Changed Composition (8)
				Changed Composition (4)	Fixed Composition (5)			
Food	*1.8*	*2.4*	52.8	10.3	18.4	−8.1	2.19	−17.7
Tobacco	*1.4*	*1.8*	4.1	0.6	1.4	−0.8	1.90	− 1.5
Clothing	*2.2*	*2.6*	15.4	3.8	5.4	−1.6	1.23	− 2.0
Footwear	*0.4*	*3.8*	3.0	−0.1	1.0	−1.1	1.32	− 1.5
Nonfarm housing (rent)	*4.9*	*1.6*	14.9	9.1	5.2	3.9	7.79	30.4
Furniture	*5.3*	*4.4*	2.5	1.7	0.9	0.8	1.50	1.2
Floor coverings, bedding and misc. durable house furnishings	*−0.8*	*6.0*	2.5	−0.2	0.9	−1.1	1.96	− 2.2
Semidurable household textiles	*1.7*	*3.8*	2.3	0.4	0.8	−0.4	1.23	− 0.5
Household utilities	*4.5*	*3.9*	5.3	2.9	1.9	1.0	3.23	3.2
Telephone and telegraph	*7.0*	*1.4*	1.4	1.4	0.5	0.9	3.94	3.5
Automobiles	*7.4*	*10.1*	6.0	6.3	2.1	4.2	1.79	7.5
Tires	*1.2*	*5.3*	1.7	0.2	0.6	−0.4	1.51	− 0.6
Gasoline and oil	*7.2*	*2.1*	4.1	4.1	1.4	2.7	3.77	10.2
Total or average	*3.0*	*1.8*	116.0	40.5	40.5	0	2.80	30.0

[a] The sources and notes for columns 1 through 8 are as follows:

1. Growth rate computed from an exponential curve fitted to annual estimates of real consumption expenditure. The estimates of expenditures in current dollars are from *U. S. Income and Output*, a supplement to *Survey of Current Business* (November, 1958), Table II-4. The price deflators are from Bureau of Labor Statistics, *Consumer Price Indexes for Selected Items and Groups* (July 1956 and later issues). The curves were fitted by the use of Glover's mean value table (J. W. Glover, *Tables of Applied Mathematics* [1923], pp. 468 ff.).

2. Index of instability is an arithmetic mean of the percentage deviations of the annual observations from the fitted exponential curve.

3. Expenditure in 1947 as calculated from the fitted curve for each category.

4. Change in expenditure between 1947 and 1957 as calculated from the fitted curve for each category.

5. Change in expenditure which would have occurred had each category started from the estimated 1947 level shown in column 3 and increased between 1947 and 1957 at the weighted average rate (3.0 per cent) for all categories.

6. Column 4 *minus* column 5.

7. Capital coefficients from Wassily Leontieff *et al.*, *Studies in the Structure of the American Economy* (1953), Appendix 1. The derivation of the estimates is described by Robert N. Grosse in Chapter 6 of the volume. The coefficients relate fixed capital to capacity output rather than actual output. Most of them are based on the average ratio of undepreciated fixed capital to capacity, although for some industries it was possible to estimate marginal ratios from engineering data or from cost data on newly constructed facilities. The coefficient for each class of final product is a weighted average of the coefficients of all industries which contribute directly or indirectly to its production. The weights consist of the dollar value of total production required from each industry per dollar of final demand of the given category, as shown in W. Duane Evans and Marvin Hoffenberg, "The Interindustry Relations Study For 1947," *Review of Economics and Statistics* (May 1952), pp. 97–142, Table 6. Since the industry classification used in the 1947 study differed from that of the 1939 study, the capital coefficients from the latter were assigned to the industries included in the former with the assistance of the comparison of classifications shown in Leontieff, *op. cit.*, Appendix 2, Tables 1 and 2. The average coefficient for all categories is weighted by the relative importance of each category in 1947 consumption as shown in column 3.

8. Column 6 *times* column 7.

during the postwar period. It is assumed that each category of consumption expenditure changed between 1947 and 1957 in an amount determined by its fitted growth line, and that just enough net investment was undertaken to adjust capacity commensurately with sales. The necessary amount of net investment per dollar change of sales in each category is assumed to be given by the capital intensities listed in column 7, which are taken from the study by Robert N. Grosse cited in the table. The coefficients reflect the capital requirements of all industries directly or indirectly affected by the given increase of final consumption expenditure, including trade, transportation, manufacturing, mining, and agriculture. Details are given in the notes to the table.

Column 6 shows the estimated gain or loss of sales in each product category resulting from expenditure shifts. For each item, it is the difference between the 1947-57 change of expenditure, as estimated from its own growth rate (column 4), and the change which would have occurred had each category increased at the same rate as aggregate expenditure (column 5). The expenditure shifts sum to zero, of course, but this is not true of the hypothetical investment effects (column 8). Since the items which grew more rapidly than total expenditures had capital coefficients which averaged higher than those of lagging items, there was a hypothetical investment gain from the shifts of $30 billion. This is a 26 per cent increase over the hypothetical amount of investment which I calculate would have occurred with the same capital coefficients and the same growth rate of total output but with an unchanged composition of output.

The large contribution of housing construction to aggregate investment in the postwar period is strikingly illustrated in the calculations. Since rent or its equivalent for homeowners is a substantial item in household budgets and the capital-output ratio is extremely high for housing, residential construction would have formed a sizable fraction of aggregate investment even if the demand for housing had grown only at the average rate of consumption expenditure. As it was, it grew much more rapidly than the average, the composition of expenditure shifted substantially toward housing, and the corresponding increment to investment demand was a large multiple of the shift. In fact, this one sector was enough to account for all of the estimated 26 per cent gain from consumption shifts. When it is dropped from the list and the calculations redone for the remaining 12 groups, the gain is reduced to $7.9 billion, or an increase of 12 per cent above the hypothetical investment estimated for an unchanged composition of output.

The foregoing estimation procedure has serious shortcomings. First, the capital intensities were estimated from 1939 data, and other estimates of capital-output ratios—unfortunately not available in the necessary detail—indicate a considerable decline from prewar to postwar years. The decline occurred over the broad range of industry, however, so that the differences which existed among industries in 1939 should have been preserved within tolerable limits, and that is what matters here. If all the coefficients were halved, this would halve the hypothetical absolute amounts of investment both with and without expenditure shifts, so that the composition effect would still augment investment by the same percentage as presently calculated.

Second, most of the coefficients are on an average, instead of incremental, basis, but again, there should be a close correlation between the magnitudes of the average and marginal coefficients, and the interindustry differences among the latter should be represented adequately by the former.

Third, the coefficients are simply the best estimates that could be made from incomplete information, and should be regarded as no more than "a set of 'reasonable' numbers of the right general order of magnitude."[23]

Fourth, since the expenditure shifts are measured against an unchanged composition of demand, they could be attributed entirely to income-autonomous factors only if the individual income elasticities of demand were all equal to one another. Since the elasticities do in fact differ, the hypothetical investment gain from compositional shifts includes an income-induced component. The induced component could be positive or negative, depending on the distribution of differences between the actual growth rates and the rates which would exist if growth divergencies were due only to differing income elasticities. The size and sign of the induced component cannot be measured in the

[23] Robert N. Grosse, "The Structure of Capital," *Studies in the Structure of the American Economy,* Wassily W. Leontief *et al.* (1953), p. 218.

absence of reliable numerical estimates of the several income elasticities. In the critical case of housing demand, however, one can scarcely argue that its rapid relative growth during the postwar decade was due primarily to the differential impact of income growth.

Despite these qualifications, it appears that high growth rates in some consumption sectors (principally housing) served to augment investment demand over the postwar decade as a whole. Neither individual nor aggregate outputs rose steadily along their growth lines, however, and a fortiori this was not true of investment. Nor were the fast-rising sectors necessarily stable. Of the six which grew most rapidly, three—nonfarm housing rent, telephone and telegraph services, and gasoline and oil—had low indexes of instability, whereas the others—furniture, household utilities, and automobiles—were rather unstable. A similar spread of stability characteristics is evident in the retarded sectors (column 2).

Other things equal, one would expect rapid growth to enhance stability in a given industry. Since its share of total demand is growing, it should be resistant to business contractions and should rise more steadily on that account. Because other factors also affect an industry's response to business fluctuations, however, some growth sectors will be more unstable than some retarded ones, even though the fast-growers will be more stable than if they themselves were growing slowly. In practice, this means that fast but unstable growers will make their major contribution to growth of aggregate investment during cyclical expansions, whereas recoveries are likely to be led by those fast or moderately fast sectors which also happen to be steady growers.

Production Shifts in Manufacturing

If the field of investigation is narrowed to the manufacturing industries, advantage can be taken of Daniel Creamer's estimates of fixed capital and output for the years 1948, 1953, and 1956 (Table 44). The estimates are in 1929 prices and were derived from balance-sheet data. Fixed capital is comprised of the value of structures and equip-

TABLE 44. *Fixed Capital, Output, and Capital-Output Ratios, Selected Manufacturing Industries, 1948, 1953, and 1956*[a] (Dollar items in millions at 1929 prices)

Industries	Fixed Capital[b]			Output[c]			Ratio of Capital to Output		
	1948	1953	1956	1948	1953	1956	1948	1953	1956
Total manufactures	*36,685*	*48,256*	*54,140*[d]	*128,719*	*161,933*	*172,971*	*.285*	*.298*	*.313*[d]
Beverages	968	959	n.a.	3,612	3,746	n.a.	.268	.256	n.a.
Food and kindred products	3,259	3,148	4,078[e]	19,872	21,710	27,007[e]	.164	.145	.151[e]
Tobacco manufactures	149	115	130	2,661	2,875	2,826	.056	.040	.046
Textile mill products	2,088	2,178	2,091	8,810	8,712	8,712	.237	.250	.240
Apparel	302	338	—[f]	5,922	6,377	—[f]	.051	.053	—[f]
Forest products	1,638	1,626	1,649	4,157	4,659	4,658	.394	.349	.354
Paper and allied products	1,526	2,002	2,412	3,240	4,197	5,057	.471	.477	.477
Printing and publishing	1,135	1,194	1,376	3,721	4,374	4,914	.305	.273	.280
Chemicals and allied products	3,309	6,865	7,493	9,066	12,928	15,546	.365	.531	.482
Petroleum and coal products	7,217	7,927	9,287	12,530	15,666	16,978	.576	.506	.547
Rubber products	480	486	568	2,743	3,447	3,572	.175	.141	.159
Leather and leather products	186	152	152	2,000	2,000	2,082	.093	.076	.073
Stone, clay, and glass products	1,158	1,456	1,740	2,888	3,658	4,339	.401	.398	.401
Primary and fabricated metals	6,363	10,004	—[g]	17,529	21,891	—[g]	.363	.457	—[g]
Primary metals	—	(6,676)	6,665	—	(11,816)	12,343	—	(.565)	.540
Fabricated metals, ordnance, and miscl.	—	(3,937)	4,035	—	(13,670)	13,771	—	(.288)	.293
Machinery, excluding electrical	2,429	2,904	3,251	9,716	13,081	14,013	.250	.222	.232
Electrical machinery	1,095	1,585	—[f]	5,887	11,321	—[f]	.186	.140	—[f]
Transportation equipment, excluding motor vehicles	791	1,770	1,970	2,071	5,364	6,024	.382	.330	.327
Motor vehicles and equipment	1,705	2,456	—[f]	8,158	10,191	—[f]	.209	.241	—[f]
Miscellaneous	887	1,091	—[h]	3,978	5,455	—[h]	.223	.200	—[h]
Instruments	—	(482)	522	—	(1,913)	2,047	—	(.252)	.255
Other	—	(4,379)	5,844	—	(27,892)	28,931	—	(.157)	.202

n.a. Not available.

[a] Source, Daniel Creamer, "Postwar Trends in the Relation of Capital to Output in Manufactures," *American Economic Review* (May 1958), p. 253, Table 2. Figures for 1956 are preliminary. Bracketed figures in 1953 are for comparison with 1956 only.

[b] Defined as sum of structures and equipment net of depreciation.

[c] Defined as gross operating receipts. The output figures were not shown by Creamer, but were implicit in the other data.

[d] Total exceeds sum of the industry groups owing to the adjustment of the total but not the subgroups for the shift away from straight-line depreciation.

[e] Includes beverages in 1956. The comparable capital-output ratio in 1953 is .161, and the comparable 1953 output is 25,509.

[f] Included in "other" grouping.

[g] Grouping comparable with other years not possible.

[h] Included with "fabricated metal products."

ment net of depreciation and output is measured by gross operating receipts.

Capital Intensity and Growth Rates: 1948-53

The capital-output ratio for total manufactures increased at an average rate of about 1 per cent per year between 1948 and 1953. The changes in individual capital intensities were often larger and there were decreases as well as increases. For the moment, I ignore these variations, and assume that the 1948 intensities prevailed throughout the interval. The 1948 capital-output ratios are applied to both the actual 1953 outputs and the outputs which would have resulted from an unchanged composition and the same over-all growth rate. The estimated gain or loss of capital due to production shifts is shown for each industry in column 5 of Table 45. The net gain from shifts is $851 million, or 9 per cent more than the increase of capital which would have occurred with a constant composition and unchanged capital-output ratios.

The distribution of gains and losses is interesting. Only seven of 19 industries grew more rapidly than the average. However, four of the seven fast-growing industries were above average in capital intensity, whereas eight of the 12 "laggards" were below average. Four industries—transportation equipment other than motor vehicles, electrical machinery, chemicals, and nonelectrical machinery—contributed the bulk of the investment gain during the period. The Korean mobilization provided a substantial stimulus to production and investment in all four cases during the last half of the period, and was especially important in chemicals and transportation equipment.

Inspection of Table 44 reveals that the rise in the over-all ratio of capital to output between 1948 and 1953 resulted primarily from large increases in the ratios of three industries—motor vehicles, metals, and chemicals. Capital rose relative to output in three additional industries, but the rise was negligible in paper and the 1953 ratio for textiles doubtless overstates the "desired" capital-output relationship, since capacity was certainly under-utilized in that year.

TABLE 45. *Hypothetical Effects of Shifts of Manufacturing Production on Investment Demand, 1948-53*[a]
(Dollar items in millions at 1929 prices)

Industry	Actual 1953 Output (1)	Hypothetical 1953 Output with 1948 Composition (2)	Hypothetical Gain or Loss from Output Shifts (3)	Ratio of Capital to Output (1948) (4)	Hypothetical Investment Gain or Loss from Output Shifts (5)
Beverages	3,746	4,542	− 796	.268	− 213
Food and kindred products	21,710	24,987	−3,277	.164	− 537
Tobacco manufactures	2,875	3,346	− 471	.056	− 26
Textile mill products	8,712	11,078	−2,366	.237	− 561
Apparel	6,377	7,446	−1,069	.051	− 55
Forest products	4,659	5,226	− 567	.394	− 223
Paper and allied products	4,197	4,074	123	.471	58
Printing and publishing	4,374	4,678	− 304	.305	− 93
Chemicals and allied products	12,928	11,400	1,528	.365	558
Petroleum and coal products	15,666	15,755	− 89	.576	− 51
Rubber products	3,447	3,450	− 3	.175	− 1
Leather and leather products	2,000	2,515	− 515	.093	− 48
Stone, clay, and glass products	3,658	3,631	27	.401	11
Primary and fabricated metals	21,891	22,041	− 150	.363	− 54
Machinery excluding electrical	13,081	12,218	863	.250	216
Electrical machinery	11,321	7,402	3,919	.186	729
Transportation equipment excluding motor vehicles	5,364	2,604	2,760	.382	1,054
Motor vehicles and equipment	10,191	10,258	− 67	.209	− 14
Miscellaneous	5,455	5,002	453	.223	101
Total or Average	161,652	161,652	0	.285	851

[a] Sources and notes for columns 1 through 5 are as follows: (1) Table 44; (2) Percentage distribution of 1948 output applied to total output of 1953; (3) column 1 *minus* column 2; (4) Table 44; and (5) 3 *times* column 4.

Observed capital intensities fell in the remaining industry groups. Creamer noted these same facts and went on to observe:

> The reversal in the long-term downward movement of the fixed capital-output ratio was restricted to chemicals and allied products, primary metals and fabricated metal products, and motor vehicles. These are branches in which product and technology innovations in these years were striking, resulting in a rapid expansion of fixed assets—more than a doubling in chemicals and allied products and an increase of about one-half in primary metals and fabricated metal products and motor vehicles and equipment. That is, when dramatic innovations in technology promising substantial cost reduction are available, competitive pressure may force management to invest in the plant and equipment incorporating the new technology, thereby extending capacity regardless of whether the additional capacity is immediately required for the satisfaction of current demand. This, of course, would result in a rising fixed capital-output ratio for the industries in which this occurs.[24]

Perhaps there is a considerable element of truth in this interpretation, but it needs to be modified. For one thing, private investment was subject to governmental control during the Korean War. Investment in the defense industries was encouraged by accelerated amortization and other devices, and it was discouraged elsewhere. Chemicals and primary metals were strongly affected by the defense facilities expansion program, and to the extent that they built capacity ahead of demand, it was perhaps due as much to this factor as to technological forces. Conversely, some part of the reductions in capital-output ratios among nondefense industries may have been occasioned by defense restrictions on investment. Second, technological change and competitive pressures need not necessarily cause capacity to be erected in excess of current demand, and capital-output ratios may rise because of deepening innovations even though capacity remains fully utilized. Third, under-utilization occurring for nontechnological reasons may also raise observed capital-output ratios. Fourth, changes in capital-output ratios may reflect underlying changes in capital-labor ratios induced by changes in factor prices. Creamer is well aware

[24] Daniel Creamer, "Postwar Trends in the Relation of Capital to Output in Manufactures," *American Economic Review* (May 1958), pp. 255-56.

of these problems, and he, therefore, advanced only tentatively the technological interpretation which I have quoted.

It is important to notice that most of these qualifications have to do with various possible causes of autonomous investment expenditure. For many purposes, it is comparatively unimportant whether autonomous investment is caused by deepening innovations or production shifts or defense needs over and above those reflected in production shifts. In this connection, it should be noted that autonomous manufacturing investment—as defined and measured by the difference between realized net capital formation in 1948-53 and the amount which would have been forthcoming at the same over-all growth rate, but with an unchanged output composition and constant capital intensities—amounted to nearly one-fifth of the realized total. Again, this definition of autonomous investment abstracts from the influence of differing income-elasticities of demand on shifts in the composition of output. For the rest, the differing growth rates among the manufacturing industries must reflect the differential impact of income-autonomous factors on final product demands, on the relationship of derived inputs and final demands, or on both.

Slowed Growth After 1953

The average annual rate of increase of manufacturing production dropped from 4.7 per cent in 1948-53 to 2.3 per cent in 1953-56.[25] A comparable decline occurred in the growth rate of manufacturers' fixed capital, which decreased from 5.5 to 3.3 per cent. This meant that the annual volume of manufacturers' net investment in plant and equipment was reduced about one-fourth between the two periods.

Several factors doubtless contributed to the retardation of national income and manufacturing production after 1953, including a decline of $12 billion or 20 per cent in federal purchases of goods and services and a swing of $14 billion from a deficit to a surplus on federal income and product account between 1953 and 1956. The restrictive monetary policy adopted during 1955 and maintained through the remainder of the expansion also inhibited the growth of real income,

[25] Growth of real GNP also slowed; the rates were, respectively, 4.7 and 2.9 per cent.

TABLE 46. *Hypothetical Effects of Shifts of Manufacturing Production on Investment Demand, 1953-56*[a]
(Dollar items in millions at 1929 prices)

Industry	Actual 1956 Output (1)	Hypothetical 1956 Output with 1953 Composition (2)	Hypothetical Gain or Loss from Output Shifts (3)	Ratio of Capital to Output (4)	Hypothetical Investment Gain or Loss from Output Shifts (5)
Food and kindred products including beverages	27,007	27,254	− 247	.161	− 40
Tobacco manufactures	2,826	3,071	− 245	.040	− 10
Textile mill products	8,712	9,308	− 596	.250	−149
Forest products	4,658	4,977	− 319	.349	−111
Paper and allied products	5,057	4,485	572	.477	273
Printing and publishing	4,914	4,673	241	.273	66
Chemicals and allied products	15,546	13,812	1,734	.531	921
Petroleum and coal products	16,978	16,738	240	.506	121
Rubber products	3,572	3,683	− 111	.141	− 16
Leather and leather products	2,082	2,136	− 54	.076	− 4
Stone, clay, and glass products	4,339	3,907	432	.398	172
Primary metals	12,343	12,625	− 282	.565	−159
Fabricated metals, ordnance, and miscellaneous	13,771	14,605	− 834	.288	−240
Machinery excluding electrical	14,013	13,976	37	.222	8
Transportation equipment excluding motor vehicles	6,024	5,731	293	.330	97
Instruments	2,047	2,044	3	.252	1
Other	28,931	29,799	− 868	.157	−136
Total or average	172,820	172,824	− 4	.308[b]	794

[a] Sources and notes for columns 1 through 5 are as follows: (1) Table 44; (2) Percentage distribution of 1953 output applied to total output of 1956; (3) column 1 *minus* column 2; (4) Table 44; and (5) column 3 *times* column 4.

[b] Uncorrected for accelerated amortization. See Table 44 for corrected ratio.

principally by depressing residential construction (Chapter 7). What can be said about production shifts as a factor in the retardation?

As far as manufacturing is concerned, production shifts assisted the expansion of industrial investment and national income after 1953 (Table 46). The production shifts were slightly larger in 1953-56 than in 1948-53 when measured relative to the corresponding increases of total output. More significant is the changed direction of the shifts in the later period. The new group of fast-growers was heavily weighted with capital-intensive industries. Two industries grew at virtually the average rate and neither gained nor lost significantly. Of the nine industries which Table 46 shows expanded more slowly than total output, a further check shows that seven had lower than average capital intensities. In contrast, five fast-growers were considerably above the average in this respect, and the sixth was not far below. Hence, the estimated net gain of real fixed capital from shifts was about 24 per cent of the increase which would have occurred with an unchanged composition, as compared with the corresponding figure of 9 per cent in 1948-53.

The compositional shifts of 1948-53 were powerfully influenced first by deferred demands from World War II and later by Korea. It was primarily the demand for durables which was favored by these exogenous forces, which were superimposed on other, presumably more lasting, factors acting to change the composition of demand. Thus, the spectacular production increases recorded by many durables during 1948-53 were sharply reduced in 1953-56, but several important branches among nondurables continued strongly ahead, as did stone, clay, and glass (Table 44).

Finally, manufacturers' net capital formation was stimulated by an increase in the aggregate capital-output ratio between 1953 and 1956. This time the gains were diffused widely and sometimes mitigated, sometimes reinforced, the investment effects of production shifts. Autonomous investment, defined to include the effects of both production shifts and changes in capital-output ratios, was almost three-tenths of the realized net capital formation of the period.

Growth Retardation and the Contraction of 1957-58

Earlier in the chapter, I discussed the hypothesis that the major contractions of the past were caused by a temporary exhaustion of autonomous investment opportunities owing to deceleration of output in those capital-intensive industries which had been growing rapidly during recent years. Was the marked slowdown in the rate of increase of aggregate production between the cyclical peaks of 1953 and 1957 a symptom of approaching exhaustion of investment opportunities, and if so, what accounts for the comparative mildness of the contrac-

TABLE 47. *Annual Rate of Increase of Output by Industrial Sector, Selected Periods, 1948-57*[a]
(In per cent)

Industrial Sector	Annual Rate of Increase[b]	
	1948–53	1953–57
Farm	0.2	1.4
Mining	1.5	2.6
Contract construction	5.3	2.7
Durable manufacturing	8.1	1.1
Nondurable manufacturing	2.9	2.4
Wholesale trade	4.4	1.1
Retail trade	4.3	3.3
Finance and insurance	8.8	5.5
Railroad transportation	−1.5	0
Other transportation	6.2	4.6
Communications	5.6	7.8
Public utilities	10.2	8.0
Services	2.0	4.6
Housing	5.3	4.4
Average	4.5	3.5

[a] Output indexes for all sectors except housing from Charles L. Schultze, *Prices, Costs and Output for the Post War Decade: 1947–1957* (1959), Table 2. Housing output is measured by real housing expenditure in constant dollars (*U. S. Income and Output*, a supplement to *Survey of Current Business* [November 1958], and *Survey of Current Business* [July 1959] Table II-5) and is not strictly comparable to the other series.

[b] At compound interest.

tion of 1957-58? In other words, was the contraction mild because investment opportunities remained favorable in the growth industries, or was it mild despite unfavorable developments in the growth industries?

Answers to these questions may be inferred partly from the growth rates of the various industrial sectors before and after 1953. Table 47 shows the average annual percentage rate of increase of output in 14 major sectors during 1948-53 and 1953-57. The rate of output growth diminished in nine of the industries after 1953, and the average rate of growth for all of the industries decreased from 4.5 to 3.5

per cent. Especially marked reductions occurred in durable manufacturing and wholesale trade. The deceleration of durable manufacturing was particularly important, both because the growth rate diminished so much and because the sector accounts for such a large share of the national income (Table 30). A measure of business output which reflects the relative importance of the various sectors[26] shows a rate of growth of 4.4 per cent between 1948 and 1953—virtually the same as the unweighted average rate for the 14 sectors—but a rate of only 2.6 instead of 3.5 per cent for 1953-57.

The consequences of retardation in durable manufacturing were less severe for the stock of private investment opportunities than for output growth. This is because the ratio of capital to output is much lower in manufacturing than in the housing, public utility, communications, or transportation industries. In these sectors, the growth rate of railroad transportation stopped its decline; housing, public utilities and other transportation decreased comparatively little after 1953; and communications increased substantially. Furthermore, all except railroad transportation continued to exceed the average growth rate for all industries by substantial margins (Table 47). Thus, rapid growth continued among most of the capital-intensive industries and output continued to shift in a direction favorable to investment demand.

As indicated in Chapter 7, favorable investment opportunities among important nonmanufacturing industries contributed substantially to economic stability in 1957-58. Residential nonfarm construction was stable throughout the contraction and rose briskly during the upswing. Moreover, investment by public utilities decreased only 8 per cent, and that of a group composed of trade, service, finance, construction, and communications only 3 per cent, between the third quarters of 1957 and 1958. In contrast, fixed investment in the manufacturing, mining, and railroad industries fell respectively 34, 29, and 59 per cent over the same interval.

Needless to say, these investment disparities cannot be attributed solely to differences in potential growth rates. It has been sufficiently emphasized that cyclical fluctuations in the level of output will induce cyclical fluctuations in investment demand, even though over the

[26] The gross business product, which is equal to the gross national product *minus* income originating in general government, households and institutions, and the rest of the world.

longer run net investment depends on the secular growth rate of output. The fact that manufacturing, mining, and transportation are among the cyclically more sensitive industries goes far toward explaining the correspondingly wide fluctuations of investment in those in-

TABLE 48. *Real Gross National Product by Type of Product and Purchaser, Selected Years, 1948-57*[a]
(Dollar items in billions at 1954 prices)

Item	Expenditures			Annual Rate of Increase[b] (Per cent)	
	1948	1953	1957	*1948–53*	*1953–57*
Gross national product[c]	293.1	369.0	408.6	*4.7*	*2.6*
Durable goods[c]	55.4	80.8	85.5	*7.8*	*1.5*
Personal consumption expenditures	24.6	33.1	38.5	*6.1*	*3.8*
Producers' durable equipment	22.8	22.5	24.6	*– 0.3*	*2.2*
Government purchases	4.4	21.8	17.0	*37.7*	*– 6.0*
Nondurable goods[c]	112.3	126.9	137.9	*2.5*	*2.1*
Personal consumption expenditures	105.1	118.3	132.6	*2.4*	*2.9*
Government purchases	4.8	10.8	4.3	*17.6*	*–20.5*
Services[c]	97.2	122.5	141.2	*4.7*	*3.6*
Personal consumption expenditures	69.6	83.7	100.1	*3.8*	*4.5*
Government purchases	27.4	40.4	41.9	*8.1*	*0.9*
Construction	28.2	38.8	44.0	*6.6*	*3.3*
Private construction	22.7	27.6	31.8	*4.0*	*3.7*
Government construction	5.5	11.2	12.2	*15.3*	*2.4*

[a] Source, *U. S. Income and Output,* a supplement to *Survey of Current Business* (November 1958), Table VII-6, and *Survey of Current Business* (July 1960), Table 66.
[b] At compound interest.
[c] Includes net exports and change in business inventories not shown separately.

dustries (Chart 30). At the same time, it is clear that other sectors would have invested much less heavily during the recent business contractions (and expansions) were it not for their strong growth potential.

The primary factor behind the deceleration of durable manufacturing between 1953 and 1957 was the decline of government purchases of durable goods (Table 48). Government expenditures of all types had boomed during the Korean War, of course. Government purchases of nondurables dropped at an even greater rate than those of durables after Korea, but over-all demand for nondurables was not retarded as much because such purchases had increased less in previous years and also accounted for a smaller part of the total than was true of durables. The rate of growth of services and construction was also retarded considerably by a marked deceleration, though not an absolute reduction, of government spending after 1953.

The decline of government spending on durables between 1953 and 1957 was largely the result of defense cutbacks after Korea. Just as military expenditure had earlier created investment opportunities in durable manufacturing, during this period it diminished them. Thus the slowdown of durable goods manufacturing and gross national product after 1953 was to a large extent a reaction from the accidental stimulus of war and only partly a symptom of a break in underlying growth tendencies in the economy. Private investment opportunities remained sufficiently favorable to prevent a severe reduction of gross fixed investment during 1958 despite substantial declines in some sectors.

Summary

Aggregate investment demand depends partly on the level and rate of change of real national income and partly on income-autonomous factors like technological change, population growth, and shifts of taste. Autonomous determinants of investment demand will usually favor some industries at the expense of others. Aggregate investment will be augmented by shifts in the composition of demand if the fast-growing industries invest more heavily per unit of output than the lagging industries, and it may be augmented even with equal capital intensities if certain lags are operative.

The empirical investigation of consumption shifts during the postwar decade indicates that they raised investment demand substantially if housing is included, and moderately if it is not—although these results rest on unverified assumptions about the relative magnitudes during the postwar years of the prewar capital coefficients on which the computations are based. The calculations for manufacturing alone are based on current and consistent estimates of capital stock and output, however, and they also indicate that compositional shifts augmented investment demand moderately in 1948-53 and more impressively in 1953-56. The data for manufacturing also make it possible to take account of autonomous investment associated with changes in capital-output ratios. Again, the amounts are found to be positive, and in the case of 1948-53 rather substantial.

The hypothesis that past severe contractions were caused partly by output deceleration in growth industries is theoretically attractive and has some empirical support. The deceleration of output growth between 1953 and 1957 did not lead to a large reduction in the stock of private investment opportunities, however, since it was due principally to cutbacks in defense spending and these cutbacks primarily affected durable manufacturing with its low capital-output ratio, whereas capital-intensive sectors like housing, public utilities, and communications continued to grow rapidly. Private investment opportunities therefore remained sufficiently favorable to prevent a severe reduction of gross fixed investment during 1958, despite substantial declines in some industries.

12 / *Residential Construction*

THE LARGE SHARE of residential construction in total fixed investment makes it an important determinant of the level of aggregate economic activity. In the postwar period, the role of residential construction has been especially prominent because investment in new housing not only has grown at a rapid average rate, but also has figured significantly in each business recovery. Similar periods of buoyancy have characterized residential building in the past, however, only to be followed by prolonged intervals of depressed activity. The causes of the long downswings of building and their relationship to the major business depressions of the past are discussed in this chapter, in order to form a judgment on the future stability of the industry and its effect on the economy.

Postwar Residential Construction

Gross private fixed investment increased at an average rate of 5.9 per cent per year between 1947 and 1958, although its uptrend was punctuated by moderate declines during the contractions of 1948-49, 1953-54, and 1957-58 (Chart 36). The business component of fixed investment behaved rather differently from residential construction, however. Its average rate of increase was slower than that of home building, but it was steadier.[1] It conformed perfectly to the business cycles of the period, moreover, rising continuously during the expansions and falling in every contraction.[2] In contrast, residential con-

[1] The growth rates and stability indexes were 5.6 and 5.4 per cent for business fixed investment and 7.0 and 8.1 per cent for residential construction.

[2] This is not to imply that each industrial sector conformed perfectly. Invest-

CHART 36. *The Growth and Instability of Gross Private Fixed Investment and its Business and Housing Components, 1947-58*[a]

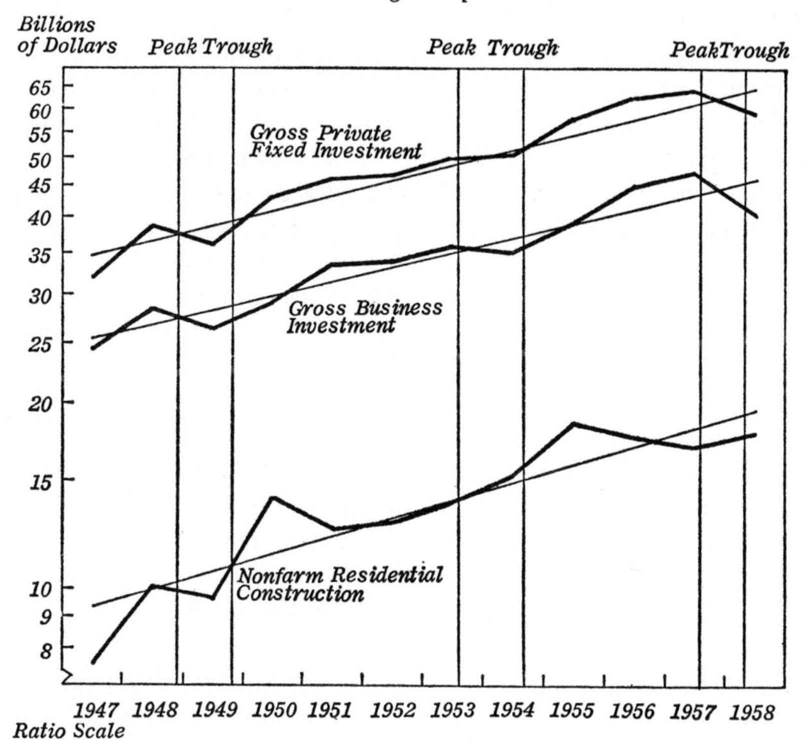

[a] The exponential trends are fitted to the annual data for 1947 to 1958 by the method described in footnote c of Table 34.

Source: Office of Business Economics, Department of Commerce.

struction moved against the cyclical tide during many of the postwar years, and not only during contractions but also during the latter portions of the expansions of 1949-53 and 1954-57.

---

ment in manufacturing, mining, and transportation conformed closely for the most part, but other sectors—public utilities and commercial and financial enterprises—displayed greater independence. These last sectors, like housing, are less sensitive to short-term fluctuations of national income than are the industries engaged in producing and transporting commodities. Farm investment has also conformed poorly to business cycles in the postwar period, again because farm income has been dominated by noncyclical factors. See discussion of the variety of investment behavior in Chapter 8.

The reasons for the contracyclical fluctuations of residential construction are not hard to find. Consumer demand for owner-occupied housing is elastic to variations in the terms on which mortgages can be obtained, and especially to the size of down payments and of monthly payments for interest and amortization. The supply of mortgage credit is also responsive to financial developments, including particularly changes in the relative returns on mortgages and other long-term investments. Since interest rates on residential mortgages are sticky—partly because of administrative ceilings on government-insured or government-guaranteed loans—the supply of mortgage credit at given interest rates has tended to move inversely (and hence contracyclically) to the rate of return on capital funds for other purposes. The reaction has been augmented by deliberate administrative changes in allowable terms on government-backed mortgages, and more generally by the discretionary contracyclical monetary and credit policies that have prevailed since 1951. Indeed, the combination of a plentiful stock of underlying investment opportunities in the housing field and its sensitivity to credit changes goes far toward explaining the success of easy money policies during the recessions of 1953-54 and 1957-58, when residential construction led and business fixed investment lagged on the upturns.[3]

The behavior of residential construction is especially significant because of its large share in aggregate investment. It accounted for almost three-tenths of fixed investment at the postwar business peaks —the only near rival being manufacturing investment, which ran a close second (Table 49). And it was an even larger proportion of the total (36 per cent) during its own peak years of 1950 and 1955.

Nor is the importance of residential building fully reflected in its own share of total investment. New houses require complementary services and community facilities. John M. Mattila and Wilbur R. Thompson have distinguished two broad categories of "completive residential-service investment": house-connected and household-oriented.[4] The first category includes investment to provide residences

[3] However, see the end of the section on monetary policy in the postwar era in Chapter 13 for a discussion of the qualified sense in which residential construction led the cyclical upturn in 1958.

[4] "Residential-Service Construction: A Study of Induced Investment," *Review of Economics and Statistics* (November 1956), pp. 465-73.

with electricity, gas, telephones, water, sewage disposal, and streets. The second embraces needs which are less closely linked in space and time to new housing but are nonetheless broadly related to it except in the case of urban redevelopment: stores, restaurants and garages, churches, schools, hospitals, and social and recreational facilities. Mattila and Thompson estimate on the basis of investment experience during 1920-41 and 1946-54, that each dollar of residential construc-

TABLE 49. *Relative Importance of Residential Construction and Other Components of Gross Private Fixed Investment at Postwar Business Peaks*[a]
(In per cent)

Sector	1948	1953	1957
Residential nonfarm construction....	27.9	29.6	29.4
Manufacturing....................	25.2	25.5	27.6
Mining..........................	2.4	2.1	2.1
Railroads........................	3.6	2.8	2.4
Other transportation..............	3.5	3.3	3.1
Public utilities....................	7.0	9.8	10.7
Commercial and other.............	19.0	17.2	18.0
Farm............................	11.3	9.7	6.7
Total............................	100.0	100.0	100.0

[a] Expenditures on new plant and equipment by business (excluding expenditures of agricultural business and outlays charged to current account) are from the U. S. Department of Commerce, Office of Business Economics, and Securities and Exchange Commission. Farm investment and residential construction are from U. S. Department of Commerce, National Income Division. See *Economic Report of the President* (January 1960), Tables D-8 and D-30. The Commerce-SEC data on business expenditures for plant and equipment are not strictly comparable to the corresponding figures for nonfarm business investment included in the national income accounts, although the differences are unimportant in the present context.

tion (1947-49 prices) induces an additional 40 or 50 cents of investment in related facilities, allowing for lags of two years or less. The estimates include several kinds of public investment, but the private components alone amount to 30 or 40 cents.

In view of the substantial contribution of residential construction to both the growth and stability of the postwar economy, the industry's past record of extreme instability demands attention. Here is another instance where an examination of past experience is an essential prerequisite for an understanding of present and future developments.

The Building Cycle and Severe Depressions

The often noted historical association between severe business contractions and long downswings of building activity is illustrated in Chart 37.[5] The middle curve depicts the volume of real building construction since 1860.[6] The lowest is an index of manufacturing production, which is used here as an indicator of general business fluctuations.

The reader will observe that building construction passed through five long cycles (or waves) between 1865 and 1944. They averaged 16 years in length if the last one is included, and 17 years if it is not. The long cycles were dominated by residential construction, but other types of building participated as well, although not without considerable short-term variability within the broad swings.[7]

Seven major business contractions since the Civil War were listed in Chapter 2. Three of them—1873-78, 1892-94, and 1929-32—were both long and deep. In each case it was six or more years from the onset of contraction before production came permanently to exceed the previous peak. Clearly these were super-depressions. A

[5] This association was emphasized by Clarence D. Long, Jr., *Building Cycles and the Theory of Investment* (1940), Chap. IX, and Alvin H. Hansen, *Fiscal Policy and Business Cycles* (1941), Chap. I.

[6] The estimates include both public and private, and both residential and nonresidential building, but exclude other forms of construction. Before 1915, they are derived by deflating the John R. Riggleman index of the dollar value of building permits as adjusted by Walter Isard to remove the influence of population. The deflator was Riggleman's index of building costs in 1913 dollars. See Miles L. Colean and Robinson Newcomb, *Stabilizing Construction: The Record and Potential* (1952), Appendix N, Tables 2 and 4. Beginning in 1915, the estimates are those of the Department of Commerce and Bureau of Labor Statistics, and measure the value of construction put in place in 1947-49 dollars. The Riggleman-Isard index was used to extrapolate the Commerce-Labor series backward from 1915.

[7] Long, *op. cit.*, Chap. VIII. Some kinds of nonresidential building are linked closely to residential construction. Other types are not, however, and the participation of nonresidential building as a whole in past long building swings is probably due more to the synchronizing power of wars and major depressions than to factors specific to the building industry.

CHART 37. *Population Increase, New Building Construction, and Manufacturing Output, Annually and Three-Year Moving Averages, 1860-1958*

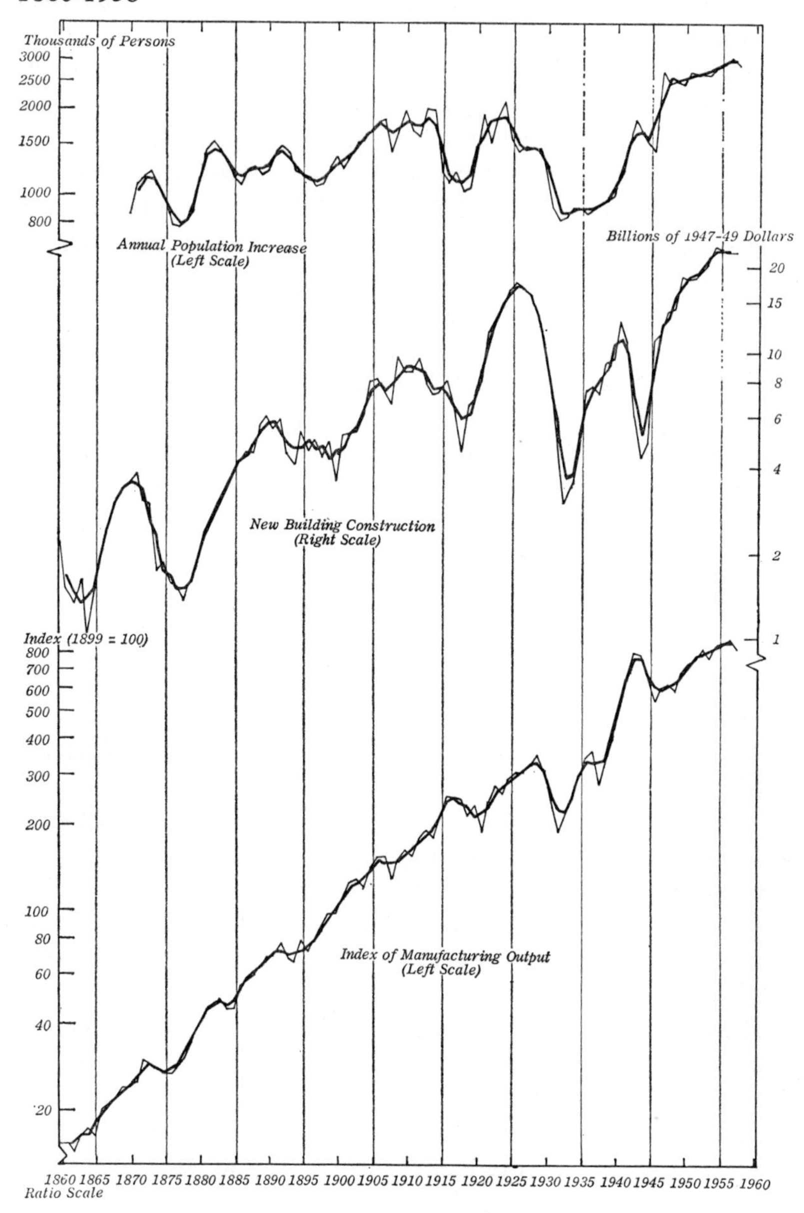

Sources: Population, Simon Kuznets for National Bureau of Economic Research; Building, see Chapter 12, footnote 6; Manufacturing production, see Table 1, footnote b.

glance at the chart will reveal that each of them coincided with a long downswing of building activity. In contrast, those major business contractions which occurred during long building upswings were either relatively moderate in amplitude (1882-85) or relatively brief in duration (1907-08, 1920-21, and 1937-38). At the outset, then, I conclude that business contractions which were sufficiently severe to cause widespread distress have sometimes occurred even when investment prospects remained favorable in housing; but the three super-depressions of the past hundred years were associated with long downswings in residential (and other) building.

The historical relation between building and business cycles is important for the analysis of business cycles primarily because of the possibility that the long swings in building affected the remainder of the economy more than they were affected by it, so that the concurrence of severe business contractions and building downswings was due primarily to independent weakness in the construction industry. However, this last hypothesis is open to serious question in view of the strong interaction between general business activity and residential construction. There are several possible explanations.

War Influences

It will not have escaped the reader's attention that three of the six building cycle troughs depicted in Chart 37 occurred during major wars. War depresses most types of building and hits residential construction especially hard. Since war depresses building but stimulates aggregate production, it is only the peacetime troughs of the building cycle which are associated with severe business depressions. There is still the question, however, whether the peacetime building cycles are not themselves a reaction to war stimuli.

There are two principal avenues by which war could set in motion a series of long building cycles.[8] A major war creates a severe housing shortage and fosters a postwar construction boom. If the structure of the housing market and construction industry is such as to cause prolonged and widespread overbuilding in response to the war disturb-

[8] *Ibid.*, pp. 161-63.

ance, the ensuing building contraction will also be prolonged and severe. Not only that, more long cycles could follow if the industry continued to overadjust to changes in demand. These possibilities will be considered later, after the effect of war on population growth—the second avenue of war influence on building cycles—is discussed.

Population Waves

Population growth and migration obviously create investment opportunities in the housing field. Moreover, there is a fairly close, though imperfect, correlation between the long swings of building and the rate of population increase (Chart 37). If the long swings in the rate of population growth could be assigned to autonomous factors, the associated fluctuations of building might be explained as a simple response. Their duration would depend on the duration of the population waves. As for amplitude, since the demand for additional dwelling units depends on population growth, the volume of new building to house additional families will tend to vary with the rate of population increase, and since the latter is susceptible of wide variation, so also will be the former.[9] If replacement demand is steady, or as seems more likely, if it gets drawn into the same rhythm as other building, population cycles could easily cause wide swings of construction.

One possibility is that the waves of population growth result from major wars which cause marriages and births to decline during the years of belligerency and to spurt thereafter. The population bulge thereby created will tend to repeat itself with diminishing intensity in each new generation. August Losch put the interval between generations at 33 years.[10] This, of course, is too great a span to account for the historical length of the American building fluctuations.[11] Thus, the building downswing of the 1870's came too soon after the Civil

[9] See Arthur F. Burns, "Long Cycles in Residential Construction," *Economic Essays in Honor of Wesley Clair Mitchell* (1935), pp. 63-104.

[10] "Population Cycles as a Cause of Business Cycles," *Quarterly Journal of Economics* (August 1937), pp. 649-62. Losch's population data were for Germany in the nineteenth century, and he was not directly concerned with the building cycle.

[11] Long, *op. cit.*, p. 163.

War for the explanation to hold, although it is not inconsistent with the building trough of the 1890's. Moreover, the interval between generations was probably shorter than 33 years in the United States even during the last three or four decades of the nineteenth century. In 1890, the median age at first marriage for males was 26 years. This interval, however, would fit neither the first building cycle following the Civil War nor the trough of the 1890's.

Difficulties are also encountered when other autonomous determinants of population growth are considered. Statutory immigration curbs contributed to the decline of population increase during the 1920's, and the growing practice of birth control reduced birth rates during the first third of this century.[12] Both these factors affected interwar developments, but neither can account for the earlier swings of population increase.

The fact that fluctuations in income and employment opportunities have pronounced effects on population growth[13] is the most compelling reason to discard the notion of one-way causation from population increase to building cycles to major business fluctuations. Before World War I, variations of income and unemployment influenced population increase principally by their effects on immigration, and thereafter because of their influence over marriage and birth rates. But the level of building activity is a major determinant of the level of national income and employment, and vice versa. Evidently, then, the swings of population increase which accompany the building cycle have themselves a large induced component. That this is so, is strongly suggested by a comparison of the variations in population increase, building construction, and general business activity portrayed in Chart 37.

Consider first the contraction phases of the cycles in population increase during the nineteenth century. Counting from peak to trough,

[12] W. S. and E. S. Woytinsky, *World Population and Production, Trends and Outlook* (1953), pp. 159-62.

[13] Harry Jerome, *Migration and Business Cycles* (1926); Simon Kuznets and Ernest Rubin, *Immigration and the Foreign Born,* National Bureau of Economic Research, Occasional Paper 46 (1954); Moses Abramovitz, "Long Swings in the Economic Growth of the United States," *Employment Growth and Price Levels,* Part 2, Hearings Before the Joint Economic Committee, 86 Cong. 1 sess. (1959), pp. 411-66.

they were: 1873-77, 1882-86, and 1892-97. These intervals sound familiar, of course, because they correspond to the major depressions of the period. The first one also corresponds to a building downswing, but its peak came in 1871. The building downswing began, in other words, two years before population growth started to decline. The decline of building helped precipitate the business contraction, but it was the business contraction which caused population growth to diminish.

The second period of retarded population increase coincided with the business contraction of 1882-85, during which building continued to rise. Thus, on the one hand, building activity was not primarily determined by current population increase, and on the other, population increase did respond to the decline of general business.

The third downswing of population growth again lagged the building downswing but coincided with the business depression of the 1890's. Both general business activity and population growth, moreover, recovered several years before building construction. The upturn of population growth doubtless contributed to the later revival of building, but the population upturn was itself induced by the business revival.

The correlation between population growth and general business activity is not as close in the twentieth century, but for reasons which do not imply that building cycles are regularly caused by autonomous population cycles. Thus the fact that both building and population growth diminished sharply during the world wars, and despite increases in aggregate economic activity, merely means that both were responding to war depressants. Finally, although restrictive immigration legislation caused population growth to decline after 1924, this one clear instance of an autonomous population lead over both building and general business, stands out precisely because it is an isolated case.

Transport Innovation and the Building Cycle

Walter Isard has stressed the considerable covariation between long swings in building and in transportation investment, and states that:

> The underlying causal force behind the cyclical movements, which, broadly, average seventeen-to-eighteen years, is the irregular emergence of transport innovation and the jerky development of the transport network, and [that] building represents more or less the culmination of the process of industrial, commercial, and population adaption to the changing character of transport.[14]

In Isard's view, major innovations in transport—canals, railroads, street and electric railways, and the automobile—successively initiated one or more long swings in residential building because of the links between transport improvement, population migration, and community development.

As for the long duration of the induced swings of residential construction, Isard argues that:

> The formation of rather regular cyclical patterns from spurts of building activity is dependent upon, and results from, appropriate monetary conditions. American experience offers a case where the speculative elements were too often given a free rein. These elements tend to distort the real phenomena of housing need. The intense speculative fever has always interpreted a sharp, sudden increase in housing needs in unduly optimistic terms, thereby causing an over-production of residential units and progressive creation of excess housing. This usually continued until a collapse of the financial structure caused an almost paralytic cessation of building activity through exaggerated pessimism, and it was only after the creation of an urgent housing demand by new transport developments that building activity regained new prosperous levels.[15]

The response mechanism which Isard advanced to explain the severity and duration of the building cycle, which embraces the assumption of speculative overbuilding due to psychological causes and to defects of financial structure and practice, has appealed to other writers.

[14] "A Neglected Cycle: The Transport-Building Cycle," *Review of Economic Statistics* (November 1942), p. 149. See also, Norman J. Silberling, *The Dynamics of Business* (1943), Chaps. 9 and 10.

[15] Walter Isard, "Transport Development and Building Cycles," *Quarterly Journal of Economics* (November 1942), pp. 90-112.

Structural Factors in the Residential Building Cycle

A powerful disturbance, like war, may initiate a spurt of housing construction lasting several years. However, such a spurt will not in itself cause even one long housing cycle, let alone a series of them. There must also be some response mechanism capable of converting the shock into a cycle or sequence of cycles. Among the possible mechanisms, a distinction must be drawn between those internal to the housing sector itself, which might cause independent housing cycles, and those which involve other sectors of the economy and affect residential building through some feedback relationship. A third possibility, which has already been dismissed, is that of independent cycles in the rate of population growth which become mirrored in residential construction and therefore in aggregate economic activity.

For a leading example of a response mechanism which emphasizes the mutual interaction of building and business activity, I cite Arthur F. Burns.[16] Among the principal elements stressed by Burns are the extreme durability of buildings, which makes the demand for new construction depend primarily on population growth; the variability of the rate of population growth; and the changes of housing standards which occur in prosperity and depression. Burns analyzed also the effects of internal migration on demand and of uncertainty on estimated demand. Uncertainty, of course, can lead to overestimates of housing demand and hence to overbuilding.

Does the record of housing construction since World War I provide evidence of the operation of these forces? Estimates of the number of nonfarm dwelling units started and the number of nonfarm households formed each year between 1911 and 1958 are pictured in Chart 38. A household consists of all persons occupying a single dwelling unit. The increase in the number of households is a better measure of potential demand for new residential construction than is the increase of total population. It is apparent from the chart that there was a fairly close correspondence between the long swings in house-

[16] *Op. cit.*

CHART 38. *Nonfarm Household Formation, Nonfarm Dwelling Units Started, and the Cumulative Difference, Annually, 1911-58*

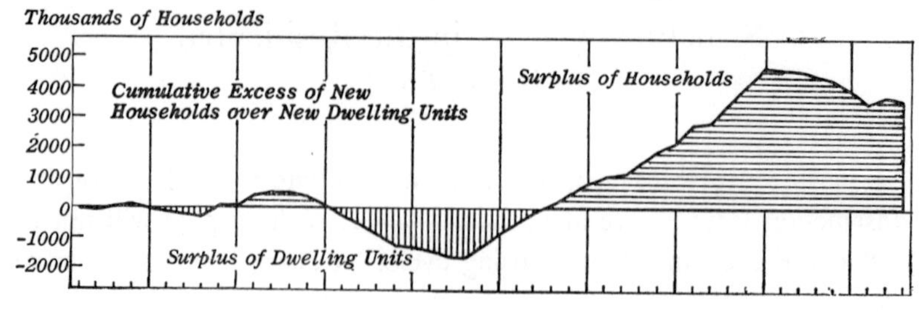

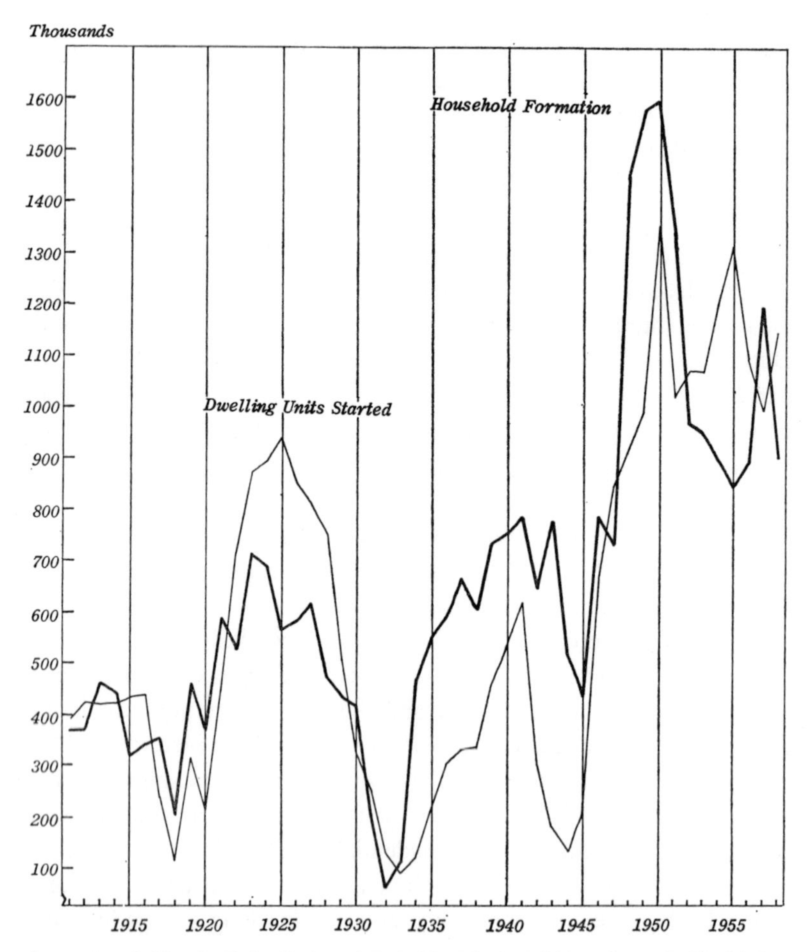

Source: Leo Grebler, David M. Blank, and Louis Winnick, *Capital Formation in Residential Real Estate* (1956); Bureau of the Census.

hold formation and those in residential construction between the world wars. Nevertheless, the fluctuations of residential construction cannot be explained as a simple response to those of household formation, for two reasons.

First, the rate of household formation was itself influenced by the level of economic activity, and hence, by the level of residential construction. Thus the observed fluctuations of household formation during the interwar period are a compound of autonomous forces—war, immigration legislation, and social attitudes—and economic influences. When per capita income plunged during the early 1930's so also did immigration, marriages, and housing standards. The rate of new household formation dropped precipitously as fewer new families were formed and as families doubled up in existing quarters.

Second, the cycles in construction are not mere replicas of those in household formation. True, the interwar turning points either coincided or differed by only a year or two, and when there was a lag, it was the expected one of housing starts behind household formation. Notice, however, the differences in amplitude of the two series. The amplitude of the cycle in construction between 1918 and 1933 was much larger than that of household formation, whereas the reverse was true of the upswing of 1933-41. Evidently forces other than shifts of demand stemming from variations in the rate of household formation helped shape the construction cycles. This brings us to structural factors specific to the housing sector.

An increase of demand for new dwelling units must be expressed through market forces before it can become an effective inducement of additional construction. Builders must anticipate profitable sale of the new units, which generally means quick turnover at steady or rising prices and with adequate profit margins. These conditions will be met for new rental units whenever the capitalized value of the anticipated income stream is high enough to provide a ready market for the new units at going prices. This capitalized value will vary directly with the level of rent (and expected rent) and inversely with the cost of funds and prospective maintenance expenditures. Similar considerations apply in the case of houses intended for owner-occupancy.

The principal determinant of prospective yields is the level of rents, which affects the value of rental property directly and that of owner-occupied units indirectly. Rents, in turn, depend primarily on the vacancy rate and the level of average family income.[17] If rents respond only slowly to conditions of excess demand or supply in the market for the services of existing buildings, or the volume of construction responds only slowly to changes in the derived demand for new buildings, or both, the conditions are present for waves of overbuilding and underbuilding relative to the underlying real opportunities created by population growth. Since rents do tend to be sticky and the construction industry does tend to expand and contract in good part through the time-consuming process of entry and exit of small contractors, it would not be surprising if the industry were especially susceptible to prolonged or amplified fluctuations. A critical question, of course, is whether these factors merely amplify fluctuations due to other causes, or actually set the duration of the observed building swings.

J. B. D. Derksen has published the major econometric investigation of endogenous building cycles; that is, of building cycles caused by a response mechanism internal to the housing sector.[18] The period studied was 1914-38 and the statistical technique was multiple regression. The principal variables affecting nonfarm housing starts were rents, building costs (lagged one year), the rate of change of average nonfarm family income, and the annual increase in the number of nonfarm families (lagged two years). Income, building costs, and family formation were considered to be largely independent of the level of residential construction, so that rent was the only endogenous variable. Rent itself was determined by an exogenous variable—average family income—and an endogenous one—the occupancy ratio. The latter, of course, is a measure of the intensity of use of the housing stock and is the complement of the vacancy ratio.

Derksen determined experimentally that the best statistical estimate of the annual level of rents was given by the current level of family income and the rate of occupancy which had prevailed two years

[17] Lowell J. Chawner, *Residential Building*, Industrial Committee of the National Resources Committee, Housing Monograph Series No. 1 (1939); J. Tinbergen, *Statistical Testing of Business Cycle Theories* (1939); J. B. D. Derksen, "Long Cycles in Residential Building: An Explanation," *Econometrica* (April 1940), pp. 97-116.

[18] *Ibid.*

earlier. A lag of this magnitude is not unreasonable in view of the imperfect nature of the rental market and the fact that dwellings are commonly rented on an annual basis. The length of the lag is important because it determines the period of the endogenous cycle of overbuilding and underbuilding. It is therefore of considerable interest to note that Lowell Chawner, using much the same data and techniques as Derksen, obtained a good correlation between rents and occupancy with a lag of about one year.[19]

Even with a two-year lag, the period of the implied endogenous cycle is only 12 years.[20] The actual cycle after World War I lasted from 1918 to 1933-34, or 15-16 years. This means that the factors exogenous to housing construction—population change, income, and construction costs—prolonged the decline from the 1925 peak by several years and actually set the duration of the building downswing. As Derksen shows, the downswing of building after 1925 would have been several years shorter and much milder had the exogenous factors remained constant. In fact, with a two-year lag, the endogenous "oscillations are very damped: the cyclical fluctuations disappear practically after completion of one cycle."[21]

Derksen suggests that, before 1914, the total lag between a change in the occupancy ratio and the resulting change in housing starts, which could involve a lag of starts behind rents as well as one of rents behind vacancies, might well have been longer than two years. A lag of three and a half years, for instance, would yield an endogenous cycle of 15 years and with a much smaller degree of damping.[22] This still falls two years short of the average duration of the building cycles prior to World War I, however. Moreover, a lag of three and a half years is intuitively too long to be reasonable. It is much more likely that, except for the war-induced cycle of 1865-79, the observed long swings of residential construction between the Civil War and World War I were more nearly the result than the cause of the associated swings of population increase and income.[23] This conviction is

[19] Chawner, *op. cit.*
[20] Derksen, *op. cit.*
[21] *Ibid.,* p. 115.
[22] *Ibid.,* p. 116.
[23] For a similar judgment, see James S. Duesenberry, *Business Cycles and Economic Growth* (1958), Chap. 7.

strengthened by the observations that the building downswing of the 1890's was heavily damped relative to that of the 1870's, and that no serious decline of residential construction occurred in the twentieth century until the United States entered World War I.

The boom and depression in residential construction during the 1920's and 1930's was intensified by overbuilding in its physical aspect, as is illustrated by Chart 38. Notice that housing starts turned upward along with household formation in 1919. Starts did lag, however, in the sense that they were fewer than the number of new households. Indeed, starts fell short of household formation in every year from 1917 to 1921. But this means that population was outstripping the rise of the housing stock even apart from demolitions and abandonments, and assuming that conversions of existing structures were not an important source of additional dwelling units.[24] The result was a growing shortage of dwelling units.

The cumulated excess of household formation over housing starts can be used as an indicator of the trend of occupancies relative to available units, beginning the cumulation in 1911 (top panel of Chart 38).[25] Assuming that vacancy rates were at the normal frictional level during 1911-14—which appears reasonable in view of the steadiness of housing starts during those years—then a negative cumulated excess indicates a surplus stock of dwelling units and a positive excess means a shortage of accommodations. The upward pressure on rents would be greatest when the shortage was increasing; but rents might be expected to rise at least as long as vacancies were below normal—as long as the cumulated excess was positive—and perhaps for a short

[24] Neither replacements nor conversions were quantitatively important in the 1920's. See Leo Grebler, David M. Blank, and Louis Winnick, *Capital Formation in Residential Real Estate* (1956), Appendix A.

[25] Each annual increase of households was compared with the number of housing starts during the preceding year in the calculation of the cumulated excess. Because of the lag of completions behind starts, the addition to the housing stock occasioned by the starts during a calendar year actually takes place from about the middle of that year to the middle of the next year. Since the stock of households is estimated as of July (or March or April after 1946), the annual increment of households plotted in a given calendar year is actually the estimated increase from the middle of the previous year to the middle of the given year, and is properly compared with the starts of the previous year to ascertain the trend of the occupancy ratio.

while longer.[26] This is just what appears to have happened in the 1920's.

Starts exceeded household formation during 1922-25, eliminating most or all of the shortage. In addition, the rate of household formation dropped considerably after 1924. For both reasons, vacancies increasingly exceeded the normal frictional level after 1925, so that rents turned down in 1925 or 1926 and starts in 1926. Starts declined through the rest of the decade, but they continued to exceed the rate of household formation, and hence the physical surplus continued to grow. By 1929, it amounted to an estimated 1.2 million units, or about three times the current rate of household formation. Why did such a large surplus develop?

One reason was that rents declined only moderately as vacancies accumulated, which is another way of saying that the economic surplus was smaller than the physical surplus, even allowing for the rental lag. Income was still rising, offsetting part of the response of rents to vacancies.[27] No doubt there was substantial upgrading of housing standards during those years, with vacancies increasing among the least desirable units in each rental bracket and depressing other rentals comparatively little.

It is probably of considerable significance that the peak in starts of apartment houses was not reached until 1927, or two years after those of single-family units and aggregate starts, and that apartment starts fell but little even in 1928. Speculation on quick capital gains doubtless played a part, and perhaps an important one, in the apartment building boom of the late 1920's. As Duesenberry has emphasized, speculative activity is likely to center on apartment houses, since they are rented more easily than single houses. Once underway, moreover, a boom based partly on expectations of short-term capital gains is

[26] This factor may be the major reason for Derksen's two-year lag of rents behind the occupancy ratio. If the peak occupancy ratio were abnormally high, rents could continue to rise for a time as vacancies increased to the normal level. The increasing vacancy rate during this (say) two-year period would not be evidence of "overbuilding" relative to "normal" demand, however.

[27] The rent index of the National Industrial Conference Board dropped 40 per cent between 1924 and 1933, but only 13.5 per cent from 1924 to 1929. The rent component of the Bureau of Labor Statistics consumer price index fell 38 per cent from its peak in 1925 to its trough in 1934, but the decline from 1925 to 1929 was merely 7 per cent.

likely to continue for some time after rents have begun to weaken, both because of the long gestation period for apartment buildings and because promoters tend to conceal the difficulty of renting new structures by granting concessions.[28] The high rate of apartment construction in 1926-28 was especially important because the dwelling units added in new structures housing three or more families accounted for three-tenths of all new units, as compared with one-tenth in the 1950's.

The gap which opened between the stock of dwelling units and the number of households during the late 1920's is the principal evidence of residential overbuilding before the onset of the depression—and that gap may readily be explained as a consequence of lagged reactions to changes in the occupancy ratio, together with the intensifying effects of speculative real estate activity. Was residential overbuilding an important deflationary factor in the downturn of 1929? This question really has two parts: Did the drop of housing construction contribute importantly to the business downturn? Did overbuilding cause the drop?

On the first point, it is clear that housing starts fell from 1925 onward, despite the continued growth of national income. It is equally apparent that this deflationary influence was overcompensated by increases in other forms of investment demand until 1929. Thus, residential construction contributed to the downturn in the same manner as any income-autonomous decline in a particular industry, but in proportion to its great size. It partly offset investment increases elsewhere and probably retarded the growth of aggregate investment prior to the downturn.

There appears also to have been residential overbuilding before the depression began, although one may accept Schumpeter's admonition that this factor is easily overstressed.[29] He had in mind speculative overbuilding—rather than overbuilding resulting from lagged responses—but there probably was some of both. At the same time, it should be emphasized that both investment opportunities and realized investment in housing were diminishing during the late 1920's, not

[28] Duesenberry, *op. cit.*, pp. 153-55.
[29] Joseph A. Schumpeter, *Business Cycles*, Vol. II (1939), pp. 744-48.

only because of overbuilding, but also because of the income-autonomous decrease of household formation.

No matter what one's judgment on the degree of overbuilding during the late 1920's, it is evident from the behavior of vacancies and rents that the supply of shelter was increasing faster than the demand at going rates of population growth and family income. The early decline of residential construction, in other words, was not due primarily to cost factors, and this meant that new home-building during the contraction could not be restored to predepression levels merely by easy credit or reduced building costs. (In this vital respect the situation differed considerably from that during the 1950's.)

Once into the contraction, moreover, there was cumulative deflationary interaction between residential construction and aggregate demand. Each decline of building reduced income, but each reduction of income depressed rents and augmented vacancies. There were also feedback relationships between real estate prices, the value of bank portfolios, and the lending policies of banks on mortgages and other securities. These factors must be kept in mind when interpreting the relation between household formation and housing starts during the depression.

New housing starts decreased along with household formation during the early 1930's, so that the calculated surplus of dwelling units was increased only 400,000 units from the predepression level by erection of new structures. However, the cumulated excess of household formation over new starts is an inadequate index of occupancy rates during the depression decade. This is because more than a million dwelling units were added to the housing stock between 1930 and 1939 by conversion of existing structures, as compared with new starts totaling 2.6 million during the same period.[30] Thus new starts lagged so far behind household formation during 1933-39 partly because of the excess supply of previously erected dwelling units and partly because of the high level of conversions during the 1930's. Real per capita disposable personal income recovered after 1933, but it did not regain the 1929 level until 1940. The deterioration of housing standards which accompanied the reduced level of income took

[30] Grebler *et al., op. cit.,* p. 329.

the form in part of reliance on inexpensive conversions rather than new structures to supply additional dwelling units.

The contraction of aggregate demand during 1929-33 was considerably aggravated by "debt deflation," including that resulting from residential mortgage indebtedness. The burden of fixed mortgage debt increased as money incomes and prices fell. Foreclosures mounted swiftly, adding to the downward pressure on real estate prices. The fall in real estate values directly reduced the profitability of new construction, but the indirect repercussions on bank assets and bank lending were probably of greater importance.

The deterioration of bank portfolios due to the fall in prices of mortgages and other securities increased the liquidity preference of banks and other financial institutions alike. Banks pressed for repayment of loans and were reluctant to make new ones. Customer fears of bank solvency increased, leading to currency withdrawals and putting additional pressure on banks to liquidate their loans and investments.

As far as mortgage debt is concerned, the deflationary consequences were powerful both because of its size and its quality. Both the nonfarm residential mortgage debt and its ratio to disposable personal income had tripled during the 1920's, and the average debt per household had more than doubled.[31] But the burden of debt is not fully measured by the debt-income ratio, both because the debt may be rotating among the population—with new families coming forward to incur new debt as the old is retired by others[32]—and because the burden is affected by the size of monthly payments, and these are not necessarily proportional to the size of the debt. And, of course, the debt was probably not unduly burdensome at the income levels of the late 1920's. Nonetheless, the marked increase of the debt-income ratio during the prosperity decade is not without significance for the developments of the 1930's, for two reasons.

First, mortgage terms changed comparatively little during the 1920's,[33] so that monthly outlays for debt service probably rose about

[31] *Ibid.*, Chap. XI.

[32] See the discussion of this subject in the section on postwar behavior of instalment credit in Chap. 10.

[33] Grebler *et al., op. cit.*, Chap. XV.

proportionately to the debt. The burden of fixed monthly payments grew heavier thereafter as incomes dropped.

Second, the size of the mortgage debt was in itself a better measure of its burden, or rather its potential burden during times of depression, than is true today. Nowadays most mortgages are fully amortized. This was not the case in the 1920's except for mortgages written by savings and loan associations. At that time, 46 per cent of the mortgage loans made by commercial banks were not amortized, and only 13 per cent were completely amortized. The corresponding percentages for loans from life insurance companies were 22 and 18.[34] Lack of amortization made little difference as long as times were good and a new mortgage could be obtained to retire the old one. After the boom collapsed, however, many a borrower was forced into foreclosure because he was unable to refinance his mortgage when it came due. Foreclosures and distress sales would have been fewer—probably substantially fewer—during the early 1930's had mortgages been fully amortized and borrowers responsible only for the monthly payment and not the principal amount. They would also have been fewer with today's government insurance and guarantee programs.

Investment in Housing After World War II

Housing construction during the 1940's was dominated by war and its aftermath. As usual, household formation plummeted during the war and skyrocketed for a few years thereafter. Also, as usual, housing starts fell even more drastically than household formation during the war, so that a backlog of demand accumulated despite the reduction in population growth. The classic groundwork had been laid for a postwar housing boom (Chart 38).

The boom did develop during 1946-50, but it failed to assume the proportions of the corresponding upsurge of household formation, so

[34] *Ibid.*, Table 66.

that the cumulated excess of new households over new dwelling units mounted steadily. Just as in the 1930's, however, the cumulated excess is a spurious index of the occupancy ratio.[35] The stock of dwelling units actually increased more than the number of households between 1940 and 1950, although new starts amounted to only 54 per cent of the increase of dwelling units. The difference was supplied by conversions, transfer of farmhouses to nonfarm residential use, and occupancy of trailers, cabins, and the like. Thus, the underlying nexus between population growth and the increase in the housing stock was maintained in the 1940's (and 1930's), but that between population growth and construction of new residential structures was not.[36]

Household formation dropped precipitously from its abnormal postwar peak after 1949-50, but new starts did not fall correspondingly. Instead, they oscillated widely about a roughly horizontal "trend" during the 1950's. The "local peak" of starts in 1955 was slightly lower than in 1950, but the seasonally adjusted annual rate of starts during the first half of 1959 (not shown in Chart 38) was slightly above the annual total for 1950. More important is the fact that the dollar amount of new residential construction rose considerably even between 1950 and 1955 (Chart 36). Nor was the uptrend of expenditure due only to price increases. Real expenditures also rose, owing to increases in the physical volume of additions and alterations and in the average amount of real expenditure per new dwelling unit.

New starts and household formation were unequal in every year and often moved inversely during the 1950's, since the timing of construction was governed more by changes in the supply of funds than by shifts in demand for new houses. Nevertheless, the long-run relationship between starts and households, which had broken down during the 1930's and 1940's, was re-established during the 1950's. That is, the number of new starts between 1950 and 1957 exceeded the growth of nonfarm households from March 1950 to March 1958

[35] At the level reached by the 1940's, the cumulative excess would have to be a spurious index of the occupancy ratio unless vacancies had been enormous in the initial year of the cumulation. This is because a household is, by definition, the social group occupying a dwelling unit, so that the number of households can never exceed the number of existing dwelling units, although it can fall short by the amount of vacant units.

[36] Grebler *et al.*, *op. cit.*, Chap. V.

by about 15 per cent. Evidently conversions were an unimportant source of new dwelling units during the 1950's, presumably because the postwar housing shortage was easing and real incomes were high. Other signs of an easier supply were a decrease in the doubling ratio (proportion of married couples living with others) from 8.7 per cent in 1947 to 5.6 per cent in 1950 and 3.1 per cent in 1958, and an increase in the percentage of dwelling units for sale or rent from 1.6 in 1950 to 2.9 in 1958.[37]

The war-induced backlog of housing demand seems to have been liquidated sometime during the 1950's. Moreover, the transition to "normal" conditions occurred without a building depression, and despite the pronounced drop of household formation after the immediate postwar upsurge of marriages and the drop in the doubling ratio. The transition occurred so smoothly, principally because such a large proportion of the demand for new dwelling units during the 1940's had been supplied by conversions. Had the postwar shortage been eliminated by new starts instead of conversions, the level of new construction would necessarily have carried much higher, and a radical downward adjustment would have followed when the demand for new dwelling units receded to a normal level.[38] Be that as it may, the transition was in fact smooth, and no substantial deflationary force akin to that of the late 1920's developed in the housing sector.

With regard to the future, there are sound reasons to believe that the housing industry will not again pose as serious a deflationary threat to the economy as it has in times past, although it may still exhibit considerable independence of national income and its movements. Residential construction—while still a substantial share of gross investment and national product—is now much less important than in the 1920's because of the secular decline in real expenditure

[37] Bureau of the Census, *Current Population Reports,* Series P-20, No. 86; Housing and Home Finance Agency, *Housing in the Economy, 1955* (1957), p. 67, and *Housing Statistics* (May 1959), p. 18.

[38] It is unlikely, of course, that without conversions the shortage could have been eliminated as rapidly as it was, given supply limitations on the volume of new construction. In the absence of conversions, and with a gradually rising limit on new construction, the building upswing would have been stretched out, and the decline after elimination of the shortage would have been smaller than is suggested by the actual course of household formation.

per new dwelling unit[39] and because national income has grown more rapidly than population. Residential nonfarm construction amounted to only 2.5 per cent of real gross national product during 1947-55, as compared with 4.5 per cent in 1920-29 (Table 27). Thus, a housing downswing as severe as in 1925-33 would be a much smaller depressant now than it was during those earlier years.

Moreover, the past long downswings of residential building would have been much milder, and probably also shorter, had they not been reinforced by contraction elsewhere in the economy. But the cyclical response mechanism of the economy has been damped somewhat by the structural changes of the past quarter century, and this will lend greater stability to the industry—and hence the economy—even apart from the potentialities of discretionary contracyclical actions. Among the important structural changes is the widespread adoption of the fully amortized government-insured or government-guaranteed home mortgage, which will act directly to diminish the amplitude of any future long downswing in residential building. In combination with other financial reforms, it will also mitigate the financial repercussions which accompany income contraction and which so often in the past have degenerated into cumulative spirals between liquidity preference and effective demand.

Together with this, it is probable that the trend of residential construction will be upward during the next two decades, or at least after the early 1960's.[40] Within a few years, marriage rates will begin to echo the upsurge of births during the postwar years, and nonfarm household formation will be further augmented if, as seems likely, the historical trends toward a smaller average household and a declining number of farm households continue to prevail. Additionally, demolitions are apt to increase in importance with greater activity under urban renewal and municipal highway programs. Internal migration and increasing ownership of vacation or weekend cottages also may add significantly to the demand for new housing.

The foregoing forces would lose much of their influence, of course, if real income failed to grow, but it does look as if the demographic

[39] Grebler *et al., op. cit.,* Chap. VII.

[40] The following discussion of the long-term outlook for residential construction is based primarily on Grebler *et al., op. cit.,* Part C.

determinants of residential construction are on the side of expansion. This does not mean, however, that residential construction will rise proportionally to aggregate investment or income. On the contrary, the anticipated rise in the absolute rate of household formation may be offset in its effect on investment, in part, at least, by a prolongation of the secular downtrend in amount of real expenditure per new dwelling unit, and per capita income growth will favor other demands relative to housing. Thus, unless there is a decline in the average propensity to save at full-employment income levels, other investment demands—including, possibly, public expenditures—will have to rise more rapidly than income if full employment is to be maintained.

13 / *Financial Reforms and Monetary Policy*

THE FINANCIAL STRUCTURE of the economy has changed markedly during the past quarter century. Many of the changes date from the mid-1930's or 1940's and consist of financial or monetary reforms which were consciously designed to augment economic stability. Others evolved out of competitive processes to satisfy private demands—as in the case of the growth in relative importance of nonmonetary financial intermediaries like insurance companies and savings and loan associations—but may nonetheless have affected cyclical behavior. Still another—the enormous growth of liquid assets and marketable federal debt during World War II—not only added to the liquidity of the postwar economy but modified both the goals and the scope of monetary policy.

These developments will be examined from three points of view. How important were financial factors in past depressions? How wise has been the conduct of monetary policy during the postwar era? To what extent, if any, has monetary policy been weakened by the growth of nonmonetary financial intermediaries and other changes in the economic environment?

Financial Reforms

The principal changes in the financial structure were described in the section on financial reforms in Chapter 8; those relating to housing finance were discussed further in Chapter 12. The remaining reforms fall into three groups. One is designed to curb potentially disequilibrating financial activities in the securities markets. Another comprises safeguards to prevent mass bank failures. The third consists of basic modifications of the monetary system in the direction of greater independence of international monetary conditions and thus of greater scope for the use of monetary policy in the interest of domestic stability.

There can be little doubt that the foregoing financial reforms have augmented the resistance of the economy to deflationary forces. One must still ask, however, whether the improvement in this respect is of major or minor significance for economic stability. The answer depends primarily on whether financial factors were of major or minor importance in the severe contractions of the past.

Financial Crises Before World War I

Several of the reforms were designed to prevent or mitigate financial crises. Financial crises may administer a powerful deflationary shock because of the abnormal demands for liquidity which they engender owing to loss of confidence in the value of goods and securities and —in the more extreme cases—of some forms of money, or because of the downshift of the consumption function which may result from a fall in the real value of assets.[1] A key point is that financial shocks can occur for reasons which are independent of the state of the "real" determinants of aggregate demand.

Each of the four major contractions between the Civil War and World War I was marked by a financial panic.[2] The national banking system was especially vulnerable because of the practice of depositing reserves with correspondent commercial banks in New York City. Such deposits could earn handsome returns because they were re-

[1] For an analysis of the various forms of deflationary pressure from financial factors, see Gottfried Haberler, *Prosperity and Depression,* 3rd ed., United Nations (1946), Chap. 10, sec. 8. These forms include outright deflation by the central bank, hoarding of gold or bank notes by individuals, credit contraction by commercial banks, hoarding by industrial and commercial firms, liquidation of nonbank debts, forced sales of assets to repay debts, sales of assets to cover business losses, and sales of assets for fear of a fall in their price.

[2] O. M. W. Sprague, *History of Crises Under the National Banking System,* National Monetary Commission, 61 Cong. 2 sess. (1910).

loaned in the call loan market to finance stock speculation. Seasonal increases in the demand for currency by country banks could force a substantial contraction of call loans and put pressure on stock prices. A reduction of security values, or a few failures in the financial community, could set off a chain reaction in which outside banks withdrew deposits, forcing correspondent banks to reduce call loans, which in turn led to liquidation of stocks which had secured the loans, which further depressed stock prices, etc. Public alarm could lead quickly to bank runs and suspensions, especially since the correspondent banks after 1873 preferred to suspend payments to interior banks rather than permit their own reserve ratios to fall below customary limits.

Crises occurred early in the depressions of 1873-78, 1892-97 and 1907-08. In each instance the proximate cause of the crisis is to be found in financial excesses which had developed during the upswing—in 1873 and 1893 in connection with railroad financing and imprudent banking methods, and in 1907 because of trust company practices. Financial factors were particularly prominent in the prolonged monetary crisis of 1907, and it is probable that the brief business contraction of 1907-08 was deep primarily because of them. The panics of 1873 and 1893 doubtless aggravated the early phases of contraction, but it seems unlikely that they contributed importantly to the extended duration of the depressions, except perhaps to the extent that they uncovered the financial weakness and poor short-term prospects of railroads and related ventures. For the rest, the panics were over in a few weeks (1873) or months (1893) and could scarcely have caused several years of depression had real investment opportunities been favorable to expansion. The economy recovered much more rapidly from comparable financial shocks at the beginning of the contractions of 1890-91 and 1907-08.

A better case for prolongation of contraction because of a financial crisis can be made for the panic of 1884. This panic occurred after more than two years of business contraction, which had, however, been comparatively mild in production, though not in prices. The panic itself was relatively minor and confined to New York City. Its main cause was loss of confidence in financial institutions owing to failures among brokerage houses and banks because of fraud and defalcation. It was over within one week, but not before it had led to a precipitous drop in share prices and a large number of failures among New York financial houses. The adverse effects on investment expectations may readily have caused the additional year of economic contraction which followed the panic.

Crises Under the Federal Reserve System

The structural weaknesses of the national banking system were important contributing causes to financial crises before World War I, but it is the sad lesson of history that the reforms under the Federal Reserve System were insufficient to prevent either the stock market crash of 1929 or the bank failures of the 1930's. Nor did the formation of the System ensure that the money supply would be so managed as to prevent monetary deflation during periods of business contraction.

There can be little doubt that the major contraction of 1920-21 was deepened by the deliberate actions which were taken to tighten money and credit: certainly its amplitude was much larger than the corresponding post-war contraction of 1948-49 despite the presence of underlying elements of strength markedly similar to those of the later experience. Deflation of bank credit and prices was regarded as a necessary and desirable aftermath of the war and postwar inflation, and the primary concern of the Federal Reserve was that the inevitable liquidation be an orderly one. As Chandler in a Brookings Institution study points out, by the standards of the day, the policy was a success: "It did, after all, succeed in maintaining gold payments and in avoiding financial crisis and 'disorderly' liquidation."[3]

The Federal Reserve grappled with the twin problems of speculation and inflation in the stock market in 1928-29, using as its weapons moral suasion and a restrictive monetary policy. The one was directed specifically at "speculative" bank loans but was ineffectual in reach-

[3] L. V. Chandler, *Benjamin Strong, Central Banker* (1958), p. 187. Chandler is perhaps overly generous in this appraisal. Bank suspensions in 1921 were eight times the number in 1919 and about three times the number in 1920. See Bureau of the Census, *Historical Statistics of the United States, 1789-1945* (1947), Table N-135.

ing them, whereas the other probably restrained real investment more than stock speculation. Margin controls were unavailable at the time, nor were they requested.

The great bull market doubtless induced some misdirected real investment and there may have occurred a general overestimation of prospective yields. However, there is little evidence in the available data on capacity utilization and capital-output ratios of generalized excess capacity before the downturn. The major damage came during the downswing, when the stock market crash exposed the weakness of the financial structure and initiated a process of cumulative monetary deflation. The fall of security prices was self-reinforcing and in time it contributed to a liquidity crisis which was abetted by deflationary central bank actions and the collapse of the international gold standard. The banking structure was not shaken seriously until the solvency crisis of late 1931—the Federal Reserve had acted to ease the commercial banks over the earlier crisis in the stock exchange—by which time the contraction was already a major one. On the other hand, the flood of bank failures during the following 18 months obviously helped prolong and worsen the contraction.

Many of the weaknesses which contributed to the financial debacle of the 1930's[4] have been eliminated. Margin requirements may now be raised to limit the pyramiding of stock market credit which may otherwise occur through the very increase in the collateral value of securities which speculation on margin encourages.[5] Margin controls cannot prevent speculation on capital gains, but they can certainly slow it, and they can mitigate the worst effects of margin calls and enforced liquidation on declining markets, since these are generally proportionate to the relative importance of earlier margin purchases. In much the same way, the extreme leverage formerly offered for inflation and deflation of security values through pyramiding of investment trusts and holding companies has been diminished by remedial legis-

[4] John Kenneth Galbraith, *The Great Crash, 1929* (1955).

[5] That is, stock purchases based on margin credit help to raise the market value of existing portfolios, thereby augmenting the collateral value of the portfolios and increasing the amount of margin credit which may be based on them.

lation and regulation. Deposit insurance should inhibit chain-reaction bank failures which might otherwise result from deposit runs on solvent banks. Contemporary practices with respect to amortization and insurance of residential mortgages should prevent wholesale foreclosures and capital losses. Finally, the problems of postwar disequilibria in the international accounts were handled this time by devices (largely governmental) which pose less danger to international financial stability during periods of domestic crisis than did the private foreign lending of the United States in the 1920's.

Other Monetary Factors in Major Depressions

The acute disturbances so far discussed are merely the most spectacular of the ways in which financial factors may adversely affect real activity. A persistent world shortage of monetary gold played some part in the downtrend of prices from the early 1870's to the late 1890's, and some economists would accord it a major role. If the failure of the gold stock and money supply to grow as rapidly as the real demand for money is attributed largely to autonomous factors—the lack of significant new gold discoveries before the 1890's and insufficient advances in techniques of extraction and refining—it remains only to establish a connection between an inadequate money supply and deficient aggregate demand in order to account for falling prices and the succession of severe contractions during the period.

The principal study of United States business cycles during the last quarter of the nineteenth century is by Rendigs Fels. Following Rostow,[6] who applied a similar argument to the British economy, Fels rejected the hypothesis that the "long-wave depression" of 1873-1897 was due primarily to inadequate growth of the money supply.[7] The reason is that interest rates were low and falling during the 1880's and 1890's, whereas an inadequate money supply would be expected to depress aggregate money demand and prices by raising interest rates and reducing investment expenditure. Perhaps this is sufficient reason

[6] W. W. Rostow, *British Economy of the Nineteenth Century* (1948).
[7] Rendigs Fels, *American Business Cycles, 1865-1897* (1959), Chap. 5.

to reject an exclusively monetary explanation of the deflationary cast of the times, but the behavior of interest rates is not inconsistent with the argument that deficient growth of the money supply was an important contributing cause.

Thus, assume that investment expenditure was inadequate to maintain continuous full employment at going interest rates because investment opportunities were not increasing fast enough for autonomous reasons; and that the effects of price deflation on investment and consumption demand were either unfavorable or not sufficiently favorable to restore full employment. Had the money supply risen more rapidly, interest rates might have declined more (assuming that the safest rate was not already at its Keynesian floor) and induced a larger volume of investment expenditure for any given schedule of investment demand, thereby putting upward pressure on prices and output. Nor is that all, for investment demand itself would probably have been augmented had prices been bolstered by monetary expansion, since the expected profitability of current investment is likely to be larger if prices show a rising instead of a falling tendency. Finally, it has been argued that the economy would have been less susceptible to political-monetary disturbances—the "resumption" controversy of the 1870's and the silver controversy of the 1890's—and less prone to bank crises had gold been plentiful. This was Fels' earlier opinion.[8] Whether or not falling prices could have been averted were gold more plentiful, Fels concludes in his 1959 study that the silver controversy itself was an important adverse factor in the 1890's, and that monetary instability also contributed significantly to the depressions of the 1870's and 1880's.

Whatever weight one is willing to give to independent monetary factors as a determinant of past long swings and severe depressions, it is clear that future dangers, if any, must lie in possible misuse of the discretionary monetary institutions, rather than in automatic internal reactions to international monetary disturbances or to autonomous variations in the world stock of gold.

[8] "The Long-Wave Depression, 1873-97," *Review of Economics and Statistics* (February 1949), pp. 69-73.

Monetary Policy in the Postwar Era

The goal of monetary policy is that of stabilization policy generally: to promote full employment and economic growth without inflation. Ideally, it should be judged on the extent to which it accomplishes this broad objective. Two formidable difficulties stand in the way of an appraisal based on ultimate results, however. The first is the analytical problem of disentangling the effects of monetary policy from other forces impinging on the economy. Second, since the three strands of the broad goal in practice may conflict, because they cannot all be maximized simultaneously, a value judgment must be made about the relative importance of each as a social objective.

Although one of the ultimate purposes of Federal Reserve policy is to foster economic growth, the operating goal of the monetary authorities appears to be simply to offset inflationary and deflationary tendencies as they develop in the short-run, rather than to attempt control of the secular growth rate itself. Thus their policy is to diminish the rate of increase of aggregate money demand when price inflation threatens and to augment it when physical contraction occurs, and their instrument to affect aggregate demand is control over the money supply (demand deposits plus currency). Since the largest component of the money supply consists of demand deposits at commercial banks, this survey of postwar monetary policy begins at the point of contact of the Board of Governors of the Federal Reserve System with the money-creating activities of the banks. This section is concerned principally with the timing of monetary policy and with its effects on the money supply and interest rates.

The capacity of commercial banks to lend by creating new money is limited by the availability of reserves to hold behind demand (checking) deposits.[9] The Federal Reserve authorities can prevent or

[9] Commercial banks may also sell old securities from their portfolios in order to raise funds to purchase new issues or make new loans. In this way, banks may foster the transfer of money balances from idle to active use, provided that the old securities are purchased by the public with money which otherwise would have been held idle. The net result is that income-autonomous expenditure on goods is financed by an increase in the velocity of circulation of

inhibit an expansion of demand deposits by curbing the creation of additional reserves, and it can encourage, but not force, an expansion of demand deposits by supplying excess reserves to the banking system. The principal instruments of monetary policy are open market transactions in government securities to provide or withdraw reserves, and changes in the legal reserve ratios to be observed by member banks of the Federal Reserve System. Additionally, variations in the rate of discount charged by Federal Reserve Banks for the temporary loan of reserves to member banks may encourage or discourage such borrowing by altering the differential between the discount rate and the rate paid for loans by customers of the commercial banks. In practice, however, reserve borrowing by member banks for purposes other than temporary protection against unforeseen reserve drains is discouraged administratively, and the discount rate is simply altered passively to keep it in line with private short-term rates. Exceptions occur on those occasions when a change in the rate is used to signal a reversal in direction of Federal Reserve policy.

The intent of Federal Reserve policy cannot be discerned merely by observing variations in open market operations, reserve ratios, or the discount rate. This is because the cyclical rise and fall in the demand for loanable funds and money balances is only one of many factors affecting the reserve position of commercial banks. Other significant influences include secular, seasonal, or sporadic variations in loan demands, gold flows, currency needs, the "floating" volume of uncollected checks, and the receipt and disbursement of funds by the United States Treasury. When these noncyclical factors are altering bank reserves in the desired direction and amount, no overt action will be required to implement stabilization policy. Conversely, open market operations may be necessary at times merely to offset noncyclical factors and to leave the reserve position unaffected.[10]

---

money instead of an increase in the stock of money. How this process complicates monetary policy is discussed in the later section on the scope and efficiency of monetary controls.

[10] Robert V. Roosa, *Federal Reserve Operations in the Money and Government Securities Markets,* Federal Reserve Bank of New York (July 1956).

The best single indicator of Federal Reserve intentions is the volume of "free reserves" in the (Federal Reserve) banking system. These consist of the excess reserves *minus* the reserve borrowings of member banks. A fall in the amount of excess reserves reduces the potential increase of demand deposits. An increase of reserve borrowings is another sign of monetary constraint, since member banks are discouraged from borrowing except to meet temporary reserve deficiencies, and are expected to get out of debt quickly by selling assets or reducing deposit liabilities.[11]

Excess reserves, borrowings, and free reserves are pictured monthly for 1947-58 in the upper panels of Chart 39. Free reserves were positive, large, and cyclically stable from 1947 through 1950. During this period, the Federal Reserve authorities were committed to a policy of stabilization of the government bond market, and this meant that commercial banks could dispose of government securities without penalty of capital loss whenever they wished to augment their private lending ability. In its capacity as residual buyer of government securities, the central bank perforce supplied reserves to the commercial banks on demand, thus undermining its control over the money supply. The commitment to continuous support of bond prices was abandoned in the Federal Reserve-Treasury Accord of March 4, 1951, freeing monetary policy for contracyclical use.[12]

[11] An individual bank may expand private loans and deposits by selling government securities to add to its reserve balance. However, the sale of the security to any other buyer than a Federal Reserve Bank will reduce the reserve balance and lending capacity of some other commercial bank. The other bank may meet the reserve drain by temporary borrowing or by the sale of some of its securities, but it cannot by Federal Reserve policy remain continuously in debt in order to expand loans, and if it disposes of securities, this causes a reserve drain elsewhere, etc. See Ralph A. Young, "Tools and Processes of Monetary Policy," *United States Monetary Policy,* Neil H. Jacoby, ed., The American Assembly, Columbia University (December 1958), pp. 33-35.

[12] "The Treasury and the Federal Reserve System have reached full accord with respect to debt-management and monetary policies to be pursued in furthering their common purpose to assure the successful financing of the Government's requirements and, at the same time, to minimize monetization of the public debt." See Joint Announcement by the Secretary of the Treasury and the Chairman of the Board of Governors, and of the Federal Open Market Committee, of the Federal Reserve System (March 4, 1951).

CHART 39. *Indicators of Monetary Policy, Monthly, 1947-58*[a]

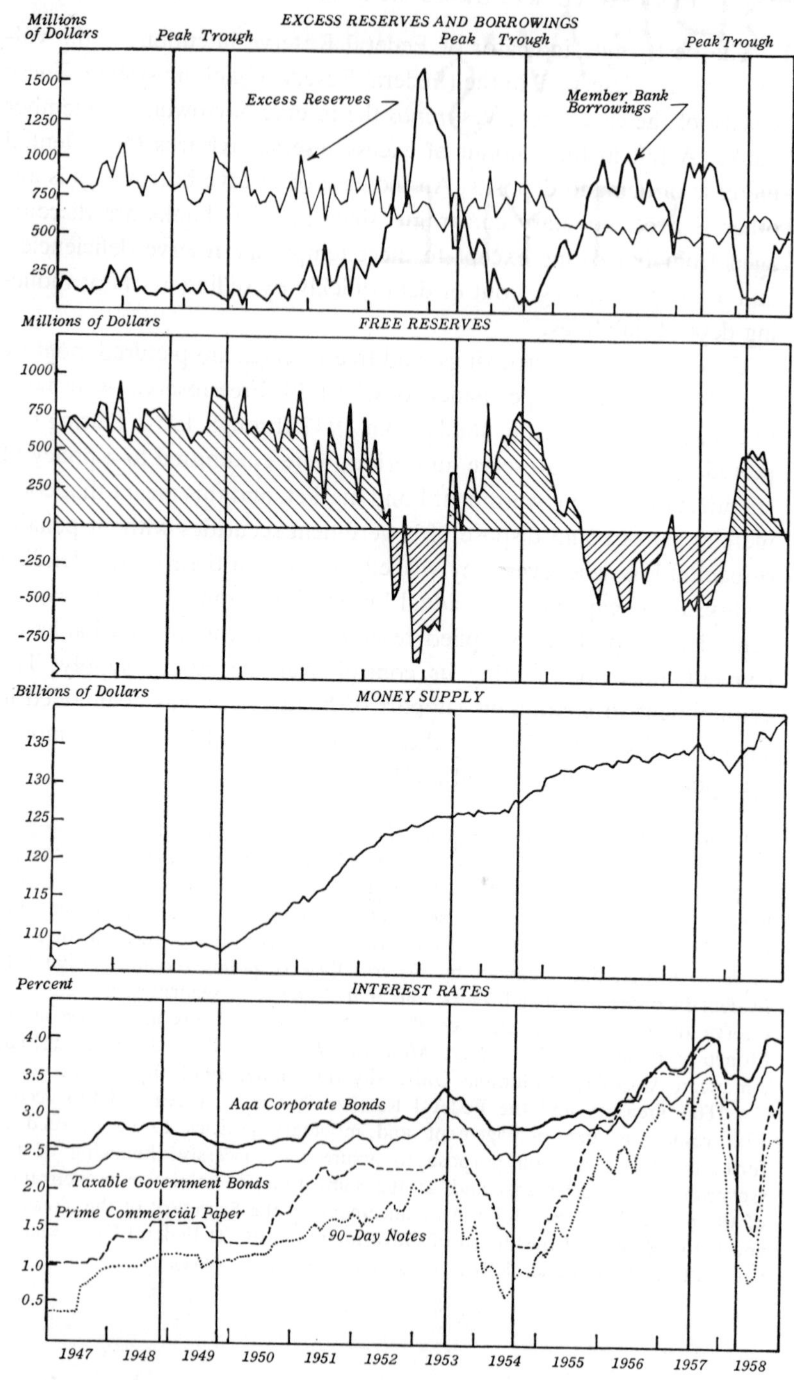

[a] The money supply includes currency and demand deposits and is adjusted for seasonal variation. Free reserves equal excess reserves *minus* borrowings of member banks of the Federal Reserve System.
Source: Board of Governors of the Federal Reserve System.

At first, little use was made of the new restrictive powers. The money supply increased more rapidly during the 15 months following the Accord than in the same interval preceding it (Chart 39). The pressure on bank reserves increased slightly during 1951 and the early months of 1952 and interest rates rose somewhat until the end of 1951, but neither change was sizable enough to exert substantial restraint. Indeed, substantial restraint would have been undesirable, since it might have interfered with the expansion of defense production and since prices were stabilized by direct controls (including specific controls over nonessential credit) and by the deflationary effects of the civilian buying lull (Chapters 5 and 14). By the same token, general monetary policy cannot be credited with the price stability of 1951-52.

Civilian production boomed after mid-1952 as the defense expansion began to taper off. The monetary authorities tightened the reserve position considerably during this period, so that, by early 1953, free reserves were substantially negative and interest rates were rising at a rapid rate. The policy of restraint was shifted abruptly to one of ease during May and June, however, when open market purchases supplied $1.2 billion of reserves to commercial banks and it was announced that a like amount would be freed in July by a reduction of reserve requirements on demand deposits.[13] Member bank borrowing dropped sharply as the reserve position eased, and free reserves increased from *minus* $353 million in May to *plus* $364 million in June. Interest rates declined after June under the combined impact of easy money and a cyclical reduction in the demand for loanable funds.

Thus, the direction of monetary policy was reversed at least two months before the business cycle peak of July 1953. Perhaps the early reversal was prompted more by "unsettled" conditions in the financial markets than by a Federal Reserve forecast of the business downturn, as is commonly alleged. On the other hand, the Open Market Committee noted on June 11 that "throughout the period since March there had been an undertone of concern about potential declines in economic activity" and that concern had been expressed "lest measures designed to limit credit expansion had become more

[13] *Fortieth Annual Report of the Board of Governors of the Federal Reserve System* (1954), p. 30.

restrictive than was desirable, setting in motion forces of decline which would be difficult to check."[14]

The policy of credit ease was pursued throughout the contraction, as evidenced by the progressive increase of free reserves through the summer of 1954. The contracyclical influence of easy money was substantial. The early recovery of residential construction, which figured so prominently in the business upturn, was fostered largely by the increased availability of mortgage credit at liberalized terms. Business loans of commercial banks declined $1.3 billion during the year ending June 30, 1954, but their real estate loans increased $1 billion over the same interval. They also added $4.9 billion to their portfolios of United States government securities. Meanwhile, mutual savings banks and insurance companies decreased their holdings of governments by $1.2 billion, so that the commercial banks in effect made available to them that amount of funds to finance mortgage loans and other investments. At the same time, commercial bank purchases of government securities from business firms and individuals augmented private liquidity during a period of general uncertainty. Thanks largely to stepped-up bank purchases of government securities, the seasonally adjusted money supply rose gradually during the recession.

The contraction ended in August 1954. Beginning with a shift from "active ease" to "ease" on December 7, 1954, monetary policy was progressively tightened until it came ultimately to be defined as "restraining inflationary developments in the interest of sustainable economic growth" on August 2, 1955.[15] The gradually increasing pressure on bank reserves was paralleled by rising interest rates during late 1954 and 1955, and the rate of growth of the money supply abated markedly after April 1955. Margin requirements on stock market credit were raised from 50 to 60 per cent on January 4, 1955, and were increased again to 70 per cent on April 22, 1955. Selective credit actions were also taken by the Federal Housing Administration and the Veterans Administration during the spring and summer to

[14] *Ibid.*, p. 93.

[15] For the successive changes in the policy directive of the Open Market Committee, see the *Forty-first Annual Report of the Board of Governors of the Federal Reserve System* (1955), pp. 97-98, and the *Forty-second Annual Report* (1956), pp. 89-90, 95, and 101.

tighten terms on federally insured or guaranteed mortgages (see section on rapid expansion in 1955, Chapter 7).

The restrictive policy established during the summer of 1955 was maintained until late in 1957. The two and one-half years of restraint had the desired monetary effects. The money supply had increased 4.2 per cent during the year ending June 1955. In the next two years, it rose only 2.4 per cent. Credit became increasingly costly during the expansion, with an especially substantial rise of long-term interest rates in 1956-57. The tight money program did not, however, succeed in preventing moderate inflation of the price level, for reasons to be discussed in the next section of this chapter.

Although the general policy was one of restraint after mid-1955, the degree of restraint was moderated on several occasions. These episodes occurred in December 1955-February 1956, in June-July 1956, and in October 1956-February 1957, and were attributed to uncertainties in the business outlook, to Treasury financing problems, or to both.[16] John M. Culbertson has suggested that the cumulative experience with this succession of abortive easings may partly account for the firmness with which the Federal Reserve pursued its restrictive policy after March 1957.[17] Be that as it may, Federal Reserve policy did not again shift in the direction of ease until November 12, 1957, and even then the policy directive called for a moderate relaxation of the degree of restrictive pressure rather than the complete elimination of restraint on credit expansion.[18] Thus the policy shift lagged the business downturn by two or three months.[19]

The Federal Reserve authorities have been widely criticized for excessive delay in reversing the restrictive policy. The criticism may be made on two levels. First, it may be argued that credit should have

[16] See the *Forty-third Annual Report of the Board of Governors of the Federal Reserve System* (1957) and *Forty-fourth Annual Report* (1958) for details.

[17] "Timing Changes in Monetary Policy," *The Journal of Finance* (May 1959), pp. 145-60.

[18] *Forty-fourth Annual Report, op. cit.*, p. 56.

[19] The lag is three months if the National Bureau of Economic Research date for the business cycle peak (July) is accepted, making August the first month of decline. It is two months if the peak is placed in August, which marks the end of a plateau in industrial production and is the peak month for nonagricultural employment and personal income.

been eased many months before it was—perhaps as early as March 1957 when the contrary decision was made to increase restraint. A change of monetary policy can affect financial markets almost immediately, but it may be several months before expenditure and production are significantly influenced by the change. The length of the lag varies with the type of expenditure, being shortest in those cases where reaction lags and production periods are brief. Thomas Mayer has recently estimated that from four to seven months may elapse before a restrictive monetary policy has achieved half its direct effect on production, and that the corresponding interval for an expansionary policy is four to nine months.[20] Unless Mayer is quite wide of the mark, which seems unlikely from the evidence which he cites on lags in the various sectors, his results indicate that an easy money policy beginning in the early spring of 1957 would have become effective at about the appropriate time to counteract recessionary tendencies in the economy. The degree of effectiveness is another question, of course, and would depend both on the intensity of the easy money policy and on the magnitude of the response of investment (including consumer durables and state and local expenditure) to changes in the cost and availability of funds.

Admittedly, it is easier to recognize a prior need for expansionary policies after a contraction is already underway than it is to foresee the need some months before the downturn. It is fair to observe, however, that the Open Market Committee of the Federal Reserve System was aware that the business expansion was losing momentum as early as January 28, 1957,[21] and that the reports of the Committee's deliberations in subsequent months refer repeatedly to the "sidewise movement" of aggregate activity.[22] Nor was the Committee unaware that business investment expenditure was leveling off and that statistical indicators of investment preparations pointed downward. While recog-

[20] These lags are exclusive of multiplier, accelerator, liquidity, or expectational effects. He also presents estimates which allow for multiplier effects, but not the others. See "The Inflexibility of Monetary Policy," *Review of Economics and Statistics* (November 1958), pp. 359-74. It should be noted that fiscal policies are also subject to lags.

[21] *Forty-fourth Annual Report, op. cit.*, p. 37.

[22] *Ibid., passim.*

nizing that the general sidewise movement was compounded of offsetting downward and upward movements in particular sectors, the Committee was uncertain in which direction the conflict would be resolved. In the face of this uncertainty, and because prices were still rising, its members decided on restraint—probably less because they believed that continued expansion was more likely than contraction than because they wished to hold the line against price increases even at considerable risk to continued expansion. Thus, it appears that it was the heavy weight given to the goal of price stability by the monetary authorities, rather than forecasting deficiencies, which lay behind their decisions during the period.

The second level of criticism for excessive delay runs in terms of failure to act promptly and vigorously once the contraction had begun. Not only did the policy shift lag the downturn by two or three months but, even then, the directive called for diminished restraint rather than active ease. It was more than two months after the November 15, 1957 reduction in the discount rate before the Open Market Committee noted that the "economic decline had acquired a definite momentum" and that "the free reserve position attained thus far by member banks had been of moderate size, and monetary expansion, which had paused in the latter part of 1957, had not yet been resumed."[23] Thus, although interest rates decreased considerably between November 1957 and January 1958, it was not until February that the free reserve position eased substantially and a six-month decline in the seasonally adjusted money supply was reversed (Chart 39). Surely monetary policy should avoid downward pressure on bank credit and the money supply during business contractions. Instead, efforts should be made to stimulate the flow of loanable funds to sectors where real demands remain high and to augment total liquidity (by increasing the size or improving the composition of the stock of liquid assets) unless the latter was clearly excessive relative to national income before the contraction began.

After January 1958, the monetary authorities moved aggressively to supply reserves to the commercial banking system through a series

[23] *Forty-fifth Annual Report of the Board of Governors of the Federal Reserve System* (1959), pp. 36 and 37 (meeting of January 28, 1958).

of reductions in required reserve ratios for member banks and by purchasing securities in the open market. As a result, the free reserve position eased substantially and the seasonally adjusted money supply increased at an annual rate of 8 per cent between January and July of 1958. Time deposits at commercial banks rose even more strikingly, at an annual rate of 20 per cent. Just as in 1953-54, the increase of bank credit was due primarily to bank acquisitions of United States government securities. Business loans increased $1.6 billion during the first half of 1958, whereas they had increased $1.3 billion in the same period of 1957. In marked contrast, commercial bank portfolios of United States government securities increased $6 billion during the first half of 1958, as compared with a decline of $1.9 billion in the corresponding months of 1957. Commercial banks also purchased $1.8 billion of state and local securities and added $600 million in real estate loans during the 1958 period of easy money. The increase of real estate loans was slightly more than a year earlier, but the increase in bank holdings of state and local securities was over four times as large as before.

Thus prompt monetary results were achieved after the reserve position was substantially eased early in 1958. Just as in the case of fiscal policy,[24] a deflationary factor was converted to an expansionary one midway in the contraction. In my opinion, however, the influence of monetary policy was comparatively minor in either of its phases during the contraction. On the one hand, the deflationary phase was too brief and mild to have done much damage. Tight money may have been partly responsible for the sharp reductions in fixed investment plans and in inventory investment during the latter months of 1957, but greater weight should doubtless be given to the adverse effects of declines in sales and profits, and the latter declines, as explained in Chapter 7, were heavily influenced by nonmonetary factors. On the other hand, the shift to active ease came too late to give monetary policy a prominent role in the upturn, in view of the lag which intervenes between investment decisions and investment expenditures. To cite one important example, residential construction expenditure

[24] See section on contraction and recovery, 1957-58, in Chapter 7.

lagged the business upturn by a month even though housing starts had led it by two months.[25] The pronounced rise of homebuilding during the latter half of 1958 did, however, contribute importantly to the vigor of the new upswing once the latter was underway.

The final policy reversal of the postwar period came during the summer of 1958. Free reserves dropped swiftly after July and became negative in December. The rate of growth of the money supply diminished markedly after July. Interest rates climbed rapidly until September and then leveled off at values which, for long-term securities, were virtually the same as at the late 1957 peaks.[26]

Thus the 1958 turnabout to a restrictive policy was accomplished more quickly and intensively than in 1954-55. Outside observers had castigated the Federal Reserve for undue delay in exercising restraint during 1954-55, and the monetary authorities had concurred in this opinion, after viewing the matter in the perspective provided by subsequent inflationary developments.[27] Probably because of the earlier experience, they acted more quickly in 1958. Indeed, the shift to restraint occurred while the seasonally adjusted unemployment rate was still over 7 per cent, and even by the end of 1958 the ratio had declined only to 6 per cent. In contrast, credit had not been tightened much in 1955 until the unemployment rate had reached the neighborhood of 4 per cent (Chart 24). The Open Market Committee was aware, of course, of the substantial unemployment which still existed when they applied the brakes to monetary expansion in 1958, but they feared that an inflationary and speculative psychology was developing which must be curbed despite the large numbers of unemployed.[28]

[25] The upturn of starts did affect production of building materials immediately, however. See Chapter 7 for an analysis of the various forces which prompted the business upturn.

[26] Speculation in the market for United States Government securities played a considerable role in the sharp swing of long-term interest notes during the contraction and recovery. See *Federal Reserve Bulletin* (February 1959), pp. 112-13.

[27] Asher Achinstein, *Federal Reserve Policy and Economic Stability, 1951-57*, Senate Committee on Banking and Currency, Report No. 2500, 85 Cong. 2 sess. (1958), pp. 47-55.

[28] *Forty-fifth Annual Report, op. cit.*, pp. 60, 63, and 66 (meetings of August 19, September 30, and November 10, 1958).

The Scope and Efficiency of Monetary Policy

Discussion of the limitations of monetary policy may conveniently be introduced with a pictorial representation of the equation of exchange (Chart 40). The top line of the chart shows the seasonally adjusted money supply (demand deposits adjusted and currency outside banks) on a quarterly basis from 1947 through 1958. The income velocity of the money supply is charted next, and the third line shows the product of money supply and income velocity: that is, the gross national expenditure in current dollars. On the fourth and fifth lines the gross national expenditure is resolved into its price and production components.

The immediate impact of monetary policy is on the money supply, and the first important limitation of monetary policy is that not even the money supply is under the complete control of the Federal Reserve authorities. This limitation applies only to periods of depressed activity, however, when an easy money policy may be thwarted at the outset by the commercial banks if they should prove reluctant to purchase securities or make loans despite plentiful reserves.[29] In periods when tight money is appropriate, the central bank has ample power to keep the money supply from rising or even to reduce it if desired.

The second major limitation on monetary policy results from the fact that the monetary authorities have no direct control over the rate of turnover of the money supply, yet monetary velocity is far from invariant during business cycles. Notice how much larger are the fluctuations of velocity, shown on Chart 40, than those of the money stock. Notice also that velocity often varies in a manner to nullify part or all of the influence of changes in the money supply on aggregate expenditure. Velocity increased during the tight money periods

[29] Even this is not an absolute limitation, however, for the central bank may achieve any given increase of the money supply despite lack of multiple expansion by the commercial banks, provided the central bank itself is in a position to increase its purchases of earning assets from the public in sufficient quantity.

MV = PQ

CHART 40. *Elements of the Equation of Exchange, Seasonally Adjusted Quarterly Totals at Annual Rates, 1947-58*[a]

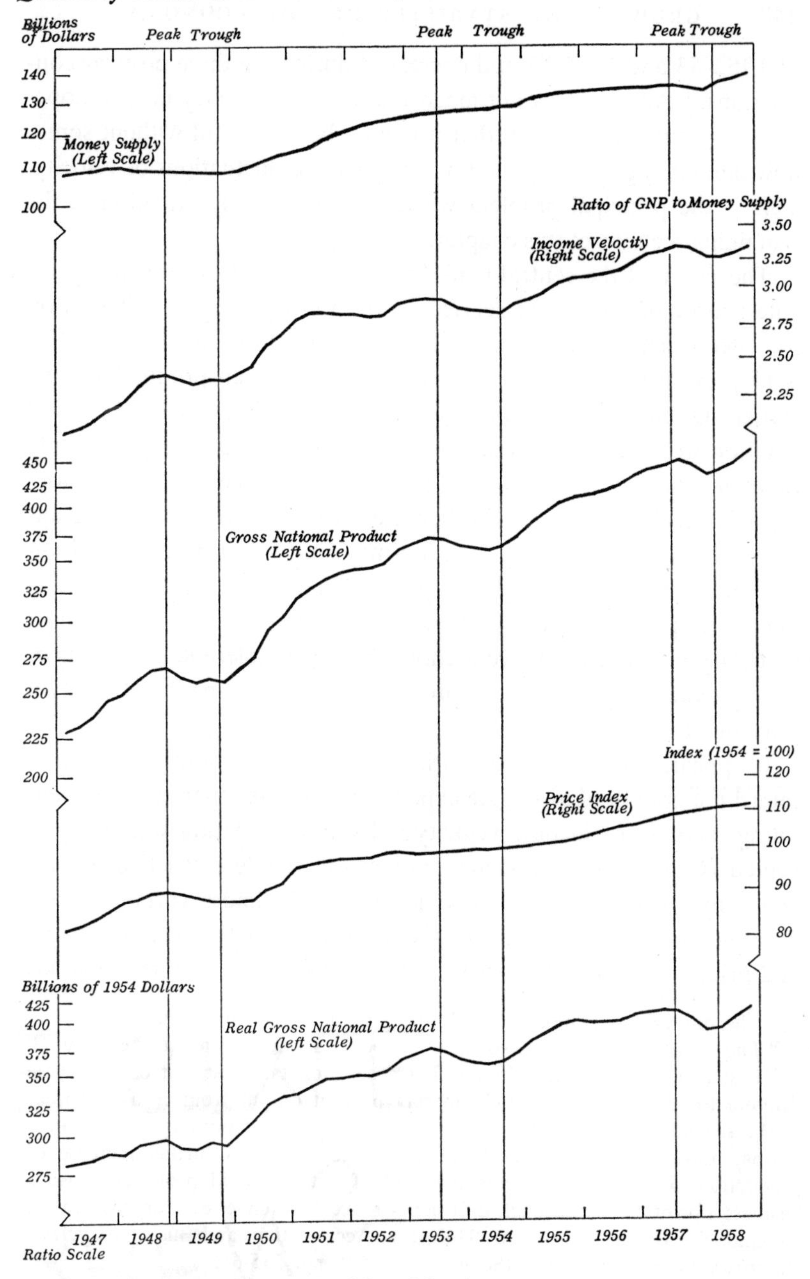

[a] The money supply includes currency and demand deposits.

Sources: Board of Governors of the Federal Reserve System; Office of Business Economics, Department of Commerce.

of 1952-53 and 1955-57 and decreased during the three postwar contractions.[30] All this does not mean that monetary policy faces a hopeless task, but it does mean that it cannot be successful without somehow eliminating or compensating for perverse fluctuations of velocity. This is the principal problem which will occupy my attention in the remaining sections of this chapter.

The fact that the central bank has no direct control over the aggregate supply of goods and services is the third principal limitation on the effectiveness of monetary policy.[31] The goal of a restrictive policy is to prevent prices from rising rather than to keep production from increasing, but under some conditions it may be impossible to prevent inflation without curbing output. For one thing, the aggregate supply function may become less than perfectly elastic before full employment is reached, owing to bottlenecks in particular sectors. For another, the aggregate supply function may shift upward because of autonomous increases in wages or prices of materials. In either case, a limitation placed on the expansion of aggregate demand through monetary policy will involve a choice between "tolerable" amounts of unemployment and foregone production, on the one hand, and of price inflation, on the other.[32]

It appears reasonable that during 1956-57 tight money did help to retard the growth of aggregate expenditure despite a partially compensating increase of income velocity.[33] Even so, inflation was not prevented (Chart 40). A monetary policy sufficiently restrictive to prevent any increase in the price level would almost certainly have prompted a physical downturn, given the upward pressures on wages and prices originating for partly autonomous reasons in durable goods

[30] The money supply also declined during the first and third contractions.

[31] This limitation applies also to fiscal policies affecting aggregate demand.

[32] It may be objected that in the first case, monetary restraint on aggregate demand to stabilize prices would merely prevent output from rising, whereas in the second case it would force an actual reduction of output. In a dynamic setting, however, monetary or fiscal actions to prevent a further increase of production along a fixed aggregate supply function would probably cause a business downturn because of diffusion or acceleration effects on investment demand. See Bert G. Hickman, "Diffusion, Acceleration, and Business Cycles," *American Economic Review* (September 1959), pp. 535-65.

[33] See section on downturn in 1957, Chapter 7.

industries during those years (Chapter 14). As it was, real gross national product increased little after 1955, and the growth of excess productive capacity during 1956-57 indicates that this was not due exclusively to supply inelasticities.[34] Tight money and other demand factors contributed importantly to the retardation of production.

Monetary Policy and the Market for Loanable Funds

Monetary policy does its work by affecting the supply of loanable funds. Its effectiveness therefore depends both on the extent to which the central bank can control the total supply of loanable funds and on the response of investment demand (including government and consumption expenditure not financed from current income) to changes in interest rates and credit availability. In recent years, qualified observers have argued that structural developments in the economy have diminished the scope and efficiency of monetary policy from both sides of the loanable funds market.[35] Let us examine the arguments.

Financial Institutions and the Supply of Funds

The total supply of loanable funds during a given period consists of planned saving, the current increase in the stock of money, and the net transfer of existing money balances from idle to active use (dishoarding).[36] Funds may be loaned directly to the ultimate borrowers

[34] For data on capacity in relation to output, see Table 17; see also *Economic Report of the President* (January 1959), Chart 3.

[35] John G. Gurley and E .S. Shaw, "Financial Aspects of Economic Development," *American Economic Review* (September 1955), pp. 515-38; Warren L. Smith, "On the Effectiveness of Monetary Policy," *American Economic Review* (September 1956), pp. 588-606; Arthur F. Burns, *Prosperity Without Inflation* (1957), Chap. III; John G. Gurley, "Liquidity and Financial Institutions in the Postwar Period," *Study of Employment, Growth, and Price Levels,* Joint Economic Committee, Study Paper No. 14, 86 Cong. 2 sess. (1960).

[36] If there is net hoarding instead of dishoarding, the amount of hoarding may either be subtracted from the supply of funds or added to the demand for funds. For an exposition and critique of the loanable funds theory of the determination of the interest rate, see Haberler, *op. cit.,* Chap. 8, sec. 2.

by savers or dishoarders, but they may also flow indirectly to borrowers through financial intermediaries. When the Federal Reserve wishes to restrict the supply of loanable funds, it puts pressure on commercial bank reserves in order to diminish the rate at which new money balances are being created. The supply of funds diminishes relative to the demand for them, and hence interest rates rise. The amount by which investment expenditure is reduced, if any, depends on the magnitude of the increase of interest rates, the interest elasticity of investment demand, and the degree of credit rationing by lenders at various rates of interest.

Modern proponents of monetary policy generally concede that planned saving and planned investment are much less elastic to interest fluctuations within "normal" limits than was once thought to be the case. Instead, they emphasize the influence of changes in interest rates on the lending decisions of financial institutions.[37] According to

[37] Irrespective of the interest-elasticity of saving and investment, still another school of thought stresses the "direct" wealth effects of changes in the real value of money on decisions to save or invest, rather than the "indirect" effects of interest rate changes on these decisions. Thus if wages and prices were sufficiently flexible, inflationary tendencies could be curbed by permitting prices to rise more than the nominal supply of money (or "net money"), thereby reducing the real value of money balances and depressing consumption or investment demand; and vice versa during periods of deflation. (See Don Patinkin, *Money, Interest, and Prices* [1956], Pt. 2.) Emphasis on the "real balance" or "Pigou" effect is sometimes coupled with the proposal that discretionary control over the supply of nominal money and the fiscal accounts of the federal government be eliminated, and that reliance be placed instead on "automatically equilibrating" changes in the price level to mitigate inflationary or deflationary tendencies. (See Milton Friedman, "A Monetary and Fiscal Framework for Economic Stability," *American Economic Review* (June 1948), pp. 245-64, reprinted in American Economic Association, *Readings in Monetary Theory* [1951].) Patinkin appears to be less sanguine than Friedman about the efficacy of major reliance on price flexibility as an equilibrating device in the real world. This is not only because institutional rigidities in fact make for price inflexibility at least in a downward direction, but also because even in the absence of "extraneous monopolistic elements" a capitalist economy would be subject to those rigidities "inherent in the very fact that the level of aggregate commodity demand in such an economy is the resultant of individual decisions to consume and to invest, and that these decisions respond only stickily to market changes in interest and prices. They are the rigidities of sovereign consumers and investors unwilling to modify their expenditure habits on short notice." (*Op. cit.*, p. 240.)

this view, the investment portfolios of financial institutions are sensitive to small changes in yields on government securities. For instance, it is alleged that during a period of tight money and rising interest rates, institutional lenders will be inhibited by capital losses from selling government securities in order to increase private lending. Thus small increases in interest rates are thought to result in a considerable reduction in the availability of credit to private borrowers. Because the national debt grew enormously during World War II and much of it is held by commercial banks and other financial institutions, and because of the long-standing trend toward increased importance of institutional lenders in the market for the loanable funds, it is asserted that central bank policy can "exert a powerful influence upon the volume and timing of changes in the general availability of credit" in the postwar economy.[38]

The foregoing line of argument has met with justifiable skepticism.[39] Commercial banks want to meet the credit demands of their customers. They can meet those demands during a period of restraint by the sale of short-term government securities without appreciable capital loss, and the losses taken on long-term maturities can be compensated by a sufficient increase in the differential between yields on private loans and government securities. This last is true also for other financial institutions, which tend to hold the longer maturities. Thus, although few will deny that a sufficiently large rise of interest rates would "lock-in" institutional holdings of government bonds, because the demand for private funds would become too elastic to permit the development of the necessary differential between yields on private and government securities, there is considerable question whether small changes will have much effect. At the very least, it may take a long period of gradually rising interest rates before the effect becomes pronounced. Thus commercial banks sold $10 billion of

[38] Robert V. Roosa, "Interest Rates and the Central Bank," *Money, Trade, and Economic Growth, Essays in Honor of John Henry Williams* (1951), pp. 270-95. For a statistical picture of the growth of financial institutions, see Raymond W. Goldsmith, *Financial Intermediaries in the American Economy Since 1900* (1958).

[39] Smith, *op. cit.;* Burns, *op. cit.;* Howard Ellis, "Limitations of Monetary Policy," *United States Monetary Policy,* Neil H. Jacoby, ed., The American Assembly, Columbia University (1958), pp. 149-70.

government securities as interest rates rose between December 1954 and December 1956, and insurance companies and mutual savings banks divested themselves of $3 billion of federal obligations during the same period. Bank holdings of government securities changed scarcely at all during 1957, however, and the holdings of insurance companies fell more slowly than in the preceding year. Perhaps the cumulative effects of two years of tight credit had reduced the liquidity —and hence, had increased the risk differential to be overcome before portfolio shifts would be profitable—of financial institutions sufficiently to inhibit portfolio shifts, although the diminished demand for business loans during 1957 may have been of equal or greater importance as a deterrent to such shifts. In any event, there is little basis in recent experience for optimism about the credit-restraining influence of small increases in interest rates during periods of excess demand for loanable funds.

The basic difficulty is that higher interest rates encourage dishoarding, since they increase the cost (foregone earnings) of holding idle money balances. Restraint on the growth of the money supply tends, therefore, to be partially nullified by induced dishoarding, with the result that interest rates rise less and credit availability is restricted less than otherwise would be the case. (The statistical reflection of dishoarding, or of a rate of hoarding sufficiently smaller than the current increase of the money supply, of course, is an increase in the income velocity of the total money supply.) As many writers have noted, from this point of view the existence of large institutional holdings of federal debt probably contributes to monetary instability by facilitating the mobilization of idle money balances for active use during periods of tight credit. This is not a fundamental factor, however.[40] Financial institutions cannot activate idle balances by selling federal securities and lending the proceeds to active spenders unless other spending units are willing to purchase and hold the federal obligations.[41] But this implies that spending units are sufficiently liquid to be willing to diminish their idle balances because of small increases in interest rates. Given plentiful liquidity and high demand for loanable funds, dishoarding

[40] Ellis, *ibid.*

[41] The principal net purchasers of federal securities during 1955-57 were individuals, state and local governments, federal trust funds, and miscellaneous investors, including some financial institutions.

would occur through other channels if this particular one were unavailable,[42] although perhaps not quite as sharply for a given increase of interest rates, since noninstitutional lenders would probably be less alert to the profitability of portfolio shifts.

There is another way in which the activities of financial institutions may foster increases in velocity, however. The claims which many financial intermediaries sell to the public in order to finance their own lending activities, are themselves highly liquid. Thus, time deposits, savings and loan shares, mutual savings deposits, credit union shares, and postal savings deposits are close substitutes for money. Hence, nonmonetary financial intermediaries, including savings departments of commercial banks, may induce dishoarding by offering their own claims as income-earning liquid assets as well as by the sale of government bonds from their portfolios. A given degree of monetary restraint will induce more dishoarding and a smaller rise of interest rates to the extent that their own claims instead of bonds are sold to the public by intermediaries, since liquidity is reduced less by the purchase of money substitutes than bonds. Again, then, a tight money policy will be partially offset by induced dishoarding through the creation of money substitutes as interest rates increase and permit financial intermediaries to offer higher returns on the claims which they sell to the public.

The foregoing problem is not new—although it may become increasingly important if there is a continuation of the present trend toward rapid relative growth of nonmonetary financial institutions and nonmonetary liquid assets. Whereas Goldsmith's data show that commercial banks accounted for only 44 per cent of the assets of all private financial institutions in 1952, it should be noted that their share was little more than one-half in either 1900 or 1922. Thus, financial institutions other than commercial banks were already important in the 1920's. Moreover, the private nonbank intermediaries grew rapidly during the 1920's, just as they have done in the years since World War II. Finally, time deposits in commercial banks also grew more rapidly than demand deposits during the 1920's—again, just as in the years since 1945.[43] Whether a new problem or a problem newly em-

[42] Ellis, *ibid.*

[43] For recent discussions of the magnitude and implications of these prewar and postwar shifts in financial structure, see Joseph Ascheim, "Commercial Banks and Financial Intermediaries: Fallacies and Policy Implications," *Journal*

phasized, however, it remains true that monetary policy must reckon with the debilitating effects of shifts from money balances to money substitutes as credit is tightened.

Despite the rather gloomy cast of the preceding paragraphs, there is reason to believe that monetary policy will be somewhat less subject to frustrating velocity increases during future periods of tight money. This is because the liquidity of the economy has been substantially reduced by the events of the past 12 or 13 years, as Table 50 shows.

As a result of wartime financial practices,[44] both the money supply and total liquid assets increased at the extraordinary compound interest rate of 18 per cent per year between 1941 and 1946 and rose sharply relative to money income. By the end of 1946, the ratio of total liquid assets to gross national product had reached 123 per cent, as compared with an average ratio of 101 per cent in 1939-41. The ratio of money supply to gross national product, which is the reciprocal of the income velocity of money, stood at 52 per cent in 1946, whereas it had averaged only 40 per cent in 1939-41.[45]

All or most of the wartime heritage of excess liquidity was wrung out of the economy during two waves of price inflation in 1946-48 and 1950-51 (Table 50 and Chart 40). Each inflation was financed mainly by a pronounced rise of velocity—the money supply increased only 2.5 per cent per year between 1946 and 1951 and actually fell during 1948 and 1949. The fact that these inflationary velocity increases occurred in the face of low interest rates and during a period when Federal Reserve policy assured an elastic money supply at those low rates, indicates the degree of excess liquidity at existing levels of real income, prices, and, in the case of Korea, price expectations. By

of Political Economy (February 1959), pp. 59-71, and Warren L. Smith, "Financial Intermediaries and Monetary Controls," *Quarterly Journal of Economics* (November 1959), pp. 533-53. These authors dispute the contention of Gurley and Shaw (*op. cit.*) that the rapid expansion of nonmonetary intermediaries has considerably undermined the effectiveness of traditional monetary controls.

[44] See discussion of the war years in Chapter 3.

[45] Since the figures on liquid assets given in Table 50 are for the end of the year, the ratio of money supply to gross national product shown in the table is not strictly equal to the reciprocal of the income velocity of money. The latter should be estimated on the basis of the average money stock for the year.

TABLE 50. *Liquid Assets of Nonfinancial Sectors and Their Proportion to Gross National Product, 1939-58*[a]
(Dollar items in billions)

Year	Total Liquid Assets	Money Supply	Time Deposits	Savings and Loan Shares	Mutual Savings Deposits	Credit Union Shares	Postal Savings Deposits	Policy Reserves in Life Insurance Companies	U. S. Savings Bonds	*Per Cent of Gross National Product*: *Total Liquid Assets*		
										Unweighted	*Weighted*[b]	*Money Supply*
1939....	95.4	36.2	15.3	4.1	10.5	0.2	1.3	25.8	2.0	*105.7*	*72.2*	*39.7*
1940....	104.6	42.3	15.8	4.3	10.7	0.2	1.3	27.2	2.8	*104.0*	*73.1*	*42.0*
1941....	115.7	48.6	15.9	4.7	10.5	0.3	1.4	28.9	5.4	*92.0*	*65.3*	*38.6*
1942....	140.7	62.9	16.4	4.9	10.6	0.3	1.4	30.8	13.4	*88.4*	*64.0*	*39.5*
1943....	175.8	79.6	19.2	5.5	11.7	0.3	1.8	33.0	24.7	*91.3*	*66.3*	*41.3*
1944....	208.7	90.4	24.1	6.3	13.4	0.4	2.3	35.6	36.2	*98.7*	*70.8*	*42.8*
1945....	240.0	102.3	30.1	7.4	15.3	0.4	2.9	38.7	42.9	*112.4*	*80.1*	*47.9*
1946....	258.8	110.0	33.8	8.5	16.9	0.4	3.3	41.7	44.2	*122.8*	*87.5*	*52.2*
1947....	271.4	113.6	35.2	9.8	17.8	0.5	3.4	44.9	46.2	*115.8*	*82.2*	*48.5*
1948....	276.7	111.6	35.8	11.0	18.4	0.6	3.3	48.2	47.8	*106.7*	*74.9*	*43.0*
1949....	283.8	111.2	36.1	12.5	19.3	0.7	3.2	51.5	49.3	*110.0*	*76.5*	*43.1*
1950....	296.2	117.7	36.3	14.0	20.0	0.8	2.9	54.9	49.6	*104.1*	*72.7*	*41.4*
1951....	310.8	124.5	37.9	16.1	20.9	1.1	2.7	58.5	49.1	*94.5*	*66.2*	*37.8*
1952....	327.2	129.0	40.7	19.2	22.6	1.4	2.5	62.6	49.2	*94.3*	*65.7*	*37.2*
1953....	341.6	130.5	43.7	22.8	24.4	1.7	2.4	66.7	49.4	*93.5*	*64.6*	*35.7*
1954....	359.9	134.4	46.8	27.3	26.4	2.0	2.1	70.9	50.0	*99.1*	*68.1*	*37.0*
1955....	376.9	138.2	48.4	32.2	28.2	2.4	1.9	75.4	50.2	*94.8*	*64.8*	*34.8*
1956....	391.7	139.7	50.6	37.1	30.0	2.9	1.6	79.7	50.1	*93.4*	*63.4*	*33.3*
1957....	405.3	138.6	56.1	41.9	31.7	3.4	1.3	84.1	48.2	*91.6*	*61.5*	*31.3*
1958....	430.5	144.2	63.2	47.9	34.0	3.8	1.1	88.6	47.7	*97.5*	*65.1*	*32.6*

[a] End of year. Source, John G. Gurley, "Liquidity and Financial Institutions in the Postwar Period," *Study of Employment, Growth, and Price Levels,* Joint Economic Committee Study Paper No. 14 (1960), p. 5, Table 1.
[b] The weighted ratios were constructed by giving the money supply a weight of unity and all other liquid assets a weight of one-half.

the end of 1951, however, both total liquid assets and the money supply alone had fallen below the prewar ratios to money income—not because of monetary constraints on the growth of liquid assets, but because inflation had swelled the money value of income, with a sizable assist from real income growth after 1949. Thereafter, spending units would require substantially greater interest returns before parting with liquidity during periods of tight money (Charts 39 and 40).

Therefore, the policy of credit restraint pursued during 1955-57 caused a further decline in the ratios of money and of total liquid assets to income, but this time interest rates rose more sharply for a given reduction of liquidity ratios than in pre-Accord years, as Gurley has demonstrated.[46] Because of the progressive reduction of liquidity during the postwar era, a given degree of monetary restraint increased the cost (and presumably reduced the availability) of credit considerably more at the end of the period than at its beginning. It follows that the monetary authorities are nowadays in an improved position to tighten the entire market for loanable funds through monetary controls. It also follows, however, that credit restraint will mean high and rapidly advancing interest rates, rather than the small increases envisaged in the doctrine of credit availability.

Structural Changes in Demand for Loanable Funds

Burns has discussed several structural changes which have acted to diminish the sensitivity of investment demand to credit restraints.[47] Two of the developments have reduced the significance of interest charges as a cost-deterrent to capital expenditure. The marked rise in rates of corporate and personal income taxation has considerably reduced the effective cost of funds for any given interest rate. "Interest charges are rarely a large element in business costs, and their practical importance has tended to become smaller as a result of high taxes. . . . Hence, allowing for taxes, a rise of interest rates from, say 4 to 5 per cent meant just about that during the 1920's, while nowa-

[46] *Op. cit.*

[47] *Op. cit.* Subsequent quotations from this volume will be identified by page references in the text.

days it means roughly a rise of only half that size—that is, from 2 to 2½ per cent—for many borrowers, at least some of whom are sure to ignore so small an increase in cost" (pp. 46-47). Moreover, amortizable loans have grown in importance in the areas of business, consumer, and mortgage credit, and the terms of such loans can be, and often are, adjusted to minimize the impact on the borrower of increased interest rates.

With regard to corporate investment, the growth in relative importance of internal financing has diminished the share of investment demand which is directly affected by changes in credit markets. "In all, the internally generated funds of business corporations exceeded their externally raised funds—that is, new capital issues, bank loans, mortgages, trade debt, and other liabilities—by 42 per cent during the decade from 1947 through 1956. Between 1923 and 1929, on the other hand, corporate internal funds appear to have exceeded their external funds by about 10 or 20 per cent" (p. 46). If it is correct to assume that internally financed investment is insensitive to moderate changes in market interest rates,[48] this part of investment demand is beyond the reach of monetary controls.[49]

Burns also argues, incidentally, that "the great expansion of governmental activities since the 1920's has reduced the economic area over which a restrictive credit policy can nowadays be effective" (p. 44). This is incorrect. The growth of federal expenditures has not been at the expense of items for which external financing is important. Rather, it is consumer expenditure on nondurable goods and services which has diminished in relative importance.[50]

[48] This assumption is implicit in Burns's argument. It could be supported either by the proposition already advanced about the interest-inelasticity of investment demand generally, or by an assumption that business firms irrationally ignore the opportunity cost of internal funds even if they are sensitive to the cost of external funds.

[49] I am assuming that the "real balance" effect on investment demand, if any, of an increase of the general price level relative to the nominal money supply is quantitatively unimportant for the sort of moderate price increase that is likely during peacetime business expansions.

[50] Compare the current-dollar shares of gross national product going to private domestic investment, state and local spending (which has an important externally financed component), and purchases of consumer durable goods in 1929 and 1957 (Table 35). For the present discussion of credit controls over the stream of money expenditure, the relevant shares are those in current dollars.

Two principal conclusions emerge from Burns's analysis. First, because of changes which have occurred on both sides of the credit market, "in order to achieve a particular effect on the nation's total expenditure in today's environment, the degree of credit restriction which needs to be taken is likely to be appreciably greater than was the case a generation ago" (p. 54). This does not mean that the monetary authorities lack the power to curb aggregate demand, but it does mean that a mild degree of restraint may be ineffective, whereas a policy of vigorous restraint not only increases the risk of prompting a business downturn but is likely also to encounter political opposition.

Second, a restrictive credit policy acts unevenly on the economy, producing side effects which although of "little consequence if the policy is applied over a few months . . . cannot be safely ignored if the policy is extended over years" (p. 64). In my opinion, this is the principal significance of the "sheltered" position of federal expenditure and internally financed private expenditure, and the fact that the terms of amortizable loans can be adjusted to mitigate the deterrent effect of higher interest charges on borrowers, as in the important example of consumer instalment credit. Monetary policy need have only marginal effects on demand in order to accomplish its aggregative objectives, at least during inflationary periods and assuming that demand controls can prevent inflation without unduly restricting output and employment. From this point of view, it is immaterial whether a large fraction of investment demand is invariant to interest rates or credit availability, as long as a sufficient margin of demand exists somewhere else to be restricted. It could make a difference for other national objectives, however, if the marginal impact tends to fall repeatedly or heavily on particular sectors of the economy.

There is convincing evidence that the brunt of adjustment to changes in the cost and availability of credit was borne by residential construction during the 1953-58 period of flexible monetary policy.[51]

[51] See Warren L. Smith, "The Impact of Monetary Policy on Residential Construction, 1948-58," *Study of Mortgage Credit*, Hearings Before a Subcommittee of the Committee on Banking and Currency, United States Senate, 86 Cong. 1 sess. (May 1959), Appendix pp. 244-64. Because of the long investment horizon in housing, the demand for new residential construction is more elastic to interest costs than is, say, industrial investment. However, the principal reason for the recent sensitivity of residential construction to changes in

Indeed, as noted several times in this book, residential construction moved contracyclically during much of the period under the influence of general monetary policy as modified by administrative changes in permissible terms on mortgages insured or guaranteed by the federal government. According to Burns, small business appears also to have experienced financing difficulties during the 1955-57 period of tight money, and state and local governments may have felt at least a minor degree of restraint (pp. 59-62).

Summary

Financial crises and monetary disturbances helped to deepen or to prolong the severe contractions of the past. Financial reforms which augment the resistance of the economy to deflationary forces may therefore contribute importantly to economic stability. On the one hand, many of the financial reforms which date from the 1930's are akin to built-in stabilizers, in the sense that they automatically inhibit the development of liquidity panics during business contractions and provide time and a congenial environment for deflationary tendencies to be overcome by the self-adjusting properties of the economic system or by favorable autonomous factors. The basic monetary reforms, on the other hand, have augmented the discretionary power of the monetary authorities and hence could be either stabilizing or destabilizing.

Any evaluation of Federal Reserve actions should take into account the inherent limitations on monetary policy. As far as timing is con-

monetary policy and credit conditions is to be found on the supply side of the loanable funds market. That is, fluctuations in market rates of interest widen or narrow the differential between alternative investments and the (temporarily) fixed interest ceilings on government-insured or government-guaranteed mortgages, thereby augmenting or diminishing the supply of funds to purchase FHA or VA mortgages. The fact that the shifts to or from the government-supported mortgages are not fully compensated by off-setting changes in conventional mortgages, reflects in part the sensitivity of total demand for residential construction to interest costs, but it is also due partly to capital rationing.

cerned, the principal difficulty is that changes in credit conditions do not affect investment expenditure for several months. (Discretionary fiscal policies are also subject to troublesome lags, for somewhat different reasons.) This means that credit restraints would have to be eased perhaps as much as six months before a downturn would otherwise occur if monetary policy were to prevent, instead of mitigate, the recession. The forecasting problem would not be as serious as first appears were it not for the threat of inflation. Enough is known about the causes of contractions and the symptoms which precede them, to warn policy makers when there is considerable likelihood of a downturn within a few months. Unfortunately, however, the systematic forces are overlaid by others which are unpredictable, so that there is always a risk that early action may unnecessarily aggravate inflationary pressures instead of offsetting deflationary ones. There might well exist a conflict between the goals of stable economic growth and stable prices in any event, but forecasting uncertainties compound the difficulty of choosing between them. Thus, both the policy decision and an outsider's judgment on its wisdom will depend not only on a probability estimate of likely outcomes, but also on the weights which are attached to the risks of wrong forecasts in either direction. The tight money policy of 1957 is a case in point.

Apart from questions of timing, there remains the issue of the scope and efficiency of monetary policy. One potential limitation—that the Federal Reserve can supply excess reserves to commercial banks but cannot coerce the banks to lend—has not proved to be an important factor during the postwar recessions. Indeed, expansionary credit policies met with considerable success during the contraction and recovery of 1953-54 and the recovery of 1958. This was not only because they stimulated the credit-sensitive areas of homebuilding and state and local construction but also because commercial banks were willing to acquire United States government securities from spending units which wished to augment their liquidity or to invest in mortgages or other private assets. It should not be inferred, however, that easy money policies will necessarily be as successful during all future contractions. An expansionary monetary policy could well prove ineffective if it were pursued so tentatively or belatedly as to encourage the formation of deflationary expectations, or if a temporary deficiency of investment demand should develop in credit-sensitive areas for autonomous reasons.

During postwar intervals of inflationary pressure, however, monetary policy has been partially frustrated by offsetting velocity increases. The growth of the national debt and of nonmonetary financial intermediaries in the loanable funds market has facilitated velocity increases during recent intervals of tight money by increasing the efficiency with which idle money balances can be shifted to active spenders and by augmenting the stock of money substitutes. The fact remains, however, that the problem is neither a new one—nonmonetary intermediaries were important long before World War II and so were low-risk financial assets possessing as much or more liquidity than government securities—nor an absolute limitation on monetary policy. If used vigorously enough, the traditional instruments of monetary policy are capable of overriding offsetting increases of velocity during inflationary periods. The principal limitations on restrictive monetary policies stem from other sources and are shared to a greater or lesser extent by fiscal controls.

First, general monetary and fiscal restraints over aggregate demand do not bear evenly on all elements of the economy. At the least, the uneven impact will arouse the opposition of affected interest groups and may therefore tend indirectly to weaken the application of the controls. More critically, the incidence of general policies may be such as to conflict with other objectives of national policy which lie outside the stabilization field.

Second, general monetary or fiscal controls over aggregate demand may be inadequate to cope with an inelastic or upward shifting aggregate supply function during inflationary periods, unless stability of the price level is granted precedence over the goals of vigorous and stable economic growth.

14 / *Postwar Price Movements: Causes and Implications*

ONE OFTEN HEARS references to "the postwar inflation," and it is certainly true that prices have moved substantially higher over the 13 years spanned by Chart 41. The consumer price index rose 59 per cent between January 1946 and December 1958. The pace of the advance was markedly uneven, however. This suggests at the outset that it would be unwise to ignore developments during the period in an explanation of the increase over the period, and that a search for a single cause of the over-all advance would be unrewarding.

These initial reflections are strengthened by the fact that the unevenness is of several kinds. First, there are variations associated with the ebb and flow of business activity during business cycles. Prices increased during the three business expansions covered by the chart, but declined during the contraction of 1948-49 and were steady in 1953-54. There is a hint here of the operation of systematic cyclical factors affecting prices: everything else the same, one would expect prices to rise during at least the later stages of cyclical expansion when demand was pressing on capacity, and to fall during contractions when excess capacity developed because of reduced demands. Notice, however, that the tendency for prices to fall during the postwar contractions was weak, and that they actually increased during that of 1957-58.

Chart 41 shows considerable irregularity in price movements during the expansions. Each successive expansion saw a smaller rise of average consumer prices, with increases respectively of 33 per cent, 13 per cent, and 5 per cent. Thus the first of the postwar expansions was highly inflationary. So also was a portion of the second—the eight to nine months following June 1950 during which consumer prices in-

CHART 41. *Indicators of Prices, Production, and Employment, Monthly, Seasonally Adjusted,*[a] *1946-58*

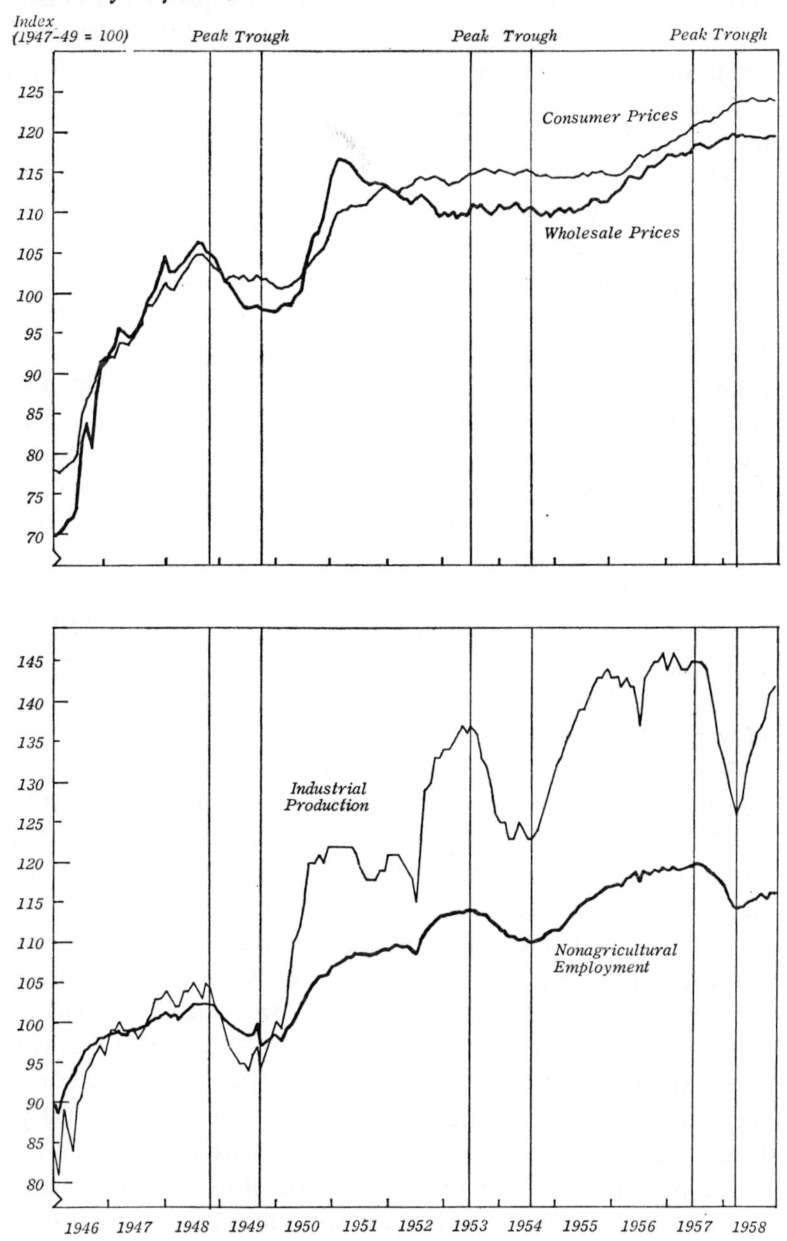

[a] Prices not adjusted for seasonal variation.

Source: Bureau of Labor Statistics; Board of Governors of the Federal Reserve System.

creased nearly 1 per cent per month. No comparable advance in the cost of living occurred during the most recent expansion. The index began to rise midway in the upswing and increased thereafter at the not inconsiderable rate of 0.3 per cent per month, however. Nor is that the end of it, for average consumer prices rose at the same monthly rate during the ensuing business contraction of July 1957-April 1958, only to level off thereafter.

The subsequent analysis has been organized to take into account differences in the causes and intensity of inflationary pressures during various portions of the postwar period. The causes of price advances during each of the three postwar expansions between 1946 and 1957 are discussed in succession, before turning to an analysis of price stability during the postwar contractions and some comparisons with prewar experience. It will then be possible to frame general conclusions about the nature of the inflationary process in the postwar American economy.

The foregoing plan is not the only feasible one. Another division with much to recommend it is between developments before and after early 1951. This division could be justified on three main grounds. First, prices increased substantially more before than after 1951, and the earlier period contains the only violent inflationary episodes since World War II. These episodes were related to war or the aftermath of war.

Second, agricultural prices weakened after 1951 (Chart 42). Since agricultural products are the raw materials for many manufactured nondurable goods, it is reasonable to expect the weakness of the former to be reflected in the prices of the latter, though not necessarily to the same degree because of changes in other components of cost or by reason of differential movements of demand at the various market levels. The expectation is confirmed by the breakdown of wholesale prices of finished goods shown in the lower panel of the chart.

Like all changes in relative prices, these disparate movements affected the distribution of national income. The question is whether they also influenced the price level. It is surely pertinent that the gap between agricultural and industrial prices opened and widened most noticeably during the only extended interval of over-all price stability in the postwar period—that is, from about mid-1951 to late 1955 or

CHART 42. *Indexes of Wholesale Prices, Monthly, 1947-58*

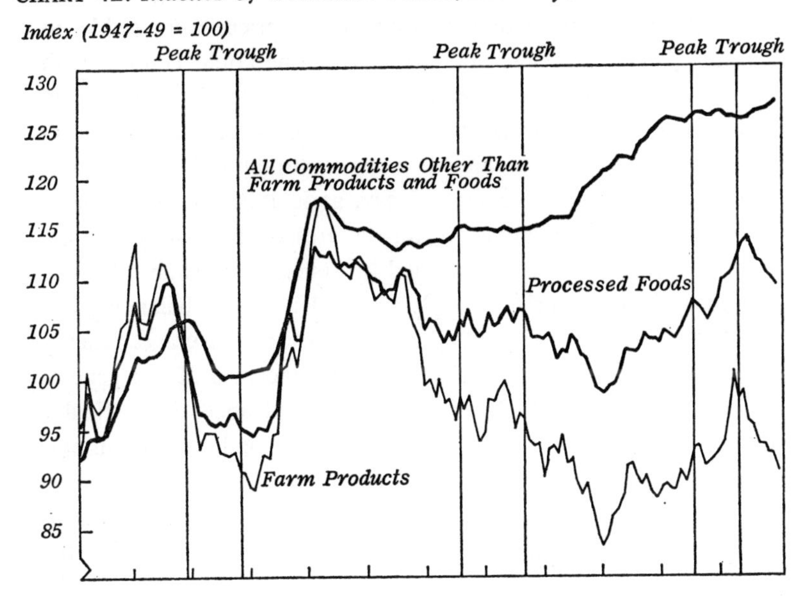

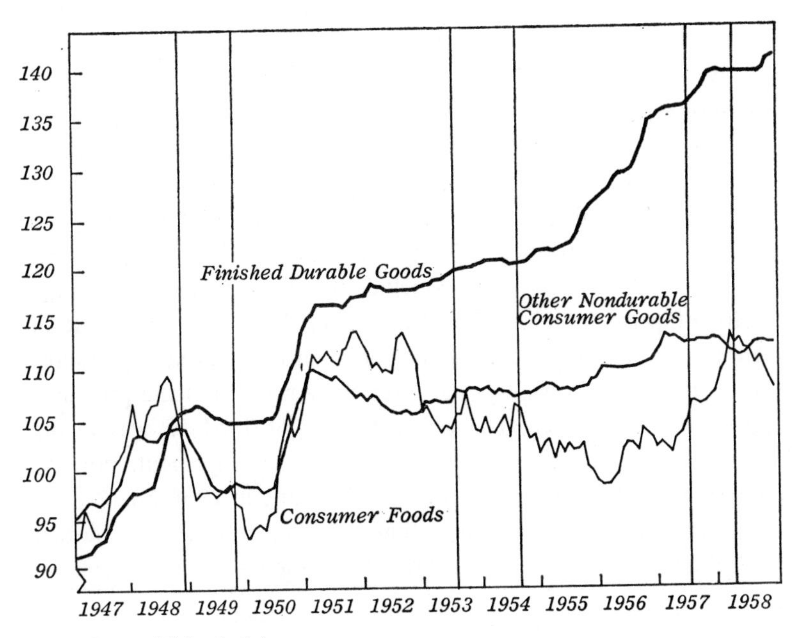

Source: Bureau of Labor Statistics.

early 1956. The observation alone is not enough to establish causation, of course. To an unsupported claim that prices were stable on the average because agricultural prices fell, one could counter with equal arithmetic justice that the rise of nonagricultural prices caused the average to remain stable. The shortcoming of this kind of statement is obvious. But it is perhaps less apparent that it also is not sufficient to show that the movement of, say, agricultural prices is due to factors peculiar to them alone; for this ignores the possibility that the height of the price level is determined by general causes and that the change in agricultural prices simply induced a counterbalancing adjustment in other prices without affecting the over-all average. Exactly the same analytical problem arises when an increase of the general price level is attributed to large autonomous advances in particular sectors as in some interpretations of the 1956-57 inflation which emphasize the role of steel prices.

The third reason for distinguishing between events before and after 1951 is the change in monetary policy which occurred following the Federal Reserve-Treasury Accord of March 4, 1951. Prior to the Accord, the Federal Reserve Authorities were forestalled from using general monetary controls to combat inflationary pressures because they were committed to the policy of support of government bond prices. When the Accord was reached with the Treasury, however, the goal of stable interest rates was subordinated to that of managing the money supply to restrain inflationary or deflationary tendencies in the economy whenever either developed. The agreement changed the environment in which inflationary disturbances could operate and meant that inflation would no longer be encouraged by easy money.[1]

It would not do, however, to conclude that the contrast between the intensity of price inflation before and after 1951 was the result of the shift in monetary policy. The power to curb inflationary pressures by monetary controls was greater after the Accord, but the pressures themselves were weaker. The price stability of 1951-55 was by no means the outcome exclusively of monetary management, nor did monetary controls prevent prices from advancing in 1956-58.

It is to avoid misinterpretations that run in terms of one or another specific factor as "the" cause of price behavior during heterogeneous

[1] See discussion of monetary policy in the postwar era in Chapter 13.

periods that the subsequent analysis is organized by cyclical units. The expansions of 1950-53 and 1954-57 were individually more homogeneous with respect to the determinants of both prices and production than was the period 1951-58 as a whole. Moreover, the analysis by cyclical units, by highlighting the influence of structural changes and autonomous disturbances, permits the integration of noncyclical factors into the analysis.

Aggregate Supply and Its Interactions With Aggregate Demand

It is apparent that the costs of production of an individual business firm can vary in several ways. If it has unutilized plant capacity, it may be able to increase production considerably without forcing costs up, but as it approaches capacity operations, marginal costs are bound to rise even when there is no increase in the prices which it pays for labor, materials, or other resources. This is because there is an optimal balance between materials, manpower, and equipment, and when that balance is exceeded, the output per additional worker or batch of materials must decrease—it will do little good to put two workers on a machine which can be operated efficiently by one. Costs may also be forced up at higher rates of utilization because prices of resources rise —premium pay for overtime is an important example—or because standby units of inefficient equipment may be pressed into service or it may become necessary to hire persons who are poorly trained or otherwise inherently less efficient than the normal complement of workers.

Analogous considerations apply when the economy as a whole is considered. When coming out of a period of recession, most firms will be operating well within capacity, and increases of demand will go primarily to stimulate production rather than prices. As national output continues to expand, however, bottlenecks will increase prices of some resources, capacity will be reached in some businesses, overtime pay will increase, and so forth. If demand continues to rise, firms will produce more, but they will also charge higher prices to cover the resultant increase of cost.

It must now be emphasized that two important cost influences were left out of account in the preceding paragraphs. This was deliberately done, for they are quite different from those discussed thus far. The variations in costs already considered were the result of changes in output which were induced by changes in demand—costs and prices would not have risen had demand not increased. The type of cost change to be considered now can occur at any given output and independently of any change of demand.

Physical limitations on output can be gradually overcome, given sufficient time, by construction of additional productive facilities and the growth of the labor force. Technological improvements, moreover, may make possible new methods of production which lower costs no matter what the rate of capacity utilization. In these cases, the same total output as before can be produced at lower prices, or alternatively, a larger output will be forthcoming at the same price level.

The second main type of independent cost change is an autonomous variation in the price paid for a resource. Wage increases negotiated in collective bargaining are sometimes autonomous, since they are not necessarily induced by a current expansion of output and will raise money costs of producing each alternative output. Independent changes may commonly occur also in the prices of raw materials imported from abroad, traded in world markets, or subject to supply interruptions due to the vagaries of weather. Provided demand remains unchanged, autonomous increases in resource prices will raise the prices of goods and reduce their output, whereas decreases will have opposite effects.

Demand will not remain unchanged in the ordinary course of events, however, and this brings me to the next major point. On an aggregative basis, supply and demand are not independent, but interact with one another in several ways. Thus in the present example, an autonomous wage boost may increase aggregate demand in addition to raising costs. This is because wages affect incomes as well as costs, and income is one determinant of demand. Suppose that a general wage increase goes into effect at a time of full employment and when businessmen have no independent reason to be pessimistic about the near-term future of sales. Under those circumstances, businessmen are likely to maintain output, increase prices, and wait to see whether the increase diminishes the physical volume of sales.

With higher wages and stable employment, consumer demand will be augmented, though not enough to match the price increase. The increase of wage-earner consumption demand will be smaller than the price increase partly because prices will usually be raised enough not only to cover the wage increase but also to increase profits, and partly because workers will save some fraction of their added incomes. If no increase of demand is forthcoming from other sources, the same physical volume of sales as before cannot be maintained at the new price level, and either prices or production or both must be cut.

It should not be assumed, however, that other demands will remain unchanged. Large components of final demand are partly or entirely independent of the level of labor income. Under the conditions of full employment assumed in my illustration, it is probable that businessmen and governmental units will pay the higher prices now necessary to carry out their previously planned physical investments. There is likely also to be sufficient flexibility in the financial arrangements of nonwage personal income receivers to permit them to increase their consumption outlays and defend their living standards even if their incomes lag somewhat in time or amount. Thus aggregate demand may rise enough to sustain the price increase without any reduction of output.

This last result is quite possible, and even probable, under the assumed conditions, but it is by no means inevitable. To cite a single important exception, financial constraints might prevent the necessary expansion of money outlays for plant and equipment, business inventories, or durable consumer goods. Thus "it all depends"—but that is precisely the point.

There are two other types of supply-demand interaction. The first occurs when the initial change on one side is conditioned by the actual or expected state of the other. Thus unions will ask for larger wage increases if they expect demand to be high or rising, and management will resist a given increase less strenuously if they hold the same expectation. Second, there is the interaction occasioned by the fact that an initial adjustment of price or output in response to a primary disturbance may induce secondary repercussions, as when a price rise caused by increased demand induces a wage increase which puts further pressure on prices.

In summary, the following points should be kept in mind in interpreting postwar price experience. What happens to prices and production depends on both supply and demand. Under given conditions of supply, prices and output will rise and fall together along with demand, and their relative movements will be correlated with the level of economy-wide resource utilization. Under given conditions of demand, autonomous cost increases will raise prices and reduce output, and vice versa for autonomous decreases. An initial change on either side is unlikely to leave the other unaffected, however, and this means that one must be alert to several forms of interaction between the two. In view of these complexities, inferences about the causes of observed behavior should be drawn with care and assertions that single factors are responsible received with skepticism.

The Inflation of 1946-48

The inflation of 1946-48 was started by the discharge of excess demand after decontrol and it was ended when final demand weakened, largely because backlogs were worked off in many lines, even as real income continued to rise.[2] This does not end the matter, however, for the progress of the inflation—its duration and magnitude and the timing of the successive waves—might have been quite different in another economic environment.

There can be no doubt, for example, that the inflation could have been terminated earlier and with a smaller over-all price rise by sufficiently vigorous monetary or fiscal actions. As it was, external monetary intervention did comparatively little to bring the inflation to a close, and fiscal actions actually prolonged its final phase (Chapter 4).

[2] See the many references to demand and expected demand in the section analyzing postwar inflation, 1946-48, in Chapter 4.

Not much is to be gained by speculating about what might have been, especially since it cannot be known how far alternative policies could have been pursued without producing consequences less attractive than the gradual diminution of liquidity through price inflation and the concomitant gradual elimination of the more pressing physical shortages.

What can be done profitably is to inquire more closely into the time path of the inflation, given the fact that external intervention was minimal. Prices did not increase at a steady rate, or even at a steadily diminishing rate, during 1946-48. Rather, intervals of slow increase or of temporary decline alternated with periods of rapid rise—with the latter periods occurring mainly in the second halves of 1946 and 1947 and in the spring and summer of 1948 (Chart 43). Why did the inflation progress in three successive waves with alternating phases of slow and fast advance, and why was each wave smaller than its predecessor? The first hypothesis to be tested is that the successive waves were recurrent phases in a wage-price spiral which was started and kept in motion by a series of wage increases. In that event, the interval between waves would be determined by systematic lags in the process of wage-price-wage adjustment, and the magnitude of the waves would depend upon the size of the successive wage adjustments.

The hypothesis is lent a surface plausibility by the fact that wages led prices during the first two waves (Chart 43). Average hourly earnings of manufacturing workers increased more rapidly than consumer prices during the first half of 1946. Prices moved ahead of wages after decontrol, however, so that by early 1947 the purchasing power of wages was considerably reduced. Wages spurted again during the spring of 1947, and after a lapse of two to three months, prices resumed their climb. Up to this point, then, there were alternate spurts of wages and prices. This neat phasing broke down in the third round of inflation, however, when prices and wages rose simultaneously in the spring and early summer of 1948. Apparently there was nothing inherent in the organization of the economy to make prices lag wages. Therefore, special circumstances may account for the two earlier instances of lagging prices. That is certainly true of the first round, when prices were decontrolled later than wages (prices in the summer of 1946, wages in August 1945). Also, unusual conditions (described in

CHART 43. *Indexes of Average Hourly Earnings in Manufacturing Industries and of Wholesale and Consumer Prices, Monthly, 1946-49*

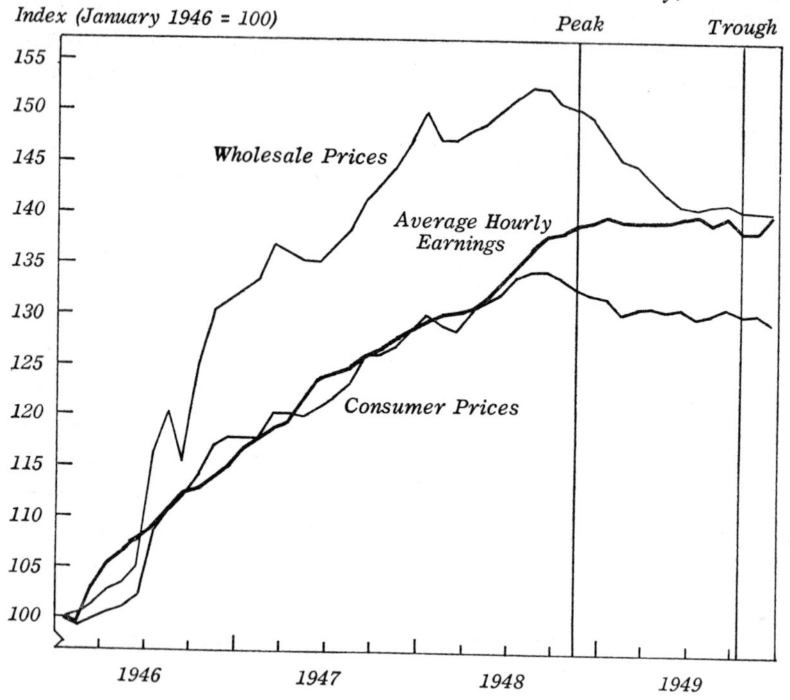

Source: Bureau of Labor Statistics.

Chapter 4) prevailed at the time of the second lag, when public attitudes and short-term expectations were unfavorable to price increases and when springtime wage increases were absorbed for a few months in steel and other heavy industries.

Apart from timing, there is the question of amplitude. May not the progressively smaller size of the price waves be due merely to the fact that each round of wage increases was a smaller percentage than the last? The answer again must be no. The reason may be seen by asking under what conditions the statement might be true. It implies, first of all, that the role of demand is permissive only; that the amount of a price increase is determined by the size of a supply-induced wage increase and a standard mark-up on labor cost and that product demand merely rises enough subsequently to sustain the higher price.

Second, applied to a sequence of damped wage-price movements, it implies that some mechanism exists to make each wage increase smaller than the last, unless, of course, this important fact is left unexplained. A plausible hypothesis for the sort of situation now under consideration is that wage demands are equal to the increase in the cost of living since the last wage increase, and that each wage increase induces a less than equal rise in consumer prices because of productivity gains or the sluggish response of prices of consumer services.

Neither of these assumptions can be accepted. With regard to the first, it is obvious that the margin of excess demand which existed at the time of price decontrol for reasons independent of the preceding wage advance was an important determinant of the size of the initial price spurt, which was, moreover, considerably larger than the preceding wage advance (Chart 43). Nor was the wage increase of the first half of 1947 as large as the price increase of the last half of 1946. All the same, there is substance in the idea that the amplitudes of the price waves in 1947 and 1948 were partly determined by the amplitudes of the corresponding wage movements. This does not mean, however, that this is an example of "cost-push" inflation.

The crux of the matter is that wages and prices may spiral under conditions of either cost-push or "demand-pull." The cost-push terminology implies that the spiral originates and is kept going by autonomous wage increases because workers are trying to increase their share of real national income, whereas demand-pull carries the connotation that prices rise because of demand pressures and induce subsequent wage increases as workers strive to maintain their real income position. A spiral may occur in either case, however, and for the same underlying reason—the attempts of contending parties to defend or increase their shares of the national product. These attempts may embrace investment goods as well as consumer goods, and the contenders are not limited to those facing one another across the bargaining table.

Since a spiral may occur for either reason, it may be difficult to decide whether a particular experience is caused by one or the other or some combination of the two. The task is complicated by the fact that lags in the process may be short or even nonexistent when current changes on either side are influenced by expected changes on the other, and the further fact that independent disturbances may enter the picture as well. Nevertheless, an examination of the movements of wages and prices during 1946-48 against the background of the earlier analysis of the period should help to overcome these difficulties.

It is easy to detect changes in basic wage rates in the statistics of average hourly earnings for a given industry, since abrupt vertical steps appear in the data whenever such changes occur. Unfortunately, these vertical movements tend to be smoothed out when hourly earnings are averaged for large numbers of industries, because the individual changes are spread over time. The smoothing is not complete, however, for some bunching does occur, and at those junctures the curve accelerates (Chart 43). If a close positive relationship exists between changes in wages and in prices, it should be possible to observe corresponding accelerations of prices. For reasons already discussed, I take the timing and amplitudes of prices and wages during 1946 as given, and inquire into the subsequent reactions to this first wave of inflation.

Small dips occurred in the indexes of wholesale and consumer prices during the second quarter of 1947. Was this the result of a prior deceleration of wages in manufacturing industries, which because of technical lags in the processes of production and distribution did not affect prices of goods to final users for several months? That is not the explanation, since the temporary price declines were confined largely to nondurable goods—especially to foods, and since wages had accelerated in the nondurable goods industries in the preceding quarter and had been accompanied at that time by accelerated increases in prices of finished nondurables at wholesale and retail. The cause of the lull in prices was the reduced inventory demand—itself influenced by the price expectations analyzed in Chapter 4—coupled with the temporary absorption of springtime wage increases in the durable goods industries at their source.

Nor should the resumption of the inflation in the second half of 1947 be interpreted merely as a delayed response to previous wage increases. For one thing, food prices were a leading element in the second inflationary wave, and their rapid advance was due to a combination of high world demand and short crops rather than to wage increases.[3] This is not to say that the general price movement was unrelated to the wage increases, however, for the latter did influence both the timing and magnitude of the former.

With regard to timing, the new round of price increases for durable manufactures was initiated by the simultaneous advance of wages and prices in coal mining during July 1947; the heavy goods industries had already absorbed wage increases during the second quarter of the year. In the short run, prices of many important durable manufactures are set by company policy instead of impersonal market forces, owing to the concentrated market structures of the industries. Although the prices of these goods are usually advanced at the same time as wages are increased—unless demand conditions are decidedly unfavorable—this had not been done in the spring of 1947. A probable reason is the public attention which had been focused by the government on the desirability of voluntary restraint in setting prices. Be that as it may, the July increase of coal prices provided the private incentive, the public rationale, or both, for a decision to raise steel prices in August, and other durable goods industries followed suit during the next few months.

The size of the price increases for durable goods was also affected by the preceding wage increases. For example, the increase of steel prices between July and August matched the previous wage increase between April and May—7.1 per cent for prices as compared with 7.6 per cent for wages. A similar close correspondence is to be observed between the wage and price increases for automobiles and agricultural machinery, after due allowance for the lag of prices behind wages. Not all durable goods industries followed this practice, however, so that although the index of prices of intermediate durable materials caught up with wages by the start of 1948, the index for finished durable goods did not (Chart 44).

The relationship between wage and price increases is less immediate and direct for nondurables as a class than for durables. Many of the important nondurable goods industries are sufficiently unconcentrated

[3] According to the economic sector indexes of the Bureau of Labor Statistics index of wholesale prices, the increases of prices of consumer foods, other finished nondurable consumer goods, and finished durable goods between June 1947 and January 1948 were respectively 14, 6.8, and 5.2 per cent.

CHART 44. *Indexes of Average Hourly Earnings and Wholesale Prices, Durable and Nondurable Manufacturing, Monthly, 1947-49*

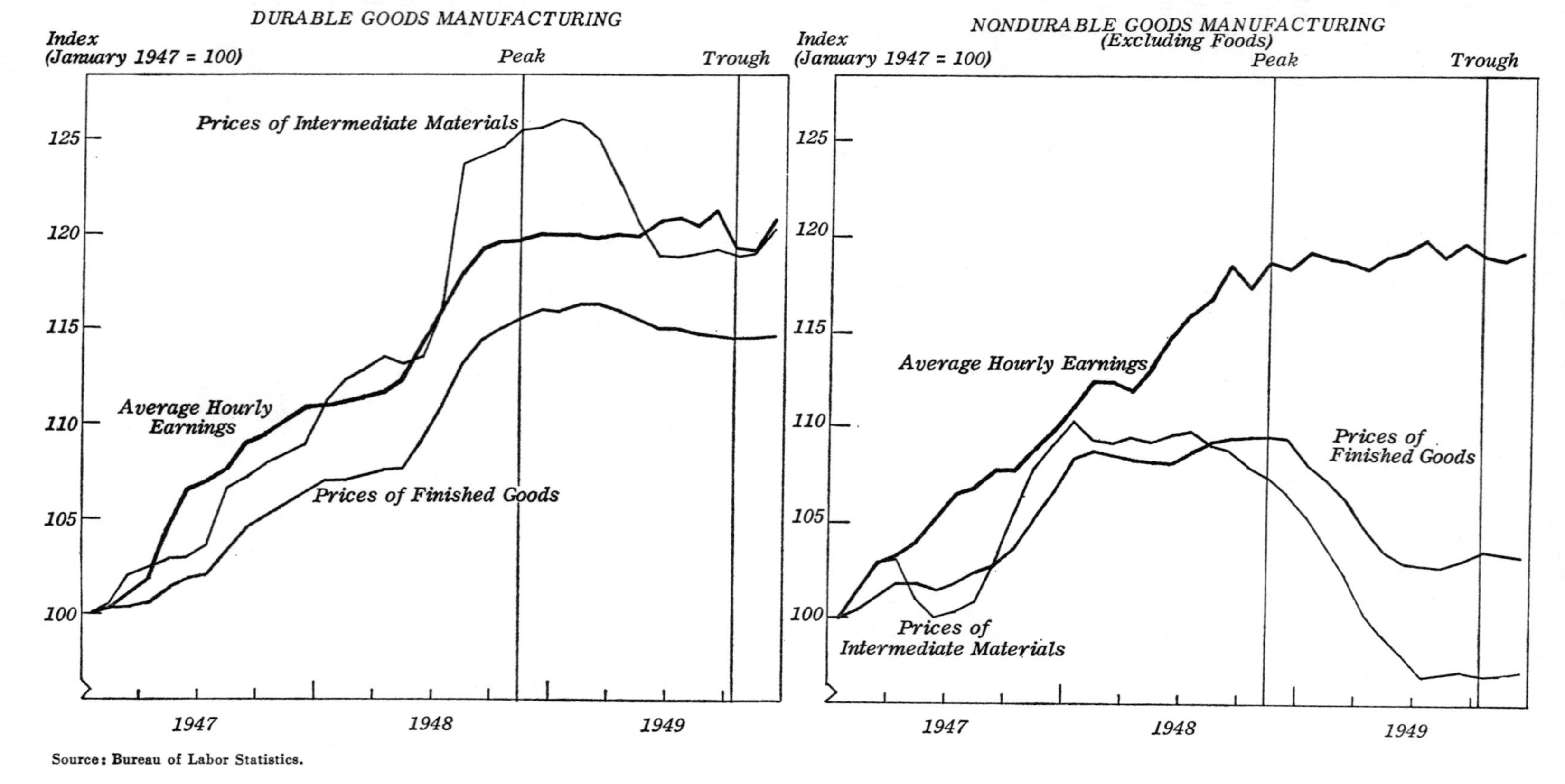

Source: Bureau of Labor Statistics.

to prevent prices from being marked up at the discretion of individual sellers. In such cases, individual wage increases will affect prices to the extent that they raise marginal labor costs; but prices will not rise proportionately with wages unless (1) other variable costs rise in the same proportion as wages and productivity relationships and product demand remain unchanged, or (2) product demand rises sufficiently to offset any cost-restraining influence stemming from productivity gains.

Wage and other cost increases doubtless contributed to the rise of prices of nondurables during the last months of 1947, but the pull of rising demand is evident also in the increase of production which accompanied the advance of prices. Economy-wide wage increases helped indirectly to raise these prices, of course, by augmenting labor income and consumption demand in money terms. Other factors also boosted demand, however. These included windfall income gains from terminal leave bonds and a resurgence of inventory demand, prompted partly by current sales increases and partly by speculative purchases in anticipation of price increases. Thus, it cannot be said that the overall average of price increases during the latter months of 1947 was fixed in size by the prior round of wage increases, although it is probably true that if the average wage increase had been considerably smaller during the spring and summer, the average price increase of later months would also have been considerably smaller.

The wage pattern of 1948 was quite similar to that of 1947, but prices behaved rather differently because independent supply and demand factors assumed greater importance. The principal price increases were for durable goods and food, with prices of nondurables other than food rising only slightly (Charts 42 and 44). Meats were still in short supply and accounted for most of the closing spurt of food prices.

The supply-induced increase of food prices not only raised the cost of living directly but also influenced industrial prices indirectly through its effect on wage negotiations. It will be recalled that one effect of the agricultural price break of February 1948 had been to augment management resistance to wage increases in the heavy industries (Chapter 4). The renewed upsurge of food prices in April undercut employer arguments that the cost of living had stabilized or was due to drop, however. And at the same time the announcement of new government programs to continue foreign aid, increase defense spending, and reduce taxes served to increase expected demand. Especially in the durable goods industries, it appeared that demand would prove to be adequate to sustain new price increases. The result of these developments was a series of wage-price increases in the major durable goods industries during the spring and summer. Average hourly earnings in durable goods manufacturing plants and wholesale prices of finished durable goods both increased 6 per cent between May and September. Wages rose about as much in the soft goods industries,[4] but in that sector demand was already weakening and prices of farm-produced raw materials were beginning to slide, so that prices of finished soft goods increased very little (Chart 44). The same combination of easier demand and enlarged supplies forced food prices downward beginning in September, so that the consumer price index declined and real wages increased correspondingly during the closing months of 1948.

This third wave is an interesting example of joint and simultaneous participation of demand and supply in an inflationary episode. Since the wage increases negotiated during 1948 were generally in line with the cost-of-living rise during the life of the previous labor contract (Chapter 4), it cannot be argued that their size was determined solely by current product demands. Perhaps a sizable "catch-up" increase of money wages would have occurred even in the absence of the new increase of food prices and the new government fiscal programs. But, if so, it probably would have been smaller than the rise which actually took place. In that event, the average price increase among nonfood items would also have been smaller.

The principal analytical lessons from the wage price behavior of 1946-48, in summary, are as follows. The existence of a wage-price spiral does not in itself show whether it is due basically to cost or demand forces. Lags between wages and prices are not necessarily indicative of causal sequences and special factors may sometimes ac-

[4] When account is taken of changes in output per man-hour as well as in wage rates, it appears that labor cost per unit of output actually rose more in the nondurable goods division than in the durable goods division of manufacturing. At least, this was the case for unit labor costs in 1948 as a whole compared with 1947 as a whole (Table 51).

count for their occurrence. Expected increases of product demand may induce wage and price reactions before final expenditure actually rises. An observed sequence of price waves may be the result of the interplay of wages and prices in response to a single initial disturbance, but there is also the possibility that autonomous forces operating outside the mechanism of the spiral may exert a decisive influence over the course of events.

With regard to the pattern of the inflation itself, it was initiated by the excess demand released by decontrol; revitalized during 1947 by a combination of short crops, catch-up wage increases which raised costs and incomes, and income-autonomous demand increments (including anticipatory inventory buying which was itself prompted by rising prices); and prolonged in its third phase by a similar combination of food shortages, wage increases, and autonomous increases of (expected) demand. The duration of the waves and the intervals between them were modified by wage behavior, but cannot be explained by systematic lags between wages and prices. The inflation would doubtless have moved faster and with fewer pauses had it been customary to negotiate wage contracts twice a year rather than annually, or had cost-of-living adjustments been written into the contracts. Whether it would have been greater or smaller in over-all magnitude depends upon a number of unknown factors. Included among these are the extent to which frequent wage-price revisions would affect price expectations, the vigor of anti-inflationary public policy under the alternative conditions, and the relative importance of real and monetary stimuli to demand under circumstances in which liquidity was reduced more rapidly by price advances, giving less time for the reduction of physical backlogs of demand.

The Korean Inflation

The causes of the violent inflation during the early months of the Korean War were analyzed in Chapter 5. This was clearly a demand inflation, touched off by expectations that wartime shortages of civilian goods were in the offing, and financed by a 3 per cent increase in the money supply and a 12 per cent rise in income velocity between the second quarter of 1950 and the first of 1951. Just as clearly, the voluntary downshift of consumer demand which followed the buying waves was a major factor in the price stability of 1951-52, but was not exclusively responsible for that stability. Although a reduction of demand *relative* to income would still have developed in reaction to the forward-buying movements, consumers probably would have both saved more *and* spent more if money income had continued to increase rapidly. Among the factors retarding the growth of money income during 1951-53 were the tax increases and credit controls that were discussed in Chapter 5. It is now time to consider the way in which direct controls over prices, wages, and materials affected the behavior of money incomes and prices.

A general freeze was announced on January 26, 1951, and prices and wages were under varying degrees of direct control from then until early in 1953. As mentioned earlier, however, it was a fascinating and unexpected feature of the times that average wholesale prices declined substantially during 1951-52 and that the prices of many nondurables actually fell well below legal ceilings. The fall in average wholesale prices was caused by the lull in consumer spending and the decline of inventory investment which it induced, but that is not to say that price and allocation controls were unnecessary or ineffective. By insulating the several sectors of the economy from one another, they gave maximum effect to the relaxation of consumer demand, with the probable result that the price level rose less than it otherwise would have done.

Suppose that no administrative controls had been imposed on prices, wages, or critical materials and that no fiscal or monetary curbs to private expenditure had been in effect when consumer demand declined in 1951. Is it not likely that bottlenecks in metals and metal products would have forced prices higher in those sectors—including prices of durable consumer goods? Consumers might have reacted to this by purchasing fewer cars or refrigerators until prices came down again, or they might have spent more on durables and less on nondurables, thereby depressing the prices of the latter. Quite possibly, however, they might have increased total expenditure even at the same level of money income, thus sustaining a higher price level.

Probably even more important is the fact that money income would not have been the same. Money wages would have risen along with prices in the durable goods industries, and the wage increases would have spread to other industries as well, raising the whole structure of prices and money incomes at the given level of real national income. Thus, the relaxation of private demand contributed so much to over-all price stability partly because it occurred in an institutional complex that constricted the normal channels for transmission of inflationary impulses between sectors and permitted deflationary forces full scope in the affected areas. By the same token, the task of containing inflationary pressures by direct and indirect controls was greatly simplified by the voluntary reduction of consumer demand and the associated inventory adjustments.

Perhaps the preceding discussion has left the reader inadequately prepared for the amplitude of the price declines in nondurables during 1951-52 (Chart 45). The reaction was especially severe for prices of intermediate materials—intimately related to basic agricultural commodities—just as the preceding rise had been under the impact of speculative inventory demand at home and abroad. Prices of finished nondurable goods did not fall nearly as much—partly because the demand for finished goods always holds up better than that for materials during periods of declining sales and inventory liquidation, and partly because wages in nondurable goods factories continued to rise along with those in durable goods industries.

Average hourly earnings of manufacturing workers kept closely in step with the cost of living until the summer of 1952 (Chart 46). Consumer prices moved ahead during the first Korean buying wave, but wages responded quickly and, by the time of the general freeze in January 1951, had achieved approximate parity with the consumer price index, not only for factory workers but for other large groups of employees as well.[5] Wages were under direct control after the freeze, of course, but gradual increases occurred as adjustments were granted

[5] Cost-of-living escalator contracts assured rapid (quarterly) wage adjustments in some industries, and similar increases were granted in others even when not required under existing wage contracts. See Benson Soffer, "The Effects of Recent Long-Term Wage Agreements on General Wage Level Movements: 1950-1956," *Quarterly Journal of Economics* (February 1959), pp. 36-60.

CHART 45. *Indexes of Average Hourly Earnings and Wholesale Prices, Durable and Nondurable Manufacturing, Monthly, 1950-54*

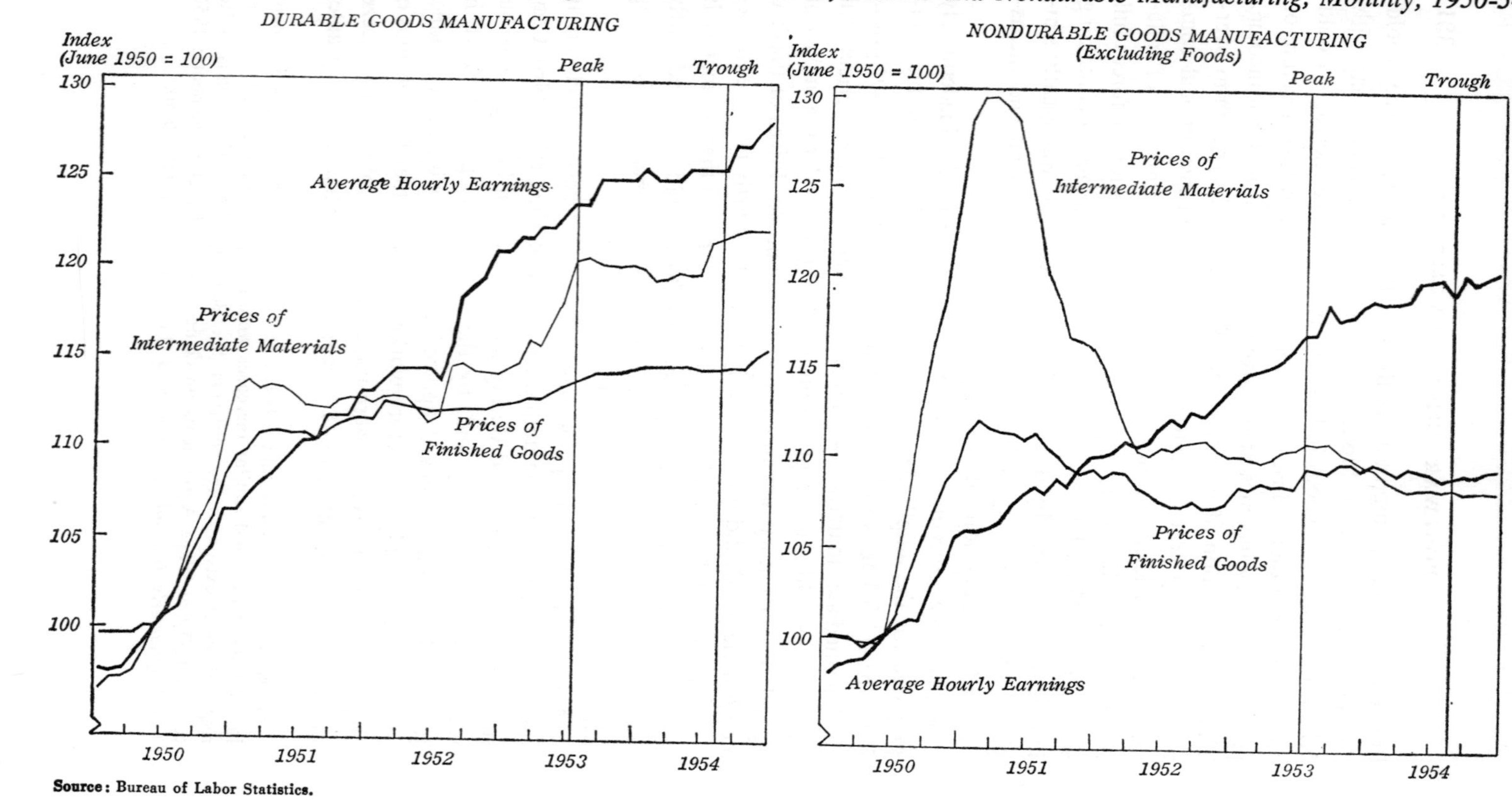

Source: Bureau of Labor Statistics.

CHART 46. *Indexes of Average Hourly Earnings in Manufacturing Industries and of Wholesale and Consumer Prices, Monthly, 1950-54*

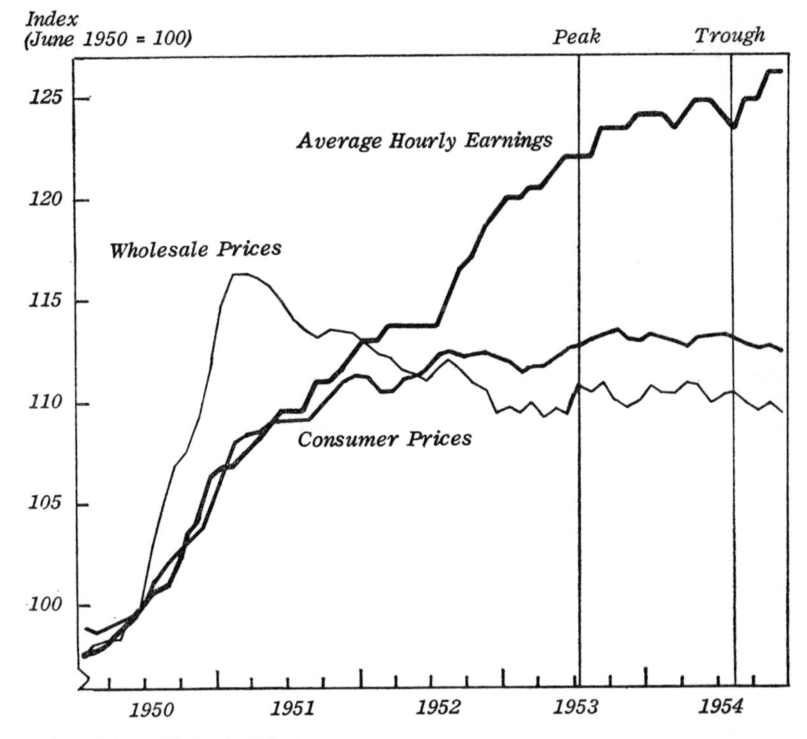

Source: Bureau of Labor Statistics.

to groups whose real earnings had lagged in 1950, and to workers in general to compensate for increases in consumer prices during the period of price control. In this way, higher wages became part of the cost-price-income structure of the economy (Table 51), thereby limiting the price declines in the weaker sectors. With the exception of foods, average wholesale prices of nondurable finished goods never did fall back to the pre-Korean peak of 1948, and not even foods did so at retail.

Wages surged forward during the last phase of direct controls in the latter half of 1952 and early 1953. The rise reflected a breakdown of the hold-the-line policy on real wages, and was part of a general movement to relax direct and indirect controls as it became apparent that this could be done without undue danger to the mobilization pro-

TABLE 51. *Indexes of Unit Labor Cost of Production Workers in Manufacturing, 1947-58*[a]

Period	Total	Durable Goods	Nondurable Goods
	Part A. Indexes (1947=100)		
1947	100.0	100.0	100.0
1948	104.1	103.3	105.1
1949	102.4	102.4	103.9
1950	100.5	99.8	101.4
1951	109.7	111.4	106.1
1952	111.9	111.7	109.6
1953	114.0	113.1	111.1
1954	111.3	110.3	110.0
1955	110.9	110.4	108.4
1956	114.3	113.8	111.0
1957	114.7	114.8	111.4
1958	112.1	113.7	108.8
	Part B. Percentage Changes		
1947–48	*4.1*	*3.3*	*5.1*
1948–50	*– 3.5*	*– 3.4*	*–3.5*
1950–53	*13.4*	*13.3*	*9.6*
1953–55	*– 2.7*	*– 2.4*	*– 2.4*
1955–57	*3.4*	*4.0*	*2.8*
1957–58	*– 2.3*	*– 1.0*	*– 2.3*

[a] Each index of unit labor cost was derived by dividing an index of payrolls of production workers (Bureau of Labor Statistics) by an index of production (Board of Governors of the Federal Reserve System). The resulting indexes reflect the influence both of changes in money wages and changes in output per man-hour on labor cost per unit of output. Source, National Bureau of Economic Research.

gram or to economic stability. Substantial advances for steel, copper, and aluminum were permitted under a corresponding relaxation of the criteria for price increases, and metal users were allowed to pass through the resulting absolute cost increases but not to pyramid them by proportional mark-ups. Were it not for the ceilings, prices of finished durable goods would doubtless have risen substantially after the steel strike of mid-1952, under the combined pressure of heavy consumer and inventory demand and the concomitant rise of resource prices. As is was, they increased only fractionally before the final elimination of price controls in April 1953.

Increases were small also among nondurables, however, where ceilings had been suspended for a large proportion of commodities, and despite a substantial upswing of wages, production, and sales. The principal depressant at work—the emergence of agricultural surpluses—has been an important determinant of prices of nondurables ever since. In late 1952 and early 1953, increased domestic production and a sharp drop of exports augmented domestic supplies sufficiently to depress prices of food at wholesale and retail and to offset increases of demand for materials important in the manufacture of nondurable goods. During the last phase of the Korean expansion, then, the spread which had initially developed between prices of durables and nondurables because of internal shifts of demand was kept open with the assistance of shifts of export demand and domestic supply.

In summary, the Korean experience provides an interesting example of a period in which changes in relative prices—declines among nondurables while prices of durables stayed at ceiling levels—definitely affected the over-all level of prices. One can be confident of this because the usual channels through which a change in one sector might induce a compensating variation in another were blocked by price and wage controls. Direct controls also inhibited bottleneck increases in wages and prices which would probably have occurred in their absence and spread to other sectors of the economy unless contained by fiscal and monetary devices. Finally, because wages and prices were under direct control, and also because their behavior during 1951-53 was heavily conditioned by the prior developments of the inflationary phase of the Korean expansion, it is invalid to conclude that the experience in itself proves that full employment and vigorous growth is compatible with stable prices under normal peacetime conditions.[6]

Expansion and Inflation: 1954-57

"Expansion and then inflation" would be more descriptive of the 1954-57 period. The business expansion which began in August 1954 lasted 35 months. During the first half of this span, the average of

[6] On this point, see John P. Lewis, "The Lull That Came to Stay," *Journal of Political Economy* (February 1955), pp. 1-19.

consumer prices kept within a range of one index point, but it rose 5.3 per cent between March 1956 and July 1957 (Chart 47). The advance of consumer prices during these months, while not nearly as rapid as in the inflations of 1946-48 and 1950-51, was nonetheless substantial, and was larger than the concomitant gain of real personal income (3.2 per cent).

In its broad aspects, this is just the sort of price behavior that one would expect of a peacetime expansion uninfluenced by postwar shortages or scare buying. Surplus capacity should prevent prices from rising much in the first stage of expansion, and the increases which come later should be comparatively small when judged against wartime or postwar inflations. However, the actual situation during 1954-57 was at once more complicated and more interesting than this simple generalization allows. I begin with an examination of wage-price developments in manufacturing and turn then to an analysis of their influence, and that of other factors, on the behavior of consumer prices generally.

A suggestion of wage-push inflation is conveyed by Chart 47, since average hourly earnings in manufacturing increased so much more than the over-all indexes of wholesale or consumer prices. This behavior contrasts strikingly with the events of 1946-48 (Chart 43) and 1950-51 (Chart 46). Money wages of factory workers lagged the cost-of-living during the earlier intervals, whereas they moved ahead of it in 1954-57. In the two earlier inflations, organized labor was reacting to previous price increases and attempting to restore the real value of money wages, whereas in 1954-57 it was seeking to augment real wage rates. It is this last fact, coupled with the observation that money wages outran below-average productivity increments and raised unit labor costs (Table 51), that has led many observers to speak of cost-push inflation during 1956-57. This is misplaced emphasis, because it ignores the initiating role of specific demands and the propagating role of permissive monetary-fiscal policies in the inflationary process.

Chart 48 shows that inflationary pressures did not permeate the economy evenly during 1954-57. There are pronounced differences between the durable and nondurable goods branches of manufacturing with regard not only to the timing and amplitude of price changes,

CHART 47. *Indexes of Average Hourly Earnings in Manufacturing Industries and of Wholesale and Consumer Prices, Monthly, 1954-58*

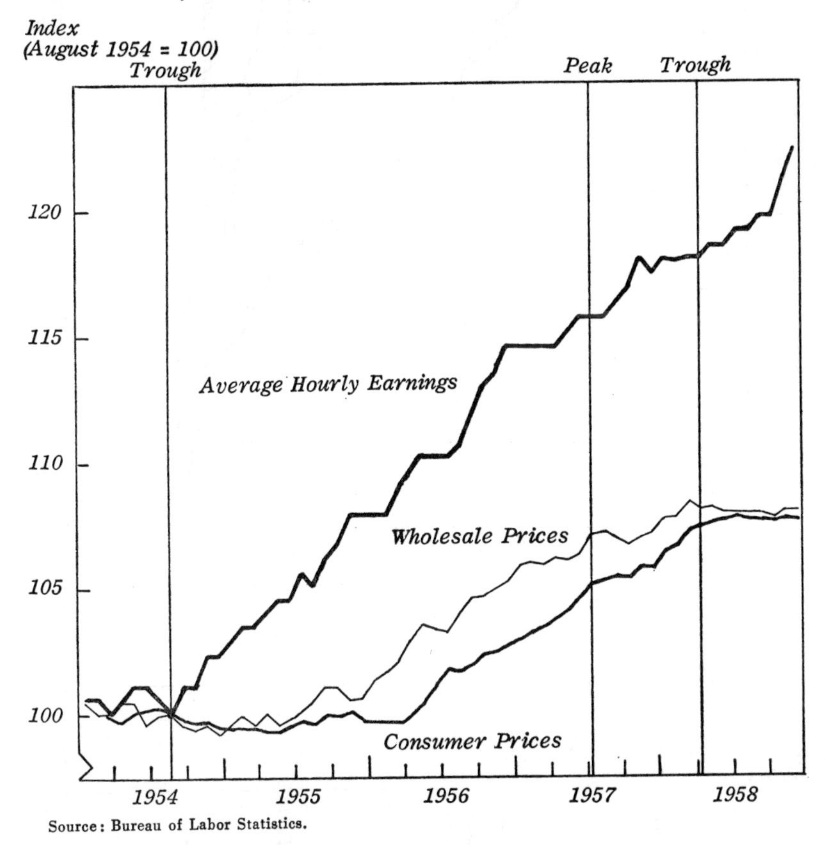

Source: Bureau of Labor Statistics.

but also to the relationship between changes in wages and prices.[7] A valid explanation of the inflationary process should be consistent with these differences among sectors.

The first thing to notice is that wages and prices moved closely together in the durable goods sector. This was not a new phenomenon, for a similar association appeared in 1948.[8] In both periods these prices

[7] Because food prices are strongly affected by independent variations in farm supplies owing to vagaries of weather or to long lags in the adjustment of supply to demand, they have been omitted from the comparisons in Chart 48 and are discussed separately at a later point.

[8] During the Korean War, of course, prices were controlled.

CHART 48. *Indexes of Average Hourly Earnings and Wholesale Prices, Durable and Nondurable Manufacturing, Monthly, 1954-58*

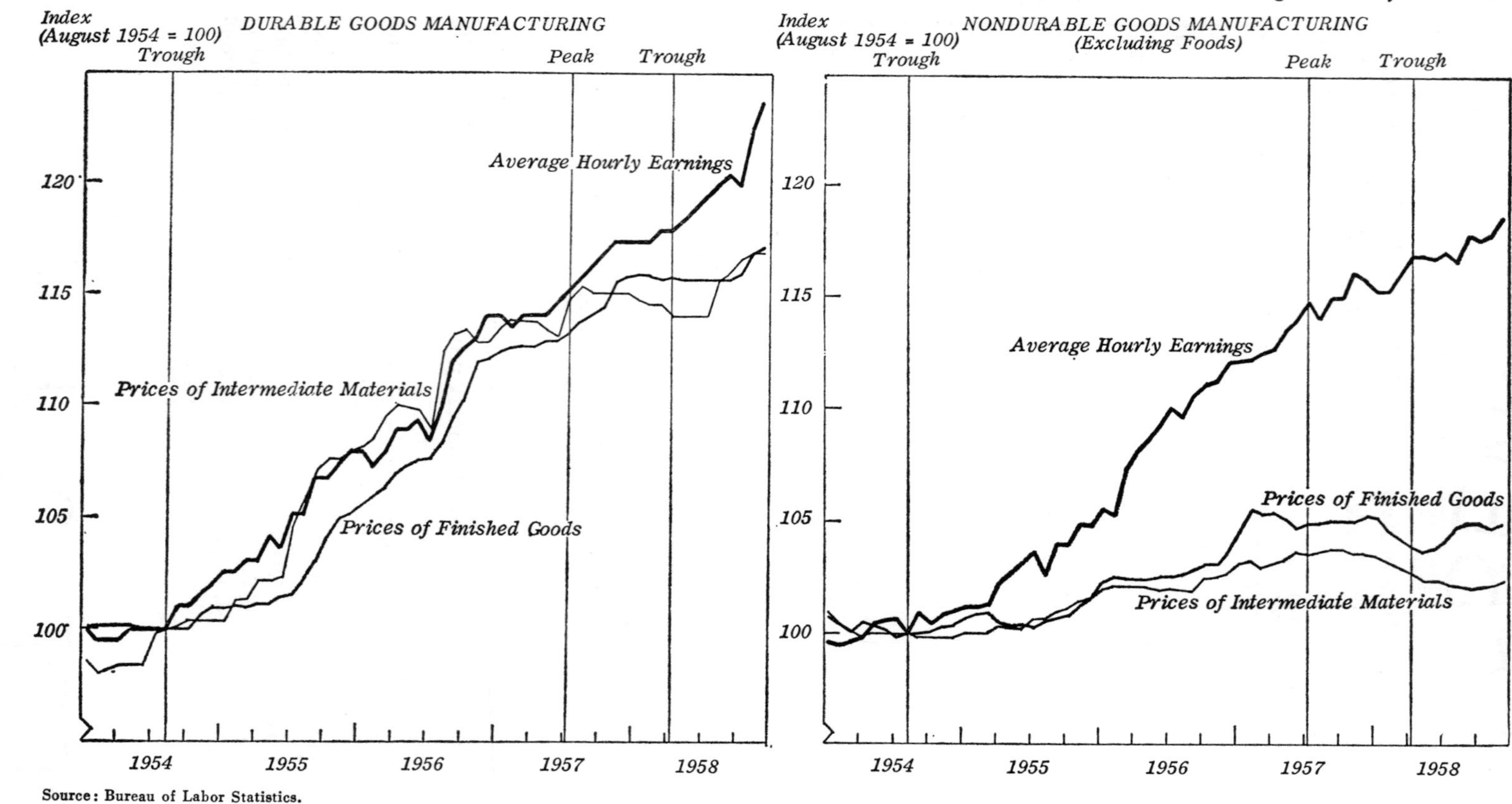

Source: Bureau of Labor Statistics.

rose swiftly, and in both the advance accelerated in those months of the year when major wage increases went into effect.

This timing relationship is certainly not surprising in view of the oligopolistic market structure of many of the important durable goods industries. Where industries are sufficiently concentrated so that individual firms recognize mutual interdependence, but there is no collusion, it is advantageous to all if prices are changed infrequently and in response to clearly identifiable factors known by each firm to affect the others in about the same way. When the individual firms are also large and in the public eye, a further advantage accrues if price increases can be attributed to wage increases, even though profit margins may be maintained or augmented in the process.

The magnitude of the increases cannot be explained simply by the fact that prices are administered, however. Even administered prices have to be set at some level—and at a level which is profitable to the company. This means that product demand cannot be ignored; it sets limits within which the firm must price if it is to attain profits which are satisfactory or better. By the same token, it sets limits within which costs must be held. These facts apparently are recognized by both labor and management, since the largest currently negotiated wage increases occur during periods of rising or high demand. (Deferred wage increases written into long-term contracts are another matter, for they may become effective during periods of low or falling demand.)

Two important features of the recovery of 1954-55, described in Chapter 7, have a bearing on the rise of industrial prices which began in 1955. One was the spectacular reception accorded the 1955 automobile models and the acceleration of consumer purchases of durable goods for which it was primarily responsible. The other was the onrush of business plans for capacity expansion during the winter and spring of 1955. These plans were a lagged response to the business upturn, so that business fixed investment did not rise strongly until the latter half of the year. The upsurge was foreshadowed during the spring, however, in surveys of investment plans and, even more concretely, in new orders for producer goods. Thus, prospects for 1955 sales and profits were excellent at the time of the wage settlements in major durable goods industries during the late spring and summer.

With product demands high and expected to rise further in many industries, sizable wage increases were demanded and received by employees in heavy industry. Parallel changes occurred in prices of intermediate materials for durable goods manufacturing—comprising principally primary metals, lumber, and plastics—and of durable finished goods. Between June and November of 1955, average hourly earnings of production workers in durable goods factories increased 3.5 per cent and prices of intermediate materials rose 5.1 per cent. Average wholesale prices of finished durable goods increased 3.4 per cent between July and December, with consumer durables up 2.4 per cent and producer goods 4.3 per cent.

Were these price raises caused by increased demands or higher costs? The answer can only be: by both. Current demands for durable goods had recovered strongly before the wage advances, and further increases of demand were in the offing and the orders were on the books. These facts certainly augmented the size of the wage increases —contrast the increases of 1954 and 1955—but the timing and magnitude of the price increases were just as definitely influenced by the behavior of wages.

Nor is that all. The bargaining decisions made in 1955 also influenced the wage-price behavior of the next three years. This is because 1955 saw a revival of labor-management interest in the long-term contract which specifies deferred annual wage increases and provides for wage escalation to protect the real value of wages against cost-of-living increases during the life of the agreement. Such contracts were renewed in the automobile and trucking industries and negotiated for the first time with the General Electric Company in 1955. They spread to steel, meatpacking, railroads, and other industries in 1956, so that by the end of that year nearly 5 million workers, or two-thirds of all those in major collective bargaining situations, were covered by long-term agreements.[9]

The deferred increases specified by "annual improvement factors"

[9] Lily Mary David and Donald L. Helm, "Deferred Wage Increases in 1957 and Wage Escalator Clauses," *Monthly Labor Review* (January 1957), pp. 50-52; Donald L. Helm and Richard G. Seefer, "Major Wage Developments in 1957," *Ibid.* (April 1958), pp. 377-83.

or "annual productivity increases" are generally in line with the long-term average rate of growth of output per man-hour for the economy as a whole, but that fact does not necessarily make them noninflationary. Annual productivity gains in the industries directly affected by the contracts may change unevenly over time and may deviate widely from the average for the economy, both in any given year and over the long term. Moreover, since the deferred increases set a minimum standard for other wages, they may lift the general level of money wages at a faster rate than over-all productivity rises in any particular year, especially since productivity growth is markedly uneven (Table 52). When this happens the upward pressure on prices from the cost side is increased everywhere, although the over-all average of prices will not rise commensurately or at all unless demand permits. In addition to all this, escalator clauses in the long-term agreements speed price-wage adjustments and provide a ready channel by which autonomous increases of food prices may quickly raise the level of industrial wages.

It would be excessive to claim that the magnitude of the average wage increase negotiated in 1956 was determined by the deferred and escalated increases specified under the long-term agreements of 1955. The 1955 agreements covered only 2 million workers. Certainly demand conditions were favorable in most industries during 1956, so that substantial wage increases were to be expected in any event.[10] Yet, given the high level of demand, it is difficult to believe that foreknowledge of the 2.5 to 3 per cent deferred increases to be received by automobile and electrical workers, plus the increases due them under escalator clauses after the consumer price index began rising in May, did not establish the general standards for wage settlements in other industries. As Benson Soffer pointed out, the modal wage increase currently negotiated in all major collective bargaining situations in 1956 was 9 to 11 cents per hour, whereas the increase to auto-

[10] Indicative of this is the fact that wage increases were negotiated during the year in several industries—northern cotton and synthetic textiles, men's apparel, and anthracite mining—which had not experienced increases for three or more years. Lily Mary David and Donald L. Helm, "Major Wage Developments in 1956," *Monthly Labor Review* (April 1957), pp. 447-52.

TABLE 52. *Annual Increases of Real Product per Man-Hour for the Private Economy, 1947-58*[a]
(In per cent)

Year	Total Private Economy	Agriculture	Nonagricultural Industries		
			Total	Manufacturing	Nonmanufacturing
1947–48	3.6	18.3	1.9	2.6	1.6
1948–49	2.9	– 4.6	3.9	2.5	5.1
1949–50	7.1	13.7	5.3	6.7	4.3
1950–51	2.5	– 1.4	1.7	1.6	1.5
1951–52	2.2	8.6	1.3	1.6	1.2
1952–53	4.1	11.3	2.8	4.7	1.3
1953–54	1.8	7.0	1.6	–0.8	3.5
1954–55	4.4	3.4	4.3	7.0	2.8
1955–56	0.6	4.8	–0.1	1.2	–0.8
1956–57	2.7	4.9	2.1	0.5	3.2
1957–58	0.8	12.8	–0.1	n.a.	n.a.

n.a. Not available.

[a] The productivity indexes were computed by the Bureau of Labor Statistics from estimates of real product and man-hours. The real product estimates, referring to 1954 prices, are based primarily on national product statistics of the Department of Commerce, Office of Business Economics, except for the manufacturing real product estimates which were developed by the Bureau of Labor Statistics. The man-hour data are primarily from the Bureau of Labor Statistics and relate to man-hours paid, rather than man-hours worked. Source, John W. Kendrick, "Productivity, Costs and Prices: Concepts and Measures," *Wages, Prices, Profits and Productivity*, The American Assembly, Columbia University (1959), p. 48.

mobile workers under their long-term contract was 12 cents.[11]

A stronger case can be made for the proposition that the size of the 1957 wage increases was set largely by earlier wage agreements. For one thing, among the 7.5 million workers covered by major collective bargaining agreements in 1957, two out of three received wage increases under long-term agreements signed in prior years. For another, the modal increase currently negotiated was again 9 to 11 cents, although increases of 7 to 9 cents, were almost as common, and the weighted average negotiated increase was 10.5 cents.[12] The increase

[11] *Op. cit.*, pp. 47-48. Soffer's data are from the Bureau of Labor Statistics. I have calculated the weighted average of all increases between 5 and 19 cents, and it comes to 10.5 cents.

[12] Helm and Seefer, *op. cit.*, Table 2. The weighted average was computed for wage increases of more than 5 cents but less than 19 cents.

for automobile workers was again 12 cents. Finally, product demands had eased considerably for durable goods by the time the principal wage increases went into effect (June-November). Indeed, factory sales of durables had been falling gradually since the turn of the year.

Clearly, then, the high demand for durable goods during 1955-56 was a principal determinant of wages and prices in those industries, not alone in those years but, through the medium of long-term wage contracts, in 1957 as well. The price and wage increases of 1955 and 1956 would probably have occurred in any bottleneck situation, with or without collective bargaining or concentrated product markets, but it does appear that the 1957 increases were fostered by bargaining decisions made a year or more in advance and were therefore autonomous with regard to current product demands.

The wage increases negotiated in key durable goods industries spread to other parts of the economy within a few months. Average hourly earnings in nondurable manufactures, for example, lagged behind durables during the last half of each year and then caught up in percentage terms during the first half of the next (Chart 49). A similar pattern of lagged adjustment to the wage increases established in durable manufacturing is observable for crude petroleum and natural gas, wholesale trade, and retailing. Wage increases in building construction and gas and electric utilities, on the other hand, were closely timed with those in durable manufacturing, suggesting that these industries may also have been pattern setters.

The fact that wages in the various industrial divisions kept pace during 1955-57 is not especially interesting in itself, for both union activities and labor market forces tend to preserve wage parities. The interesting point is that the wage increases in the durable goods sector set the pace for advances elsewhere, and for reasons partly independent of the level of aggregate demand in 1955-56 and even of the demand for durables themselves in 1957.

It by no means follows that the inflation of the general price level was necessarily caused by the wage increases negotiated in heavy goods industries. There are two reasons why the price level might not rise despite a general wage increase which was autonomous from the point of view of most of the economy. First, productivity advances

CHART 49. *Indexes of Average Hourly Earnings, Selected Industries, Monthly, 1954-58*

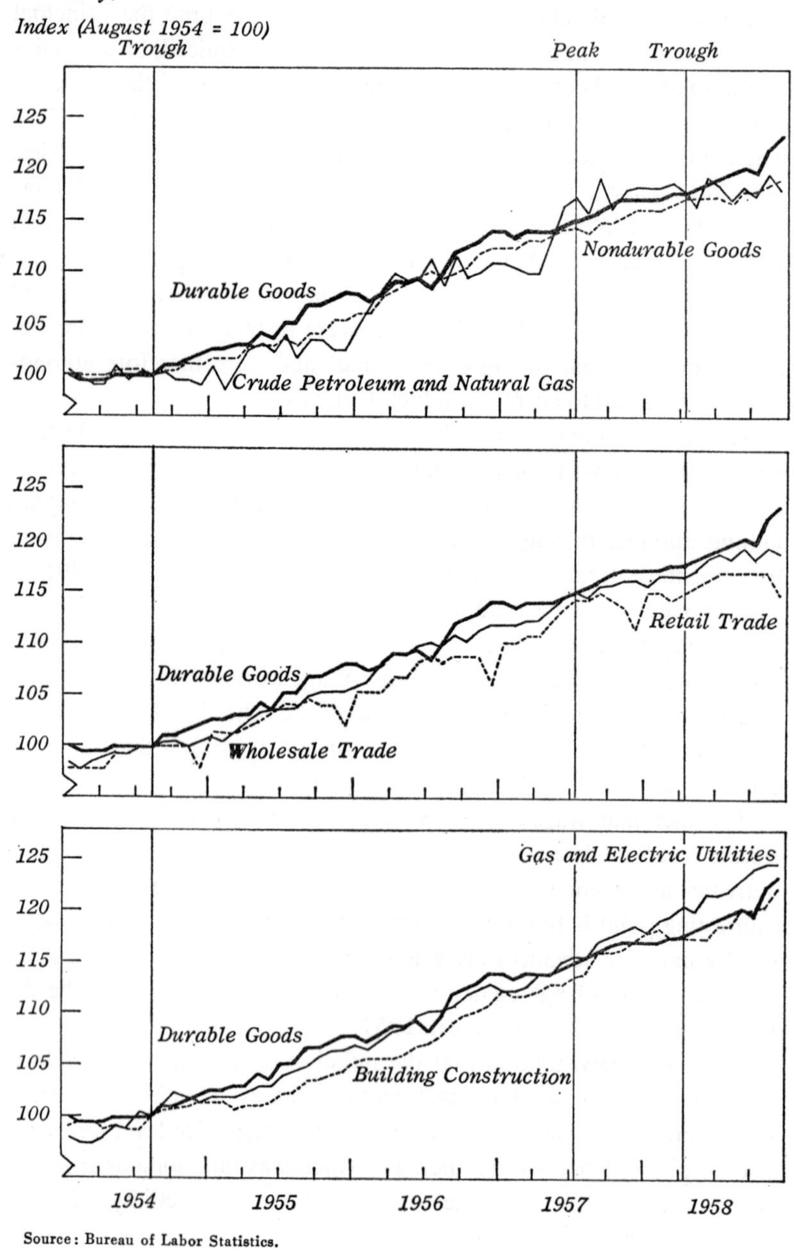

Source: Bureau of Labor Statistics.

might offset the cost-raising influence of wage increases. Secondly, even if costs went up, aggregate money demand might not rise sufficiently to sustain a general price increase without forcing a reduction of production and employment. It is interesting, therefore, that many of the major concentrated markets for products and labor are located together in the durable goods sector—a fact which tends to foster the initiation and spread of inflationary impulses from these markets to others, and does this from the side of demand as well as cost.

Durables are more subject than nondurables to income-autonomous increases of demand under normal peacetime conditions. But demand increases of this type, financed by new money or from idle balances, will augment the income stream and induce increases of demand elsewhere in the familiar multiplier process. Thus, ordinarily, we would expect a cyclical expansion to be led by an increase of investment or government expenditure and to spread to consumer goods as personal incomes rose.[13] Now, if supply conditions in the durable goods sector make it necessary for buyers to pay higher prices for additional goods and for producers to pay higher wages for additional labor, the autonomous increase of expenditure will contain a price-wage as well as a production-employment component. Moreover, the increase of money expenditure will then be larger than otherwise by virtue of the price increases, provided demand is inelastic.

All this could also occur in the absence of monopoly elements in labor or product markets. In fact, bottleneck price-wage increases could easily be larger during expansions if all markets were perfectly competitive and hence sensitive to short-term shifts of demand. Given the existence of oligopolistic product markets, however, the added presence of labor unions increases the likelihood that moderate inflationary pressures will develop during the usual cyclical expansion. Because of uncertainty about what rivals will do and the threat of public intervention, individual firms are reluctant to advance prices even during periods of rising or high demand unless the action can be justified by cost increases. Since labor unions will press for higher money wages, however, it is likely that under favorable demand conditions,

[13] Income-autonomous increases of demand for consumer durable goods may also start or amplify an expansion with similar results.

and even at other times if deferred wage contracts are widespread, wages and prices will rise together in the durable goods industries in the familiar pattern of recent years.

Assume, as appears realistic, that final demands for durable goods as a class are inelastic to moderate price increases, so that the price increases will leave production and employment largely unaffected but will increase money expenditure in the durable goods industries. Then not only will the associated wage increases in these industries set standards for other workers, but the higher money incomes generated in the process will increase other product demands.

This is just what appears to have happened during 1955-57. The durable goods boom stimulated specific wage-price-income increases which spread to other sectors. However, prices did not rise as evenly as wages over the economy, for several reasons. Labor costs depend on physical productivity as well as money wages. Industries with small productivity gains were pressed especially hard by wage advances. Differences were also encountered among industries with regard to other aspects of cost. Many raw materials originating on farms were in chronic excess supply, with the result that prices were stabilized at levels governed by federal programs and the entire cost structure of products fabricated from these materials or their substitutes was anchored—a fact which is responsible for much of the pronounced contrast between price increases for durables and nondurables during 1955-57. There was no important difference between the two divisions insofar as the 1955-57 increases of unit labor cost in manufacturing were concerned (Table 51).

Relative demands also differed among the various goods and services. Among durables, this shows up in the fact that prices of producer goods rose more than those of consumer items, and within the latter group, those of automobiles more than household appliances, despite the similarities in prices of materials and labor. As between durables and nondurables, the comparative strength of market demands is difficult to judge. The demand for durables as a class doubtless increased more than was true of nondurables—witness the fact that production as well as prices of durables outpaced nondurables during the expansion. The substantial difference between the two divisions in the behavior of material costs, however, also accounts for much—perhaps most—of the contrast in the amounts of average price increase.

The factors analyzed thus far were not the only important determinants of price change during the expansion. Although industrial wholesale prices rose fairly rapidly after mid-1955, the consumer price index did not begin a sustained advance until the following April. For a time, the effects of higher industrial prices on the cost of living were offset by other forces which were noncyclical in origin.

The persistent agricultural surpluses not only affected prices of farm-produced raw materials used in the manufacture of many nondurables, but also had other effects on the consumer price index. When agricultural prices broke sharply downward during the last half of 1955, retail food prices dropped, though by smaller amounts, tending directly to reduce the consumer price index (Charts 42 and 50). Consumers probably took advantage of lower food prices partly to increase their food consumption, their rate of saving, or both, but partly also to increase expenditures for other items. If so, the induced shift of demand was probably insufficient to raise other prices enough to compensate for the decline of food prices. Supplies of many consumer goods and services are fairly elastic in the short run—in good part because of market imperfections and sluggish price responses—so that a shift of demand toward nonfood items is likely to raise their sales more than their prices for some months at least.

The other important noncyclical factor helping to stabilize the consumer price index during 1955 and early 1956 was a fall of retail prices of durable consumer goods in the face of rising wholesale prices. This was not a new development, however, for retail margins on durable goods had been narrowing for several years under the competitive pressures associated with the growth of the discount house and emergence of a buyers' market in automobiles. The potential for retail price reductions from this source appears to have become exhausted about mid-1956. Prices of household appliances did fall slightly over the next two years, but furniture prices rose slightly, and those of automobiles more substantially.

Foods accounted for one-fourth of the 1956-57 increase in consumer prices. This was due partly to an autonomous reversal of the

CHART 50. *Indexes of Consumer Prices, Quarterly, 1946-58*

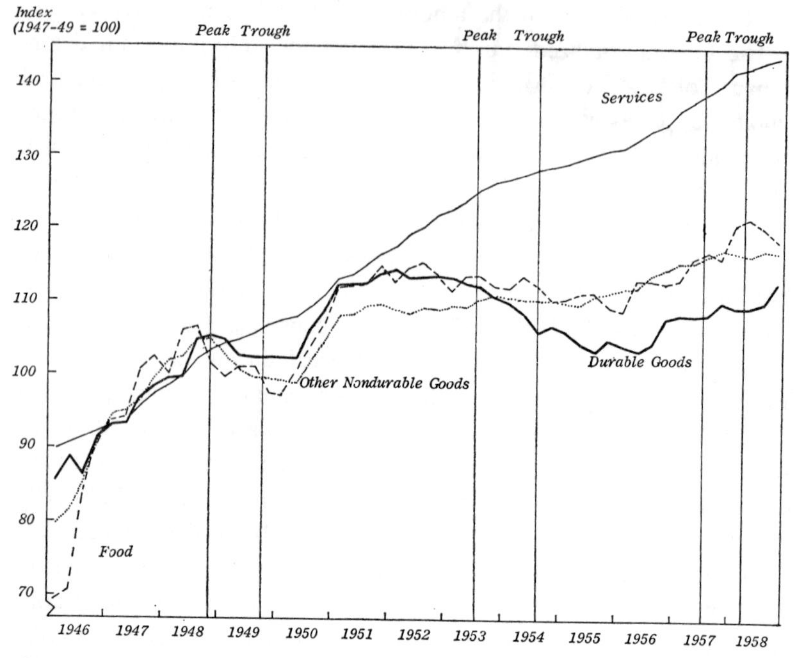

Source: Bureau of Labor Statistics.

earlier downslide of farm prices, with reduced meat supplies contributing prominently to the reversal. Just as the prior fall of food prices had probably reduced the over-all price level despite substitution effects, so now their increase probably raised it. Nor were food and industrial prices linked only by demand factors, for the advance of food prices was quickly matched by industrial wage increases under escalator clauses.

The relationship between food and other prices did not run in one direction only, however. Apart from meats, higher food prices during 1956-57 were due mainly to increased costs of processing and distribution and to quality improvements.[14] Wage increases to workers engaged in food processing and distribution contributed to these cost increases, and, as we have seen, the standards with respect to wage raises were set in the durable goods industries.

[14] *Economic Report of the President* (January 1958), p. 24.

Services also figured prominently in the rise of average consumer prices during 1956-57, accounting for four-tenths of the increase in the over-all index. Indeed, service prices have risen throughout the postwar era, but the rise since 1951 has been especially noticeable because prices of consumer goods have not kept pace. Like farm commodities, prices of services are subject to special influences which set them somewhat apart from industrial prices, especially with regard to sensitivity to current shifts of cost or demand. Since they are produced as used, they are unaffected by the shifts of inventory demand on the part of households or businesses which are responsible for much of the cyclical variation in prices of goods. As a class, moreover, they are slow to respond to changes in cost or demand, because some are subject to public regulation (utilities) and others are influenced by market imperfections of one sort or another (rent, medical care, personal services, etc.). Because of these characteristics, services reveal in purest form the underlying inflationary cast of the postwar period. Their rise relative to prices of goods since 1951 must reflect a tendency toward lagging productivity, growing relative demand, or both, but their absolute increase need not have occurred had gains in real national income due to advancing productivity been distributed in the form of general price reductions at a constant level of money income.

The Recessions and Creeping Inflation

Prices rose during each of the expansions after 1946, but as Chart 41 has shown they declined relatively little in the 1948-49 contraction, were steady during that of 1953-54, and increased during the 1957-58 contraction. Barring war scares and crash armament programs, there is no reason to anticipate the recurrence of an inflation as violent as in 1946-48 or 1950-51. Moderate price increases during business expansions, however, are neither unusual from the perspective of history nor unlikely from the point of view of the institutions and attitudes of the present-day economy. But even moderate increases during expansions will lead to a secularly rising price level in the absence of compensating decreases during contractions. What are the causes and implications of the resistance shown by the postwar economy to price deflation?

The Contraction of 1948-49

Deflationary forces were mild during 1948-49. Prices and production declined, but so little as to be scarcely detectable against the background of fluctuations since the Civil War (Chart 1). Analysis of the principal features of the contraction in Chapter 4 led to the conclusion that it was mild because speculative excesses had not been a feature of the postwar inflation; because institutional factors and public policies minimized actual and expected declines of incomes, sales, and prices and prevented cumulative deterioration of short-term expectations; and because, in those favorable circumstances, the forces for expansion inherent in the postwar population upsurge and remaining backlogs of public and private demand could quickly assert their influence.

The price declines which did occur were orderly and conformed to the usual pattern of changes during periods of economic contraction. That is, prices of finished goods fell least and those of materials experienced greater reductions (Chart 44). This is typical of contractions because deflationary impulses are propagated backward with increasing intensity from final sellers to manufacturers and thence to suppliers of raw materials; since, in their desire to trim inventories, firms at each stage of production or distribution curtail purchase orders by more than their own sales decline. The pressure on prices resulting from the magnification of downshifts of demand at each stage is especially powerful in markets where large numbers of sellers are actively engaged in price competition and where output changes slowly in response to demand. And, of course, the more prices of purchased materials weaken at each market level, the greater is the scope for reductions in prices of finished goods. It is in the light of these facts that the importance of agricultural supports as a cushion to the price structure should be viewed, since farms supply the basic materials for a large number of nondurable goods. It is relevant also that a good part of the potential decline of farm prices during 1948-49 came before the contraction of aggregate business activity was actually underway, largely because of the sharp increase of crop output which had occurred here and abroad in 1948 (Chart 42).

Additional support to prices was forthcoming from the downward inflexibility of wage rates (Chart 43). Now, wage rigidity during minor contractions is not a new phenomenon confined to the postwar economy. Wages also lagged by long intervals during the business cycles of the interwar period, and responded scarcely at all to the mild downswings of 1923-24 and 1926-27 (Chart 51). Hence, it cannot be asserted with absolute confidence that wages were stable during 1948-49 because organized labor was stronger than in prewar years. Wages may have remained firm simply because the contraction was mild and short-lived, so that management determination to seek lower wage schedules was never put to the test, and might not have been even in the absence of labor unions.

That is not the end of the matter, however. If businessmen become convinced for any reason that wage rates will not fall, they are, in the same measure, convinced that substantial declines in prices of finished goods are not in the offing. These dual convictions must have been cultivated by the growth in the power of organized labor. Indeed, there is some evidence of this in the behavior of wages and prices during the severe contraction of 1937-38, which occurred after the mass production industries were organized. It is inconclusive evidence, because that contraction, though severe, was short-lived, and fell within the range of the normal time lag of wages behind business downturns (Chart 51). All the same, the fact that the wage and price reductions of 1937-38 were comparable to those of 1923-24 and 1926-27, rather than 1920-21, is consistent with the a priori prediction of greater rigidity.

The expectation was probably widespread after the war, then, that wages would hold firm even under considerable deflationary pressure. This factor would be particularly important in a contraction such as 1948-49, which followed a sharp inflation. Such a belief would modify price expectations which might otherwise become quite pessimistic, and, by so doing, help to prevent the contraction from becoming severe enough ever to press heavily on wages. Were wage rates to

CHART 51. *Indexes of Wage Rates and Factory Employment and Average Hourly Earnings, All Manufactures, United States, 1919-39*

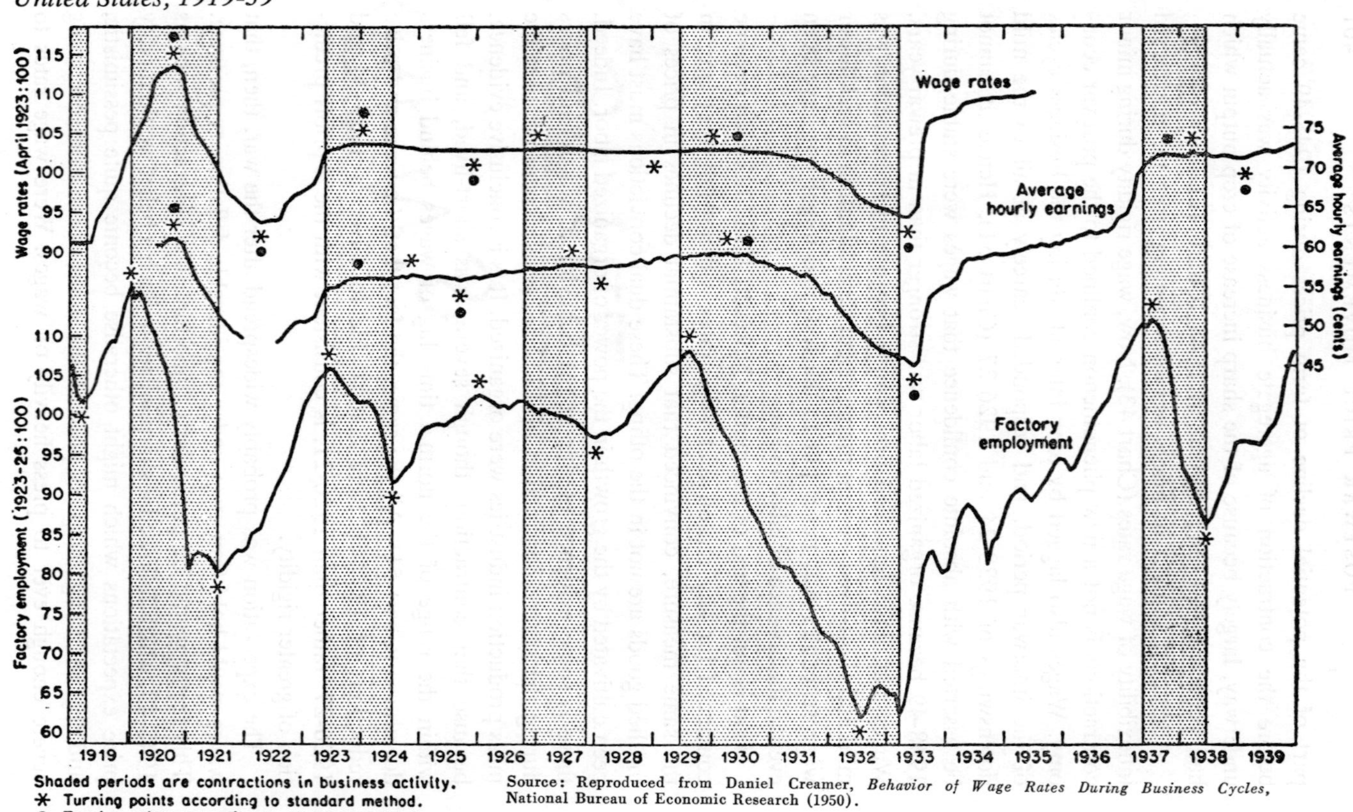

Shaded periods are contractions in business activity.
* Turning points according to standard method.
● Turning points according to alternate method.

Source: Reproduced from Daniel Creamer, *Behavior of Wage Rates During Business Cycles*, National Bureau of Economic Research (1950).

fall from the beginning of the contraction, the chances of widespread postponement of purchases in anticipation of future price declines would be greatly enhanced.

The final aspect of wage-price rigidity to be discussed is, perhaps, the most important of all in connection with the contraction of 1948-49. It is doubtful that there existed then or exists now any sizable segment of opinion in business or government circles that widespread wage reductions are beneficial as a means of combating unemployment, or that a deflation of wages and prices is a necessary, though painful, penalty for permitting an inflation to run its course. To quote the Council of Economic Advisers in mid-1949:

> There would be no purpose, and much potential damage, in an attempt to get back to some drastically lower price level by wage cutting, since incomes are now geared to prices substantially higher than before the war or immediately after the war. Such an effort would involve a deep and vastly unsettling decline in wages as the accompaniment to a prolonged period of severe depression. From that, practically no one would gain; the economy would lose tragically.[15]

This attitude was reflected in the fiscal and monetary policies of the day. It contrasts strikingly with the situation of 1920-21, when deflation was regarded as a necessary evil, and when Federal Reserve actions were taken to tighten rather than ease credit. The differing attitudes toward the inevitability and desirability of wage-price deflation, and the associated differences in public and private actions, go far toward explaining the greater severity of the earlier experience despite the presence of underlying elements of strength similar to those following World War II.

Prices and Wages During the 1953-54 and 1957-58 Contractions

Does the fact that the index of consumer prices fell in 1948-49, changed little during the 1953-54 recession, and increased noticeably during the contraction of 1957-58 mean that prices are becoming in-

[15] *The Economic Situation at Midyear 1949, A Report to the President by the Council of Economic Advisers,* p. 8, included in *Midyear Economic Report of the President* (July 1949).

creasingly resistant to business contractions because of postwar trends in economic structure? There are indications that this may be so.

The principal reason is that wages appear to be less sensitive than ever to reductions in labor demand. There was a hint of this in the slight increase of average hourly earnings in manufacturing during 1953-54 (Chart 46), although much of that rise should be discounted because it occurred during the early months of the contraction when the unemployment ratio was still low by peacetime standards. The seasonally adjusted unemployment rate did not exceed 3.5 per cent until November or December of 1953.[16] The substantial increase of average hourly earnings during the 1957-58 contraction is on a different footing, however (Chart 47). Unemployment was 4 per cent or more of the labor force from the beginning of the contraction in August, and reached 7.5 percent at the April trough.

More important, the wage increases that went into effect during the latter contraction were largely the lagged result of prior agreements under long-term contracts. Not only did wages rise because of deferred increases; they were also boosted under escalator clauses as the consumer price index rose contracyclically. The latter rise was caused primarily by autonomous increases in food prices. Clearly the chances of wage increases during periods of depressed employment will be enhanced if long-term agreements continue to be popular with labor and management and continue to spread. Even should the consumer price index decline, the induced wage reductions under escalator clauses would have to be substantial enough to swamp the annual deferred increases in order for wage rates to fall.

Wage increases may not lead to price increases, of course, and especially not when they occur during depressed periods. It is useful to distinguish between durables and nondurables in this connection. It has been shown that average prices of durable manufactures tend to rise in concert with average hourly earnings during periods of business expansion, and to take major jumps at the time of the annual wage increases. But these annual wage-price increases may easily come during the early months of a business decline, since the transition from

[16] The particular month depends upon the method used for seasonal adjustment.

expansion to contraction often occurs gradually and prices of durables are slow to respond to demand shifts. This is what happened in 1957 (Chart 48). The situation was similar in 1953, except that the price increases which occurred just before and after the cyclical peak were prompted by price decontrol (Chart 45). In 1948, the business peak came late in the year, so that the "third round" of wage-price increases in durable goods factories was completed prior to the contraction (Chart 44).

Thus, price increases for durable goods in the neighborhood of cyclical peaks are not especially surprising. The consequences are different from those which follow similar increases during the early or middle phases of a boom, however. At those times, money expenditure and money income are likely to increase as a result of the price hikes and to cause demand to rise elsewhere. This probably will not happen, however, if demand for durables is already declining at the time of the price increases. It also will not happen if demand for durables becomes elastic to price increases near the top of the upswing, although (for reasons discussed in Chapter 11), this is less likely to occur than in prewar days. In either event, money income will not rise autonomously to increase existing demand for nondurables, and hence prices of nondurables will merely hold their own or decline, and this despite the spread of wage increases from the durable to the nondurable goods sector (Chart 48).[17]

The contrast between the price behavior of durables and nondurables during periods of depressed demand may be partly fictitious. The quoted prices which enter the official indexes are not always representative of actual market conditions, and discounts and concessions may reduce market prices even though administered list prices are unchanged.[18] This does not appear to be a serious qualification, how-

[17] This is not to say that wages in nondurable goods industries will rise as fast as those in the durable goods sector during periods in which product demands are generally depressed. Long-term labor contracts are especially common among durables, whereas the annually negotiated increases typical of other industries are apt to be sensitive to current product and labor demands. Notice that although average hourly earnings kept pace in the two divisions during the expansion of 1954-57, durables went considerably ahead of nondurables during the ensuing contraction and recovery.

[18] See Martin J. Bailey, "Administered Prices in the American Economy,"

ever. Price concessions would surely become important during a prolonged contraction, but it does not follow that the increases which have occurred in the average price tags of finished durable goods at the onset of each postwar contraction have been rescinded during the brief periods those contractions have spanned.[19] Furthermore, the wage increases which accompany price advances at those times—which are possible precisely because prices and wages in concentrated markets are loosely circumscribed rather than closely determined by current conditions—place a floor under subsequent price reductions, not only in those markets but elsewhere as well.

It should be reiterated that wage stability during business contractions has a positive as well as negative aspect. Wage stability inhibits the formation of adverse price expectations which could amplify deflationary pressures and reduce production and employment along with prices. Moreover, wage increases which occur after a contraction has been underway some months and product demands are already depressed, may augment real income and contribute to a business upturn. Under those circumstances, oligopolistic firms may temporarily absorb wage increases without raising prices or reducing production and employment. If so, the resulting stimulus to consumption demand might outweigh the adverse effects, if any, of the wage increase on investment.

Wage stability was not the only factor limiting price reductions from the cost side during the contractions of 1953-54 and 1957-58. In prewar contractions, the scope for price reductions of finished goods was augmented by substantial declines in prices of materials. Even this

---

The Relationship of Prices to Economic Stability and Growth, Compendium of Papers Submitted by Panelists Appearing before the Joint Economic Committee, 85 Cong. 2 sess. (March 31, 1958), pp. 89-105.

[19] The official consumer price index of retail prices of new cars, for example, showed the usual seasonal decline in the early months of 1958 but stayed above the corresponding months of 1957. This index reflects dealer concessions from list prices. In general, one would expect the downward pressure on list prices during a contraction to be greater for materials than for finished goods, since the downshift of demand for materials is amplified by inventory disinvestment, and since materials are more homogenous than finished goods and more open to price competition on that account. A high proportion of the scanty quantitative evidence on price concessions is for materials.

avenue was closed during 1953-54, however, partly because prices of nondurable materials had been forced down previously—the adjustment which ordinarily would come with a general contraction had already occurred because of the isolated contraction in that sector during 1951-52. Still, these prices did decline a little in 1954, and would have decreased more were is not that prices of crude materials were lent independent support by the agricultural program. As for 1957-58, not only did supports keep crop prices from falling much, but average food prices rose contracyclically because of autonomous declines in supplies of fruits, vegetables, and meats.

The contracyclical rise of food prices during 1957-58 was due to accidental factors that might or might not be repeated during future contractions, and could readily go the other way. To the extent that agricultural supports remain a feature of the economic structure, however, and especially when prices have been under support before contraction begins, they will minimize cyclical declines in prices of important classes of goods. Any diversion of purchasing power which might arise during a contraction, if prices of foods and other nondurables were lower in the absence of supports, would tend to stimulate larger purchases of durables rather than higher prices for them. Thus, it is likely that the over-all average of prices would be kept higher by the supports than it otherwise would be. And, of course, the net injection of income from government sources via the support operation helps to firm demands generally. If the cost of living were, indeed, prevented from falling as much as it would without supports, this would reinforce the tendency toward price stability by diminishing wage reductions under escalator clauses.

Expansion and Creeping Inflation

For the postwar period as a whole, the economic environment was consistently hospitable to expansion and inflation and hostile to contraction and deflation. Prices rose during each expansion and fell little or not at all during the contractions. But price increases during cyclical expansions are the historical rule. This is made clear in Table 7, which shows 27 business expansions between 1834 and 1944. In 18 of these expansions, wholesale prices increased, and in four they held virtually steady. Of the five exceptional cases of price deflation during the period, all except that of 1927-29 occurred during the business expansions between the Civil War and 1892.

Prices fell sharply during each of the seven major contractions which plagued the economy between 1873 and 1938 except that of 1907-08. There is no doubt that a severe contraction of aggregate demand would again reduce prices; and also no doubt that employment and production would fall sharply as well. A principal reason for the continued inflation of the postwar years, then, is that depression has been avoided. But the same factors which have combined to prevent a severe contraction—stabilizing changes in economic structure, a plentiful stock of investment opportunities, and discretionary anti-recession policies—have also inhibited price deflation. To a large extent, the inflationary bias exhibited by the postwar economy has been merely another aspect of its expansionary bias. Nor is this a unique association in American experience.

The period of rising prices from 1897 to 1914 was marked by only one severe contraction—1907-08—and that one short-lived. Prices at wholesale did come down during the last three contractions of the 1897-1914 period, but the reduction in prices was smaller in each contraction than the increase in each preceding expansion. Consumer prices rose during every contraction except that of 1907-08 (Table 53). It was a time of creeping inflation, with the increase in consumer prices averaging 1.3 per cent per year from 1899 to 1914.

Such comparisons are useful as reminders that the economy may behave similarly in rather different economic environments, and this gives perspective on those features of contemporary experience which are relatively new. Labor unions were unimportant before World War I, for example, and yet prices followed a rising trend during more than 15 years of fairly stable economic growth and in the absence of war inflation. Nor was inflation prevented by the fact that the economy was on the gold standard at that time. On the contrary, just as a world shortage of gold had contributed to the deflationary trend of the 1880's and 1890's, so now rapid expansion of the money supply was fostered

TABLE 53. *Indexes of Wholesale and Consumer Prices, 1897-1914*[a] (1897 = 100)

Year	Wholesale Prices	Consumer Prices
1897	100.0	100.0
1898	104.0	99.3
1899 (P)	111.9	99.3
1900 (T)	120.5	101.3
1901	118.5	102.7
1902	126.4	103.7
1903 (P)	127.7	105.7
1904 (T)	128.1	106.7
1905	129.0	106.4
1906	132.7	108.4
1907 (P)	139.9	112.8
1908 (T)	135.0	110.1
1909	144.9	109.8
1910 (P)	151.2	113.8
1911 (T)	139.3	114.5
1912	148.2	116.8
1913 (P)	149.8	118.9
1914 (T)	146.2	120.2

[a] The initials (P) and (T) indicate cyclical peaks and troughs as dated by the National Bureau of Economic Research. Wholesale price index from Bureau of Labor Statistics. Consumer price index from Albert Rees, "Patterns of Wages, Prices and Productivity," *Wages, Prices, Profits and Productivity*, The American Assembly, Columbia University (1959), pp. 15–16, Table 1.

by important gold discoveries.[20] This autonomous development diminished the strength of the monetary check against overexpansion of aggregate demand in the face of supply inelasticities during business upswings.

Thus, creeping inflation is not a new phenomenon newly created by the growth of trade unionism or by fiscal or monetary mismanagement. Even so, the totality of our postwar institutions and attitudes has fostered the initiation and propagation of inflationary impulses during business expansions, while guarding against their liquidation during periods of contraction.

Although the economic environment for the postwar period as a whole has been hospitable to inflation, this was less true after 1950

[20] Milton Friedman has estimated that the money stock expanded about 7 per cent per year between 1897 and World War I, as compared with an average rate of 5 per cent per year from 1881 to 1897. *Thirty-fifth Annual Report* of the National Bureau of Economic Research (1955), p. 32.

than before. This was partly because excess liquidity and demand backlogs had been largely worked off by that year, and partly because of the shift of monetary policy dating from the Federal Reserve-Treasury Accord in 1951. Yet even during 1955-57, the constraints placed upon expansion of the money supply were insufficient to prevent sizable price increases, in good part because during most of the upswing the Board of Governors of the Federal Reserve System was alert to the danger of prompting business contraction by restrictive monetary actions—and wisely so from the point of view of the national commitment to the goals of full employment and stable growth.[21] As for federal fiscal policy, it was automatically deflationary during much of the expansion, but a step-up of federal purchases of goods and services about mid-1956 contributed to the increase both of production and prices thereafter.

Perhaps the major change with regard to the initiation of inflationary pressures is that nowadays unions can maintain upward pressure on money wages during periods in which demand is high or rising but employment is not extraordinarily high. It is not so much the fact that wages have not declined during contractions which distinguishes recent experience from the 1920's, as the fact that wages have risen rapidly during the recent expansions (compare Charts 43, 46, 47, and 51). Considerable attention has been given to the consequences of this development for the peacetime behavior of administered prices and the price level as a whole. Suffice it is to say that it increases the difficulty of containing moderate inflationary pressures by the usual monetary or fiscal devices.

Summary—The Inflationary Process in the Postwar Economy

The postwar economy has been troubled less by two kinds of inflation, as commonly alleged, than by two degrees of inflation. The two earlier inflationary episodes of the postwar period were more vigorous

[21] Restrictive monetary policies were a contributing cause to the downturn of 1957, however (Chapters 7 and 13).

and more widely diffused among the various sectors of the economy than the third. Prices tended everywhere to move upward in common surges. One reason for this was that market demands generally were more intensive and less easily discouraged by price increases than in the third; and this, in turn, was due to the powerful inflationary potential supplied by deferred demands and postwar liquidity in 1946-48 and by generalized war-inspired expectations of physical shortages and price advances during 1950. That is not to say, however, that cost pressures and, more specifically, wage increases were unimportant in 1947-48, for they did affect the timing and size of the price waves in those years.

Demand pressures were clearly less intense in 1956-57, but that does not render them unimportant in the gentler inflation of those years. If one insists on a distinguishing categorization for this inflation, "bottleneck" is more suitable than "cost-push." The former term at least carries the connotation of increased demand as well as increased cost in the sectors where prices rise strongly. It also has the virtue of emphasizing the fact that inflationary pressures may originate in particular sectors and spread to others, rather than appearing simultaneously everywhere.

That, in fact, is what one must expect under normal peacetime conditions. Widely diffused, powerful surges of excess demand are easily recognizable precisely because they are abnormal. Such abnormal conditions aside, inflationary forces will tend to fan out from initial areas of disturbance. If the postwar American economy does indeed have an inflationary bias—and I think it does—it is because its institutional framework favors the initiation and propagation of inflationary impulses but guards against their reversal.

With regard to the initiation of inflationary impulses, there is the fact that organized labor groups will press for money wage increases during periods of business expansion, since this is the variable affecting real income over which individual unions have some degree of direct control. Their success in winning wage increases will depend in part upon management estimates of the extent to which wage increases may profitably be passed on in product prices. This will mean that wage levels will tend to be determined by the increases which occur in the industries whose profit prospects are most favorable.

And it is at this point that high demands for specific products become crucial in helping to set standards for wage increases. The standard-setting wage increases may or may not exceed the long-term average rate of over-all productivity increase, but they are quite likely to exceed the increase for any given year and especially for years of full-employment expansion.

Nor is that all. The heavy industries will usually experience the greatest demand increases during a normal business boom, and the concentrated nature of labor and product markets in these key industries leaves a considerable area of discretion in the determination of wages and prices. Sizable increases in both are likely when demand expectations are favorable and are judged to be inelastic. If these expectations are realized, the income stream will be augmented by a larger increase of autonomous money expenditure than would occur with stable prices (and probably than would occur were only the product markets concentrated). As a result, money demands for other goods and services will also tend to rise.

Apart from acute inflationary disturbances like price decontrol or Korea, then, a problem of adjustment is posed for the economy each time wages and prices go up in the key durable goods industries. If productivity advances enough in flexible price sectors to outweigh the resulting increase in the general wage level, the over-all average of prices may not rise. If not, the question is whether aggregate money demand will rise sufficiently, either in response to the specific increases or for autonomous reasons, to sustain a higher level of prices and money incomes. This question, be it noted, is the same no matter what the cause of the specific increases: whether, for example, they are heavily influenced by expected demand as in 1948 or 1955, or are the lagged result of bargaining decisions made one or more years previously, as in 1957.

The additional money demand will be forthcoming when real demands are strong and financial constraints are insufficiently restrictive, as in the early and middle phases of a business expansion. After an expansion has been underway for sometime, however, current (as contrasted with expected) real demands are apt to diminish because of the price increases or for independent reasons, including restrictive fiscal or monetary controls. The weakness may appear in the heavy industries themselves, as in 1957, so that employment reductions cancel or more than cancel wage and salary increases and prevent a secondary expansion of income and demand. Or it may happen that the secondary expansion of demand fails to materialize because consumers choose not to increase expenditure in line with the growth of income, as in 1948. In either event, prices will not rise in other industrial sectors despite the increase of labor costs.[22] The increased level of labor costs, however, will limit price declines in response to demand reductions even in unconcentrated industries.

The inflationary bias of the economy is apparent also when it comes to this question of the propagation of inflationary impulses. The money supply is managed, and it is managed with regard to domestic stabilization objectives. This means that monetary controls will be used to curb an expansion of money expenditure under conditions of "full employment," and this whether aggregate demand is surging forward on a wide frontier because of powerful external forces, or rising unevenly in response to the gentler prodding of demand or cost increases in specific sectors. It means also, however, that monetary or fiscal curbs are apt to err on the side of too little restraint for a stable price level, since the goal is not stable prices at any cost, but stable prices accompanied by full employment and economic growth.[23] Thus anti-inflationary public policies are unlikely to be carried far enough to prevent price increases during business

[22] Prices of services or farm products may still rise for autonomous reasons.

[23] A distinction is sometimes drawn between demand inflation and cost inflation on the grounds that the former can be stopped at a given level of real income by eliminating excess demand, whereas even if that is done, autonomous cost increases will renew the latter type of inflation and force either a relaxation of the demand constraint or a reduction of output. I suspect that this contrast is more a property of static equilibrium models than of the dynamic economy. In the first place, autonomous demand shifts might also disturb a stable equilibrium if the latter were achieved through fiscal or monetary controls—and autonomous demand shifts occur frequently in the real world. Credit controls would have to be tight indeed to prevent a price advance fostered by new autonomous demands and financed by the activation of idle money balances. Secondly, financial constraints powerful enough to keep prices from rising under demand pressures, would almost certainly prompt a contraction of physical activity. If they did not lead directly to a downturn, they would do so indirectly by retarding or stopping the expansion of physical activity, with adverse consequences for investment demand (see Chapter 11). Such considerations argue for that cautious application of inflationary controls which is observable in practice, no matter what the origin of the inflationary pressures.

expansions, although they may be pursued to the point of retarding growth or raising unemployment in the interest of smaller price advances than would otherwise occur.

Finally, present American institutions and policies forestall the liquidation of inflationary pressures. Deflation brings not only lower prices but unemployment and lost production, and these are adjudged worse evils than inflation. Instead of forcing credit deflation, the monetary authorities pursue easy money policies during contractions. Expansionary fiscal actions—increased government spending, tax reductions, or both—are not unlikely. Automatic stabilizers cushion the drop of income and demand. Agricultural supports slow or prevent price declines, and administered prices are preserved by company policy. General wage reductions are neither recommended nor anticipated. In short, the preponderance of public and private economic forces work directly, and in many instances deliberately, against price reductions during business contractions.

The economy's bias toward price inflation has been largely a byproduct of properties of the postwar economy which most persons would agree were desirable. This fact should be kept in mind when judging the performance of the economy during these past years, and it should come to the forefront whenever the benefits of alternative goals and the risks of alternative policies are to be weighed.

Index

Index